HISTORICIZING THE ENLIGHTENMENT

HISTORICIZING THE ENLIGHTENMENT

Volume 1

Politics, Religion, Economy, and Society in Britain

MICHAEL MCKEON

Lewisburg, Pennsylvania

Library of Congress Cataloging-in-Publication Data

Names: McKeon, Michael, 1943– author.
Title: Historicizing the Enlightenment / Michael McKeon.
Description: Lewisburg, Pennsylvania : Bucknell University Press, [2023] | Includes bibliographical references and index. | Contents: V. 1. Politics, Religion, Economy, and Society in Britain—v. 2. Literature, the Arts, and the Aesthetic.
Identifiers: LCCN 2022054831 | ISBN 9781684484713 (v. 1 ; paperback) | ISBN 9781684484720 (v. 1 ; hardcover) | ISBN 9781684484737 (v. 1 ; epub) | ISBN 9781684484744 (v. 1 ; pdf) | ISBN 9781684484768 (v. 2 ; hardcover) | ISBN 9781684484751 (v. 2 ; paperback) | ISBN 9781684484775 (v. 2 ; epub) | ISBN 9781684484782 (v. 2 ; web pdf)
Subjects: LCSH: Great Britain—Intellectual life—18th century. | Enlightenment—Great Britain. | Great Britain—Civilization—18th century.
Classification: LCC DA485 .M35 2023 | DDC 941.07—dc23/eng/20230203
LC record available at https://lccn.loc.gov/2022054831

A British Cataloging-in-Publication record for this book is available from the British Library.

Copyright © 2023 by Michael McKeon

All rights reserved

No part of this book may be reproduced or utilized in any form or by any means, electronic or mechanical, or by any information storage and retrieval system, without written permission from the publisher. Please contact Bucknell University Press, Hildreth-Mirza Hall, Bucknell University, Lewisburg, PA 17837–2005. The only exception to this prohibition is "fair use" as defined by U.S. copyright law.

Credit lines for previously published material are listed in the Source Notes section.

References to internet websites (URLs) were accurate at the time of writing. Neither the author nor Bucknell University Press is responsible for URLs that may have expired or changed since the manuscript was prepared.

∞ The paper used in this publication meets the requirements of the American National Standard for Information Sciences—Permanence of Paper for Printed Library Materials, ANSI Z39.48-1992.

bucknelluniversitypress.org

Distributed worldwide by Rutgers University Press

Contents

Introduction — 1
    Periodizing the Enlightenment — 2
    Understanding Enlightenment Thought — 6
    Enlightenment Separation and Conflation — 10
    Experimental Method — 13
    Quantification — 15
    Politics — 16
    (Civil) Society — 17
    The Public Sphere — 17
    Capitalist and Enlightenment Universality — 19
    Imperialism — 22
    Macro-pastoralism — 23
    Conjectural History — 24
    Slavery — 25

1 Tradition as Tacit Knowledge — 28
    Tradition — 28
    Ideology — 37
    The Aesthetic — 42

2 Civil and Religious Liberty: A Case Study in Secularization — 49
    Accommodation — 49
    Civil Society — 54
    The Empirical Criterion — 56
    The Sociology of Group Formation — 57
    Accommodating God's Will: Thoughts, Speech, Actions — 59
    Defining Spheres of Discourse — 62
    The Three Negative Liberties — 65
    Secularization — 71

3 Virtual Reality — 75
    Religion — 76
    Corporation — 77
    Polity and Economy — 78
    Capitalist Universality — 84
    False Consciousness and Uneven Development — 84
    The Commodity Form — 87
    The Trope of the Fetish — 91
    Parody — 93
    The Trope of the Invisible Hand — 94
    Conceptual Abstraction — 97

Capitalist and Enlightenment Universality — 98
Superstructure and Dialectics — 105
Conjectural History — 107
Polity and Society — 108
The Public Sphere — 109
The Two Publics — 111
Print — 115
Experimental Science — 118
Experience and Experiment — 121
Instruments: Experimental versus Artful — 125
Extending Experiment I: Political Philosophy — 129
Extending Experiment II: Beyond Observables — 131
The Imagination — 139

4 Gender and Sex, Status and Class — 141
From Patriarchalism to Modern Patriarchy — 141
From Domestic Economy to Domestic Ideology — 144
Separate Spheres? — 146
Sex and Sex Consciousness — 148
The Two-Sex Model? — 148
The Three-Gender System: Conflation I — 151
Gender as Culture: Conflation II — 153
The Dialectic of Sexuality and Class — 156
The Common Labor of Sexuality and Class — 159
Sodomy and Aristocracy — 159
Types of Masculinity — 163

5 Biography, Fiction, Personal Identity — 167
Biography, Fiction, and the Common — 167
Biography, Fiction, and the Actual — 170
Biography, Fiction, and the Virtual — 171
The Self behind Self-Fashioning — 173
From Secret History to Novel — 175
The Rise of Personal Identity — 178

6 Historical Method — 182
Distance and Proximity — 184
Historicizing Empiricism — 185
Historical Method: Matching Particulars
  and Generals — 187
Dialectical Opposition I: History as Focalizations
  of Perspective — 189
Dialectical Opposition II: History as Moments
  of Temporality — 191
Dialectical Opposition III: History as Levels
  of Structure — 195

Acknowledgments — 201
Notes — 203
Source Notes — 241
Index — 243

HISTORICIZING THE ENLIGHTENMENT

Introduction

To historicize is to enclose what we think we know in a spatiotemporal frame that transforms its meaning. To historicize the Enlightenment requires that we try to imagine what it was like to live through the first emergence of concepts and practices that are now commonplace.

"Enlightenment" is a cognitive state or action. "The Enlightenment" situates this state or action in a particular historical period. My concern in this study is with the period of the English—after 1707, the British and Scottish—Enlightenment, which by loose convention comprises the century and a half from 1650 to 1800.[1] But because my argument will be that with the Enlightenment came a new way of thinking about the world, my concern is also with Enlightenment thought as such. This point requires emphasis. *Historicizing the Enlightenment* is an exercise in intellectual history that seeks to overcome misconceptions about what we refer to when speaking of Enlightenment as the innovative mode of understanding that characterizes the period of the Enlightenment. I'm not concerned to claim that this innovative way of thinking has no precedent before this period. My central aim is to argue the nature of Enlightenment thought by showing its continuity and integrity across a broad range of conceptual domains. To be clear, what I mean by Enlightenment thought is not its high philosophy (although philosophy will have an important place in the sources I rely on), but its way of thinking, the concepts and ideas that underlie what makes the Enlightenment distinctive and innovative as a way of thinking. So, along with philosophical texts my sources will include writings in advocacy and controversy on political, social, economic, and religious topics, works of literature and reflections on the aesthetic, and a broad range of cultural commentary.

Historicizing the Enlightenment consists of two volumes: volume 1 concerns "Politics, Religion, Economy, and Society"; volume 2 treats "Literature, the Arts, and the Aesthetic." Together they construct an overarching perspective on the nature of Enlightenment thought: how it has shaped our views of both tradition and modernity and the revisionary work that needs to be done in order to understand our place in the future. In the process, *Historicizing the Enlightenment* exemplifies a distinctive historiography and historical method. This introduction will begin with the fundamental terms of my argument, the relationship between Enlightenment as a period and as a new way of thinking. On this basis I'll then turn to the most important criticisms that have been leveled at Enlightenment thought, and to a brief summary of how I'll counter those criticisms in the body of this volume.

Periodizing the Enlightenment

Never mind that *the Enlightenment* is an invention of the late nineteenth century, *the Scottish Enlightenment* a fabrication of the early twentieth century, *the Enlightenment Project*, of more recent pedigree than the Manhattan Project, just a scheme largely devised in the past two decades. What possible bearing can genuine scholarship have upon claims about the conceptual roots of modernity which are writ large and on stilts?[2]

Like any historical period, the Enlightenment has undergone fluctuations in the way it's been understood by its posterity. For a great number of thinking people, the historical significance of the Enlightenment—what it "stands for"—is a matter of great cultural importance, a touchstone of critical belief about not only how modernity in the West came to be but also what it amounts to. Especially in recent decades, the Enlightenment commitment to principles of analysis, division, reduction, abstraction, objectification, quantification, and universalization has been acutely criticized both in itself and as bearing responsibility for some of the most destructive developments of modern life.[3] My purpose in this volume is to correct the defective understanding of Enlightenment thought in itself, and of the Enlightenment as a period phenomenon. To be clear at the outset, I don't suppose that this basic misconception has dominated the majority of recent studies of the Enlightenment. That notion is belied both by projects in the general and explicit reappraisal of the Enlightenment,[4] and by the work of numerous scholars whose treatment of particular topics in the field of literature implicitly affirms a considered approach to it.[5] My concern is rather with a diffuse and pervasive conjecture about the nature and sources of modernity whose influence has required, at least in part, that it not be looked into very deeply. Evidence of it isn't hard to find, as this introduction will document from time to time. I'll begin with the period problem: the misconception of the Enlightenment in its relation to its past, self-reflectively to its present, and to its future. My argument is that the critique of the historical period of the Enlightenment has abstracted it from its past, present, and future—from its history.

1) The modern reaction against the Enlightenment, largely confined to a problematic view of its future influence, ignores the Enlightenment's past—that is, the Enlightenment's own explicit and self-conscious reaction against the traditional domination of unexamined authority. When we criticize the innovations of the Enlightenment, we do so as human agents who are capable of both action and passion—who can both act in pursuit of our choices and suffer effects we haven't chosen. However, our conception of Enlightenment agents is too often by this standard partial: we ascribe to them the former but not the latter capacity, and if we suffer the consequences of their actions we tend not to ask what they may have suffered and whether their actions may be a consequence of that suffering.

My aim is to overcome this partiality in structural rather than evaluative terms. My point is not that the negative effects of Enlightenment innovations may be balanced by adducing their positive effects. This can and has been argued;

but it's a method of qualitative accounting that leads in a different direction. My point is, first of all, not evaluative but structural because historiographic actions have consequences, but they are also the consequence of antecedent actions. "Consequence" has two distinct meanings. As "chronology" consequence is clearly evident: one event follows another. Consequence as "determinacy" in the strong sense of causation must be rigorously demonstrated; in the broader sense of the setting of outer limits, it may be assumed in the spirit of further inquiry. I observe below that the determinacy of Enlightenment thought on what follows it has been too routinely asserted without examination. We need to ask how Enlightenment thought might be a reaction against, and therefore determined by, what precedes it. By the same token, we must ask if Enlightenment thought is not in opposition to, but continues, extends, and is determined by, modes of thought antecedent to its own. These are not quibbles, but a ramification of taking periodization seriously as a tool to think with, one that puts in practice the fundamental premise that historical understanding is a matter of both continuity and discontinuity.

2) Propelled by its initial momentum, the Enlightenment extended its reactive analysis of the past to its own present through self-analysis and self-criticism. There's no doubt that the Enlightenment played a determinant role in initiating the divisions that characterize the modern world. But by the same token, the Enlightenment is also responsible for modern impulses that complicate, mitigate, or overcome those divisions in the ongoing process of historical change. The modern critique of the Enlightenment, largely oblivious to these immediate and local reactions to division, tends to look beyond the Enlightenment itself for the kind of conceptual movement that, set going by categorial division, elaborated methods of synthesizing the new categories that division generated, a movement that began in the Enlightenment itself. A classic example of the Enlightenment's self-analytic and self-critical impulse can be seen in the trajectory of thinking about the grounds of empirical epistemology in the half century between the writings of John Locke and David Hume. Challenging the metaphysical view of mind, Locke posited two separate operations of the understanding: *sensation* of experience and *reflection* on the mental experience of processing that sensation. Inspired by Locke's empirical method, Hume used it to for a closer analysis of these mental operations and found that they're not really separate: what we know is a function of how we know.[6]

3) On the one hand, a common modern devaluation of what the Enlightenment achieved is unhistorical because measured against modern achievement, and incongruous with what might be expected when Enlightenment innovation is first underway. On the other, what can look from a modern perspective like the failure of the Enlightenment must be distinguished from the failure of its posterity—of its future—to sustain Enlightenment principles. Belated and distorted versions of Enlightenment principles have then been read back retrospectively into the Enlightenment. Behind these errors, which are to a real degree subject to empirical inquiry, lie more profound and difficult questions, central to historiography, that I've

already alluded to. When we say that the Enlightenment "led to" or was "responsible for" or "determined" later developments, the nature of the relation we posit is unavoidably more problematic than the language itself suggests. What concepts or events might have entered into the process of transmission to influence the nature of what was transmitted? Is the relation between earlier and later phenomena thought to be one of cause and effect, or are the earlier phenomena thought to result from a motive that foresees and affirms the nature of the later phenomena? *Post hoc non est propter hoc.* The stringent requirements for showing a causal relationship are well known; and what has been called the law of unintended consequences makes tenuous the assumption that an original function or purpose will be replicated in the minds of those who preside over and sanction what's taken to be its later fulfillment. Easy outrage at our forebears for having promoted policies that we take to be the straightforward antecedents of what is currently outrageous can assume on our part a comparative moral rectitude that is facile and unearned.

Again, my purpose is not to apologize for the Enlightenment but to take history seriously. However, because my aim is to defend the Enlightenment on its own terms, I run the risk of appearing to denigrate the tradition that the Enlightenment defined itself against. In correcting the historical balance at one end I inevitably, but only temporarily, overbalance at the other. My aim is to think historically, not to take sides. The distinction between "tradition" and "modernity" is central to my argument; but although it has substance in my own thinking, to give it substance for my readers I must first formulate it heuristically in the schematic form of the bare distinction itself.[7] However schematic, I intend the distinction between tradition and modernity to be understood as a dialectical relationship, whereby the two are constituted over against each other as what the other is not. By this understanding, the period of the Enlightenment, mediating between these two greater periods, must partake of both.

I ask readers to understand this distinction, like periodization itself, as a tool to think with, a methodological generalization whose plausibility and utility will be tested by the argument that follows. My generalization is likely to be refuted especially by readers whose specialist knowledge, in this case of what I've called "tradition," will quickly and reasonably adduce concrete instances that defy my abstraction. I urge them to suspend the impulse to reject my argument until they've had an opportunity to test it more fully by sampling a more extensive portion of it, as well as on the basis of this consideration. Like any tool, periodization leaves its mark on its material. It imposes on the fluid medium of temporality a chronological quantification that gives categories like "tradition" and "modernity" the definitive difference of "before" and "after." However, *Historicizing the Enlightenment* is an intellectual history, and the difference between these periods is substantive and conceptual. This being the case, where tradition ends and modernity begins varies according to variations between particular concepts under study, as well as between the particular national and regional traditions that constitute "tradition" in general. I urge specialists to read with a confidence that although tradition refers to a period, the fact that this period is defined conceptually means that it's adjustable according to differences in specific and local conceptual histories. The chronological breadth of the English Enlightenment as I define it, 1650–1800, acknowledges this variation; and in particular cases these dates should also be seen as adjustable.[8]

The method of reading history I've entered into is itself a product of Enlightenment thought. By this I mean not periodization as such, which was practiced long before the Enlightenment, but the hypothesis of a difference between periods produced by a method that attends closely to testimonies and evidence both of a continuity between them and of discontinuities within each. (By the same token, I speak of "the Enlightenment" in the hope that this, too, will be read as a manner of speaking, appearing to take in the generality of Enlightenment thinkers in order to throw into relief particular thinkers and modes of thought as a distinguishable part within a greater whole.) This attention to the empirical grounds for periodization aims to adduce and analyze relevant evidence in order to achieve an increasingly precise understanding of difference based on standards of not certainty but probability. These categories—empirical evidence, probability, historicity itself—are themselves products of the period and the method of thought this inquiry aims to define, and they must guide the reader's judgment of its adequacy in defining the Enlightenment in relation to, and in distinction from, tradition and modernity.

To characterize periodization as a tool to think with runs counter to the anti-Enlightenment view that formulating categories like historical periods is a technique of abstraction that overrides and erases the concrete particularity of things. The chapters that follow will argue the fallacy of this view by showing, across a broad range of subject matters, that the Enlightenment innovated and undertook to practice a method of abstraction that was sanctioned and authorized by an ongoing, self-conscious attention to the adequacy of totalities to the divisions they subsume, of generalities to the particulars they enclose, and of abstraction to the concrete entities it abstracts from. My claim is not that this attention was fully and regularly sustained, but that Enlightenment abstraction was committed in principle to accounting for the plurality of concrete instances, because this was the end for which Enlightenment abstraction was undertaken. So too, the rhetoric of periodization. Although the period is spoken of as though a singular self-identical subject, this should not be taken to conflict with the principle, evident in the multiple contingencies that affect the discrimination of the Enlightenment from both tradition and modernity as I've just discussed them, whereby periods are probable and relative constructions based on a plurality of testimonies and evidence.

My analysis of the Enlightenment's role in crucial historical developments like scientific method, capitalism, and imperialism should be read in the light of the foregoing discussion of periodization. Any attempt to discriminate the period of the Enlightenment runs up against the ongoing nature of temporal existence, which from an ontological perspective precludes analysis. My analysis of the

Enlightenment period aims to acknowledge rather than ignore this perspective by proposing a dialectical historiography.

I'll turn now from the Enlightenment as a period to Enlightenment as an innovative mode of thought, which will involve a summary account of, and challenge to, the criticisms that have been lodged against it. I'll abstract from this discussion a conceptual framework that's also a chronological framework for understanding Enlightenment thought as it emerged from tradition and precipitated modernity. I'll then summarize several period developments selected from the following chapters that clearly exemplify this framework, as well as significant criticisms of Enlightenment thought that are specific to these exemplary cases. Along with these exemplary cases, I'll underscore several others that exemplify the failure of the Enlightenment to pursue its distinctive program of innovation. These are not "exceptions that prove the rule." Some may be seen as failures to overcome, or even to identify, the tacit force of traditional thought. In others, Enlightenment thought may have aggravated the dogma of tradition by assimilating it to contemporary practice. I don't think these failures countermand the distinctive program of innovation I advance as a corrective to fundamental misconceptions of Enlightenment thought. I mark them here because I think no revisionary effort can succeed without the will to specify what lies beyond revision.

Understanding Enlightenment Thought

Let me recall the terms I used to summarize the critical denunciation of Enlightenment thought: analysis, division, reduction, abstraction, objectification, quantification, universalization. These principles are criticized for imposing on human experience a dominating structure of dichotomous opposition. In this view, rational and empirical analysis reduces and abstracts the full variety and rich multiplicity of existence to one model. Objectification fragments the fluid continuity of experiential process into static products divested of their ties to each other and of their generative, often subjective, sources. Quantification—spatiotemporal measurement, statistical computation, experimental method, commodity exchange—sacrifices concrete qualitative difference to a universal standard of comparability and knowledge. The effect is to make differences absolute and irreconcilable except in quantitative terms. Enlightenment claims to inclusiveness and universality, made in the guise of egalitarian pluralism, are belied by the actual effects of methods like these, which erase difference and promote the entrenchment of traditional prejudice and privilege in the name of change, aggravated by the pretense of actual innovation and reform. Taken together, these elements of Enlightenment thought are condemned as having transformed knowledge as inquiry into power as domination.

The proponents of Enlightenment thought saw things differently. Based on the cognitive premise that knowledge is the product of our sensible experience and our empirically valid inferences—in related terms, the product of our logically cogent discernment and the judgments it dictates—Enlightenment thought excludes what fails or evades these empirical and rational trials. It directs us toward what can be known empirically and rationally, and away from what, although justified by tradition, custom, and other kinds of authority, cannot. Enlightenment quantification created not a problem of partiality but a solution to it, because it vastly improved on the results of assessing the whole according to one or another standard that are qualitatively different and therefore inevitably partial.

The Enlightenment emerged in reaction against a traditional wisdom that took knowledge to be an integral whole whose integrity was entailed in the qualitative priority and determinacy of one of its parts, commonly religion or theology, or any part that fostered the being and purpose of the whole, over all others.[9] The rule of that part was taken to be self-evident; Enlightenment thought asked if its rule was affirmed by an independent standard of evaluation that was separable from its own tacit conviction, providing grounds for comparing it with other parts. The impulse of Enlightenment thought was to reduce phenomena to their simplest and smallest units, or (what amounts to the same thing) to abstract phenomena from the context or practice that they exist in but that are not integral to them. In other words, Enlightenment thought disintegrated the presumed integrity of traditional cognitive wholes by applying rational and empirical standards to their analysis. Tradition tacitly assumed that the being and purpose of the parts that composed these wholes subserved only the greater being and purpose of those wholes. Enlightenment partialization found that this assumption obscured or denied the integrity of the parts themselves, which were knowable and epistemologically self-sufficient wholes, in their own right. Subsumed under greater wholes, the particular qualities and character of what traditionally were deemed mere parts of wholes were rendered not simply insignificant but invisible.

Traditional and customary authorities are *tacit* and total: they "go without saying" and possess the "self-evidence" of what's "taken for granted" as true. To analyze authority is to make the tacit *explicit*, dividing its supposedly irreducible integrity into parts in order to discover their relationship to each other and to the whole.[10] In their self-evidence, traditional wholes are absolute abstractions and preclude the acknowledgment of their concrete parts; or, in other terms, they're concrete abstractions. Enlightenment knowledge abstracts the parts that compose abstract wholes and thereby gives them concretion. Another way of figuring the difference between traditional and Enlightenment knowledge is in terms of their epistemological procedures. Tradition begins at the top of the hierarchy of what can be known and derives all lower knowledge from that premise. Enlightenment begins at the bottom, where the actual units of knowledge have been rendered indivisible, and derives all higher knowledge from this lowest level.

I've been invoking empiricism and the empirical in the familiar terms of a knowledge based on experience and derived from our sense impressions of the material world around us. On the authority of nothing less than Enlightenment thought itself, empiricism is customarily opposed to the notion that knowledge is innate and a priori, based in an extrasensory, indwelling or transcendent, realm of pre-existent ideas. This understanding of empirical knowledge conceives it in terms of its *source*, which I point out not to question it but to observe that empiricism also involves, less familiarly but consequentially, a *method* of knowing. And to make this point I intervene in my exposition of Enlightenment thought because empirical method is another way of characterizing the method of making tacit knowledge explicit. This principle has an importance that invites overstatement: empiricism is not matter but method, not content but form, not the actual but the virtual. As I'll elaborate later on in this volume, its Enlightenment proponents practiced empirical method on phenomena, beyond actuality, that inhabited the virtual realm of the ideational and the mental. And as a practice, empiricism entailed the analysis of wholes into increasingly particulate units that were susceptible in turn to further breakdown. The fundamental difference between experience and experiment in the Enlightenment theory of scientific method might seem, by implication, to separate the experimental attitude of active attention from the undiscriminated mass of brute experience on which it focused its systematic inquiry. But experience and experiment have the same root; and whereas the French language has no separate word for experiment, the English separation intimates the conflationary impulse that is already implicit in experience itself as a dialectical negation of what's truly unsusceptible of analysis by virtue of its a priori givenness.

To return to my exposition: arguing the negative consequences of Enlightenment partialization, the critique of the Enlightenment evokes as its alternative the traditional vision of wholeness. Yet the positive standard of this critique—the value of difference, multiplicity, particularity, quality, subjectivity, and the like—is not the traditional and tacit norm of the integral and overarching whole, but the modern norm of Enlightenment partialization and the integrity of the part. And on reflection this isn't surprising, because anti-Enlightenment thought is also modern, devoid of the tacitness of tradition and armed with the instruments of explicit and self-conscious analysis that it has learned from the Enlightenment to deploy. In other words, the critique of the Enlightenment affirms the traditional vision of a singular wholeness, but in the partializing terms of that vision's critique. Are the Enlightenment and its critique, although different in substance, therefore epistemologically equivalent?

The partiality entailed in Enlightenment thought is not absolute but operational and heuristic, which is to say that its negative aim of exclusion predicates a positive consequence of inclusion. The Enlightenment analysis of the traditional whole excludes the presumption of its integrity in order to disclose and include the integrity—the existence and coherence—of the part-turned-whole that the tradition's presumption renders invisible. But Enlightenment partiality does not thereby exclude the traditional whole as such from epistemological understanding. Rather, it mobilizes the rational and empirical method of inquiry that reframes traditional and analyzes emergent knowledge through the experimental interplay of parts and wholes, which entails simultaneously the negative exclusion and the positive inclusion of knowledge. The Enlightenment reframing of tradition's tacit whole results, moreover, in a new and dynamic whole, a totality composed of multiple wholes and subject to ongoing totalization fueled by this ongoing experimentation.

Anti-Enlightenment partiality that criticizes Enlightenment partiality precludes the movement from negative exclusion to positive inclusion. Its critical focus on the Enlightenment is absolute because, paradoxically, it can conceive no alternative to it. Derivative of what it criticizes, anti-Enlightenment is itself the positive future that it cannot conceive because it is immobilized, one foot still rooted in the period it would negate. But anti-Enlightenment is also compromised by its opportunistic endorsement of a past, the wholes of tradition, that is recommended by little more than its repudiation by the Enlightenment and therefore offers no ground for positive inclusion. Hence the need to historicize the historical period of the Enlightenment by historicizing anti-Enlightenment.

The difference between *tacit* and *explicit* conceptual relations clarifies why the new whole of Enlightenment knowledge can be figured as a totality subject to ongoing totalization. Traditional knowledge is tacit in that it acknowledges distinctions between the parts of a whole but not their separability. Enlightenment separation has several consequences. Most important, only when parts are detached and separated from each other sufficiently to be conceived as such can they be entered into active relation. Moreover, because the nature of the relationship between parts contributes to their meaning, their separation subtly alters and sharpens their semantic and substantive force. Enlightenment separation creates the conditions for a new sort of power, the self-constitution of knowledge. Once separated, conceptual parts become subject to actively willed reconception and resituation in relation to other parts, whether in reciprocal mutuality or competitive conflict, but in either case as parts of a whole that is new by virtue of its ostensive, self-conscious fabrication. This may enable the resolution of old problems that had not been amenable to solution, but also the conceptualization of new problems that couldn't have risen to awareness under the aegis of tradition.

So, if we step back from the Enlightenment partialization of categories that traditionally were distinguishable but not separable from each other, we gain perspective on how, in its analytic division of *distinction*, *separation* creates the conditions for innovative *conflation* that, because knowingly undertaken, cannot be taken for granted but is subject to debate and ongoing reconception and resituation. The fruit of Enlightenment thought is therefore not only division or separation but also the innovative conflations that are consequent on separation. By "conflation" I mean convergence not blending, which might suggest an illusory revival of a whole consisting of distinct but inseparable parts. The result of Enlightenment conflation is instead a dialectical category, a self-standing whole that's both divisible into its component parts and subsumable into a greater whole of which it constitutes one part. I hope to show that the broad historical trajectory from tradition to enlightenment is defined in conceptual terms by the schematic movement from tacit difference to explicit separation, and then, sometimes quite punctually, to conflation. If the foregoing account strikes some readers as an idealization of Enlightenment thought, I urge them to recall that my aim is just that: to define the body of ideas that distinguish Enlightenment thought in itself, and as it sought to distinguish itself from tradition.

Enlightenment Separation and Conflation: Some Examples

In the following chapters I'll offer arguments and evidence to support the thesis that Enlightenment thought across a range of fields[11] underwent the kind of development that's schematically represented by the movement from distinction to separation and, to different degrees, conflation. I'll now sample several examples of this conceptual development.

And because it's important that the reader have a concrete sense of the anti-Enlightenment criticism that I'm responding to, I'll also sample excerpts of that criticism keyed to the relevant examples of conceptual development. One appraisal holds that "While the Enlightenment has enabled emancipation, human rights, democracy, and freedom through its much-celebrated exercise of reason, it has also led to colonialism, imperialism, slavery, and crimes against humanity, ironically through the same 'reasoning'. . . . Enlightenment rationalism and empiricism also created 'scientific racism' consolidated by a power and knowledge system used to justify colonialism and subjugate other knowledges."[12] Another critic speaks of the Enlightenment's "faith in a universal Reason," "the transcendent subject of Enlightenment theories," "totalizing and universalistic theories such as those of the Enlightenment."[13] In the words of another, "One finds in the writings of the Frankfurt School a clinging to the Enlightenment notion that freedom depends on the reason of the individual and the individual can exercise reason best in a condition of autonomy. . . . By excluding mental operations from the domain of historical materialism, Marx remains within the traditional, Enlightenment metaphysic."[14] Another critic maintains that "privileging abstraction over historical accounts of difference, I suggest, is one of the forms of mystification that characterizes all Enlightenment 'knowledge.'"[15] And the judgment of another is that "The legacy of the Enlightenment, of the scientific and critical effort of the Enlightenment . . . to separate fact from the values of a crumbling tradition, separated fact from all values—bequeathing a world in which fact is a measurable quantity while value is man-made and illusory. . . . It was when superior individuals of eighteenth-century intellect discovered in themselves the new imaginative faculty that they became romanticists."[16]

There's a broad consistency in anti-Enlightenment critique. In one appraisal, "Enlightenment thinkers . . . understood difference as only an external phenomenon and therefore inconsequential and ephemeral, while the internal structure of the mind and reason were universal, eternal, and essential. . . . Governed by epistemological interests in order and knowledge produced through a largely taxonomic discourse, Enlightenment thinking focuses on the empirical study, the Cartesian paradigm."[17] Another thought that scientific method epitomized the problem, because it entailed the belief that "the more metaphysically comfortless and morally insignificant our vocabulary, the likelier we are to be 'in touch with reality' or to be 'scientific,' or to describe reality as it wants to be described and thereby get it under control."[18] But the following critic argues that at the heart of the problem was the fallacy of enlightenment itself. "From the seventeenth century onwards it was a commonplace that," unlike the scholastics and Aristotle, "we moderns . . . had stripped away interpretation and theory and confronted fact and experience just as they are. It was precisely in virtue of this that those moderns proclaimed and named themselves the Enlightenment. . . . The Enlightenment is consequently the period par excellence in which most intellectuals lack self-knowledge."[19]

Some of these denunciations betray the influence of the two best-known misconstructions of the Enlightenment. Because their critiques are unrivaled in their celebrity I'll take the liberty of going beyond citation to summary, and summary refutation.

The first, Max Horkheimer's and Theodore W. Adorno's *Dialectic of Enlightenment*, holds that the Enlightenment promotes the "universality of ideas," a "domination in the conceptual sphere [that] is raised up on the basis of actual domination."[20] Horkheimer and Adorno partialize the Enlightenment and confuse it with the tradition it would replace—and it's a confusion on which they insist: "The Enlightenment recognizes as being and occurrence only what can be apprehended in unity. . . . Its rationalist and empiricist versions do not part company on that point." "The unity of the manipulated collective consists in the negation of each individual. . . . Abstraction, the tool of enlightenment, treats its objects as did fate. . . . It liquidates them." "The whole as whole . . . necessarily leads to the execution of the particular" (7, 13, 22). "The execution of the particular" describes from the other end "the universality of ideas" that is in their view the Enlightenment project. To affirm this reduction of Enlightenment thought to an a priori and unqualified universality requires that the critics erase the recourse to particularity that grounds universality in empirical rationality. Moreover, "the dominant conventions of science" are the "same conventions [that] define the notion of linguistic and conceptual clarity," the "false clarity" of what is actually "an impoverished and debased language" (xiv).

Like my *Historicizing*, their *Dialectic* observes the relation between the Enlightenment and enlightenment as such, but only to render it absolute. "It is not merely the Enlightenment of the eighteenth century that . . . is relentless but . . . the advance of thought itself." By this logic, the Enlightenment only exemplifies the problematic nature of knowledge as such: all thought, by construing, enclosing, incorporating, universalizes and thereby dominates, in its implacable progression, what it thinks about. Speciously indicting the Enlightenment of a transhistorical claim to universality, *Dialectic of Enlightenment* is really a universalizing polemic against the historicity of knowledge (20). Moving swiftly from Homer to Sade, the culture industry, and fascist antisemitism, the grand sweep of enlightenment entails, "with the inevitability of necessity," a perpetually repeated effort to progress (in the terms of this study) beyond the tacit whole of the moment by demythologizing what's taken for granted and goes without saying. But the will to progress is illusory, canceled by the irony that it only repeats the same impulse that motivated what it would now replace. "The curse of irresistible progress is irresistible regression." So, the old myth is replaced by a new one: "Myth is already enlightenment; and enlightenment reverts to mythology" (11, 36, xvi). Adorno, master dialectician, knows that dialectic is structured as a relation of sameness and difference. Here sameness cancels difference and history is sheer repetition. *Dialectic of Enlightenment* is the classic articulation of anti-Enlightenment thought: abstract generality at the expense of particularity; methodological progress equated with the will to material progress; the aim to dominate through both universalization and exclusion; empiricism cast in the shadow of instrumental reason; the failures of posterity imputed to its present; period reduced to thought, history flattened to concept.

The second notable critique of the Enlightenment is that of Michel Foucault. I have in mind not his later statements "What Is Enlightenment?" (1984) and "What Is Critique?" (1990) but his early *The Order of Things* (1966), which, despite the view of some that he soon moved beyond this tour de force, remains a key to his thought. This is where Foucault classifies the largely discontinuous epistemes of the human sciences, among them the Classical Age, which is Foucault's term for the Enlightenment. His bibliography is overwhelmingly French, which means that his guiding category in the analysis of the Classical Age is Reason, not empiricism, and its tutelary genius, despite a multitude of others, is Descartes. Foucault treats "the sciences" in chapter 5, whose title, "Classifying," suggests the path he'll follow. Although he begins by invoking Bacon and the physical sciences, within the space of a page Foucault passes from a mention of experiments and observations to the "adjacent realm of living beings," Descartes, "the possibility of classifying living beings," and Linnaeus, and he scarcely looks back. Foucault's narrative fiction in this chapter is that he's following "the historians," who lead him quickly to "natural history" and its consuming interest in classification and taxonomy.[21] Observation is centrally important, not in its empiricist sense but as it limits inquiry to concentrating on vision alone and on what it gives access to: namely, surfaces. The microscope serves the purposes of natural history, Foucault argues, by focusing attention on the relation between things and the human eye and between one generation and the next. The four visual variables are number, form, proportion, and situation, and to observe them precisely is to disclose structure. The aim of science is to describe the surface of structure, which allows structure to be transcribed into language and the ordered articulation of the living body as a taxonomy. This is, for Foucault, the discourse of nature that organizes the sciences of the Classical Age, and that created a priori the foundation for a natural history based on the existence of genera, the stability of species, and the transmission of characters from generation to generation (132–134, 158).

Whether this is an accurate account of taxonomy and natural history is another question from the one I raise. As an account of Enlightenment science Foucault's partiality, what it leaves out, is obvious. Earlier in this introduction I wrote that the "impulse of Enlightenment thought was to reduce phenomena to their simplest and smallest units, or (what amounts to the same thing) to abstract phenomena from the context or practice that they exist in but that are not integral to them." This sounds superficially like Foucault's statement that "classification requires the principle of the smallest possible difference between things" (159). However, by "smallest" Foucault refers to a strictly superficial standard of visibility, one appropriate to his limitation of science to Linnaean classification. What I refer to is not a visual but a conceptual standard, which calls for an understanding of Enlightenment thought that includes empirical experiment and much else besides—all, in fact, that Foucault excludes from his episteme the Classical Age. Foucault's method exemplifies what I've described as the failure of anti-Enlightenment critique. Derivative of what it criticizes, Foucault's partiality can't go beyond Enlightenment method and is condemned to an absolute exclusion rather than heuristically enabling a more informed inclusiveness.

The concept of the Anthropocene, spurred by the relatively recent global awakening to the crisis of climate change, has generated an enormous amount of discourse that has not simply altered environmental studies but fundamentally revised our understanding of how, and how quickly, the earth has been exploited and degraded by the presence of human beings. Periodizing the Anthropocene has been subject to widespread debate, ranging from the prehistorical effects of deforestation and the earliest agriculture to the late eighteenth-century invention of the steam engine. On the one hand, the Anthropocene period debate is a macro-version of disagreement about the chronology of the Enlightenment—although the definitional complexity of how to date the earliest human alterations of "nature" is a far greater challenge than giving pride of place to one or another European national culture. On the other, the proponents of steam power have tended to identify it with the origins of the Enlightenment, which then becomes a period—from 1800 on—that no nationalist contenders would recognize. The likely explanation for this chronological solecism is that the Enlightenment and the Anthropocene tend to be associated with similar modern developments. But the effect of this dovetailing is to lock into an interpretation of the former the utter negativity of the latter. "The Anthropocene" names, and justly describes with a force that accrues both from its empirical detail and from its summary power, a long-term process of corruption whose climax we've come to identify in "climate change." To identify the Anthropocene with the Enlightenment imposes on it an absolute condemnation that precedes and precludes actual interpretation and analysis.[22]

Experimental Method

Not taxonomy but experiment is the method we're most likely to associate with the emergence of modern science in early Enlightenment England. Experimental method explicitly concentrates and applies those principles that are generally characteristic of Enlightenment thought, and it therefore epitomizes what the anti-Enlightenment critique both refutes and misconstrues. It was developed by members of the Royal Society in an effort to formulate as a methodical procedure Francis Bacon's seminal arguments about the need for an inductive mode of pursuing knowledge that was based on "experience" and the evidence of the senses rather than on an a priori deduction from general principles. Experience, the basis of all knowledge, consisted of our individual sense impressions of the multitude of concrete natural entities we encounter in the actual world. But although natural philosophers held the evidence of the senses to be the basis of all knowledge, they also recognized that the sense impressions of any single individual only recapitulate in another form the absolute partiality—meaning the liabilities of both fragmentation and bias—of deductive assumptions. Experimental procedure—"trials"—proposed a solution to this empirical problem of the partial by collecting and comparing, for a multiplicity of samples of a given entity, the sense impressions of a multiplicity of individuals so as to identify and strain out those variables that are not shared by all. What remains is the natural constant, its virtual integrity ensured by the abstraction of all concrete qualities found in the actual samples that had been subjected to experiment. The analytic separation of constant from variables enables the conflation of all those elements that have been found to be more or less constantly present so as to constitute an abstract understanding of the thing itself. The aim of the experimental process is to test the data of experience across as broad a range of circumstances as possible—times, places, participants in the experiment—to be able to generalize about the abstract nature of the thing, and to repeat these trials to the same end. Bacon had still conceived the final state of knowledge that would result from experiment as "certainty." By the middle of the century, the status of knowledge had been reconceived as an ongoing and continually retested "probability."[23]

This understanding of Enlightenment experimental method suggests what's wrong with its critiques. The premise of experiment is not that it will confirm conclusions already agreed on in advance but that it will provide an empirical basis for drawing probable conclusions. Experimental abstraction is not a universalizing end in itself. It's a conflation of concrete data to the end of constituting a representation of knowledge about natural things, which is achieved only if experiment toggles back and forth between abstraction and concretion in a continuous and provisional confirmation of their correspondence. Scientific method doesn't posit that the pursuit of scientific knowledge requires that language be purified of metaphorical, emotive, evaluative, and subjective expressions. Experimentalism doesn't dispute the notion that knowledge is a social product. On the contrary, it requires the collective contribution of many people and relies on the authority of consensus. Experiment is motivated by the aim to gain universal knowledge of the nature of things, and unprecedented in its intuition of a means to that end. The critique of experimental universalism confuses this aim with the conviction that knowledge already gained in the Enlightenment ipso facto has universal application. The case I'd like to make for Enlightenment experimentalism is that it was not a totalizing theory that assumed a transcendent subject, nor even that it had certain demonstrable practical effects, but that it was a remarkable conceptual innovation that bears a singular analogy with others of the period.

Among other things, specious criticisms of Enlightenment experimentalism obscure this radical historicity.

Applied to the realms of political, social, and economic relations, the logic of scientific method offers the clearest argument, only momentarily surprising, that the exclusion of particularity and difference aimed at in quantification creates the grounds for equality. What the partiality of quantification excludes is not different individuals, but the variables whose difference obscures the constant that makes individuals equal, and it thereby conflates and includes them on an empirical basis. My point here is central to my aim in historicizing the Enlightenment by concentrating on its conceptual and methodological innovations and discoveries. The question is not how well or badly they were practiced or applied. A study that concertedly ignored these questions would be problematic, and I don't intend to do that. But to ignore them is first of all what needs to be done (and the analogy with the purpose of quantification should be clear) if attention is not to be distracted from the conceptual heart of the matter.

Quantification

Enlightenment quantification is criticized for reducing the three-dimensional richness of human actuality to one dimension, at best so as to secure the technological precision and productive efficiency that come with the aggregation of particulars according to a common standard. As critics of the Enlightenment have argued, the upsurge of quantification has a multitude of "at worst" consequences that counterbalance what may at best be said of it. In the specific historical focus of my argument, however, quantification becomes visible as not by definition a problem of partiality but a solution to it, because it vastly improves on the results of assessing the whole according to one or another standard that are qualitatively different and therefore inevitably partial. The reduction or bracketing of qualitative difference is not a stealthy liability of quantification but its explicit purpose. Like the aristocratic maxim "birth equals worth," the eighteenth-century custom of referring to nobility and gentry as "quality" bespeaks a restriction of value to one fraction of the whole. Statistical analysis, an Enlightenment invention, promised to subject qualitative judgment to rational and empirical standards. With quantification, value becomes a neutral standard of universal application, a constant that rules out variant and partial criteria of judgment. Granted: in cases where the constitution of the relevant unit itself is crucially contested (like the parameters of a neighborhood but not of an automobile), quantitative bleeds into qualitative judgment. Broadly speaking, however, numerical measurement is equally true to all empirical entities.

Today this is a counterintuitive notion because the criterion of quantity has gained an extraordinary authority in the assessment of what's real. "Big data" has a presumptive value despite the recognition that statistical displays may select phenomena that can be measured and omit what can't; that they may select some measurable phenomena over others that would yield different numerical results; that they may track phenomena from a baseline that has been selected over others that would yield different results. Not the quality but the amount of information is valued as being itself qualitatively valuable, so much so that the positive value of knowledge depends on its quantifiability. The idea of progress isn't itself biased toward the standard of quantity, but quantifiable progress or "improvement," because it's measurable, is implicitly accorded greater value. The epigone of such thinking is the ambition to convert qualitative to quantitative progress in order to give it value. I think these are post-Enlightenment deformations of the Enlightenment impulse to quantify.[24]

Politics

In the representation of sovereignty, the pastoral trope of Eden and the indivisible authority of God's Word here below gave way to the pastoral trope of the state of nature and the political compact to which all people consent.

The totality of *political power* was analyzed and separated out into that of the magistrate, the father, the master, the husband, and the lord. The criticism that domination is thereby explicitly stabilized and authorized within these realms misconceives the force of explicit analysis, which subjects the tacit affirmation of what goes without saying to self-conscious question and debate.

Once it became subject to explicit debate as the theory of patriarchalism, the traditional, tacit analogy between two distinct but inseparable entities, the *state* and the *family*, was dissolved by the recognition that the state is one kind of thing and the family another. This separation inaugurated the modern inquiry into the nature of both the family and the state as not simply distinct but distinctive and separate institutions.

The conception of *England's interest*, coextensive with the royal interest at the outset of the Enlightenment, by the beginning of the eighteenth century was being reconceived as the sum of the multiple private interests of English people.

Over the course of the Enlightenment, the traditional rule of "the king in parliament" evolved into the concept of *representative democracy* ruled by the suffrage of individual citizens, with an increasingly elaborate system of maintaining an ongoing correspondence between the multiple voting individuals and their collective representation. Critics of democratic suffrage in the Enlightenment censure the severe limitations its practice placed on the right to vote: men were held to a minimum property qualification and women were altogether debarred from voting. However, this criticism of Enlightenment democracy addresses its failure to achieve immediate comprehensive application to all (approximated only two centuries later and still politically contested) rather than the simple fact of its conception and existence. This is an anachronistic critique made from the viewpoint of late modern practice (although the failure in suffrage was also criticized by radical thinkers of the Enlightenment), which obscures the significance of innovation by ignoring its radical departure from tradition.

The traditional ideal of *positive liberty*, the notion that freedom is a collective condition found in relations with others, was superseded in the West by the modern ideal of *negative liberty*, or individual freedom from the external constraints of other people and institutions. In very broad terms this historical trajectory reflects a shift from one model of human value to another. The model of positive liberty focuses on the level of the whole (or on the apex of the hierarchy) and assumes that the well-being of the whole accrues to the parts, and that attention to the well-being of any part must damage that of the whole. The model of negative liberty focuses on the level of the particular parts and their individual well-being (or on the bottom of the hierarchy) and abstracts from that level to analyze how far their well-being is consistent with that of the generality, sometimes with an aim to adjust the conditions of individual liberty on that basis or to seek a balance between the well-being of individuals and collectivity. The emergence and normalization of the model of negative liberty is a major feature of Enlightenment thought. As a generalization, this historical trajectory has a heuristic, but also a descriptive, validity. However, its broadest sweep from one model of value to the other is complicated by the ambition of modern socialist and communist movements to exploit the economic productivity of capitalism to establish societies based on values of the collective that self-consciously promote the development of individual potential.

(Civil) Society

Newly constituted in the Enlightenment as a whole over against the state, *civil society* was conceived as a general category comprised of multiple particulars that were themselves conceived as self-standing individuals. In the context of its historical emergence, the *individual* became visible first of all not as an isolated fragment of "society" or as the self-authorizing engine of capitalist enterprise, but as the standard by which the putative wholeness of society could be affirmed or denied by accounting for its individual parts. This is the origin of the individualism of the "individual," which in time will assume a dialectical relationship to modern society as its constituent parts whose autonomy and integrity are threatened by the totalizing forces of socialization. By the same token, the emergence of "society" challenges the tacit integrity and authority of the state by explicitly accounting for the great majority of the population who are not part of the state but are affected by its policies because they are part of the greater whole of the English people.

The Public Sphere

Following the analysis of Jürgen Habermas, (civil) society was conceived in relation to, but in separation out from, the actual institution of the state as a virtual body of private citizens who without precedent played a public role in debating and shaping policy. One result was the establishment of "public opinion" as a central factor in English politics.[25] This modern sense of a virtual public or *public sphere*, like "society" itself, was a complex and self-conscious phenomenon, bound up with the coalescence of the category of *the private*; with the transition from a traditional, status-based to a modern, class-based model of social relations; and with the growing importance of the market and commodity exchange. Moreover, as Habermas describes it, the public sphere first coalesced in the self-consciousness of *printed publication* and the virtual network of communication that gave rise to the idea of a "republic of letters." As modern usage confirms, unlike in tradition "the public" refers both to the actual institution of the public state or government and to the virtual realm of the public.[26]

However, the revolutionary significance of the public sphere, and thereby of Enlightenment thought, has been obscured or erased by reading *The Structural Transformation of the Public Sphere* as though it were a text of modern political and social theory aimed at (mis)describing early Enlightenment practice rather than an effort to characterize the thought of the early Enlightenment in the historicity of its formation. The effect has been, first, to conform Habermas's effort to capture the fluid process of social emergence to a static social-scientific model. Second, critics have imported into the experience of the Enlightenment the putative data of later periods. Third, critics have ignored Habermas's focus on the radical importance of the public sphere as an emergent concept in the history of sociopolitical thought, seeing little value in thinking about what it replaced and reducing his thesis to the claim that a naively utopian reduction of that concept had been achieved in practice.[27]

The Enlightenment coalescence of society and the public sphere gave visibility and efficacy to the vast majority of English people, who traditionally had amounted to an undiscriminated and inconsequential mass of "commoners." This was also the effect of the Enlightenment shift in the dominant conception of social relations from *status* to *class*. Before the Enlightenment, nobility (or aristocracy) was conceived as a qualitative whole consisting of reciprocal and inseparable parts: noble lineage, political authority, wealth, physical beauty, inner virtue. This was a whole whose indivisibility bespoke a unity of external and internal honor, which as a touchstone of human value was taken to be universally shared but as a condition of being was seen to exclude commoners, who were without honor. This status system was static: nobility was unalterable and natural because determined by birth. By the latter decades of the Enlightenment, the parts of nobility were being explicitly acknowledged to be neither reciprocal nor inseparable. The aristocratic status system was in the process of being replaced by the system of class, which classified people by income and, because income was quantitative and therefore variable, assumed the possibility of upward and downward social mobility. This change in thinking, although widely assumed in modern thought, typically has been muddied in substance (the rise of the class system is reduced to the rise of the middle class) and in chronology ("the middle class is always rising").

A further complication has been the association of the middle class with the bourgeoisie, a term that obscures the quantitative significance of the new standard of difference and makes one middle-class region and profession a synecdoche for the class itself. This Franco-German usage dovetails with a broadly West European (or Anglo-American) usage that situates the change specifically in the eighteenth century, and, especially in its Marxist development, associates it specifically with the rise of capitalism and thereby feeds the confusion of the Enlightenment with capitalist universality (to which I return below). The complication here is not only that in England capitalism arose in the seventeenth century, in the countryside, and in the context of an agrarian economy rather than in the context of an industrial economy in towns and cities. The equation of the middle class with the bourgeoisie also has skewed the broad empirical study of socioeconomic history by accommodating it to one particular model.

For many years Marxist thought has guided my own. I value it, among other reasons, for its attention to empirical history, and in that spirit I read Marx attentive to the relation between the theoretical dimensions of his historiography and the historical practice it seeks to interpret. I aim to follow Marxism but not to be ruled by it. This is inevitably a hermeneutic task, nowhere more obviously than in questions, like this one, of how formulations that refer to one historical context can be transported to a different one.

Capitalist and Enlightenment Universality

The following quotations indicate the magnitude of the problem.

> Ever since the Age of Enlightenment, Reason in its universalizing mission has been parasitic upon a much less lofty, much more mundane, palpably material and singularly invidious force, namely the universalist urge of capital. From at least the middle of the eighteenth century, for two hundred years, Reason has travelled the world piggyback, carried across oceans and continents by colonial powers eager to find new grounds for trade, extraction and the productive expansion of capital.[28]

> Historically, the process by which the bourgeoisie became in the course of the eighteenth century the politically dominant class was masked by the establishment of an explicit, coded and formally egalitarian juridical framework.... But the development and generalization of disciplinary mechanisms constituted the other, dark side of these processes.... The real, corporal disciplines constituted the foundation of the formal, juridical liberties.... 'The Enlightenment,' which discovered the liberties, also invented the disciplines.[29]

> Bourgeois universalism came into being at the end of the seventeenth century and the beginning of the eighteenth century, then, as a deeply conflicted set of interests: Its universal claims on freedom are defined by a universalizing logic far greater and more powerful than the 'rights of man,' namely, the growth of the money form and the rise of colonialism. In this way the radical parochialism of bourgeois universalism would define what the mercantile and later industrial bourgeoisie will want from reason and faith in the period of Europe's imperialist expansion and development of the nation state in the late eighteenth and nineteenth centuries: a rationalization of national progress and identity.... The universal claims of bourgeois enlightenment are

> *built from* the exclusionary and hierarchical judgements *of* disenlightenment as the necessary means of developing and maintaining bourgeois progress and economic power globally.[30]

> The ideas of the Enlightenment changed the world. Their legacy was western modernity.... The West's inheritance from the intellectual battles of the 18th century was liberalism and capitalism. These have made the West, for good or ill, what it is.[31]

As these passages make clear, a central criticism of Enlightenment thought has been the notion that Enlightenment universalism is the velvet glove that conceals the iron fist of capitalist universalism. Certainly the Enlightenment is known for doctrines of universalism and inclusivity—natural rights, religious toleration, equality before the law, and others. In the face of these doctrines, skeptics have leveled at the Enlightenment charges of naivete, bad faith, hypocrisy, even the seeming pursuit of equality as a cover for its stealthy ongoing subversion. One aim of this introduction is to question the basis for those charges as they arise in particular areas of thought. Given the forceful and widespread indictment of capitalism as both doctrine and practice, we might expect its frequent association with the Enlightenment to substantiate this kind of critique. However, the assumption that early capitalism was an expression of Enlightenment thought because it emerged in the Enlightenment period is one that Enlightenment analysis itself has taught us to make explicit and thereby to question. What we mean by capitalist universalism is less straightforward, moreover, than these passages, as well as Horkheimer and Adorno's polemic against a totalizing absolutism, would suggest. The importance of the topic deserves extended treatment that goes beyond introductory purposes, and I'll return to it later on.[32]

In the meantime, it's worth noting that the relation between capitalism and the Enlightenment may be temporal but not necessarily causal or ideological. It's been argued that very different ideals of universal and inclusive equality unmarked by limiting conditions come to the fore in a broad range of belief systems during the long eighteenth century, and that the thesis of a single "Enlightenment project" can

> obscure the multiplicity of universal-isms [sic] across eighteenth-century European political thought, each with distinct foundational claims, varying relationships to conceptualizations of human diversity and to humanity (which themselves differ from thinker to thinker, and even from text to text), and different political orientations toward the nature and limits of state power in theory and in practice. These philosophical sensibilities and approaches can yield remarkably different political arguments toward foreign peoples, international justice, and imperialism. Thus, rather than ask whether 'the Enlightenment project' and 'Enlightenment universalism' are compatible with an appreciation of cultural pluralism or whether they are at bottom imperializing ideologies, it is more constructive to pose more precise and

historically accurate versions of such questions with regard to particular texts and thinkers.[33]

This cogent observation suggests that analysis begin by decoupling the Enlightenment and early capitalism in order to analyze each in its own right, understanding that reason and empirical evidence may then justify recoupling them on a firmer and more explicit basis. Moreover, if we assent to the notion that ideals of universality and inclusivity preponderate in the Enlightenment and modernity across a broad and varied range of thought, we may want to proceed at the outset on the hypothesis that these ideals affirm nothing more ideologically specifiable than the value of a speculative detachment that comes when knowledge is not tacitly affirmed but explicitly questioned. Finally, we may ask if the aspiration to universalism, rather than culminating at this historical juncture, only becomes thinkable when the impulse to make knowledge explicit has become broadly available as a habit of cultural inquiry.

Feudalism was a socioeconomic order structured as a hierarchy of qualitative differences in station, kind of service, and degree of dependence. It cohered on the basis of a tacit conviction that the reciprocal relations between all levels rendered it a whole that obviated the analysis of its parts. Capitalism is an order structured by a quantitative understanding that entails the explicit analysis of what was once tacit. How was the transition from a tacit to an explicit, from a qualitative to a quantitative order, materially mediated?

The discrimination of capitalist from Enlightenment universality requires that we do justice to what they have in common. Extrapolating from Marx's formulations in the terms of this study, the emergence of capitalism from feudalism entailed the partialization of a seemingly self-evident integrity, its rational and empirical division into parts, their further subdivisions, and their implicit ramifications. The major categories that were in dynamic transformation are labor, property, value, exchange, and structure. More specifically: historical materialism describes how labor is initially and successively divided; labor as a qualitative and singular act of personal service is abstracted to the quantitative, variable, and impersonal measures of productive and wage labor; aspects of existence that seem internal, coextensive with, and essential to personal individuality are revealed to be accidental and contingent on external circumstance; the absolute oneness of royal sovereignty devolves into the absolute private property of great overlords who formerly had held land in fealty to their royal lord; customary, common, and conditional use-rights shared with others are undermined by absolute ownership of property as alienable and disposable; property as personal propriety (one's own) is abstracted from personhood as impersonal property (what one owns); value is divided into the singularity of qualitative use and multiple units of quantified exchange; production is divided into serving the consumption of material products and enabling the accumulation and reproduction of abstract capital; material infrastructure, once totalized as a determinant foundation, generates and makes available for further analysis an indeterminate range and number of superstructures;

the self-evident correspondence of superstructural "forms" to infrastructural "forces" of production is the precondition for uneven development, when forms come to be experienced self-consciously as the "fetters" that bind and contradict production.³⁴

At the same time, the historical logic of capitalism is not a teleology but a dialectical process. Hegel's formulaic "thesis-antithesis-synthesis" is not a closed system: achieved syntheses are also new theses. To invoke an overarching formula of the present study, only when distinctions become intelligible as separations does conflation become possible. Capitalist partialization precludes a return to the tacit belief in qualitative wholes but sanctions the explicit creation of new wholes both within, and through the conflation of, former parts. For example: the division of collective labor entails a narrowing of focus and purpose, establishing the conditions for a more precise knowledge and an enhanced productivity that lay the ground for specialized ventures and corporate consolidations of labor; by the same token, in the passage from policies of positive to those of negative liberty, the removal of monopolistic constraints on individual enterprise encourages competition and growth through acquisitions and mergers, which in turn reduce the field of competing companies and prepare for twentieth-century monopoly capitalism; commodity exchange, by abstracting from the simple reciprocity of production for consumption, establishes the conditions for the virtual, and thereby vastly inclusive, collectivity of the market. The self-conscious virtuality of the capitalist market replaced the tacit actuality of a feudal order whose wholeness seemed to go without saying.

Imperialism

The critique of imperialism during the Enlightenment assumes, like the critique of capitalism, that Enlightenment and capitalist universality are the same:

> The subaltern studies historians argue that Indian nationalism is impoverished because it is *too* philosophical. It is a historical repetition in colonial space that reveals the particularistic limits of the European Enlightenment's universalist ambitions . . . the Eurocentric limits of Enlightenment universalism.³⁵

> The Enlightenment's universalizing will to knowledge (for better or worse) feeds Orientalism's will to power.³⁶

> Euro-American postmodernism dissolves the notion of a homogeneous "West" as it has been constructed within Enlightenment literary and philosophical categories.³⁷

> The urge toward the systematization of all human knowledge, by which we characterize the Enlightenment, in other words led directly to the relegation of black people to a lower rung on the Great Chain of Being.³⁸

It's not surprising that imperialism, less theoretically weighty and more figuratively expansive than capitalism, has been linked even more insistently to

Enlightenment universalism. An unusually discerning and thoughtful survey of recent readings of the Enlightenment by postcolonial scholars makes one aware of an unstated but powerful inclination in recent years to see the Enlightenment, chronologically poised between the early modern voyages of discovery and the great European empires of the nineteenth century, as therefore responsible for both the corruption of what came before and the generation of what came after.[39] The latter implication is succinctly expressed, in works critical of the period, by the phrase "the Enlightenment project."[40]

The postcolonial critique has tended to subsume the broad range of activities undertaken by Enlightenment expeditions and correspondence—gathering scientific, geographical, and cultural information and commercial exchange—under the narrowly colonial activities of conquest, the extraction of natural resources, and the exploitation of the labor and goods of native populations. Scholars have been concerned recently to rebalance this partial perspective by documenting the interrelated nature of these activities and the ambitions that motivated them, which had the effect, among other things, of fundamentally reconstructing Europe's knowledge of itself. In the same spirit, there's been a concerted effort to complicate what's been the prevailing assumption that the influence and exchange of ideas, of entrepreneurial energy and invention, and of cultural curiosity and interest, was a unidirectional movement from engaged metropolitan to passive periphery.[41]

British Enlightenment colonialism, seen in its actual concrete specificity rather than, in a late modern postcolonial retrojection as a totality ranged against its external other, takes shape internally as a dialectical relation of colonial parts. The totality or whole, the international British Empire of the eighteenth century, was precedented by the intranational colonial histories of Scotland, Wales, and Ireland, and decentered by those internal relations. As colonial peripheries to England's metropolitan, these countries also helped constitute the greater metropolitan of Great Britain that was ranged against external peripheries like India and the American colonies. So, the internal parts of Britain have double and contradictory functions.[42]

Macro-pastoralism

The Enlightenment relation between the peripheries internal to Great Britain and metropolitan Britain is itself rooted ultimately in the traditional but shifting relation between rural and urban England, whose history is told by the ancient genre of pastoral poetry and by its punctual Virgilian extrusion, georgic. Pastoral has always represented the relation between country and city as a dialectic, an opposition subtilized by connection. In the long history of English pastoral poetry, it became conventional in the Renaissance for their connection to be represented in the absolute terms of allegory. Rural life was imagined to signify the actions and passions of courtly and urban personages, a poetic representation that roughly paralleled the imagination of Scotland, Wales, and Ireland in terms of, and as parts of the whole of, Britain that were distinct but not separable from it.

The political relations of each country to England were too different to warrant general terminology; in the sixteenth century only Ireland had the effective status of an English colony. However, by the early seventeenth century, the separateness of England on the one hand and all three countries on the other was being felt more sharply, no doubt under the broad influence of incipient nationalism and perhaps in early evidence of the Enlightenment impulse toward making the tacit explicit. This impulse became very clear in the striking redirection of the pastoral genre over the course of the following century and a half, through self-consciously skeptical experimentation with traditional generic categories and a newfound attention to the empirical reality of cities, countryside, and the nature of their relationship. In both material geography and its literary representation, the country was being absorbed by the city even as it retained its rural identity in the interstices, and at the heart, of urbanity, while the industry for transporting produce from the country to urban markets increasingly infiltrated the countryside. It's instructive to think of the peripheral and metropolitan identity characteristic of contemporary empire, as it recapitulated and coextended this domestic sociopolitical complexity, as an imperial *macro-pastoralism*.[43] The preceding account of Enlightenment empire is at odds with a common view that the relation between metropolitan and periphery was definitively and invariably unequal because constituted as a dichotomous structure of domination and exploitation. There's no doubt that the inequality of this macro-pastoral relationship had those features; but it was an inequality that also partook, like the domestic relationship, of nuanced similarity and reciprocal interchange.

Conjectural History

Imperialism was first of all a geographical or spatial relationship. But the empirical and rational understanding of Enlightenment thought encouraged contemporaries to reflect on empire as it emerged and developed in time. One of the great achievements of Enlightenment intellectuals in three different nations of Europe was the notion that history, traditionally taken for granted as consisting in chronology alone, has another, "spatial" dimension as well.[44] The best-known elaboration of this method of reading history is that of Karl Marx and Friedrich Engels in the nineteenth century, whose separation and conflation of the levels of "infrastructure" and "superstructure" is crucial to their analysis of historical change. Abstracting a single "moment" from its chronological or diachronic temporality, they in effect ask two questions. First, how might the different levels of thought and action in this synchronic slice, now explicitly separable from one another (e.g., modes of material production, social organization, political system, natural knowledge, intellectual knowledge, artistic representation), be seen as unified by their formal or structural similarities? Second, what does the structural homology of this moment suggest, once we return it to chronology, about its sequential relation to other moments that precede and follow it? These questions were inspired by the Enlightenment predecessors of Marx and Engels, who were stimulated in turn by the voyages of discovery, exploration, and imperial expansion that flourished from the sixteenth to the eighteenth centuries.

Travel narratives generated a vast amount of data about other cultures that differed fundamentally from the European norm. This data, contemporary with the European voyagers, offered what was in effect a spatial, synchronic register of different cultural levels that invited coordination with the temporal, diachronic register of different stages that Europeans knew their own cultures had passed through. Once compared and analyzed, the results seemed to testify to the correlation of similar levels of thought and behavior across a broad range of cultures, both past and present and both European and non-European. The innovation of conjectural history, which required a characteristically Enlightenment separation and conflation of chronological stages and structural levels, coincided with and fed ethnographic and anthropological speculation about what came to be seen as "human culture." This was, in effect, the origin of the "social sciences," which, although confronted by kinds of variables far more daunting than those encountered in the physical sciences on which they were modeled, proceeded in a comparable spirit of probabilistic inquiry. Conjectural history exemplifies the Enlightenment's ambition to quantify data and thereby to universalize knowledge. Ethnocentric bias was to some degree inevitable; however, the aim was not to impose particular standards on the generality, European standards on the world, but to generalize about the world on the empirical basis of multiple particulars.[45] From this aim emerged a "stadial" theory that all cultures went through the same three or four stages of material development correlated with cultural development. Typical of the Enlightenment concern with the relationship between separation and conflation, stadial theory was susceptible to evaluative theories of hierarchical superiority, but it's also enjoyed descriptive application. Anti-Enlightenment polemic can be gratuitously harsh and absolute.[46]

Slavery

But if the partial and one-dimensional view of Enlightenment imperialism must be complicated in the ways I've suggested, that dimension must also be seen head-on as—to recall my previous words—conquest, extraction, and exploitation. The Enlightenment wasn't the linchpin of British imperialism, either chronologically or in practice, but it was deeply invested in the surging empire, and the trade in slaves was an Enlightenment institution. What does this mean? On the one hand, the slave trade ended only after the eighteenth century; on the other, its end culminated the momentum created by the unrelenting abolition movement of the later eighteenth century. On the one hand, the slave trade began well before the Enlightenment; on the other, it peaked around the turn of the eighteenth century, an indispensable cog in the profitable machinery of transatlantic commerce. Some apologists have gone so far as to commend the British Enlightenment for having abolished slavery, remaining silent on its role in fomenting it.[47] The significance of the abolition movement as an Enlightenment phenomenon is not that it countered what was a profoundly unenlightened policy that the Enlightenment had vigorously pursued, but that in repudiating that policy it pursued principles that are rightly associated with Enlightenment thought. This is to note, again, that to generalize about a period doesn't reduce all particulars to sameness—the British slave trade spoke for some Britons but not for others—an awareness we owe to Enlightenment thought. But to periodize is by definition to generalize.

Slavery is the most flagrant failure of Enlightenment universalism, defying the terms of my abstract model of Enlightenment thought—from distinction to separation and conflation—and making plain that a more concrete analysis is required. Over the course of the seventeenth century, the royal ownership of England's demesne, implicit in doctrines of royal absolutism, foundered and devolved into the principle of private property owned absolutely by landholders. In the American colonies, the extraction of raw materials invited the extraction of laborers from Africa. British traders were facilitated in this by African leaders, for whom political and chattel slavery were a familiar practice. In the transatlantic shipment of raw materials this practice was concentrated into a trade in human property. Absolute ownership authorized English landholders to buy and deracinate others who were beyond the real if meager common-law protections of native-born English people.

Early modern exploration and conquest arguably first confronted white Europeans with Black people in a physical and extended proximity. Did this unprecedented degree of contact give rise to a color racism and a sense of separation palpable enough to frustrate conflation so far as to justify human property and make slavery acceptable? During the Enlightenment, the grounds of human difference had become an explicit and much-debated question, and the category of otherness acquired a lability across the threshold between the human and the nonhuman. "Race," "nation," and "state" were overlapping and competing terms for sociopolitical collectivity, and the implications of "race" ramified in several directions. It's been argued that by erasing and incorporating indigenous "national" territories and identities, imperial expansion laid the ground for the replacement of the concept of nation by that of race, at least with reference to the people who were thereby incorporated. The modern language of race, "racial" and "proto-racial thinking," "racialism," and "racism" is one of the tools scholars use to discover the nature and sources of slavery in this period, which also is fed by a complicated historical genealogy of slavery that would seem to point in a different direction from the discourse of race after the Enlightenment slave trade. Yet one inheritance of that emergent discourse is the Greco-Roman difference between, and entanglement of, political tyranny and chattel slavery. Color difference and white supremacy are inseparable from modern racial discourse; but that's not true of Enlightenment discourse, in which speculation about climate, and by no means only its relevance to color, occupies a great deal of attention. Underlying all this, the ancient distinction between nature and nurture, sophisticated by modern thought, asserted its perennial authority. The post-Enlightenment development of racial science may have required—counterintuitively?—a consensus that Black people were not nonhuman but a lower form of humanity.[48]

Because it's hard to conceive that economic factors played no part in this failure of the schematic sequence of distinction-separation-conflation, slavery may exemplify in the Old World the capacity of capitalist universalism to dovetail with and to subsume Enlightenment universalism. And in the New: the revolutionary break from Great Britain demanded of the American colonies the explicit promulgation of the grounds of union. The presence of enslaved Black people blatantly contradicted the ideal of a republic founded on freedom from tyranny. But it proved pragmatic to include them in population counts that attested to national prosperity, and to count them as three-fifths of a white person in order to assuage the slave states and preserve the union itself. These practical inducements, along with the profitability of slave labor, sponsored the solidification of the racial category of whiteness and set the terms for the culture of white supremacy—slavery in other terms—that runs like a wound through American history and the daily lives of Black Americans: civil war; the defeat of Reconstruction; the lynching epidemic; Jim Crow segregation; voter suppression; mass incarceration; the routine denial of benefits and services routinely enjoyed by other citizens; brutal racial violence; the continuing and intractable inequality of Black people.[49] There's no greater testimony than this to the failure of Enlightenment conflation.[50]

1   *Tradition as Tacit Knowledge*

This chapter is an effort to explore the meaning of "tradition" from the perspective of English Enlightenment culture. The perspective seems promising because we commonly see Enlightenment thought as predicated on a more or less absolute repudiation of tradition. My inquiry is motivated by two basic questions. First, how does the idea of tradition coalesce under the powerful pressure of its wholesale critique? My second question grows out of the notion that once valued ideas and institutions do not simply disappear when their force has been undermined. What "does the work" of tradition after it has lost its authority in modern culture? The short answer to my first question is that tradition fails because it is seen to be a mode of "tacit"[1] knowledge. The short answer to my second question is that in the modern world, the tacit knowledge embodied in "tradition" is replaced by the tacit knowledge embodied, in different ways, in "ideology" and "the aesthetic." Throughout this chapter, when I speak of "modernity" as the opposite number of "tradition," I mean to refer to both the chronological and the anthropological—both the diachronic and the synchronic—senses of those terms. My argument will be broadly temporal in focus; but I think the general idea of tacit knowledge is relevant also to our spatial sense of the difference between tradition and our own cultural "modernity."

Tradition

I will begin with four quotations that span the English Civil Wars of 1642–1660.

In 1628, Parliament petitioned Charles I to affirm his support of what it argued were the English people's accustomed freedoms from arbitrary governmental demands. In the debate that followed it was suggested that the Petition of Right also affirm the customary locus of "sovereign power" in the monarchy. Sir Henry Marten argued strenuously against such an affirmation, however, because it would invite controversy too explicitly. "This petition will run through many hands," he pointed out, and people will "presently fall to arguing and descanting what sovereign power is—what is the latitude? whence the original? where the bounds? etc.—with many such curious and captious questions. . . . Sovereign power is then best worth when it is held in tacit veneration, not when it is profaned by vulgar hearings or examinations."[2] Fourteen years after the Petition of Right, on the eve of civil war, Charles himself made a similar prediction about the consequences of disturbing the constitutional balance:

> So new a power will undoubtedly intoxicate persons who were not born to it, and beget not only divisions among them as equals, but in them contempt of us, as become an equal to them. . . . All great changes are extremely inconvenient,

and almost infallibly beget yet greater changes, which beget yet greater inconveniences . . . till . . . at last the common people . . . discover this *arcanum imperii*, that all this was done by them, but not for them, and grow weary of journey-work, and set up for themselves, [and] call parity and independence liberty.[3]

Although Charles's prophecy came strikingly to pass, in the end "the common people" grew weary of the commonwealth as well, and Charles's son was restored to the throne in 1660. On the eve of the Restoration, however, George Monck, its chief military engineer, claimed that the anti-monarchical consequences of the civil war were probably irreversible: "Before these unhappy Wars the Government of these Nations was Monarchical in Church and State: these wars have given birth and growth to several Interests both in Church and State heretofore not known; though now upon many accounts very considerable. . . . *That Government then that is most able to comprehend and protect all Interests as aforesaid must needs be Republique.*"[4] Of course, Monck was wrong. But if the most immediate political consequences of the civil war could thus be reversed by military and legal means, its more long-term implications could not. Five years after the Restoration, Edward Waterhouse, bemused by England's changing social landscape, ruefully reflected in similar terms on the limits of legal authority. Our ancestors, he observed, distinguished between their social stations by tacit social practice, by their "Garb, Equipage, Dyet, Housholdstuff, Clothes, [and] Education of Children . . . not by sumptuary Laws, or Magistratique sanction, but by common agreement, and general understanding."[5]

What interests me about these four passages is how they articulate the discovery of what might be called "tradition," which paradoxically is found in and through the very process of realizing that it has been lost. "Tradition" owes its force to what Marten calls the "tacit" veneration by which it goes without saying, it's taken-for-granted-ness, its deep embeddedness within customary social practice. To "discover" tradition is to abstract it and throw it into relief, literally to remove the cover afforded by its customary embeddedness. Thus Charles predicts the common people will discover the *arcana imperii*, which, no longer woven invisibly and mysteriously into the fabric of collective necessity, now appear nakedly before them, one interest among many. It is in this sense that Monck sees the civil war as having "given birth" to the present multiplicity of interests, which did not exist previously in that they were "heretofore not known" or acknowledged as such.[6] The metaphor of tradition as a kind of invisible clothing is also pertinent to Waterhouse's insight into the way dress and other kinds of customary behavior enforce a rule of tradition that is very different from the rule of law. Sumptuary legislation announces not tradition but its decay, the point at which the law discloses the social symbolism of clothing for what it is, obviating its tacit authority in the very act of proclaiming and exploiting it explicitly.

In speaking this way I am of course pursuing a special understanding of the concept. By this understanding, a "modern tradition" is, strictly speaking, a contradiction in terms, in that it posits a tacit knowledge under cultural conditions—especially, the condition of explicit enunciation—that prohibit it. Although I will soon be moved to modify the strictness of this understanding, it has some advantages over other ways of conceiving the relationship between tradition and modernity. In the fruitful hypothesis of the modern "invention" of traditions, the tacitness of tradition, although acknowledged, plays a less prominent role in defining the nature of tradition. As a result, the problem central to my inquiry—how the tacitness of tradition can survive the self-consciousness of invention—is not fully pursued there.[7] One aim of the present argument is to pose the problem of tradition in modernity in terms of the persistence or invention not of tradition as such, but of the tacitness that "traditionally" distinguishes tradition as a mode of knowledge.

The most concrete and powerful model for what happens to tradition when knowledge becomes explicit involves an epochal change in the material technology of knowledge production and consumption: the long-term "replacement" of orality by literacy and of script by print. (Needless to say, the impression of irreversibility and permanence associated with change in the technology of knowledge when conceived as an epochal "discovery" is belied by the temporal and regional multiplicity of such changes. By the same token, "replacement" is really a matter of changing dominance under continuing conditions of overlap.[8]) When knowledge is rendered relatively ostensive, objective, and permanent by such technologies, it undergoes a transformation that is akin to less material processes of rationalization, which also concentrate attention on knowledge that previously had been customary and "taken for granted."[9]

In early modern England, this insight proved most immediately useful, perhaps, in the context of religious dispute, where the self-consciously "objective" religion of the Book was understood to improve upon the defects and corruptions attendant on the tacitness of the Roman Catholic "tradition." Justifying his Protestantism against the skepticism of Father Richard Simon in 1682, John Dryden was quick to make the crucial point:

> If *written words* from time are not secur'd,
> How can we think have *oral Sounds* endur'd?
> Which *thus* transmitted, if *one* Mouth has fail'd,
> Immortal Lyes on *Ages* are intail'd:
> And that some such have been, is prov'd too plain;
> If we consider *Interest*, *Church*, and *Gain*.

In fact, Dryden is content to use the term "tradition" to refer to the legitimation mechanisms of both Christian churches, so long as the superiority of the Protestant version is clear:

> Must *all Tradition* then be set aside?
> This to affirm were Ignorance, or Pride.
> . . . .
> *Tradition written* therefore more commends

> *Authority*, than what from *Voice* descends:
> And this, as perfect as its kind can be,
> Rouls down to us the Sacred History.

Before Gutenberg and Luther, priests could be infallible with impunity:

> In those dark times they learn'd their knack so well,
> That by long use they grew *Infallible*:
> At last, a knowing Age began t'enquire
> If *they* the *Book*, or *That* did *them* inspire

Dryden's confidence may suggest that contemporaries of this "knowing age" were ambivalent about the discovery of tradition, which could mean by turns a debilitating loss of social cohesion and a liberating gain in enlightenment. Indeed, it could mean both to the same person. Having defended himself against the demands of the priest, the Anglican Dryden now joins forces with Charles I in defense against the demanding common people:

> The Book thus put in every vulgar hand,
> Which each presum'd he best cou'd understand,
> The *Common Rule* was made the Common Prey;
> And at the mercy of the *Rabble* lay.[10]

Where the context of debate was not religious, Protestant English people found it even harder to dispense with the doctrinal authority of tradition. Largely in relation to the developing conflict between king and Parliament, seventeenth-century common lawyers had propounded a theory of English history that explained and legitimated present practice by reference to "fundamental law," to the traditionality of unwritten, indeed immemorial, custom. According to Sir John Davies, "The *Common Law of England* is nothing else but the *Common Custome* of the Realm: and a Customes which hath obtained the force of a Law is always said to be *Jus non scriptum*: for it cannot be made or created either by Charter, or by Parliament, which are Acts reduced to writing, and are alwaies matter of Record; but being onely matter of fact, and consisting in use and practice, it can be recorded and registered no-where but in the memory of the people."[11]

Sir William Blackstone, meanwhile, observed that "Aulus Gellius defines the *jus non scriptum* to be that which is '*tacito et illiterato hominum consensu et moribus expressum*.'"[12] The "common-law interpretation of English history" is one of the most radical, and paradoxical, attempts to sustain the credibility of tradition under conditions of its increasingly epidemic disclosure, a subservience to the notion of historical precedent so absolute as to seem, with hindsight, a counterintuitive "stop in the mind" vainly postponing the modern recognition of historical change and difference. Already in 1649 John Warr was writing, "The notion of fundamental law is no such idol as men make it. . . . For what, I pray you, is fundamental law but such customs as are of the eldest date and longest continuance? . . . The more fundamental a law is, the more difficult, not the less necessary, to be reformed."[13]

Francis Bacon was conventional in grounding his account of "tradition" etymologically in the process of transfer: "The expressing or transferring our knowledge to others. . . . I will term by the general name of Tradition or Delivery." But the very effort to enunciate the tacit nature of such a transfer leads Bacon to remark on its epistemological undependability—on the conflict, that is, between belief and knowledge: "For as knowledges are now delivered, there is a kind of contract of error between the deliverer and the receiver: for he that delivereth knowledge desireth to deliver it in such form as may be best believed, and not as may be best examined; and he that receiveth knowledge desireth rather present satisfaction than expectant inquiry and so rather not to doubt than not to err. . . . In this same anticipated and prevented [i.e., anticipated] knowledge, no man knoweth how he came to the knowledge which he hath obtained." And like Dryden, Bacon associates the fallibility of tradition with that of orality: "The most ancient times . . . are buried in oblivion and silence: to that silence succeeded the fables of the poets: to those fables the written record which have come down to us. Thus between the hidden depths of antiquity and the days of tradition and evidence that followe there is drawn a veil, as it were, of fables, which come in and occupy the middle region that separates what has perished from what survives."[14] Thomas Hobbes made a similar point about the opacity of the fabulous, but his emphasis was political not epistemological and his judgment was positive not negative. In the year of the regicide, Hobbes observed there was no shortage of rationales for rebellion:

> I think that those ancients foresaw this who preferred that the knowledge of Justice be wrapped up in fables rather than exposed to discussion. Before questions of that kind began to be debated, Princes did not lay claim to sovereign power, they simply exercised it. They did not defend their power by arguments but by punishing the wicked and defending the good. In return the citizens did not measure Justice by the comments of private men but by the laws of the commonwealth; and were kept at Peace not by discussions but by the power of Government. In fact, they revered sovereign power, whether it resided in a man or in an Assembly, as a kind of visible divinity. . . . The simplicity of those time evidently could not understand such sophisticated stupidity. It was peace therefore and a golden age.[15]

For Hobbes, tradition is to be valued as a guarantor of political peace. But for Bacon, tradition is problematic as a mode of knowledge because it precludes the detachment necessary for "examination" and "inquiry," the separation of the "what" from the "how" ("No man knoweth how he came to the knowledge which he hath obtained") that is encouraged by literacy and especially by print. The idea that knowledge presupposes detachment itself may be seen as a modern development, in that it entails the fundamental principle of empirical epistemology. To know something requires that it be constituted, over against the knowing subject, as an object of knowledge. In Robert Boyle's formulation, this condition is met in the separability of "opinion" from "experiment": let the experimenter's "opinions be never so false, his experiments being true, I am not obliged to believe the former, and am left at liberty to benefit myself of the latter; and though he have erroneously superstructed upon his experiments, yet the foundation being solid, a more wary builder may be very much furthered by it in the erection of more judicious and consistent fabrics."[16] John Locke articulates the same principle when he denies the authority of religious enthusiasm as a ground of assent: "Every Conceit that thoroughly warms our Fancies must pass for an Inspiration, if there be nothing but the Strength of our Perswasions, whereby to judge of our Perswasions: If *Reason* must not examine their Truth by something extrinsical to the Perswasions themselves; Inspirations and Delusions, Truth and Falshood will have the same Measure, and will not be possible to be distinguished." In Locke's formulation, the problem with tradition is that it confuses chronological with epistemological detachment, antiquity with truth; whereas in fact, "*in traditional Truths, each remove weakens the force of the proof.*"[17]

The critique of religious knowledge—the cornerstone of Enlightenment thought and here exemplified in Locke—provided contemporaries with their first and easiest access to a more comprehensive formulation and critique of traditional knowledge as such. In his most notorious work, Bernard Mandeville followed the deist lead in conceiving the system of moral virtue as a plot of "moralists" and "politicians" to govern the multitudes. John Toland had lately argued that "the *natural Man* . . . counts Divine Things mere Folly, calls *Religion* a feverish Dream of superstitious Heads, or a politick Trick invented by States-men to aw the credulous Vulgar." Later in his career, however, Mandeville explicated this argument as a kind of shorthand for describing a social process that is really neither so intentional, so personalizable, nor so punctual in its effects as this account suggests. He gives the names "Moralists" and "Politicians"

> promiscuously to All that, having studied Human Nature, have endeavour'd to civilize Men, and render them more and more tractable, either for the Ease of Governours and Magistrates, or else for the Temporal Happiness of Society in general. I think of all Inventions of this Sort [as] the joint Labour of Many. Human Wisdom is the Child of Time. It was not the Contrivance of one Man, nor could it have been the Business of a few Years, to establish a Notion, by which a rational Creature is kept in Awe for Fear of it Self, and an Idol is set up, that shall be its own Worshiper.[18]

Retaining as metaphor the religious language of idol worship already familiar from Bacon's four "idols," "which by tradition, credulity, and negligence have come to be received," Mandeville's crucial qualification affords us the germ of social theory.[19] The calculating corruption of governing personages and institutions provides a means of conceiving the process of socialization itself—of conceiving the "institution" of society as having a transpersonal, supraintentional agency. But this is also to describe the production of tacit knowledge: tacit not only for the recipients of moral doctrine (as in the relatively crude model of politico-religious conspiracy), but also for its promulgators.

If the critique of religious knowledge gives Enlightenment writers their first access to the critique of tradition as tacit knowledge, religion retains a special status thereafter as the one branch of knowledge for which the emergent norm of epistemological explicitness, of skeptical detachment, may yet be questionable. Locke distinguished between the credibility of religious "faith" and "revelation," which are confirmed by "reason," and the credulity of religious "enthusiasm," which is not. And of enthusiastic modes of knowledge he wrote, "If such groundlesse thoughts as these concerne ordinary matters and not religion and possesse the minde strongly we call it raveing and every one thinkes it a degree of madnesse, but in religion men accustomed to the thoughts of revelation make a greater allowance to it."[20] Jonathan Swift alters Locke's terminology by using "enthusiasm" as the general category for all religious belief, whether credible or credulous; but the division of knowledge he proposes is nonetheless similar. With respect to the other two realms of knowledge, Swift's attack on false knowledge is unqualified. With religion alone he is willing to affirm the existence of a realm of faith or "inspiration" in which knowledge is properly tacit.[21] Except in the extreme and relatively uncommon case of agnosticism, religion remained the one category in the ongoing disclosure of "tradition" for which a tacit dependence on authority—that is, for which "faith"—was deemed not only proper but requisite.

For this reason alone, my opening account of tradition's "discovery" by modernity—the doubleness whereby what is found is also lost in the very same movement—stands in need of revision. For under the aegis of empirical epistemology, tradition is not so much obliterated in the modern experience as vastly discredited—or consigned, where still acceptable, to the narrow and increasingly besieged enclosure of religious faith. In the modern world, "religion" explicitly defines the territory of normative tacit knowing once tacitly encompassed by the vast domain of "tradition." When tacit knowledge is acknowledged to be inescapable in emergent "political" theory as well, it can only cause problems. A case in point is the contractarian refutation of patriarchalism. Sir Robert Filmer began his famous treatise by assuring the reader that "I have nothing to meddle with mysteries of the present state. Such arcana imperii, or cabinet councils, the vulgar may not pry into. An implicit faith is given to the meanest artificer in his own craft; how much more is it, then, due to a Prince in the profoundest secrets of government[?]" Algernon Sidney's reply was acerbic: Filmer "renounces these inquiries through an implicit faith, which never enter'd into the head of any but fools. . . . Such as have reason, understanding, or common sense, will and ought to . . . suspect the words of such as are interested in deceiving or persuading them not to see with their own eyes, that they may be more easily deceived."[22] But how does the contractarian justify the notion of a consensual "original" compact that can bind later generations? Distinguishing between "an express [i.e., a verbal] and a tacit consent" to "the Laws of any Government," Locke remarks that "the difficulty is, what ought to be look'd upon as a *tacit Consent*, and how far it binds, *i.e.* how far any one shall be looked on to have consented, and thereby submitted to any Government, where he has made no Expressions of it at all."

Locke's solution to the problem is that tacit consent to the laws of a government is given by anyone who owns land and/or resides "within the Territories of that Government," a solution that, by shifting the burden of binding obligation from a temporal to a spatial register, detaches the notion of tacit consent from its problematic proximity to the idea of tradition.[23]

So Enlightenment "politics" was weaned of its dependence on the tacit knowledge of tradition as "religion" was consecrated its last bastion. These observations may help clarify the paradoxical logic of our premise that the coalescence of "tradition" as a category occurs in the early modern period through its abstraction from the ground of social practice in which it is "traditionally" embedded. Another way to say this is that "tradition" coheres as a category when it is judged not by the standards that pertain to a comprehensive and manifold social practice that is more or less coextensive with experience itself, but by the more acute and concentrated standards of empirical epistemology. In emphasizing "political" over epistemological considerations in the evaluation of tacit knowledge (and hence in defending the *arcana imperii* against the open discussion of public policy), Hobbes evinces a view of tradition as social practice, for which the maintenance of peace and communal collectivity subsumes all considerations of accuracy and precision of judgment. In the writings of Bacon, Boyle, and Locke, the division of knowledge that elevates epistemology to its modern position of dominance is already evident: not simply in their preoccupation with questions of epistemology, but also in the conviction—less explicit in Bacon and Boyle than in Locke—that like all things, social practice is subject to epistemological scrutiny. This rigorous process of definition and delimitation both brings "tradition" (and "religion") into categorial being and, by plucking them from the ample ground of experience, radically diminishes their being. In calling the tacit knowledge of which tradition partakes "the science of the concrete," Claude Lévi-Strauss claims for it the status of a rigorous method of knowing that avoids the abstraction characteristic of epistemology and thereby has the efficacy of (not a material but) a social practice.[24]

But this formulation is still too crude, relying as it does on a reductively partial view of Enlightenment thought. For the discovery of tacit knowledge that gains momentum during the early modern period does not simply demystify the credulity of tradition so as to underscore (although it surely does this too) the benightedness of the European past and the non-European present. Once set in motion, the engine of empirical epistemology and its servant social theory also turns upon modernity itself, discovering within enlightenment a systematic structure of tacit knowledge so deeply implicated in the material fabric of everyday life as to be well-nigh ineradicable.

The early modern effort to throw into relief this invisible but palpable force had frequent recourse to the available categories of "custom" and "education." Mounting a wholesale critique of customary bans on divorce in England, John Milton observed that "Custome still is silently receiv'd for the best instructer . . . because her method is so glib and easie, in some manner like to that vision of

Ezekiel [2:8–3:3], rowling up her sudden book of implicit knowledge, for him that will, to take and swallow down at pleasure."²⁵ The insensibility with which custom instructs us Milton compares to the prophet's physical ingestion of the divine book that tastes as sweet as honey. I have already alluded to the Mandevillian inquiry into the process of socialization as a discovery of tacit knowledge in our most familiar and domestic precincts. Female chastity is a case in point. "The Lessons of it," writes Mandeville, "like those of *Grammar*, are taught us long before we have occasion for, or understand the Usefulness of them.... A Girl who is modestly educated, may, before she is two Years old, begin to observe how careful the Women, she converses with, are of covering themselves before Men; and the same Caution being inculcated to her by Precept, as well as Example, it is very probable that at Six she'll be ashamed of shewing her Leg, without knowing any Reason why such an Act is blameable, or what the Tendency of it is."²⁶

Mary Astell similarly stresses the tacitness (the "ignorant," "irrational," "customary," and "habitual inadvertency") of women's socialization as crucial to its force: "Thus Ignorance and a narrow Education lay the Foundation of Vice, and Imitation and Custom rear it up.... 'Tis Custom therefore, that Tyrant Custom, which is the grand motive to all those irrational choices which we daily see made in the World.... Having inur'd ourselves to Folly, we know not how to quit it.... We have little time and less inclination to stand still and reflect on our own Minds.... By an habitual inadvertency we render ourselves incapable of any serious and improveing thought."²⁷

In these authors, "education" may be felt to stand in relation to socialization as, more generally in Enlightenment thought, "religion" does to tradition. Mandeville's analogy with the teaching of grammar is particularly telling here, since it evokes both a pedagogic scene of explicit instruction and a habituation in tacitly but rigorously rule-bound behavior. Like "religion," "education" suggests the concrete specificity of an institutional and personalized agency, and feminist authors of the period (rightly) return again and again to the deficiencies of a "narrow education" to explain why the status of women is a matter of nurture rather than nature. Ultimately, however, the explanatory force of "education" is most powerful as it leads these authors to the more encompassing notion of socialization, in which the intentional promulgation of educational programs plays only one part. Of course, not all tacit knowledge is traditional knowledge, at least in the commonly accepted sense of that term. But the association of "education" with "custom" suggests a close connection between tradition and even the more limited and intentional idea of pedagogic practice, which can be felt to operate at the micro-level of individual formation, as tradition does at the macro-level of cultural formation.²⁸

In other words, the Enlightenment that gave us the empirical critique of tacit knowledge also gave us the critique of enlightenment and of empirical knowledge itself. Thomas Kuhn's famous figure for the social (or "community") constitution of "normal" science, the figure of the "paradigm," recalls not only Mandeville's comparison of tacit social knowledge to the rules of grammar, but also David

Hume's insistence that what we experience as the immediate perception of a causal relationship is really nothing but "custom." For "we call every thing CUSTOM, which proceeds from a past repetition, without any new reasoning or conclusion.... Objects have no discoverable connexion together; nor is it from any other principle but custom operating upon the imagination, that we can draw any inference from the appearance of one to the existence of another."[29] Kuhn's work is indebted to that of Michael Polanyi, who has argued that although

> the declared aim of modern science is to establish a strictly detached, objective knowledge[,] ... tacit thought forms an indispensable part of all knowledge.... Since a problem can be known only tacitly, our knowledge of it can be recognized as valid only by accepting the validity of tacit knowing.... It appears then that traditionalism, which requires us to believe before we know, and in order that we may know, is based on a deeper insight into the nature of knowledge than is a scientific rationalism that would permit us to believe only explicit statements based on tangible data and derived from these by a formal inference, open to repeated testing.[30]

In this sense, then, the modern critique of tradition as tacit knowledge is inseparable from the modern recognition that the "traditionalism" of tacit knowledge is inescapable.[31] And of course common usage, less invested than I either in the distinction between tacit and explicit knowledge or in that between tradition and modernity, is content to accord modernity its own traditions. The interest of these distinctions, however, lies in their historical status, their powerful and pervasive plausibility to early modern commentators. For them, in fact, false dichotomy is a necessary precondition for the rapid, revisionist insight that opposition is also interconnection. I have already observed contemporaries' ambivalence toward the "discovery" of tradition, which seemed to entail both a gain in the power of knowledge and a loss in the experience of community. In the second half of this chapter I will argue that the Enlightenment articulated this ambivalence by elaborating two innovative kinds of discourse. One of these discourses enabled the confident and ongoing critique of tacit knowledge despite the apparent decay of its traditional medium, tradition itself. The other promised a way of continuing to experience the affective and communitarian rewards of tacit knowledge without suffering its epistemological consequences.

Ideology

When Dryden remarks, in *Religio Laici*, that the fallibility of Roman Catholic tradition is "prov'd too plain;/If we consider *Interest, Church,* and *Gain*" (ll. 274–275), he departs momentarily from his primary concern, which is soteriological and epistemological, to pursue what appears a related, material, view of tradition's tenacity. The critique of tradition can be made not only on epistemological, but also on material grounds—on the grounds not of "custom" but of "interest." I have already suggested how Mandeville's emergent theory of socialization sophisticates Dryden's claim by implying that society may exercise a transpersonal, supraintentional agency that is yet "political" in its effects. In other words, Mandeville discovers a kind of knowledge that is at once tacit and "interested." The disclosure of tradition as a customary formation is close here to the disclosure of tradition as an interested formation—that is, as an "ideology." If the Enlightenment "theory" of tradition disempowers it by disembedding knowledge from customary social practice, the Enlightenment theory of ideology finds a related power of knowledge in its embeddedness in material interest. "Ideology" is the category the Enlightenment elaborated to acknowledge and to understand the ongoingness of tacit knowledge despite modernity's apparent triumph over the tacitness of tradition. "Material interest" is a modern elaboration of "custom's" invisible efficacy, now operative even in a setting of explicit rationalization, of "enlightenment." "Material interest" substantializes the force of the customary so as to account for a condition of motivation so deeply rooted that it flies under the radar of conscious motive.[32]

However, the "theory of ideology" as it has become familiar to us is not the same as the theory of "ideology" from which it was derived. In fact, the term was first used, at the end of the eighteenth century, to name the new, rational and explicit, science of ideas by which the tacitness of tradition might be criticized and replaced. "It is in this way that ideologies in the restricted sense first came into being. They replace traditional legitimations of power by appearing in the mantle of modern science."[33] "Ideology thus entailed the emergence of a new mode of political discourse. . . . It separated itself from the mythical and religious consciousness; it justified the course of action it proposed, by the logic and evidence it summoned on behalf of its views of the social world, rather than by invoking faith, tradition, revelation or the authority of the speaker." But it was also "one of ideology's essential social functions . . . to stand outside of science itself, and to reject the idea of science as *self*-sufficient or *self*-grounded."[34]

Thus in its original, late-Enlightenment meaning, "ideology," so far from being the mode of knowledge that extends tradition's tacitness in other terms, instead articulates the commitment of empirical rationality to the explicitness that derives from epistemological detachment. This earliest sense of "ideology" as nothing but the rational "discovery" of tradition fed, as I have already observed, the experience of both gain and loss. If "ideology" in this sense of the term plausibly liberates us from the prison house of tradition, by the conservative understanding its explicitness could rather be felt as a deforming reduction, an "abridgment" of the knowledge bound up within traditional implication: "The ideological style of politics . . . is a traditional manner of attending to the arrangements of a society which has been abridged into a doctrine of ends to be pursued. . . . The complexities of the tradition which have been squeezed out in the process of abridgment are taken to be unimportant."[35]

The speed with which the term "ideology" came, in the early nineteenth century, to mean not an explicitating technique for disclosing tacit tradition but a category of tacit knowing itself in need of disclosure is testimony to the fact that empirical epistemology could not long rest without turning its weapons on itself.

In this way, the theory of "ideology" was quickly supplanted by "the theory of ideology," which conceived ideology to be an idealism, in its stealthy tacitness as vulnerable to criticism as tradition itself. Henceforth ideology could be seen as a "replacement" of tradition in the sense not of a correction but of a modernization. "It is, in fact, precisely at the point at which a political system begins to free itself from the immediate governance of received tradition . . . that formal ideologies tend first to emerge and take hold . . . That such ideologies may call . . . for the reinvigoration of custom or the reimposition of religious hegemony is, of course, no contradiction. One constructs arguments for tradition only when its credentials have been questioned. To the degree that such appeals are successful they bring, not a return to naive traditionalism, but ideological retraditionalization—an altogether different matter."[36]

But if retraditionalization is an ideological process, so is tradition itself. "For tradition is in practice the most evident expression of the dominant and hegemonic pressures and limits. . . . What we have to see is not just 'a tradition' but a *selective tradition*: an intentionally selective version of a shaping past and a preshaped present, which is then powerfully operative in the process of social and cultural definition and identification. . . . What has then to be said about any tradition is that it is in this sense an aspect of *contemporary* social and cultural organization, in the interest of the dominance of a specific class. It is a version of the past which is intended to connect with and ratify the present."[37] So the distinction between custom and material interest is not a simple one. Just as it has proved possible to descry "tradition" operating in the modern world in much the same way as we might expect of a comparably tacit "ideology," so "ideology," now generalized beyond its Enlightenment moment of identification, could be discovered within premodernity, uncertainly related there to "tradition," but most often helping to redirect the epistemological critique of tradition in a sociopolitical direction.[38]

The influence of an emergent "ideology theory" on the critique of tradition (or, to put it differently, the sociopolitical expansion of "tradition theory" itself) can be felt even in authors to whom the term "ideology" was not yet available. The Enlightenment demystification of aristocratic status provides an example. Daniel Defoe knew the fragility of this perhaps necessary fiction: "All Great things begin in Small, the highest Families begun low, and therefore to examine it too nicely, is to overthrow it all."[39] Tom Paine's repudiation of titles of rank carries the argument further: "Imagination has given figure and character to centaurs, satyrs, and down to all the fairy tribe, but titles baffle even the powers of fancy and are a chimerical nondescript." "The romantic and barbarous distinction of men into kings and subjects," he continues, "though it may suit the condition of courtiers, cannot that of citizens, and is exploded by the principle upon which governments are now founded." But Paine also saw that the logic of his argument implied a systematic correspondence between knowledge and its material conditions that took in both traditional and modern cultures: "Whether the forms and maxims of governments which are still in practice were adapted to the condition of the world at the period they were established is not in this case the question. The older they are, the less correspondence can they have with the present state of things. Time and change of circumstances and opinions have the same progressive effect in rendering modes of government obsolete as they have upon customs and manners."[40] From here it is a relatively short distance to Marx's theory of uneven development and to his rhetorical question: "Is the view of nature and of social relations on which the Greek imagination and hence Greek [mythology] is based possible with self-acting mule spindles and railways and locomotives and electrical telegraphs?"[41]

Broadly speaking, the critique of tradition learns from the critique of ideology the explanatory utility of having recourse to material interest as the grounds of knowledge; the critique of ideology learns from that of tradition an epistemological emphasis on illusion. They have in common a concern with the tacitness of knowledge, its inseparability from and determinate dependence upon its customary or interested conditions of existence. Ideology theory soon learns to complicate the relatively simple model of intentional motivation that first colors the notion of "interest" with which it is bound up. Indeed, "it is essential to the concept of interest that it is ambiguous as to whether the gratification it entails for persons is 'known' to them." Ideology therefore "is pushed toward rationality by the interest on which it is grounded, but is limited in this rationality by that same interest." Ideologies "are not simply a mask for self-interest: they are also a tacit and a genuine offer of support for different groups."[42] This transintentional feature of ideologies is supported not only by the view that they are, like traditions, collective and shared ("class") beliefs, but also by the analogy between ideological and specifically religious belief, the way in which a subject is insensibly "called" to acknowledge and inhabit its ideological identification.[43]

In its most sophisticated development, the theory of ideology deepens the theory of tradition as tacit knowledge by specifying more concretely, but also by opening out, the conditions under which tradition loses its tacitness. In the theory of tradition, the more or less monolithic loss of tradition is ultimately grounded in the advent of innovative technologies—literacy, print—for the production, objectification, and disembedding of knowledge. In their classic account of "the German ideology," Marx and Engels describe history itself as though it were the limit case of tradition, a more continuous and ongoing generation, corruption, and regeneration of knowledge whose material explanation requires a more densely articulated field of productive determinacy. This is a general "correspondence theory" of ideology of the sort already exemplified by Paine, which binds together the "external" explanation of how tacit belief is materially determined and redetermined with an account of what this feels like "from the inside."

To speak in the abstract of the determinate relation between "infrastructure" and "superstructure"—between "forces of production," "relations of production," and "ideology"—is to describe a dialectical relationship that is experienced as a tacit correspondence—that is, as an internal and necessary condition of existence. But the relationship is unstable because it is historical. Its component parts change at different rates, so that their abstract "correspondence" at different moments becomes more or less "contradictory." The relationship comes to feel not necessary and internal but "accidental" and "external":

> The difference between the individual as a person and what is accidental to him, is not a conceptual difference but an historical fact. . . . What appears accidental . . . is a form of intercourse which corresponded to a definite stage of development of the productive forces. . . . The conditions under which individuals have intercourse with each other, so long as the above-mentioned contradiction is absent, are conditions appertaining to their individuality, in no way external to them. . . . The definite condition under which they produce, thus corresponds, as long as the contradiction has not yet appeared, to the reality of their conditioned nature, their one-sided existence, the one-sidedness of which only becomes evident when the contradiction enters on the scene and thus exists for the later individuals. Then this condition appears as an accidental fetter. . . . These various conditions, which appear first as conditions of self-activity, later as fetters upon it, form in the whole evolution of history a coherent series of forms of intercourse, the coherence of which consists in this: in the place of an earlier form of intercourse, which has become a fetter, a new one is put, corresponding to the more developed productive forces and, hence, to the advanced mode of self-activity of individuals—a form which in its turn becomes a fetter and is then replaced by another.[44]

In this fashion, the theory of ideology takes over from the theory of tradition, explaining the discovery and rediscovery of tacit knowledge as a perpetual historical process because it is grounded in the complex multiplicity of material history. The argument can be made, at least in part, in non-Marxist terms:

> If it is an established fact for the enlightenment that all tradition that reason shows to be impossible, i.e. nonsense, can only be understood historically, i.e. by going back to the past's way of looking at things, then the historical consciousness that emerges in romanticism involves a radicalization of the enlightenment. For the exceptional case of nonsensical tradition has become the general rule for historical consciousness. Meaning that is generally accessible through reason is so little believed that the whole of the past, even, ultimately, all the thinking of one's contemporaries, is seen only "historically." Thus the romantic critique of the enlightenment ends itself in enlightenment, in that it evolves as historical science and draws everything into the orbit of historicism.[45]

The theory of ideology may therefore be said, in its strongest articulation, to sustain the theory of tradition even as it goes beyond it.

The Aesthetic

In that articulation, the theory of ideology has the neutrality of an objective method for disclosing the material conditions by virtue of which knowledge comes into being. In its historical development, however, the "discovery" of ideology has been colored most commonly by the triumphalism of a demystifying and liberatory enlightenment. And this in turn supports the plausibility of seeing the growth of ideology theory as only a partial accounting for the persistence of tacit knowledge in the modern world. True, the discovery of tradition, and the resulting insight into the customary embeddedness of knowledge, often met with a comparably optimistic response. But as I have already observed, the discovery of tradition also evoked the apprehension that an inestimably valuable condition of social coherence was being sacrificed in the process. How does modernity not only extend the former but also the latter experience of the loss of tacit knowledge? How do we perpetuate, in a culture "beyond" tradition, the nostalgic recognition of a normative coherence lost—but also, in that very recognition, vicariously repossessed for a moment?

In the book that provoked Paine's experiment in ideology theory, Edmund Burke had accepted the challenge of defending tradition from an (inevitably) enlightened perspective. To this end he exploited the capacity of empirical epistemology to turn its weapons on itself. For Paine, the tradition of inherited nobility is "chimerical" because it is tacit, unrationalizable apart from its own antiquated belief system. For Burke, the modern doctrine of "the rights of men" is "metaphysical" so long as it remains untested against its moral, political, and historical context. The putative rationality of the doctrine hides the unreflectiveness with which it is espoused: "What is the use of discussing a man's abstract right to food or medicine? The question is upon the method of procuring and administering them. In that deliberation I shall always advise to call in the aid of the farmer and the physician rather than the professor of metaphysics."[46]

Burke's and Paine's mutual recriminations, if not quite the same, nonetheless sustain an analogy. In Burke's analysis, abstraction is no safeguard against the stealthy tacitness of knowledge. The abstract detachment of enlightened reason generates the tacit knowledge of reason itself. If all ages are ruled by their illusions, should we not most suspect those rational beliefs that most closely "correspond" to our modern enlightenment? Indeed, in the very antiquity of tradition may be found a principle of historical detachment that crucially supplements, and thereby corrects, the epistemological detachment whose formidable powers are nonetheless vulnerable to its own metaphysics. "Aristocracy" is preferable to "the rights of men" because our historical detachment from it ensures our epistemological detachment from it. Locke had rejected the historical detachment of tradition on empirical grounds.[47] One hundred years later, Burke can embrace it on similar grounds. In fact, we can believe in aristocracy despite our epistemological detachment from it, precisely because of our historical detachment from it. This is the perspective from which "tradition" may be cherished, startlingly enough, as "prejudice": "You see, Sir, that in this enlightened age I am bold enough to confess that we are generally men of untaught feelings, that, instead of casting away all our old prejudices, we cherish them to a very considerable degree, and, to take more shame to ourselves, we cherish them because they are prejudices; and the longer they have lasted and the more generally they have prevailed, the more we cherish them" (98–99). To be sure, Burke can sound very much like Sir Henry Marten, in an earlier age of revolution, on the dangers of explicitly "arguing and descanting what sovereign power is": "It has been the misfortune . . . of this age that everything is to be discussed as if the constitution of our country were to be always a subject rather of altercation than enjoyment" (104).[48] Burke's genius, however, is to turn this problem into its own solution.

To return to my opening figure for cultural embeddedness as a kind of invisible clothing, in his most famous passage Burke makes a virtue of tradition's disclosure—of the clothing's visibility—by deploring not the clothing itself but the logic whereby its visibility dictates its removal. Rather than strip it off, he would seize the occasion to admire its pleasantly and self-consciously artful properties:

> But now all is to be changed. All the pleasing illusions which made power gentle and obedience liberal, which harmonized the different shades of life, and which, by a bland assimilation, incorporated into politics the sentiments which beautify and soften private society, are to be dissolved by this new-conquering empire of light and reason. All the decent drapery of life is to be rudely torn off. All the superadded ideas, furnished from the wardrobe of a moral imagination, which the heart owns and the understanding ratifies as necessary to cover the defects of our naked, shivering nature, and to raise it to dignity in our own estimation, are to be exploded as ridiculous, absurd, and antiquated fashion. (87)

Although Burke shares the epistemological detachment of ideology theory, the idea that tradition loses its efficacy when it becomes explicit plays no part in his argument. On the contrary, he employs the language of aesthetic response to suggest that for us there is a middle way between the unavailable tacitness of traditionality and the crude ostensiveness (or, the undetectable tacitness) of modernity. By this middle way, pragmatic social efficacy becomes available to belief at the moment it loses its tacit social efficacy. In fact, our historical distance from the antiquated politics of the ancien régime—from the tradition—gives them an imaginative power over us that fuels their pragmatic efficacy. We cherish tradition not because of its essential value, but because it gives us pleasure to do so, and in our affective response to tradition lies the ground of its social utility: not the immediate coherence of cultural embeddedness, but the mediated pleasure of self-conscious reenactment. This sort of skepticism lies at the heart of the modern strain of conservative political philosophy that emerged toward the end of the eighteenth century. Contemptuous of the notion that traditional social hierarchy bears any but an "accidental" relation to virtue, Johnson nonetheless told Boswell that "I would no more deprive a nobleman of his respect, than of his money. I consider myself as acting a part in the great system of society.... I would behave to a nobleman as I should expect he would behave to me, were I a nobleman and he Sam. Johnson.... Sir, there would be a perpetual struggle for precedence, were there no fixed invariable rules for the distinction of rank, which creates no jealousy, as it is allowed to be accidental."[49] Once ideologized and aestheticized, we might say, tradition becomes traditionalism.

But what is "the language of aesthetic response"? How is it related to tacit knowledge? Like "ideology," the term "aesthetics" was coined in the latter half of the eighteenth century. As the word itself suggests, the aesthetic is that subcategory of empirical epistemology which involves strictly sensible—as distinct from rational—knowledge; it was soon narrowed to refer more specifically to our knowledge of the beautiful and the sublime. In this more limited sense of the term, the aesthetic, rooted like empirical reason in sense impressions, provides a different avenue of detachment from them: not rational abstraction but imaginative distance. Its conceptual formulation precedes the term itself, especially in English Enlightenment thought.[50]

In one of his celebrated papers on the pleasures of the imagination, Joseph Addison wrote that they

> are not so gross as those of Sense.... A Man of a Polite Imagination ... meets with a secret Refreshment in a Description, and often feels a greater Satisfaction in the Prospect of Fields and Meadows, than another does in the Possession. It gives him, indeed, a kind of Property in everything he sees, and makes the most rude uncultivated Parts of Nature administer to his Pleasures.... A Man should endeavor... to make the Sphere of his innocent Pleasures as wide as possible, that he may retire into them with Safety, and find in them such a Satisfaction as a wise Man would not blush to take.

In this view, the pleasures of the imagination are "innocent" of the corruptions to which merely physical pleasures are vulnerable. They are also innocent of the dangers of empirical reality, so much so that aesthetic pleasure requires—even, consists in—the consciousness that it is not empirical. "How comes it to pass," asks Addison,

> that we should take delight in being terrified or dejected by a Description, when we find so much Uneasiness in the Fear or Grief which we receive from any other Occasion?... The Nature of this Pleasure ... does not arise so properly from the Description of what is Terrible, as from the Reflection we make on our Selves at the time of reading it. When we look on such hideous Objects, we are not a little pleased to think we are in no Danger of them. We consider them at the same time as Dreadful and Harmless; so that the more frightful Appearance they make, the greater is the Pleasure we receive from the Sense of our own Safety.... This is, however, such a kind of Pleasure as we are not capable of receiving, when we see a Person actually lying under the Tortures that we meet with in a Description; because in this Case, the

Object presses too close upon our Senses, and bears so hard upon us, that it does not give us time or leisure to reflect on ourselves.[51]

Addison's pleasures of the imagination obviate by their very immateriality the prudential critique of physical pain and corruption. They are akin to the pleasures of sense experience yet detached from their material implications. They mimetically capitalize on the empirical powers of sense perception while avoiding their physical consequences. Through the replacement of physical and sensible activity by a representation or imaginative enactment, the pleasures of the imagination escape both the crude literalism of empirical epistemology and the risks attendant on physical experience. What Addison calls "the leisure to reflect on ourselves" is a special version of the epistemological detachment Locke had identified at the heart of empirical epistemology. In the aesthetic attitude, merely sensible knowledge finds the detachment characteristic of rational knowledge.

The insight that the pleasure derived from artistic imitation is predicated on an emotional state that is both immediate and mediated is as old as the Aristotelian doctrine of mimesis. However, it finds new life in Enlightenment thought and becomes canonical in Coleridge's account of "that willing suspension of disbelief for the moment, which constitutes poetic faith."[52] To willingly suspend disbelief is to authorize belief within a skeptical framework. It is also to revive the social coherence and solidarity of "traditional" cultures, but now at the level of, not physical presence, but imaginative identification. "The illusion is lasting and complete," wrote an enthusiastic novel reader. "I interrupt the unhappy Clarissa, in order to mix my tears with hers: I accost her, as if she was present with me. No Author, I believe, ever metamorphosed himself into his characters so perfectly as Richardson."[53] Clara Reeve thought that the perfection of the novel "is to represent every scene, in so easy and natural a manner, and to make them appear so probable, as to deceive us into a persuasion (at least while we are reading) that all is real, until we are affected by the joys or distresses, of the persons in the story, as if they were our own."[54]

Coleridge's famous words remind us that even at its historical emergence, the aesthetic attitude was being associated with religious (and by that association, I would suggest, with traditional) "faith." It is a commonplace that one end of art in the modern world is to secularize religion, to replace its traditional functions and responsibilities by a thoroughly humanized mode of spirituality. In the context of my present argument, art can be seen to secularize religion by purifying it of tacit knowledge. Hedged about as it is by empiricist skepticism, aesthetic belief is a curiously guarded and notional belief. The aesthetic substitutes for the powers of divinity and spirituality an internalized and humanized replacement that evades the demystifying strictures of empirical epistemology by avoiding the metaphysical claims of religious spirituality—at least in principle. In practice, the skepticism that framed the aesthetic pleasure experienced by readers of the novel was also capable of obstructing it. At such times, the definitive gap between the aesthetic and the religious could be felt to dissolve. Not only the special authority exercised by aesthetic belief, but also the social solidarity putatively encouraged by it, could seem as illusory as those associated with a discredited religious enthusiasm. "In the enthusiasm of sentiment," wrote one reader, "there is much the same danger as in the enthusiasm of religion, of substituting certain impulses and feelings of what may be called a visionary kind, in the place of real practical duties, which, in morals, as in theology, we might not improperly denominate good works." Another reader was "afraid lest the same eye which is so prone to give its tributary tear to the well-told history of fancied woe, should be able to look upon real misery without emotion, because its tale is told without plot, incident, or ornament."[55]

This soon became a minority response. And in the more general confidence that in these respects the aesthetic "improves on" the religious, we can detect a tendency to make "religion" bear some of the weight of "tradition" itself. This is suggested, at least, by the historicizing language writers use to describe the peculiar sort of detachment afforded by aesthetic experience. The madness of Don Quixote is first of all epistemological, consisting in the confusion of romance illusions with reality. But throughout *Don Quixote* (1605, 1615) this epistemological error is hard to separate from the historical error of confusing chivalric tradition with contemporary social practice. From the old romances Don Quixote has extracted what may justly be called the "tradition" of chivalry, the complex body of semiotic codes and rituals of a bygone culture. To be thus embedded in tradition is to experience madness—the loss of reason—in two forms that are distinguishable but coextensive: the inability to detach illusion from reality and the inability to detach the past from the present. For European culture, the ultimate solution to Don Quixote's madness required that the state of mind capable of entertaining the empirical reality of illusion be reconceived not as madness, but as aesthetic response. This demanded an appreciation of the aesthetic attitude as a special mode of epistemological detachment, to which the posture of historical detachment was quite closely tied.

The process by which "romance" error had, by the end of the eighteenth century, been positively revalued as "romantic" truth was bound up with the emergence of the cult of the medieval and the gothic during the same period. At first demystified and repudiated by empirical epistemology, in time these barbaric archetypes of "the traditional" had become sufficiently distanced from enlightened modernity to afford it the pleasure of aesthetic enjoyment. Ann Radcliffe was supreme among gothic novelists at facilitating this pleasure, in part because her insistence on "explaining" her supernatural effects ensured that the reader's disbelief would be willingly suspended. As one reviewer wrote of *The Mysteries of Udolpho* (1794), "The reader experiences in perfection the strange luxury of artificial terror, without being obliged for a moment to hoodwink his reason, or to yield to the weakness of superstitious credulity."[56]

Once subjected to the transformative machinery of the aesthetic, moreover, the pleasures of tradition and its tacit knowledge could even yield a genuine species of truth, rightly conceived. In "An Ode on the Popular Superstitions of the

Highlands of Scotland" (written 1750), William Collins urged his friend John Home to exploit the traditionality of his homeland for its poetic yield. The key to this process is a detachment at once historical and aesthetic:

> There must thou wake perforce thy Doric quill,
> 'Tis Fancy's land to which thou sett'st thy feet;
> Where still, 'tis said, the fairy people meet
> Beneath each birken shade on mead or hill.
> ....
> Let thy sweet muse the rural faith sustain:
> These are the themes of simple, sure effect,
> That add new conquests to her boundless reign,
> And fill with double force her heart-commanding strain.
> ....
> Nor need'st thou blush that such false themes engage
> Thy gentle mind, of fairer stores possessed;
> ....
> Proceed, in forceful sounds and colours bold
> The native legends of thy land rehearse:
> To such adapt thy lyre and suit thy powerful verse.
>
> In scenes like these, which, daring to depart
> From sober Truth, are still to Nature true,
> And call forth fresh delights to Fancy's view,
> The heroic Muse employed her Tasso's art![57]

Like Burke, Collins reverses the Lockean critique of tradition as historical detachment by reconceiving sensible as aesthetic judgment. Collins argues the value for poetry of what he frankly calls the "false themes" of archaic Scottish culture—fairies, wizard seers, runic bards, the little people—a value that depends entirely on the fact that they are articles not of credulous belief but of fanciful "superstition." No longer either commanding religious faith or eliciting "enlightened" incredulity, such themes are resonant with the secularized spirituality of the poetic passions. No longer tacitly embraced as tradition, they may now be self-consciously embraced as "tradition." Collins urges Home to recover the "naive" poetry of the ancient Celts, as Schiller soon would do with respect to that of the ancient Greeks. To be a naive poet today, however, requires the double consciousness of the aesthetic attitude, which re-creates the naive immediacy of tradition within the "sentimental" framework of an inevitable (indeed, constitutive) mediation.[58] Only because they are historically outmoded may Scottish superstitions be taken up aesthetically as articles of poetic "faith." Collins's poem was composed five years after the last military gasp of archaic Jacobite politics, the '45, whose romance aura reinforced (as it later would for Walter Scott) the sense of a landscape that is the last refuge of the spirit in the modern world. By conflating the melancholy anachronisms of religion and politics—of Celtic myth, aristocratic honor, and the "feudal" Highlands—Collins's poem participates in an emergent reconceptualization of tradition as, like the aesthetic, a mode of tacit knowledge that may be pleasingly evoked at will.

To conclude: if the Enlightenment is responsible for our most intense and implacable "discovery" of tradition, by that very same movement it is also responsible for elaborating those categories, ideology and the aesthetic, by which modernity has most successfully theorized and extended the idea of tradition in other terms.

2

Civil and Religious Liberty: A Case Study in Secularization

In 1659, England was once again in political crisis. Ten years earlier, the Civil Wars had culminated in the beheading of the monarch Charles I, an event that had no precedent in European history. Soon after, Oliver Cromwell had seized the reins of power and ruled, as England's Lord Protector, until his death in 1658. Eighteen months later Charles II, the executed king's eldest son, would be restored to the throne of England. In the months between the death of Cromwell and the Restoration of Charles II, hundreds of tracts were published debating what should be done now that the nation once more was without a sovereign ruler. In 1659, John Milton, republican and poet, hopefully addressed to the English Parliament his own contribution to that debate, calling Parliament "next under God, the authors and best patrons of religious and civil libertie, that ever these Islands brought forth." It has been suggested that this is the first time, at least in print, that "religious liberty" and "civil liberty" were conjoined as analogous concepts and political policies.[1] Why wasn't the conjunction of political and religious liberty explicitly articulated before this? After all, ever since the Protestant Reformation more than a century earlier, the developing conflict between English monarchs and parliaments had been over religious as much as political affairs; not so many years ago historians were still referring to the period of the Civil Wars as the "Puritan Revolution." Why did the conceptual and experiential alliance of the two liberties become explicit only on the eve of the Restoration? My answer to this question will take the form of a paradox: the conjunction of civil and religious liberty could occur only once they had been separated out from each other, which in turn required the separation of positive from negative liberty. By unfolding this paradox in the following pages I also hope to shed some light on the idea of "secularization," a concept whose meaning and even utility are much disputed in contemporary scholarship yet one that seems indispensable if we are to acknowledge a fundamental historical phenomenon.

Accommodation

In the early tradition of Christian communities, the "civil" and the "religious" spheres of experience are tacitly understood to be compatible and inseparable. True, these spheres become incompatible if their relation is seen as coextensive with the ontological antithesis between the secular and the spiritual, the profane and the sacred, the creature and the Creator. Even so, the theological doctrine of accommodation holds out the possibility of mediating between these seemingly incompatible domains. In Milton's words, "our understanding cannot in this body found it selfe but on sensible things, nor arrive so cleerly to the knowledge of God and things invisible; as by orderly conning over the visible and inferior creature."[2] Milton's pragmatic affirmation of the doctrine stands in sharp contrast to George Herbert's application of it in his sonnet "Redemption":

> Having been tenant long to a rich Lord,
> Not thriving, I resolved to be bold,
> And make a suit unto him, to afford
> A new small-rented lease, and cancel th' old.
> In heaven at his manor I him sought:
> They told me there, that he was lately gone
> About some land, which he had dearly bought
> Long since on earth, to take possession.
> I straight returned, and knowing his great birth,
> Sought him accordingly in great resorts;
> In cities, theatres, gardens, parks, and courts:
> At length I heard a ragged noise and mirth
> Of thieves and murderers: there I him espied,
> Who straight, *Your suit is granted*, said, and died.[3]

The speaker's reliance on Milton's "sensible things"—the figure of a landed tenancy—to arrive at "things invisible"—spiritual salvation—is an accommodation that succeeds, at the moment of its failure, through God's gratuitous grace, which substitutes for the speaker's naively materialistic accommodation that of His own materially embodied son.

Herbert's accommodating figure of the landlord, however mistaken, is nonetheless grounded in the theological foundation of Christian faith, the accommodation of God's will in human form through the Advent, Passion, and Resurrection of Jesus Christ, a mediation of human sense and divine spirit that overcomes their seemingly insuperable antithesis. The institutional foundation of Christian faith inevitably proved more controversial. The early growth and consolidation of Christianity depended on the conviction that divine authority is justly accommodated by the Roman Catholic Church. Learned discourse on the distinction between civil and religious authority, and on how differences between them should be adjudicated, is at least as old as the writings of Thomas Aquinas. But before the Protestant Reformation, the Roman hierarchy alone was understood to possess supreme authority over the Christian doctrines and ceremonies that mediate, like Jesus Himself, between the word of God and the human ends of worship and salvation. With the Protestant schism this authority fell, in England, to the Anglican Church—the Church of England—and to the English monarch, who after the Reformation bore the official title of Defensor Fidei or defender of the faith.

The early sixteenth-century schism entailed in the Reformation was arguably the culmination of centuries of incremental reform movements within the Roman Church. But to many it seemed suddenly to have made explicit and problematic what before had been a tacit and universal faith in the capacity of the church to accommodate divinity to humanity, a capacity that in their disparate practices the Protestant churches now took to be their mission. Those that were, like the Church of England, also national churches participated in an Erastian melding of church and state whose aim was to renounce the legitimacy of the Roman Church without sacrificing its capacity, as an institution simultaneously sacred and secular, for the apparently seamless accommodation of God's will to human understanding and action. And in the later years of the sixteenth century, this dynamic tension became closely entwined with analogous demands that were entailed in the flowering of absolutist doctrines of royal sovereignty, Tudor doctrines that were passed on to Stuart rulers. The tensions that animate absolutism point both inward and outward. First, absolutist theory would dissolve the limitations imposed by feudal social reciprocity without also dissolving the implicit sanctions of feudal hierarchy. Second, the ambition of absolutism is to give to the authority bestowed upon the sovereign from without the illusory aura of self-generation. That is, absolutist doctrines, like the divine right of kings, the king's two bodies, and the patriarchal theory of political obligation exalt the will of the sovereign by deriving his power from an elevated source in such a way as to stress the present reality of authority while de-emphasizing the reality of subordination to a higher power that is implied in the very fact of derivation.[4]

The Civil Wars of the mid-seventeenth century tested the viability of these experiments in absolutism and national Reformation. Their failure, which in this context amounted to a failure to prevent the conceptual separation out of the religious from the civil, was the precondition for the modern alliance of civil and religious "liberties" that Milton articulated on the eve of the Restoration. Only when the realms of the civil and the religious were explicitly detached from each other was it possible to conceive them in themselves, as separate entities, and on that basis to conceive them anew as subject to alliance through comparison and analogy with each other. Crucial to this process was a prolonged and wide-ranging debate about the meaning of "politics," the "civil," "religion," and "liberty," a debate that precipitated the emergence and prevalence of a new consensus on the reference of each of these terms. In its concern with the nature of the relationship between civil policy and religious doctrine and practice, the debate also concerned the meaning of "liberty" as a descriptor of that relationship.[5] One way of understanding how civil and religious liberty came to appear analogous is through the emergence of the modern idea of negative liberty.

Charles I came to the throne in 1625. Within three years he found himself in conflict with Parliament over its refusal to unconditionally vote him supplies. In a sermon preached shortly before the 1628 Petition of Right, Roger Manwaring, chaplain to Charles I, addressed the topic of Parliament's duty to the king. Although schematic in its conventionality, this sermon represents a position on political sovereignty that spoke to many English people before the Civil Wars. Manwaring's text is Ecclesiastes 8:2, "I counsell thee, *to keepe the Kings commandement, and that in regard of the oath of God.*"

As the King is the sacred & supreme Head of *two* Bodies, the one *Spirituall*, the other *Secular*: so, this high and royall Text containes in it two parts correspondent: The one *Civill*, which is a *Counsell of State*, or a politique caution; *I counsell thee to keepe the Kings commandement*: the other *Spirituall*, which is a *deuout* or *religious reason; And that in regard of the oath of God.* The *First* part is founded vpon the *Second*, the Second is the ground of the First. . . . Royalty is a Preheminencie wherein *Monarches* are inuested, *immediately* from God; for *by him doe they raigne*. . . . And yet notwithstanding this; they are to bee sustained, and supplied by the hands and helpes of men. . . . *To Kings* therefore, in all these respects, nothing can be denyed (without manifest and sinfull violation of Law and Conscience) that may answer their *Royall state* and *Excellency*. . . . [Obedience] of right, may euery *Superiour* exact of his *Inferiour*, as a due debt: And euery *Inferiour* must yeeld it vnto his lawfull *Superiour*, for the same reason. *Children*, to *Parents*, in discipline, and Domesticalls: *Seruants*, to their *Lords*, in their respectiue and obliged duties: *Souldiers*, to their *Commanders*, in Martiall affaires, and feates of Armes: *People* to their *Pastours*, in Conscientiousduties and matters of Saluation: Subjects, to their lawfull *Soueraignes*, in the high Concernements, of State and Policie. . . . But, there be Pretenders of *Conscience*, against *Obedience*; of *Religion*, against *Allegiance*; of *Humane* Lawes, against *Diuine*. . . . And therefore, if, by a *Magistrate*, that is Supreame; if, vpon *Necessity*, extreame and vrgent; such Subsidiary helpes be required very hard would it be for any man in the world, that should not accordingly satisfie such demaunds; to defend his Conscience, from that heauy preiudice of *resisting the Ordinance of God*, and *receiuing* to himselfe *Damnation*.[6]

Manwaring justifies Parliament's financial supply of the king in absolutist terms, as mandated by the many-linked (if in this version unidirectional) chain of subordination and obedience that extends from God down to common people and that renders all *"Civill"* action inseparably *"religious"* in the same fashion as the king's *"Secular"* and *"Spirituall" "Bodies"* are "two parts correspondent," distinct but inseparable. "Violations" of "Law" and "Conscience" are also inseparable: to resist the secular demands of the monarch is to suffer spiritual damnation. Manwaring's sermon is broadly consistent with what has been called a concept of "positive liberty," the notion that freedom is a fulfillment achieved collectively, through relations with others. It is opposed to "negative liberty," conceived as freedom from the external constraints of other people and institutions.[7] Positive liberty is also consistent with Robert Filmer's patriarchalist argument, composed and circulated in the late 1630s as civil war approached, that "the greatest liberty in the world (if it be duly considered) is for a people to live under a monarch. It is the Magna Charta of this kingdom; all other shows or pretexts of liberty are but several degrees of slavery, and a liberty only to destroy liberty."[8]

Two years after the execution of the king repudiated this absolutist vision of positive liberty, Thomas Hobbes made public his very different theory of absolutism. Hobbes's mechanistic materialism led him to define the liberty of the subject in broadly negative terms, as "the absence of externall Impediments of motion." However, his absolutism led him to affirm, "for him that lives in a Commonwealth," a principle in keeping with positive liberty "because the Law is the publique Conscience, by which he hath already undertaken [by contractual assent] to be guided. Otherwise in such diversity, as there is of private Consciences, which are but private opinions, the Common-wealth must needs be distracted, and no man dare to obey the Sovereign Power, farther than it shall seem good in his own eyes."[9] What is innovative in Hobbes's usage is not the distinction between "private conscience" and the "public conscience" of the state,[10] but his use of that distinction to analyze the nature of absolutism, in which he replaces the unanalyzable accommodation of divine authority by the materiality of state power. Where Manwaring begins with "the oath of God," which authorizes the monarch's civil "law" and thereby also the subject's "conscience," Hobbes begins with the subject's will to subject his own conscience to civil authority, which opens up a space of freedom that separates his "private opinions" (whether religious or civil) from the public policy to which he subjects them. Grounded in a crucially temporalized version of natural law theory, which imagines a state of nature before government, Hobbesian absolutism posits for the precivil subject an original moment of absolute autonomy, of self-"absolutism."

Filmer's *Patriarcha* was recirculated in print in 1680 at the height of the Exclusion Crisis. Forty years earlier his model of positive liberty was perhaps still normative, if only because no coherent alternative to it had coalesced. In 1680 negative liberty was well on its way to replacing positive liberty as the modern norm. By the middle of the century, political theory (like that of Hobbes) was being empowered by developing methods of natural philosophy that sought to abstract principles from practical experience by an empirical process of analytic separation. In this respect Locke's celebrated opening of *The Second Treatise of Government* (1690), composed during the 1680s in explicit refutation of Filmer, provides a fruitful contrast to Manwaring's sermon of 1627: "The Power of a *Magistrate* over a Subject, may be distinguished from that of a *Father* over his Children, a *Master* over his Servant, a *Husband* over his Wife, and a *Lord* over his Slave."[11] We may be tempted to conclude that Milton's conjoining of political and religious liberty in 1659 marks a general recognition of the separability, and therefore the conflatability, of the two concepts. And it is true that the depth and passion of debate before the Restoration generated formulations—not only Milton's "religious and civil liberty" but even Hobbes's "private versus public conscience"—that articulate separation in language that suggests a complementarity of the religious and the political. The Restoration of the House of Stuarts resolved none of the problems that had precipitated the interruption of its rule. And the fears of "a return to '41" that arose during the next few decades whenever disputes flared up on public issues can create the impression that the response of contemporaries to the events of the past two decades was strictly one of defensive avoidance.

But the return of the Stuarts brought the possibility of renewing past terms of dispute under conditions that were both old and new. The former grounds of engagement could seem both restored and distanced, a reflexive projection onto the present whose comparative framework enhanced the empirical recognition and analysis of what was different. Of course the evidence of innovative forces, especially material ones—commerce, capitalism, technology—was not far to seek. But just as important as these new conditions was the experience of having lived through an unprecedented experiment in political and religious thought and action, which, however repugnant its results were to many English people, had denied irrevocably the ethos of the given that the prewar ancien régime had fostered. The dissolution of the preordained induced a mental habit of empirical skepticism in all spheres that in part created—made actual what had been potential in—the very conditions that were for that reason new. And, as we shall see, reflections on the meaning of the English Reformation provided a distanced perspective on the present moment that was only slightly less instructive than were those on the Civil Wars and Interregnum.

Civil Society

My argument in this chapter is guided by a heuristic understanding that posits the historical movement from premodern to modern culture as one characterized by a change from thinking organized in tacit relations of distinction to thinking that extends those distinctions into relations of separation and thereby lays the ground for their self-conscious conflation predicated on the understanding that conflation presupposes separate entities. The most important development in this respect, one that overarches and enables all others, is the separation of "civil society" from the "state." So far I have been speaking of the realm of the "civil" as though it had exclusive reference to the state and its apparatus. But to speak of "civil liberty" is also to designate as "civil" the experience of English people who were neither magistrates nor administrative servants of the state but its subjects—that is, those subject to state policies of liberty or restraint. This doubled reference is clear and makes sense; yet it became available to English people only around 1600, whereas the word "civil" in its several political senses long precedes that date.[12] Around 1600, the category of the "civil" began to admit of a number of disparate subcategories—trade, the press, religion, and many others—that entered into relation with each other by virtue of the fundamental separation out of "civil society" from "the state."

In the influential argument of Jürgen Habermas, which I discuss elsewhere in this volume, civil society (in modern parlance, "society") is part of a new private realm that also includes the "internal" culture of the family and the "public sphere" of private—that is, nongovernmental—citizens where people come together as a public to discuss and influence state policy. Habermas tends to equate civil society specifically with the economic activity of commodity production and exchange. Modern usage is as likely to construe civil society more broadly as the categorial container of capitalist economics, the public sphere, and the internalized family, the three basic subcategories that give civil society its definitive character as the realm of the private that comes into being over against the publicness of the state.[13] This construction is fruitful because it makes clear that when contemporaries speak of civil society they are acknowledging the newfound capacity of citizens to reflect at a distance on the authority of the institution to which they are subordinated with a self-conscious explicitness by which that subordination is re-experienced and mitigated. "Civil society" names the perspective from which the idea of civil liberty assumes its meaning as a relation to the civil rather than as one part of it, the perspective from which the modern idea of negative liberty becomes intelligible. The detachment of civil society from the (civil) state makes possible a detachment of the civil from the religious that allows them to be conceived as subject to different but analogous kinds of liberty.

The conceptual change represented by the emergence of civil society was both precipitated by and productive of material change. Although my concern here is with the former, it's useful in passing to describe one of the most important material developments associated with the distanced perspective of civil society, the separation of the polity from the economy and the emergence of absolute private property. The parliamentary act of 1646 abolishing feudal tenures and the Court of Wards officially authorized practices already in operation by giving rights of unconditional ownership and transmission of landed property to larger landholders (but not to copyholders) who previously had held their land in fief from the monarch.[14] Before the end of the century, John Locke famously filled the gulf left by this disappropriation of monarchy with a labor theory of private appropriation and a productivity theory of perdurable and absolute ownership.[15] Separated out from the polity, the economy emerged as a powerful component of civil society, and in the institution of absolute private property, contemporaries recognized a bastion of negative liberty that transformed the dependence on monarchy that had obtained under feudalism.[16] John Lilly believed that "an absolute proprietor hath an absolute Power to dispose of his Estate as he pleases, subject only to the Laws of the Land."[17] Visiting the Royal Exchange, Joseph Addison's Mr. Spectator

> fancied one of our old Kings standing in Person, where he is [now] represented in Effigy, and looking down upon the wealthy Concourse of People with which that place is every Day filled. In this Case, how would he be surprized to . . . see so many private Men, who in his Time would have been the Vassals of some powerful Baron, Negotiating like Princes for greater Sums of Mony, than were formerly to be met with in the Royal Treasury![18]

Daniel Defoe thought that

> the glory of the English gentry above all the nacions in the world [is] that their property in [their] estates is in themselves; . . . that they inherit their lands *in capite*, absolutely and by entail. . . . All the knight's service and vassalage is abolish'd, they are as absolutely posess'd of their mannours and freehold as a prince is of his crown. . . . A gentleman's estate in England is worth 5 times the income in pensions or governments which are at the will of the

granter, or than lands, however settled or entail'd, that are subject to the . . . ravages of the Sovereign, I should have said, the *tyrants*, which is the condicion of allmost all the inheritances in Europe.[19]

The Empirical Criterion

One way to learn in more detail how the alliance of religious and civil liberty became explicit might involve tracing the pertinent acts of religious legislation, both successful and failed, over the course of the Restoration period, such as Charles II's promise of a "Liberty to Tender Consciences" in the Declaration of Breda in 1660; Parliament's Corporation, Uniformity, Conventicles, Five Mile, and Test Acts of 1661–1673, which debarred from certain secular and clerical positions all those who refused to swear to, abide by, or receive Anglican oaths, declarations, and sacraments (these are the parliamentary bills that transformed "Puritans" into "nonconformists" and "dissenters"); Charles's and James's failed Declarations of Indulgence (1662, 1672, 1687, and 1688); and the Toleration Act of 1689. Rather than take this route through civil legislation, however, I will try to shed light on this period as one of secularization by asking how a reflexive view of the past through a lens of empirical skepticism might have empowered these and other more concrete developments.

Months before his army was called upon to facilitate the return of the king, George Monck described the emergence of the empirical criterion of "interest" as a product of the Civil Wars. Hitherto the national interest had been tacitly assumed to be the unity of church and state under monarchal rule; now its assessment required that all of the diverse interests that had proliferated during the past twenty years be explicitly accounted for:

> Before these unhappy Wars the Government of these Nations was Monarchical in Church and State: these wars have given birth and growth to several Interests both in Church and State heretofore not known; though now upon many accounts very considerable, as the *Presbyterian*, *Independent*, *Anabaptist*, and *Sectaries* of all sorts as to Ecclesiasticks; and the Purchasers of the Kings, Queens, Princes, Bishops, Deans and Chapters, and all other forfeited Estates; and all those engaged in these Wars against the King as to civils. These Interests again are so interwoven by Purchases and intermarriages and thereby forfeited; as I think upon rational grounds it may be taken for granted; *That no Government can be either good, peaceful or lasting to these Nations, that doth not rationally include and comprehend the security and preservrtion [sic] of all the foresaid Interests both Civil and Spiritual.* . . . *That Government then that is most able to comprehend and protect all Interests as aforesaid must be Republique.*[20]

It is difficult to imagine a report from the field on England's condition more divergent from the absolutist ideal than the one Monck gives on the eve of the Restoration. Dividing a purportedly integral civil whole into antagonistic parts, civil war played out the logic of negative liberty. The unit "church and state" that the Reformation had established as a national entity became unglued, both revealing and creating subdivisions in each of its parts. First, following Charles I's disastrous eleven-year attempt at personal rule, the English state was subdivided through the military defeat of its monarchical by its parliamentary component, the king's no-longer-silent partner in government, which in turn subdivided Parliament's House of Commons from a defunct House of Lords. Second, the Church of England escaped fragmentation only by the evisceration of its episcopal government and by the widespread local adoption of Puritan ecclesiastical reforms. Monck most emphasizes not the revelation and aggravation of fissures in already existing structures but the emergence of new entities, "very considerable" but "heretofore not known." But it is his concerted use of the term "interest" that most effectively draws attention to the pressure that's being exerted on discourse to modulate from the language of positive to that of negative liberty.

What had been distinguishable parts of a whole have now become analytically if not experientially separate parts or interests. The absolutist Hobbes leaves unanalyzed the "private consciences" or "opinions" of his Commonwealth citizens because to account for them would only distract lawgivers from the overarching "public conscience" entailed in state law. Monck's language of interest concretizes and materializes these "private" entities, including "spiritual" ones, in their politico-economic specificity, separable enough to be conflated or "interwoven" with each other. (Since the Reformation, the only religion whose threat had seemed as much political as spiritual was Roman Catholicism.) This was not to abandon the ideal of national unity but to shift the means for its achievement from a top-down to a bottom-up model, from the a priori assumption of a whole that hierarchically comprehends the many to the empirical, quasi-computational assessment of the many so as to arrive at the rational sum or whole. In 1672, Richard Cumberland wrote that "the common good or public good [is] the whole aggregate or sum total of all those various and several kinds of good, from which all individual, rational beings, collectively considered, can be benefited."[21] Under absolutism it had been customary to equate the "public good" or the "national interest" with the rule and welfare of the monarch. If this notion survived the Restoration, it was only in the mode of the purely conventional, like the maxim "the king can do no wrong."

The Sociology of Group Formation

During the winter of 1662–1663, months after the Uniformity Act became law and while Charles's Declaration of Indulgence was under consideration, the Earl of Clarendon made the point that the several Puritan sects of former years had little in common but their nonconformity:

> Whoever therefore shall design to Reduce so great a Multitude of differing Judgments to an Uniformity of Profession, by the way of Rigour and Infliction of paenalties, can reasonably expect no better Success, then to fill the

Church with Hypocrites, and the State with Subjects train'd up, and principled for Rebellion What is this but to nourish and Foment in our Bowels the Seeds of a Civil War . . . ?

For when they are all in a suffering Condition they are united together in one Common Cause and Concern of easing themselves from the pressure they are under; and (being so different in their other Principles) this is the only point they can center in, and Knit together in to a Body, and the only Band that binds them up in a Bandle. But when they are Indulged, and left Free, (the Cement of a joint Interest being taken away) they will naturally, and necessarily fall in sunder, and remain as divided in point of Faction and party, as they are in tenets and principles. Of this we have a fresh and convincing Example in the late Revolutions, for before the War, when all Sectaries and Nonconformists lived under the Curb and penaltys of the Law, [they] appeared to the World but as one Sect, and were generally known only by the Common Name of Puritans: And to what Power and Strength they grew by this union, was too fatally known by the Famous Mischiefs they did.[22]

However, if diversity of worship is indulged rather than punished, those whom persecution unites in rebellion will be divided and ruled.

More than most people, Clarendon—a major player in the politics of the past twenty years, Charles II's lord chancellor, and author of the six-volume *History of the Rebellion and Civil Wars in England*—was in a good position to draw lessons from past experience. One lesson taught by his "second thoughts" is that the virtues of a state bound together by the bands of positive liberty are limited in their capacity to persist in being taken for granted. For Clarendon, Charles I's absolutism kept him from realizing at the end of his personal rule that the reformed national church no longer had (if it ever had) this capacity, and that the explicit enforcement of a formerly tacit conviction would only generate a negative spirit of liberty whose powerful bands amounted to the shared consciousness of being constrained by the very state that sought its conformity. The lesson for Charles II was that the positive liberty of the ancien régime could not be legislated, that the only available liberty was the negative liberty of religious indulgence, consisting in being "left free" of what were felt to be external constraints. Prudence dictated that Clarendon's tract be published anonymously. His policy recommendations were not supported by the Cavalier Parliament, and for his pains he was unjustly associated with the harshness of the new penal laws ("The Clarendon Code") and unjustly impeached for England's humiliating defeat in 1667 in the Second Anglo-Dutch War.

Among those who shared Clarendon's perspective was the young John Locke. In 1667, he wondered "what understanding man in a disordered state would . . . by giving one common name to different parties, teach those to unite whom he is concerned to divide and keep at a distance one among another." Dissenters "are yet crumbled into different parties amongst themselves, and are at as much distance one from another as from you, if you drive them not farther off by the treatment they receive from you, for their bare opinions are as inconsistent one with another as with the Church of England. . . . But if you persecute them you make them all of one party and interest against you."[23]

Locke's language of "opinions" and "parties" is striking. It recalls Hobbes's view that ("private") conscience is tantamount to "opinion," and it reminds us that little more than ten years after Locke writes, the modern discourse of political parties (the "Whigs" and the "Tories") coalesced in the heat of the Exclusion Crisis. There may be some justice in viewing that discourse as a long-term "replacement" for the discourse of religious sects, so long as we recognize that the word "party" already was being applied to sects during the 1660s. Looking back, these commentators are also bemused by the proliferation in numbers and names of sects that appeared in the years following the outbreak of civil war and the curtailment of government control of the press. Unlike Thomas Edwards's famously relentless *Gangroena* (1646), however, their interest is less in the heretical than in the sociological, particularly (like Clarendon and Locke) the role of naming in the formation of group identity. And in Locke especially, the sociological perspective is so concentrated that the unique soteriological end of religious faith and practice is dissolved in the skeptical analysis of how, in political society, opinions "interweave" (in Monck's phrase) with other opinions:

> Since men usually take up their religion in gross, and assume to themselves the opinion of their party all at once in a bundle, it often happens, that they mix with their religious worship, and speculative opinions, other doctrines absolutely destructive to the society wherein they live. . . . Whether the distinction [of their group] be religious or ridiculous it matters not, otherwise than as the ties of religion are stronger, and the pretences of conscience fairer, and apter to draw partisans, and therefore the more to be suspected and the more heedfully to be watched. . . . So that they are not restrained because of this or that opinion or worship, but because such a number of any opinion whatsoever, who dissented, would be dangerous. (117, 118, 119)

From this perspective, all religious doctrine concerns "things indifferent."

Accommodating God's Will: Thoughts, Speech, Actions

But what precisely is the danger of dissent? I've argued that the skepticism we encounter in Clarendon's and Locke's perspectives on the question of religious toleration is grounded in their perspectives on the Civil Wars and the Interregnum. But the confrontation with Stuart absolutism and the Church of England was grounded in turn in the confrontation with papal absolutism and the Church of Rome. In its explicit repudiation of the Roman Catholic hierarchy, the Reformation schism repudiated an ecclesiastical accommodation that required a tacit faith not only in God's will but also in that of its human representatives. In his *Book of Martyrs*, John Foxe narrates the story of how one of his martyrs told his Catholic inquisitors that thanks to "your rules of religion," before his conversion "I made no conscience of sin, but trusted in the priest's absolution, he for money doing some penance also for me, which after I had given, I cared no further what offences I did so long as I could for money have them absolved."[24] Foxe uses the word "conscience" in the still active sense of a "consciousness" that before his conversion had been drained of its acuity by automatic and impersonal rules, rituals, and payments.[25] "Liberty of conscience" is in this sense a liberty of consciousness, the negative liberty of a mental detachment from what otherwise would be taken on trust as authoritative. In place of the "unconsciousness" enforced by the external tradition and ceremonies of the Roman Church Protestants elaborated covenant theology and its idea of the "covenant of grace," a direct and personal contract with Christ replacing Adam's covenant of works and devoid of ecclesiastical mediation.[26] Instead of what they saw as the corrupt and hypocritical "works" of soteriology sponsored by the church hierarchy, Protestants relied on the unmediated and immaterial accommodations of conscientious faith and God's "calling," and their humble places of worship, shorn of the idolatrous trappings that alienated the soul from its salvation, enabled those seeking grace to come together in community. It's been argued that Protestantism, intending to resanctify religion, had the unintended consequence of secularizing it.[27]

It was an empowering scenario: from the ceremonial splendor of exalted spaces redolent of incense and other seductions of the senses, Christian worship devolved to the inward mind of the believer and the outward sociability of the like-minded faithful. But if this was the aim of the Reformation revolt against Roman Catholic rule, it also had been the aim of the Puritan revolt against Anglican rule. Now that the Church of England had returned to power and was using civil law to enforce what seemed to Puritans only a lesser version of the ritual mediations required by Rome, how might the national church protect the nation from the danger of religious dissent without confirming that its early role as righteous rebel against ecclesiastical tyranny had been traded in for the role of tyrant?

Of course this question had been raised long before 1660. The Puritan charge that the Anglican Church had preserved far too many rituals and ceremonies of the Roman Church was already central to late Tudor controversy, and the Civil Wars were fought by many in the hope of returning to the pristine modes of worship attributed to the primitive church, in which the material means of accommodating the invisible and intangible spirit had been minimized. So the restoration of Anglican church government in 1660 also restored these former debates, intertwined with debates on absolutism. But the Civil Wars—the ultimate expression of politics by other means—fundamentally altered these debates because they threw into the highest relief the material consequences of using civil means to religious ends, and thereby also the crucial differences between the civil and the religious. In 1672, looking back on the outbreak of war over thirty years earlier, Andrew Marvell appeared agnostic on the conceptual question of where the line should be drawn even as he left no doubt about the ultimate answer on the level of action: "Whether it were a War of Religion, or of Liberty, is not worth the labour to enquire. Whichsoever was at the top, the other was at the bottom; but upon considering all, I think the Cause was too good to have been fought for."²⁸ After the Restoration, a likely consensus that war was to be avoided at all costs decisively weighted where and how the answer was to be found in favor of strategic political empiricism. If avoiding war was the acknowledged terminus ad quem, how close to that should the line of civil policy be drawn? Where does civil prudence bleed into religious persecution and engender religious dissent too dangerous to be countenanced? What is religion?

In the name of civil peace, Marvell's antagonist Samuel Parker exploited the nonconformist animosity toward material mediations by arguing that "all Matters of meer Conscience, whether purely Moral or Religious, be subject to Conscience meerly; *i.e.*, Let men think of things according to their own perswasions, and assert the Freedom of their Judgments against all the Powers of the Earth. This is the Prerogative of the Mind of Man within its own Dominions; its Kingdom is intellectual, and seated in the Thoughts, not Actions of Men. . . . Liberty of Conscience is Internal and Invisible, and confined to the Minds and Judgments of men." Invoking the idea that state law is the "public conscience," Parker argued that in "Cases and Disputes of a Publick Concern, private men are not properly sui Juris, they have no Power over their own Actions, they are not to be directed by their own Judgments, or determined by their own Wills; but by the Commands and determinations of the Publick Conscience."²⁹ Parker's standard for separating the civil from the religious assumes a seemingly definitive form in the separation of public words and actions from private thoughts. And to the complaint that civil prohibitions persecute religion he could reply that if it is subject to persecution, it is by definition not religion. Locke emphasizes the secular ends of peacekeeping in order to win for religion the same commonsense negative liberty possessed by other expressions of "opinion." Parker emphasizes those same ends in order to prohibit all religious expression except Anglican orthodoxy.

In his reply to Parker's *Discourse*, Marvell shrewdly analyzes the relationship between Parker's dichotomization of the civil and the religious, on the one hand, and on the other his confidence that Anglican modes of accommodation bring them back together. Conformists like Parker "define a Sacrament to be an Outward visible sign of an Inward Spiritual Grace," and they require nonconformists to partake of the sacraments of the Church of England if they are to participate in communion. However, nonconformists of tender consciences, Marvell continues, "object to some of the Rites of the Church of England under the name of Symbolical or significant Ceremonies," which lack the scriptural warrant of divine law definitive of a true sacrament, "and they complain that these things should be imposed on them with so high Penalty, as want nothing of a Sacramental nature but Divine Institution. And because an Humane Institution is herein made of equal force to a Divine Institution, therefore it is that they are aggrieved" (1:94, 96, 98).

By scriptural warrant, the holy sacraments accommodate the divine spirit to human communion. But if some of the Anglican sacraments are strictly human symbols lacking spiritual force, their accommodation is a false one—and yet civil law prohibits nonconformists from partaking of any others. Their liberty of conscience is constrained to the inward realm by a civil authority that usurps God's clear authorization of freedom in outward means of worship. Civil liberty cannot flourish alongside religious liberty if civil law defines religion as extra-civil, as thoughts insusceptible to civil prosecution. But as Marvell remarks, "If the freedom of thoughts be in not lying open to discovery, there have been wayes of compelling men to discover them; or, if the freedom consist in retaining their judgments when so manifested, that also hath been made penal" (52). In other words, the civil magistrate has the power of the sword to transform private thoughts into public acts and to punish them severely. William Penn declared that "if men must be Restrain'd uopn [sic] pretended Prudential considerations, for the Exercise of their Conscience . . . this makes Religion, State-pollicy; and Faith and Worship, subservient to the Humors and Interests of Superiors."[30] By relocating in America, Penn established in spatial and actual terms the separation of private conscience from the public conscience of the state that Hobbes hypothesized in the temporal and virtual terms of the state of nature.

When, as in Manwaring's pre–Civil War absolutism, the relationship between the civil and the religious is one of implicit distinction and the former is understood to be grounded in the latter, the precise definition of the boundaries between these spheres is not a matter of pressing interest or inquiry. Once their relationship is, as in post-Restoration discourse, one of explicit separation, the boundaries between the civil and the religious are perforce subject to close analysis in order to determine just where the line between the civil and the religious is to be drawn.

Defining Spheres of Discourse

As I have already documented, one of the most striking aspects of Restoration debates on religious policy is their reflexive, meta-discursive tendency to raise substantive argument to the level of self-conscious inquiry about the meaning and reference of the most basic categories in current use. Detachment from the old modes of religious controversy seems to have been sufficient to allow the topic to be conceived in physical, empirical, and analytic rather than only in metaphysical, doctrinal, and a priori terms. Leveled to the same secular playing field as were other "opinions" or components of "England's interest," "religion" became subject to the most basic definitional questions. When Roger Palmer, Earl of Castlemaine, made a plea for the indulgence of Roman Catholics, William Lloyd, Bishop of Worcester, replied: "We hold it Necessary to maintain the Authority of the King, and the Peace of the Nation. If you call any thing *Religion*, that is contrary to these, must we therefore alter our Laws? Or ought you to mend your Religion?"[31]

In 1661, Peter Pett—barrister, member of the Irish Parliament, and original Fellow of the Royal Society—published a tract in which he discussed some "generall Reasons" for liberty of conscience. Pett takes as the consensus that there is a

> necesary connexion between Civil liberty, and that which is Spiritual; and therefore they that would devest any of their spirituall liberties, do alarm

them with just causes of fear about their losing civil liberties by the same hands.

For . . . it must necessarily be presumed that such persons intend to be judges how far mens civil and spirituall liberties reach, and what are the frontires of both. . . . And 'tis most certain that he who doth impose any thing upon the people under the Species of Religion, would not leave them a power to judge whether it be in order to it or no. For if they are the Judges of it, they will say that any thing in Religion which displeaseth them opposeth their civil liberty, and so nothing at all will therein be enjoyned.

If it be said that a man may think himself bound in Conscience to oppress people in spiritual things, but not in civil; I answer, most certainly then his Conscience will lead him to put them out of a condition to assert their spiritual liberties so opprest. It is with restraining the freedom of Conscience as the denying of a *mare liberum* to neigbouring [sic] nations, which any Prince that doth must not trust to prescription of long time, or imaginary lines in the heavens whereby the compass of his dominion of the Sea may be determined, but to powerfull Fleets.[32]

On the face of it, Pett's post-Restoration inquiry into "the necesary connexion between Civil liberty, and that which is Spiritual" might sound compatible with Manwaring's necessitarian position, before the outbreak of civil war, that the civil and the spiritual are "two parts correspondent." But Pett's "connection" contradicts Manwaring's "correspondence" because it assumes the separability of the two, opening up a space in the chain of correspondence in which it can be asked "how far mens civil and spirituall liberties reach, and what are the frontires of both," a question that elicits the understanding that civil power is the efficient cause of religious restraint. Manwaring's "correspondence" is an a priori unity grounded, through the doctrine of accommodation, in a spiritual authority that cannot be rationalized in its own terms but is authoritatively interpreted by civil power. But Pett's norm of liberty of conscience presupposes a civil power whose policy decisions on religious affairs are not by definition coextensive with its spiritual grounding. That civil power is analytically separable from the chain of correspondence is evident in the fact that it can grant liberty of conscience as one of a number of possible strategies for achieving the "welfare of the nation," an end that is no longer presumptively coextensive with the will and welfare of civil power itself. Not that Pett necessarily would challenge the model of unity entailed in the doctrine of accommodation and the theory of correspondence, but that those component parts of the chain that have an empirical existence are methodologically and heuristically detachable from it and made available for independent analysis.

Manwaring's necessity is that of divine will mediated by royal law; Pett's is a generalization of secular experience. Once the question of first causes has been bracketed, religious persecution can be contemplated as the outcome not of God's will enacted through the agency of His earthly vicegerent but of a conflict between two different versions of conscience. Evidently the spirit is susceptible to oppression through physical impositions by some people on the physical conditions of others. Therefore spiritual restraint is also civil restraint, and spiritual liberties are also civil liberties. In Manwaring's sermon, the distinction between the religious and the civil is taken to be grounded in the realm of the spirit. In post-Restoration discourse, the conflation of the religious and the civil is seen to be located in the secular realm and self-consciously based on the knowledge that the religious and the civil are separate categories of experience brought together by civil exigency. Indeed, Pett reminds us that other civil restraints, like commercial prohibitions, also have been tacitly justified on grounds that discourage explicit analysis of the physical conditions under which they are imposed. The prohibition of mare liberum can be justified by "prescription of long time or imaginary lines in the heavens," but it is enforced by "powerfull Fleets."

However, Pett justifies a policy of liberty of conscience not only on the strength of skeptical analysis but also by arguing that this sort of thinking has deep roots and a broad reach in English culture. First, the Reformation itself was a liberation of "private" from institutional judgment, a program in negative liberty that sanctions liberty of conscience: explicitly from papal, but analogously also from state, persecution. And in making this argument Pett rescues the Church of England from the high-church posture of imitative orthodoxy that was manifestly belied by its origin in heterodox revolt, although for that very reason, perhaps, also its default posture under Stuart absolutism.

> The Protestant Religion doth indemnifie us in the Court of Conscience, for believing in matters of Religion according to the Dictates of our private Judgements, or rather oblige us to it. Doubtless, if it be not lawful for every man to be guided by his private judgement in things of Religion, t'will be hardly possible to acquit our separation from the Romish Church from the guilt of schism. The Genius of the Protestant Religion doth make it . . . naturall to us to weigh and consider any notions, though recommended to us by our Ministers. . . . And certainly it is much more consonant to that Religion [Christianity], and especially that form of it which hath asserted its spirituall freedom from the impositions of others, to allow spiritual liberty to others. Nor doth it seem worthy of Christ, who hath left us a Religion full of Mysteries, and not any visible Judge of them, to have design'd about those any visible Executioners. (41–43)

Like Monck's "several interests" in civil affairs, Pett's "private Judgements" in religion are the autonomous units on which public policy must be built.

Second, "a considerable part of the Gentry of England is grown more inquisitive in matters of Religion within these late yeares than formerly."

> Where this inquiring temper is not, no opinion so horrid but may be universally believ'd. Thus the Turks may be induced to think that there is a Devil in the juyce of Grapes, and the Papists that there may be a God therein. But

when men are neither by Religion or temper restrain'd from searching into the causes of things, they will not in civility to other mens understandings believe propositions to be true or false. And that which makes me (beside my own observation) to conclude that many of the Gentry of late are grown more inquisitive in Religious things then formerly, and are likely so to continue, is, because, they are more then heretofore inquisitive in civil things. (47)

Pett quickly effects a second rescue, this time of himself, from appearing to champion no more than an English inquiry into the grounds of religion by observing the international foundations of his own country's enlightenment: "Since the late introduction of reall Learning into the World by *Galilaus, Tycho Brahe*, my Lord *Bacon, Gassendus, & Des Cartes*, neither the knowledg of elegant words, or nice Speculations, wil yield any man the Reputation of being Learn'd that is altogether rude in Mathematicks" (48).

As Pett makes the case, both Protestantism and the new philosophy teach the wisdom of empirical inquiry and intellectual tolerance. Thomas Sprat, historian of the Royal Society, suggested "that all wise Men should have two Religions; the one, a *publick*, for their Conformity with the People; the other, a *private*, to be kept to their own Breasts."[33] And as civil war has led English people to "search into the causes" of civil affairs, so this civil inquiry has led them to religious inquiry. At the same time, the effect of this methodological alliance of the civil and the religious has been to detach the civil from the religious and religion from superstition. And it is Pett's very skepticism about a causal relationship that cannot be confirmed on empirical grounds and that is not available for rational debate that encourages him to use those methods to suggest an alternative and more persuasive account of the nature of that relationship. On the basis of empirical observation, the civil and the religious are not reciprocally co-implicated: religious policy is a subcategory of civil policy. A civil policy of persecution dictates that religious behavior will be restrained by civil law; a civil policy of liberty of conscience ensures that restraints will not be imposed. So, empirically speaking—that is, limiting our judgments to the realm of observable phenomena, hence to the civil realm—religion inhabits the same civil category as commercial trade and the circulation of knowledge (or, as it increasingly was called, freedom of the press). These three are allied in their vulnerability to, and in their capacity to flourish in the absence of, civil restraints.

The Three Negative Liberties

Free trade, freedom of the press, liberty of conscience: by the end of the seventeenth century, these spheres of thought and action had already coalesced in people's minds as prototypically exemplifying the freedom of private enterprise from public interference. Struggles against mercantilist protectionism, pre- and postpublication censorship, and religious penal laws persisted through the century and beyond, and the coalescence of each of these—trade, the press, and religion—as a sphere of private liberty was both the cause and the consequence of its dispute with the assumption, definitive of positive liberty, that its subordination to state control was the condition of its well-being. But, whereas both trade and printing were material processes and therefore clearly susceptible both to control and to freedom from control, the case of religion was more complicated.

When the idea of a comprehensive national church was implicitly bound up with the authority of the state, the question of what was meant by "religion" never arose. However, as the "necessary" relationship between church and state that was bequeathed by the Reformation settlement was increasingly questioned, it became unavoidable to ask just what status religion has in the world. It sounds more than a bit odd to suggest that this question had not been asked before, but it all depends on the question's conceptual context, which dictates the kind of answer that will be deemed satisfactory (if not demonstrably correct). If the aim of Christianity was to redeem fallen humanity, the Catholic Church and its elaborate rituals had tacitly been taken for granted to be the mandatory mediator between fallen sinners and divine redemption. Reformation analysis, the culmination of earlier schismatic protests, began at the bottom rather than the top of this great hierarchy and found that one of its parts, ecclesiastical mediation, was separable from the others because it was both unnecessary to and obstructive of that relationship. This became explicit in the Protestant calling and the priesthood of all believers. Then was Reformed religion spiritual or civil? If spiritual, because "religious liberty" refers to the subject's freedom from sin?[34] "Liberty of conscience" gained increased use during the middle of the seventeenth century, the same period in which the tacit authority of the national church, like that of the Catholic Church before it, was being systematically questioned. So, if "liberty of conscience" retained a residual sense of spiritual liberty from sin, it also signified an empirical liberty from civil restraint. Is it a positive freedom to be saved through reliance on the overarching community of ecclesiastical observance, or a negative freedom from the threat to salvation posed by state persecution? Is liberty of conscience a spiritual or a material condition? In its theology of salvation, Protestantism drew a sharp line between the inefficacy of "works" (as epitomized in Roman Catholic ritual) and the power of "faith," between outward acts of devotion and an inward state of grace. Does blessedness lie in the performance of works or is it strictly a matter of conscientious inner faith? And if the latter, what is the relationship between inner faith as a spiritual state and inner faith as a mental state? The distinction between external religious observance and internal religious belief is immanent in Christian experience; but in the later seventeenth century it became hard to ignore the experimental hypothesis of their separability. This seems evident, at least, in the analytic efforts I've described to divide religion into the component parts of thought, speech, and action, and to identify it with one or another of these (although this sort of analysis also figured in other, nonreligious sorts of adjudication). Another piece of evidence is the legislative rise and fall of Occasional Conformity, which was practiced by nonconformists who "occasionally" took Anglican communion to be eligible to hold public office but otherwise worshipped outside the Church of England. Occasional Conformity was prohibited by a statute passed under a Tory ministry in 1711 that was repealed by the Whigs in 1719.

What most sharply distinguished it from trade and the press, however, was that only religion was directly subject to another authority far greater than that of the state, whose will and guidance the state embraced but whose immateriality made its dictates inferable only through fallible judgments of accommodation. For this reason, perhaps, arguments for liberty of conscience often enough were conjoined metonymically or metaphorically with arguments for free trade and freedom of the press, as though to avail the former of the more empirically evident claims of the latter. Whatever the merit of this conjecture, the discussion that I will summarize makes clear that the alliance of civil and religious liberties with which this chapter is concerned was achieved through the alliance of religion with other private spheres whose civil status was unambiguous.

At least since the outbreak of civil war, many had detected an intimate association of the Presbyterians and sectarians with the powerful trading interests of the nation (as well as with more humble domestic "tradesmen"). The association goes back to the reformers' rejection of the theology of works—the belief that works were effective toward salvation—and their advocacy instead of a labor discipline consonant with the calling and effective in the glorification of God. The case for the toleration of Protestant nonconformists by reference to the interweaving of religious and commercial interests became common after 1660. The point was made succinctly in the title of John Corbet's *The Interest of England in the Matter of Religion* . . . (1661)—and succinctly questioned by Surveyor of the Press Roger L'Estrange: "I would fain know what is meant by, *The Matter of Religion*, as it stands here related to Civil Interest?"[35] In another tract, Corbet, using Monck's metaphor, wrote that "by Relations and Commerce [dissenters] are so woven into the Nations Interest, that it is not easie to sever them, without unraveling the whole." In fact, "to suppress those that are reckoned among the chief in Trading, and whose Commerce is so general, . . . may help to drive away Trade it self."[36] In his *Second Thoughts*, Clarendon wrote that "the Sea-fareing Men, and the Trading Part of the Nation, dos [sic] in a great measure consist of Non-conformists; and that much of the Wealth and Stock of the Kingdom, is lodged in their Hands, who have no great Devotion for the present Liturgy, & Hierarchy of the Church of *England*. Wherefore we need go no farther to find out the cause of that general Damp upon Traffique and Commerce, then the Strictness of our Laws upon that sort of People." (7)

Affirming more closely the metaphorical as well as the metonymic relation between civil and religious liberty, Charles Wolseley wrote that "men will never trade freely, where they do not live and converse freely. . . . A man conscious to himself that he cannot comply with the Law, will avoid medling with any thing, and choose privacy as his best security."[37]

The tolerationist position was refuted most eloquently by Herbert Thorndike, not by refuting the empirical evidence of an alliance between the interests of trade and dissent but by rejecting it out of hand as a transgression of Christian dualism:

> Men may amuse themselves, with the instance of the *United Provinces*; which, they say, flourish in trade and riches, by maintaining all Religions. But the question is of Religion, not of Trade, nor Riches. If it could be said, that their Religion is improved, with their Trade, the example were considerable. But, they that would restore and improve the Religion, that flourished in *England* thirty years ago, must not take up the *base Alloy* of that which is seen in the *United Provinces*. Nor is this a reproach to them, but a truth of God's Word; that Religion and Trade cannot be both at once at the height.[38]

Thorndike's is an absolute separation whose logic repudiates the doctrine of accommodation, one based not on an empirical analysis of recent history (and certainly not an anticipation of religion and trade's potential conflation) but on the simple intuition of the "truth of God's Word." The eloquence of his rhetoric is bound up with its belatedness.

In his dispute with Samuel Parker, Marvell reminds his readers that Protestant reform has long been associated not only with a flourishing trade but also with the power and freedom of the press. Parker's *Discourse* appeared in print when the Cavalier Parliament was working to renew the Conventicle Act of 1664, which had prohibited meetings of five or more people for the purpose of religious exercises contrary to the liturgy and practice of the Church of England. A revised version of the act was passed in 1670. Quoting Parker's self-characterization as *"none of the most Zealous Patrons of the Press,"* Marvell with mock indignation apostrophizes

> the Press (that *villanous* Engine) invented much about the same time with the Reformation, that hath done more mischief to the Discipline of our Church, than all the Doctrine can make amends for. 'Twas an happy time when all Learning was in Manuscript, and some little Officer, like our Author, did keep the Keys to the Library. When the Clergy needed no more knowledg then to read the Liturgy, and the Laity no more Clerkship than to save them from Hanging. But now, since Printing came into the World, such is the mischief, that a Man cannot write a Book, but presently he is answered. Could the Press but once be conjured to obey only an *Imprimatur*, our Author might not disdain *perhaps* to be one of its most zealous Patrons. There have been wayes found out to banish Ministers, to fine not only the People, but even the Grounds and Fields where they assembled in Conventicles: But no Art yet could prevent these seditious meetings of Letters. Two or three brawny Fellows in a Corner, with meer Ink and Elbow-grease, do more harm than an *hundred Systematical Divines* with their *sweaty Preaching*. . . . *O Printing!* how hast thou disturb'd the Peace of Mankind! that Lead, when moulded into Bullets, is not so mortal as when founded into Letters! (44–46)[39]

Looking back on the past of Roman Catholic positive liberty from the Protestant present of negative liberty, Marvell finds Parker's religious policies to be indistinguishable from those of the pre-Reformation Church, when sedition was personal, palpable, and easily suppressed by keeping information and knowledge under official lock and key. Printing transforms the actual into the virtual ("meetings of Letters"), the personal into the impersonal, the publicness of face-to-face meetings into the publicness of optionally anonymous publication and circulation, where the physical, local, and subjective character of speech is transformed into the abstract, perdurable, and impalpable objectivity of typographical reproduction. Thoughts can become acts without ever having been spoken, and the publication of heterodoxy is a civil act of great personal and political force that often enough evades both personal identification and political punishment. The severity of the penal laws entailed in the revised Conventicle Act is at least mitigated by the availability through publication of virtual conventicles of many more than five people.

Protestantism was of course the religion of the Book. The printing and circulation of multiple Bibles facilitated Luther's priesthood of all believers by breaking the priestly monopoly on scripture. In *Religio Laici* (1682), John Dryden figures scripture as the divine "Will" that adjudicates the inheritance of the landed "Estate" of salvation. Through terms of art of estate settlement—"conveyances," "search," "fair title"—Dryden represents the Reformation as the just appropriation of the means to salvation from the corrupt grasp of the Roman Catholic Church. Before the schism,

> *Mother Church* did mightily prevail:
> She parcel'd out the Bible by *retail*:
> But still *expounded* what She *sold* or *gave*;
> To keep it in her Power to *Damn* and *Save*:
> *Scripture* was *scarce*, and as the Market went,
> Poor *Laymen* took *Salvation* on *Content*;
> As needy men take Money, good or bad:
> *God's* Word they had not, but the *Priests* they had.
> Yet whate'er *false Conveyances* they made,
> The *Lawyer* still was *certain* to be paid..
> . . . .
> At last, a knowing Age began t' enquire
> If *they* the *Book*, or *That* did *them* inspire:
> And, making narrower search they found, tho late,
> That what they thought the *Priest's*, was *Their* Estate:
> Taught by the *Will produc'd*, (the written Word)
> How long they had been *cheated* on *Record*.
> Then, every man who saw the Title fair,
> Claim'd a Child's part, and put in for a Share:
> Consulted Soberly his private good;
> And sav'd himself as cheap as e'er he cou'd.[40]

Dryden's *Religio Laici* invites comparison with Herbert's "Redemption." Both poems accommodate spiritual salvation through the figure of a landed estate. Herbert's speaker, who would renew his rented lease, is in immediate contact with his landlord Jesus Christ, and for that reason the question of how his spiritual liberty may be related to his civil liberty never arises. However, Dryden's poem narrates the historical passage that brought English believers, like Herbert's speaker, into immediate contact with Jesus from the earlier, pre-Reformation necessity of relying on corrupt ecclesiastical mediators. The reformers obviate this enforced reliance through a "narrower search" of scripture, the divine "Will" and title to the estate of salvation, which reveals that it is owned not by the Roman Catholic Church but by all Christian believers (ll. 390, 392). Whereas Herbert's concern is with the mystery of divine accommodation, Dryden's is with the false accommodation—in real estate, the "false conveyances" (line 384)—undertaken by the Roman Church, which is corrupt both in its financial mediations and in the inevitable corruptions of its oral tradition, whose falsity is proved by "the written Word" and "Record" of scripture (ll. 392–393).

In *Religio Laici*, religious liberty is a negative liberty from the constraints of papal absolutism. Dryden works at the empirical and institutional level of human mediation (his "narrower search" of title recalls Pett's "searching into the causes of things"[41]), not at the ontological level that preoccupies Herbert.[42] And although this is not his point, in Dryden's account the religious liberty enabled by Protestantism is by implication secured by the technology of print and the freedom of the press. But he writes in the midst of the Exclusion Crisis and, at this point an Anglican, he is silent on the false accommodations—not the priestly monopoly on scripture formerly held by the Roman Church but penal laws against non-Anglican worship—that have been charged against the state and Church of England. Instead, he depicts his church, conventionally, as a via media of religious liberty between the absolutist oral tradition of Catholicism and the anarchic license of dissenting scripture reading, which is rightly constrained by civil law when it violates the peace:

> *A Thousand daily Sects rise up, and dye;*
> *A Thousand more the perish'd Race supply.*
> ....
> What then remains, but, waving each Extreme,
> The Tides of Ignorance, and Pride to stem?
> ....
> And, after hearing what our Church can say,
> If still our Reason runs another way,
> That private Reason 'tis more just to curb,
> Than by disputes the publick Peace disturb.
> —(ll. 421–422, 427–428, 445–448)

After he converted to Roman Catholicism in 1686 and in the absence of a liberty to tender consciences, Dryden wrote that "Conscience is the Royalty and prerogative of every Private man. He is absolute in his own Breast, and accountable to no Earthly Power, for that which passes only betwixt God and Him."[43]

By the turn of the eighteenth century, the three negative freedoms of trade, religion, and the press could be spoken of analogously and in the same breath. Well before that, in fact, the argument for religious freedom as an exemplary negative liberty from civil restraint can be found providing exemplary and metaphorical support for other sorts of private experience. William Lawrence was a radical advocate of reform in the realm of marriage and divorce law and sought to liberate both from ecclesiastical, governmental, and parental control. In 1680, he wrote that "Private Marriage, or carnal knowledge, is of two sorts, the one without publick Witness, the other without any Witness at all. . . . The Law of England makes all private Marriage, and carnal knowledge, without publick Witness, Fornication. . . . All persons ought to be left liberty of Conscience, to marry publickly or privately, with or without Witnesses, as it suits best with their conveniences and occasions, as is the use and practice in all other civil Contracts."[44] In Thomas Shadwell's play *The Lancashire Witches* (1682), Theodosia agrees with her friend Isabella's resolve to resist a suitor forced on her by her parents: "And Faith, Girl, I'le be a mutineer on thy side; I hate the Imposition of a Husband, 'tis as bad as Popery."[45] Here the demands of a domestic tyrant are compared to the putative tyranny of the Roman Catholic Church. In one of Richard Steele's *Spectator* papers of 1712, the liberty of the religious subject is assigned the opposite moral character. A correspondent of Mr. Spectator, Chastity Loveworth, writes indignantly about "that looser Part of our Sex" that "indulge the Males in Licenciousness whilst single, and we have the dismal Hazard and Plague of reforming them when married." Recently no less than four suitors "would face me down, that all Women of good Sense ever were, and ever will be, Latitudinarians in Wedlock; and always did, and will, give and take what they profanely term Conjugal Liberty of Conscience." Here liberty of conscience is opportunistically invoked by men in order to justify sexual libertinage, hence "liberty" really means "license." But the force of the critique depends on the assumption that its framework, the broad alliance between conjugal and religious morality, makes sense.[46] As we've seen, Protestantism had its own version of contractarian thought;[47] and if the differences between covenant theology and the conjugal contract were as great as their similarities, the conflation of the two provided a comparative register by which the norm in each realm might be adjusted and established.

Secularization

There is no more persuasive evidence that by the end of the seventeenth century religious liberty has come to be seen as a civil liberty in alliance with other civil liberties than this sort of metaphorical usage, whose offhand humor proclaims its idiomatic status. To understand the significance of this alliance, I've argued, we need to distinguish it sharply from the traditional and tacit assumption that the civil dispensation is an accommodation of God's great plan. This assumption had to be rationally analyzed into its two separable parts before a recognizably modern understanding—that the existing religious dispensation is a matter of civil policy comparable to other such policies—could take hold. Is this an episode in the history of secularization?

The theory of secularization has been controversial for many years, although not for as long as the Enlightenment has confidently been deemed the great epoch of secularization. Much more recently, a revisionist movement has grown up among historians of the Enlightenment that challenges the association of the Enlightenment with secularization.[48] As many people have pointed out, it all depends on what you mean by secularization—and religion. As in earlier periods, the majority of Enlightenment publications concerned religious topics; whether this refutes the secularization thesis may require more particular knowledge of what they say. Data on the increase or decrease in church attendance offers one kind of measure; does it matter which churches? Radical antinomian sects proliferated with the breakdown of Stuart authority during the Interregnum. Methodism and the evangelical movement emerged in eighteenth-century Britain. Does this have the same evidentiary meaning as the eighteenth-century proliferation of "a set of cultural institutions and practices whose relationship to religion was complicated and diverse"?[49] By the end of the eighteenth century the hard-fought battles for liberty of conscience, indulgence, and toleration had largely been won. Is this the triumph of religion, or the sign that religion has lost its political importance? Or is the political importance of religion itself a sign of its dilution qua religion?

To say that secularization was the unintended consequence of Protestant reform is a paradox akin to the recognition that the Enlightenment critique of religion was the result of taking it seriously as never before. Physico-theology, the argument from design, the notion that nature was God's other book, the notion that religious worship is a civil right: these were efforts to justify religion through the conflation of categories—empirical rationality and faith in the evidence of things not seen—that were undergoing estrangement. In traditional cultures, religion is intrinsically political in the sense that it saturates and gives meaning to all social practice. The movement from tradition to modernity is one from "ritual" to "proposition," from "external" to "internal."[50] In the culture of the Reformation, and in the Enlightenment impulse to render the tacit explicit, religion is dislodged or disembedded from its tacit authorization and analytically separated out as one of a number of human capacities, like politics, which thereby can be compared with, and set in relation to, other aspects of human life. This momentum continues in the ongoing breakdown of religion itself, separating it into diversely related "cultural institutions and practices." Thus delimited, religion coheres as a ramified complexity, articulable as a set of suppositions and propositions or experienced as a personal and private authenticity that used to be involved in the outmost perimeters of collective existence. But as I've tried to suggest, this radical transformation may be understood not as the loss of human connection and alliance but as the long-term replacement of one by another sort of connectedness.

The privatization of religion is often seen as the deracination of Christianity. But like the modern category of the "private" itself,[51] the privatization of religion results from (among other things) the skeptical discrimination of wholes into their separate parts, which is the precondition for a species of connection that is able to experience and value not only the totality of the whole, but also the totality of each of the parts that give the whole its coherence. The etymology of "religion" is uncertain. According to the *OED*, the Latin *religio* was associated by Cicero "with *relegere* to read over again," "so that the supposed original sense of 'religion' would have been 'painstaking observance of rites,' but by later authors (especially by early Christian writers) with *religāre*," "'religion' being taken as 'that which ties believers to God.'"[52] Both derivations denote connection or alliance, through communal enactment and through common belief, and together open up a semantic space that suggests that the private and the personal, far from being antithetical to the communal and the collective, can articulate their constitution.

When we speak of the "disembedding" of religion in the modern world we refer to the separation out of what was part of a greater whole only three or four centuries ago and that came into being over against another modern invention, the idea of the secular. In this sense, the secularization of modern life is coextensive with the constitution of "religion." I suggest this not as an idle paradox but in an effort to conceive the complex doubleness of the secularization process. On the one hand, the bracketing of first causes and the narrowing of our focus to the empirical may seem to stand the doctrine of accommodation on its head—not the material realm as an adumbration of the spiritual but the spiritual as a conundrum to be solved by material means. On the other, perhaps modern religion obviates the doctrine of accommodation, whose equivocal indeterminacy, an essential premise of its merely human authority, makes it an open invitation to spectacularly anti-Christian misuse. What takes its place is a less ambitious and more pragmatic impulse to translate otherworldly moral principles into concrete and quotidian ethical practices, a process that always has been at the heart of Christianity. In these terms we might see secularization not as an antagonist of religion but as its enabling condition of possibility.

What the skeptical examination of religion is willing to sacrifice is the otherworldly. Belief in the existence of another world that is both immaterial and real may have been mandatory for a fledgling monotheism that, although in this respect Judaism's heir, superseded "the Old Testament" in aspiring to an ideal of catholicity predicated on the notion that no tangible, no particular and local ties of kinship, tribe, family, or custom might limit the universality of its moral force. From this perspective, modern secularization preserves the moral center of Christianity as an immaterial, virtual reality while superseding the promise of an all-embracing world beyond this scattered one, which, having shown the way to that center, is now no longer necessary. Nor need modern skepticism deny the reality of an afterlife. The epistemology that nourished Enlightenment secularization also fed the growth of imaginative belief, what Coleridge called "the willing suspension of disbelief," a new kind of knowledge whose province is not just the way we respond to "art objects" but the human capacity to credit the reality of what we imagine to be true.

The secularization thesis continues to be criticized in many quarters as theoretically incoherent, and as an optic too crude to discern the myriad modes of religion in the modern world. The idea of the "postsecular," perhaps aiming to pass beyond these problems, has recapitulated them more overtly. These criticisms may be elicited not by the weakness of the secularization thesis, however, but by the formidable complexity of the historical phenomenon it seeks to understand. The outpouring of debate on secularization and postsecularism in recent years may have obscured the fact that in all its contradictory multiplicity, the secularization thesis may be currently the most sophisticated and generative body of thought on the nature of historical change. For Marx and Engels, religion was the paradigm case of ideology or "false consciousness." Today, secularization theory is the paradigm case of historiography.

3   *Virtual Reality*

The virtualization of reality can be associated with four great innovations in methods of cultural production: orality, literacy, typography, and digital technology. However, the contemporary consensus is that the phenomenon of virtual reality coalesced into being only in our era of digital technology, because it requires the technology of the computer. A typical definition of virtual reality today might be: a computer-generated and totally immersive simulation in which a person can, with the additional aid of devices like a head-mounted display, interact within an artificial three-dimensional environment with no sense of its difference from actuality. Those who subscribe to this computer-dependent definition often look back to lesser, predigital versions of virtual reality: Sensorama (1962), 3D cinema, the View-Master (1939), the stereoscope (1838), panoramic paintings, anamorphic art, Renaissance perspective. Some cite Antonin Artaud's *Le Théâtre et son Double* (1938) for its use of the term *réalité virtuelle*, obliquely acknowledging perhaps the precursory status of theater.[1] Second Life, a virtual reality platform launched in 2003, has been studied by an anthropologist "resident" as though it were an actual community (his own field work has been in Indonesia), inspired by Bronislaw Malinowski to conceive anthropology as the virtual study of actual communities.[2] Recently the word "Metaverse" has been coined to refer broadly to three-dimensional technologies that create virtual realities that may or may not aim at total immersion. Yet more lately, Mark Zuckerberg announced the renaming of Facebook as Meta in accord with its ambition to advance from existing hardware to body sensors in building an immersive virtual environment that will be a "successor to the mobile internet."[3]

In this chapter I'll argue that despite this ongoing upsurge in digital technologies, virtual reality became a permanent and explicitly distinctive phenomenon with the preceding innovation in cultural production, the invention and dissemination of print. Two points will be helpful at the outset.

First, the Enlightenment played a major role in authorizing the virtual extension of the human body, but it was not itself so fully invested as modernity would be in the technological solution of human problems, nor did it see the illusion of total immersion as an effect of virtual reality that was to be sought or valued.[4] The Enlightenment technology that held the greatest promise of creating the illusion of total immersion through increasingly sophisticated techniques of theatricality was dramatic representation. But in contrast to the French, the English showed a marked preference for drama and narrative that represents actuality while simultaneously acknowledging its virtuality, and to this end they labored to perfect the theory and practice of realism and the aesthetic.[5] The most important difference between the contemporary and the Enlightenment concepts of virtual reality is that although both are grounded in the visual image, their focus has been very different. In recent years the ambition has been to sophisticate material technologies that have the power to create the visual illusion of being immersed in the actual world. The Enlightenment discovered the power of the imagination to create virtual spaces that took off from the actual ones of tradition, improving on their deficiencies by extending beyond their actual and conceptual limits. The result was a broad field of innovation, including three areas in particular that have been stressed by scholars as transformations crucial to modern culture: the contractual nation-state, the public sphere, and market exchange.[6]

Second, the creation of what has been called "print culture" has been attributed retrospectively to the Enlightenment; but typography was only one important factor in the overdetermined emergence of what might be called more broadly a "virtual reality culture." To pursue this argument, I'll bring together several of these other factors, some of which I've already discussed for other reasons as central to Enlightenment thought—that is, the explicit analysis of traditional wholes into parts that the modern world treats as coherent wholes susceptible to further partialization. These developments can be exemplified and situated in a context of virtualization that substantiates the argument that virtual reality was institutionalized in the Enlightenment. But how is the culture of virtual reality a function of the Enlightenment project in making the tacit self-consciously explicit? To answer this question I'll begin by clarifying the difference between the Enlightenment culture of virtual reality and earlier historical developments that might be compared to it.

Religion

No conception of Enlightenment thought is more fundamental than its skeptical attitude toward religious belief—the prototype, in the terms of this study, of the tacit knowledge of tradition.[7] However, in this regard English Protestantism had a checkered and contradictory career in its first two centuries because although exemplary of that tradition, it was also a revolt against it from within. Faith in the divine and the supernatural differs fundamentally from the modern kind of virtuality I refer to as virtual reality because its objects are seen to have a real existence, if anything by virtue of their being nonphysical and nonsensible, and to possess a reality that owes nothing to human powers. *Creatura non potest creare*: the creature cannot create. Traditional forms of religious experience are tacit and taken for granted in that they suffuse all of life though the media of sacred time and spaces, habitual and ritual behavior, common practices, and unrationalized convictions. Christian ontology is traditional in all these senses. And in the Catholic Church, it went without saying that the material accommodation of the divine will to human experience is achieved through ecclesiastical ceremonies that embed all worshippers in a matrix of symbols and behaviors that bind them individually to the institution through the mediation of the priest and the ritual of salvation.

The Reformation protested what it took to be the ecclesiastical ambition to exploit and corrupt the virtuality of the spirit by the material intrusions of the human will, by priestly mediations and profane works, which fragmented the pristine integrity of apostolic devotion and undermined the accommodation of spirit to matter by making its instrumentality explicit. Reform was an endeavor to resanctify, to return to the tacit unity of Christ's teachings. Even Henry VIII's fusion of church and state could be extenuated as fulfilling the promise of traditional culture—religion cannot be separated from secular life—although in the very explicitness of that fulfillment it laid the ground for its eventual undoing. Reformation iconoclasm, in England especially that of Puritan sectarians, aimed to purify worship of its material mediations and replace them by the unmediated guidance of God's "calling," whose spiritual truth was sanctified by the conviction of each believer that it was so. Orthodox salvation depended on the tacit authority of mediation by an external church hierarchy, but whose integrity had come to seem contingent and vulnerable. Puritan salvation had the personal authenticity of divine communication and the immediacy of an internal state of grace, but one that required constant and self-conscious vigilance and was therefore unstable. Moreover, by disembedding worship and salvation from the stability of the institutional, social, and cultural contexts of their traditional practice, English Protestantism's explicit program of personalized reform made explicit and unavoidable the role of human motive not just in the accommodation, but in the construal, of divine purpose, completing by a very different route what the Catholic Church had undertaken less ostensively by institutionalizing and bureaucratizing salvation.[8] It's been argued that secularization was not the work of a mechanical separation of religion from politics and science, but a consequence of Protestantism's own inner logic.[9]

So, as it ceased to command tacit belief as a real but immaterial creation of a suprahuman power, the traditional virtuality of Protestantism had the potential to invite credence as a virtual reality in the modern sense of the term. What hindered it in this regard was precisely its status as a religion, as manifested in the early modern inroads of skepticism, demystification, and secularization, the paradoxical evidence of its effective proximity to what it ostensibly had gone beyond. But if modern Protestantism failed to sustain the notional belief of virtual reality, it planted the seed of the self-governed individual, which became essential to that belief.[10]

Corporation

But the virtuality of religion was not alone in adumbrating modern virtual reality. Rooted in Roman law, the idea of the corporation was refined by Christian doctrines of doubleness that were formulated to account for the double nature of the son of God, who, as head of the Christian church, also endowed the church itself with the sempiternal status of a *corpus mysticum*. In time the state too was seen to have a quasi-sacred capacity. Like *Christus*, the *fiscus* possessed a double nature, an idea expressed most famously by the legal doctrine of the king's two bodies, which named the natural and the political, the private and the public, aspects of monarchy, distinguishing without separating the merely human from the more-than-human sources and capacities of sovereignty.[11]

In this long development, attitudes toward secular institutions found the ontological doubleness bequeathed by the body of Christ increasingly useful for its temporal implications. Whoever the present, human embodiments of the corporation might be, its continuity as a sempiternal body transcends those bodies and therefore limits corporate legal liability for their errors, crimes, or lapses in continuity owing to death. But in order to ensure that the corporation was itself accountable it had to be accorded the standing of a person in a court of law—in the older terminology, its body political itself possessed a body natural—which was a legal fiction in the sense that its factual untruth was thought to be justified by the equitable decisions it enabled.

The idea of the corporation comes closer than divinity does to the modern idea of virtuality. The corporation lacks a real (i.e., a nonphysical and nonsensible) existence, and its agency, unlike divine agency, is understood to be that of a human institution. But the constitution, the continuity, and the fictionality of a corporation, although secular, have their source in a juridical decision to achieve a limited end for a limited body of beneficiaries. And although corporations persist into the modern world, their ontological rooting in legally sanctioned purposes for transient embodiments distinguishes them from the open-endedness of modern virtuality.

For when we speak of virtual existence in the modern sense we refer not simply to a human creation, but to one that is, like the Protestant calling, self-authorized in the sense that it has no ontological or material grounding beyond its own self-consciousness. The constitution and continuity of virtual entities are coextensive with matters of consciousness: to ask how people come to belong to, participate in, or inhabit them is the same thing as asking how people come to think of themselves in this light. We tend to think of virtual entities less as fictional than as notional, not so much made up as made of mental attributes, concepts, and emotions. The realm of the virtual can have important ontological consequences, but it's an epistemological phenomenon. And because it's also a modern phenomenon, virtuality is a function not just of thinking, but of a change in the way people think—and about the nature and authority of thinking itself. This suggests a link between virtual reality and the Enlightenment project of making the tacit self-consciously explicit, and why we must have recourse to the concrete historical context in which this change in thinking occurred.

Polity and Economy

The conventional terms in which we conceive the transition from feudalism to capitalism offer a template for the transition from traditional to modern communities.[12] In premodern England, physical mobility beyond the immediate circle of daily routine was limited. Social relations were local and face-to-face, between people who knew each other as fellow members of a relatively closed community through which the passage of strangers was unusual. People thought of themselves less as singular, autonomous, and mobile individuals than as constituent parts of a greater whole. The feudal economy, in this respect akin to the Roman Catholic Church, was hierarchically stratified into status groups, each of which had prescribed, but reciprocal, relations with those above and below them. Reciprocity depended on the understanding that what characterized each group was qualitative in nature and relative to the quality of other groups on a differential scale that was common to them all. Inferiors deferred to superiors, and were obligated to them, through land service or knight service, as their superiors were mutually obligated to afford them protection in return. Payment in these exchanges was in kind—that is, in goods and services. The ultimate authorization of hierarchy came from a nonphysical God and God's nature; its ultimate experience was visible and palpable dependence. As Marx puts it: "Here, instead of the independent man, we find everyone dependent—serfs and lords, vassals and suzerains, laymen and clerics. Personal dependence characterizes the social relations of material production. . . . There is no need for labour and its products to assume a fantastic form different from their reality. They take the shape, in the transactions of society, of services in kind and payments in kind."[13]

In such a system, social, economic, and political relations were embedded in daily life, interwoven into a single fabric whose wholeness conveyed a sense of existence as a tacit givenness, what goes without saying. In the system that replaced it, these relations were disembedded from their common substratum, separated out, and felt to need and assume their own distinct rules of operation, all of which tended to abstract what before had been experienced in more concrete and personal terms. This account of the transition from feudalism to capitalism can evoke the nostalgic retrospect for an absolute prelapsarian existence whose relativity Raymond Williams has unmasked through the figure of a diachronic escalator taking us back through the multiplicity of falls from an ideal "natural economy" that stops only at Eden, or Hesiod's Golden Age.[14] But the distinction I've made is obviously schematic. "The vast majority of cultures make some space for exchanges which display many of the features which are sometimes, as in our own society, associated with monetary exchange (a degree of impersonality, considerable scope for individual gratification and a concern for pure instrumentality, for example)."[15] This caveat is in keeping with the distinction between tradition and modernity as it's employed in this study, a methodological necessity whose overarching schematism must be assessed at every point in terms of specific levels of analysis and evidence. At the same time, it must be kept in mind that of these several features my focus is on impersonality in particular, and in the specific sense of the virtualization of actual embodied relationships.

One of the most important results of the early modern disembedding of feudal relations was the separation of the economy from the polity. At the beginning of the seventeenth century, the terms "state" and "estate" were used interchangeably because the political state was inseparable from the king's economic estate.[16] By the end of the century, the monarch had ceased to own the kingdom as the feudal fee or public estate of his body political and became instead the supreme administrator of the public state, against whose protectionist interference the liberty of private property owners came to be defined. The elite nobility's feudal obligation of land service to English monarchy waned in the sixteenth and early seventeenth centuries, affording great landholders absolute ownership of their property and full autonomy to use and invest it according to their own economic interests. After the king had been defeated in civil war, this process was officially ratified in 1646 by the parliamentary abolition of feudal tenures. Daniel Defoe thought that the English gentry thereby held and inherited "their lands in capite, absolutely and by entail. . . . All the knight's service and vassalage is abolish'd, they are as absolutely possess'd of their mannours and freehold as a prince is of his crown."[17] Those who worked the land of the great, no longer participating in face-to-face reciprocity through shared use-rights to common land and remuneration in kind, increasingly were paid in wages, the abstract, quantifiable, and therefore universal medium of exchange for qualitatively different sorts of products and services. The circulation and exchange of commodities translated the qualitative nature of actual things into the abstract virtuality of quantitative sums.

The transition from the "actual" social relations of feudalism gains a more material specificity when understood, in the formulation of Robert Brenner, as a transition from a "direct" mode of appropriating the produce of agrarian laborers. Before capitalism, or in early modern states like France, where the breakup of feudal jurisdictions hadn't proceeded as far as in England, peasant farmers had customary and delimited use-rights to land held in service to their landlords, whose service was directly ceded to the state in the form of rent, taxes, or officeholding. Following Marx, Brenner describes this as an "extra-economic" or "politically-constituted" mode of property relations, in contrast to the "indirect," "economically-constituted" relations that already were emerging in England, where landlords shouldered the benefit of absolute ownership with the obligation to increase labor productivity in competition with other landowners, and propertyless laborers sold their labor power in exchange for wages, as determined by market levels of exchange value.[18]

The transition to the "indirect" system of wage payment virtualized—abstracted and universalized—labor, which no longer was tied of necessity to the same actual relations. The traditionally static nature of rural life was transformed by the mobilization of laborers and the creation of a mobile labor market. In 1650, Henry Robinson proposed the establishment of a "Register of Addresses" in response to the fact that "at present, poore people, and others, spend much time, in running up and down, from one place to another to seeke employment, and sell their work." Currently jobs "are scituate some distance from one another, oftentimes unknown & In number Infinite." At such a Register people "can but leave their names, with the place of their abode," and "they may keepe at home" until something turns up. A century later, Henry and John Fielding described their similar proposal as the next step in a logical development: "Man is . . . by Nature a Social Animal." Society both creates "Wants" and supplies them by creating "Publick Meetings for carrying on Trade and Commerce between Men"; but these "fail to be universal." What's needed is therefore "some Place of universal Resort, where all the Members of the Society may communicate all their mutual Wants and Talents to each other" and "bring the World, as it were, together into one Place." At first the public will "come to the Office themselves"; but soon business "may be done with as much Ease by Letter as by their presence," replacing actual by virtual presence and virtualizing many actual places into the universality of one. From another perspective, these proposals offer a concrete realization of my abstract model of Enlightenment thinking: Distinction: the tacit relation of master and man; Separation: the detachment of masters from men by the shift to wages; Conflation: the rationalized relation of masters and men.[19] As we'll see, Adam Smith had no illusions about the availability to wage laborers of a society of universal resort.

On a greater scale, the "Financial Revolution" of the 1690s established those instruments and institutions—the Bank of England, the National Debt, Public Credit—that both responded to and facilitated the virtualization of economic activity.[20] Visiting the Royal Exchange in 1711, Joseph Addison's Mr. Spectator was struck "to see so many private Men, who in [past] Time would have been the Vassals of some powerful Baron, Negotiating like Princes for greater Sums of Mony than were formerly to be met with in the Royal Treasury . . . thriving in their own private Fortunes, and at the same time promoting the Publick Stock."[21] Like Defoe, Addison imagines the autonomy of private men lately liberated from the actual "vassalage" of feudal dependence into efficient investment practices on the virtual "market." Over the course of many centuries, the market has undergone a complex development in denotation and connotation, from an actual marketplace in proximity to human settlements and physically frequented for the purpose of different sorts of social exchange, to buying and selling according to the price or exchange value of goods and services, to the governing concept of commodity exchange for the primary purpose of capital accumulation. Already by the end of the eighteenth century, "the gradual separation of the generality of a market process from the particularity of a market place" had led to the locution "market overt" to refer to the original sense of an actually situated locale.[22] Mr. Spectator puts the virtuality of economic exchange in the most inclusive light. The Exchange kindles not only his domestic but also his cosmopolitan imagination. "I look upon High-Change [the Royal Exchange] to be a great Council, in which all considerable Nations have their Representatives. . . . I am infinitely delighted in mixing with these several Ministers of Commerce, as they are distinguished by their different Walks and different languages."[23] Others had harsher words for what was happening, especially on the domestic front. One attacked all "Improuers of our Land [who] study to do such acts, and invent such projects, as may vndo the publique for their priuave and inordinate desires, [who] liue in this world as *in a market* [and] *imagine there is nothing else for them to doe, but to buy and sell, and that the only end of their creation and being was to gather riches, by all meanes possible.*"[24] Commoners less upwardly mobile than Defoe and Addison were undergoing the painful process of having to substitute, for their tacit and personal trust of actual creditors who were also friends, a speculative and suspect trust in the abstract notion of a virtual "public credit" guaranteed not by personal reputation or by supernatural sanction but by the Bank of England. But again, the substitution was by no means absolute: for the network of private credit and debt continued to enmesh men and women in relationships with actual people where trust was based on personal reputation.[25]

Contemporaries became aware of these changes on several levels. For years, the national revenue had been thought to be primarily a joint function of land and trade, which were understood to be opposed to each other along the ideological lines of hereditary gentility versus upstart commoner, the unchanging countryside versus urban mobility. By the end of the seventeenth century this formulation no longer seemed adequate. Land and trade, the traditional opponents, had come to be seen as having more in common than not, and the traditional terms of conflict had been superseded by the emergent conflict between the "landed interest," which possessed "real" estate, and the financial "monied interest," whose virtual possessions seemed to many not only insubstantial but imaginary. Jonathan Swift wrote that "the Wealth of the Nation, that used to be reckoned by the Value of Land, is now computed by the Rise and Fall of Stocks." He supported the Property Qualifications Act of 1711, which sought to restrict parliamentary membership to landowners, because he thought it would ensure that "our Properties lie no more at Mercy of those who have none themselves, or at least only what is transient or imaginary."[26] Defoe, an enthusiastic supporter of both trade and credit, was at least ambivalent about what he calls the "Power of Imagination" that increasingly ruled the modern world of exchange value. For those who created "imaginary Value" by playing the stock market Defoe had only contempt. But he was deeply preoccupied by the abstract virtuality of public credit, "the great Mystery of this Age," "neither visible [n]or invisible," "a Being without Matter, a Substance without Form." Defoe expresses his bemusement here through the most virtualizing mode of figural re-presentation, an allegory of Lady Credit. Addison records his dream of public credit as the allegorical figure of a "beautiful Virgin." In 1720, the material consequences of immaterial imaginings were brought home by the world's first stock market crash, the South Sea Bubble.[27]

There are other registers by which contemporaries became conscious of the seemingly ineluctable transformation of actual into virtual economic value. Mercantilist policy had sponsored the trade wars of the mid-seventeenth century because it was based on the belief that the wealth of the world was actual and fixed, and therefore subject to zero-sum rules: if England became wealthier, the Dutch became that much less wealthy. According to John Graunt and William Petty in 1662, "There is but a certain proportion of Trade in the world, and Holland is prepossessed of the greater part of it." Two years later Samuel Pepys wrote: "The trade of the world is too little for us two, therefore one must down."[28] But by the end of the seventeenth century, people were learning that wealth depended not on the intrinsic value of actual objects but on subjective desire and the demand for things, and that wealth therefore was unlimited. In the words of Nicholas Barbon, "Things have no value in themselves . . . it is opinion and fashion brings them into use and gives them a value." "The Wants of the Mind are infinite."[29] The recognition that wealth was generated by the creation of capital through the circulation and recirculation of commodities made policy based on prioritizing and legislating the actual embodiments of wealth seem misguided. Overseas merchants protested against mercantilist trade wars. Domestic merchants protested the monopolistic policy of state protectionism and called instead for free trade that would in principle universalize opportunity and level the playing field.

The difference between objective and subjective value helped contemporaries understand the difference between (actual) use value and (virtual) exchange value, which was conceptualized by the translation of qualitative difference into the quantitative and universal medium of exchange, the quintessential virtuality money. Exchange value was created through the market circulation of commodities, which gave the Financial Revolution its foundation. Over the course of the Enlightenment, debate about the material form in which the circulation of value might securely be embodied shifted in focus from bullion to coinage to paper bills. The old conviction that the medium of exchange itself had to possess intrinsic qualitative value was displaced by an acceptance that it expressed a "credible commitment" to its representation.[30] In 1705, a defender of paper money was convinced that this was the case: "To the virtuality of this Paper-money, which is already of equivalent Extrinsic value, with Gold and Silver money, there shall be added a Reall & equivalent intrinsicall worth: And if these pieces of paper, shall carrie along with them, a proportionable value in Land, the things of most certain & obvious value in the world: Then these pieces of paper, shall be no more pieces of paper, but Signatures and Symbols of Land, equivalent, and consequently of more intrinsicall value than Gold and Silver money."[31] Years later this commitment wasn't entirely credible to Adam Smith, among others: "The judicious operations of banking, by providing, if I may be allowed so violent a metaphor, a sort of wagon-way through the air; enable the country to convert, as it were, a great part of its highways into good pastures and corn fields. . . . The commerce and industry of the country, however, it must be acknowledged, though they may be somewhat augmented, cannot be altogether so secure, when they are thus, as it were, suspended upon the Daedalian wings of paper money, as when they travel about upon the solid ground of gold and silver."[32]

The effect of economic change is registered in how language comes to be used. Until the seventeenth century, the word "propriety," sometimes spelled "property," signified what was proper or fitting to oneself as a social being. Drawing on recent writings in natural law theory, John Locke expanded the reference of these ideas to include those extensions of one's own body that seemed appropriate to it or that had been appropriated by it. Locke theorized that because "every man" has a property or "ownership" in his own person, whatever in the common state of nature he mixes with his own labor he removes from that state, whereby it becomes "properly" his own "property," although now depersonalized and disembodied. By the end of the century, this sort of usage had become too great a burden for a single term to bear, and the two words went their separate ways, the one referring to the sphere of being of one's own or actual self, the other to one's virtual extensions, or what one owns.[33] Of course, Locke was drawing not only on recent theory but also on recent practice, in particular the transfer of "absoluteness" from the political sovereignty of Stuart monarchy to the abstract private property rights of its landowning subjects. One of the things gained in this process was the facilitation of new agricultural technologies and increased production for market exchange. What was lost was the traditional custom of treating land as subject to the collective and conditional use rights of commoners. Both the royal and the commoner notions of property were also notions of social propriety; the capitalist notion was not. With only apparent paradox, the modern idea of "society" came into being at the same moment when the unspoken imperative of social connection was being challenged by the imperative of individual separability and autonomy.

Capitalist Universality

In the introduction to this volume I cited a number of critics who have argued that in eighteenth-century Britain, Enlightenment thought and capitalism teamed up as the good and bad cop of universality. I registered my skepticism, suggesting that the relation between the two was chronological rather than ideological and citing the view of one commentator that in the Enlightenment period there were many other bodies of thought that sponsored ideals of universality and inclusion. At that point I postponed serious consideration of capitalist universalism, what it means and what it may be shown to occasion or infiltrate, until it could be given the attention it requires. This seems to me the right place to take it up because virtuality and universality are related concepts. In fact the aim of this chapter is to argue the preponderance and multiplicity of virtual claims and institutions in the Enlightenment period, an argument that dovetails, I think, with the view that a distinctive ideal of universality motivated a multiplicity of Enlightenment projects. As I pursue this inquiry into the relationship between capitalist and Enlightenment universality, I'll also pursue the question: What's the relation between universality and virtuality in Enlightenment thought?[34]

False Consciousness and Uneven Development

Marx's writings are the most common source both for the concept of capitalist universality and for its critique. In an early text, *The German Ideology* (1846), Marx and Friedrich Engels generalize about the consciousness of individuals at each stage of historical development in terms of what Engels later characterizes, under the name "ideology," as "a process accomplished by the so-called thinker consciously, it is true, but with a false consciousness. The real motive forces impelling him," the determinacy of social materiality, "remain unknown to him."[35] In the epigrammatic words of a decade later, "It is not the consciousness of men that determines their existence, but their social existence that determines their consciousness."[36] In the terms of this study, the former describes a tacit whole that goes without saying; the latter separates out the working parts of that whole and thereby renders false consciousness true.

The German Ideology accounts for false consciousness both at the micro-level of the individual and at the macro-level of historical development. The course of history is a sequence of eras each unaware that the particular conditions of its materiality determine its general or ruling consciousness of itself. This is the key to the universalist illusion that characterizes each era in turn. But it's in the nature of historical development to require a more and more abstract and absolute denial of material determinacy and a progressively inclusive and saturating principle of universality: "Increasingly abstract ideas hold sway, i.e., ideas which increasingly take on the form of universality. For each new class which puts itself in the place of one ruling before it, is compelled, merely in order to carry through its aim, to represent its interest as the common interest of all the members of society, that is, expressed in ideal form: it has to give its ideas the form of universality, and represent them as the only rational, universally valid ones."[37] So, at the macro-level of historical development, the false consciousness of an era is the key to the character of its illusion of universality.

The German Ideology describes the historical conditions for false consciousness as a synchronicity between the prevailing material "productive forces" and the prevailing "form of intercourse"—social, "mental, political, religious." The latter, superstructural, forms of life, tacitly confirmed by the material reality that gives them being, come to seem inseparable from that reality, with which they fit so seamlessly as to conceal its force by taking it on as their own. The differences between universalisms therefore can be understood by inference on the basis of a broad perspective on material change. Because history is always in process, material forces change, and at a rate that tends to outstrip their "forms" and that makes individuals aware of them as accidental "fetters" that constrain and contradict what they earlier had expressed:

> These various conditions, which appear first as conditions of self-activity, later as fetters upon it, form in the whole evolution of history a coherent series of forms of intercourse, the coherence of which consists in this: in the place of an earlier form of intercourse, which has become a fetter, a new one is put, corresponding to the more developed productive forces and, hence, to the advanced mode of the self-activity of individuals—a form which in its turn becomes a fetter and is then replaced by another. . . . Furthermore, [this] takes place only very slowly; the various stages and interests are never completely overcome, but only subordinated to the prevailing interest and trail along beside the latter for centuries afterwards. . . . This explains why . . . consciousness can sometimes appear further advanced than the contemporary empirical relationships, so that in the struggles of a later epoch one can refer to earlier theoreticians as authorities. (pt. 1, D)

This is the phenomenon of "uneven development," the condition whereby at the macro-level of historical change, infrastructural forces, and superstructural forms periodically go out of sync, with a potentially broad and indeterminate range of consequences. The best-known instance of uneven development in Marx's canon apart from political revolution is the disparity between ancient Greek art and its material conditions. This also exemplifies the rare instance when forms are more advanced than and outstrip their forces of production.[38]

Uneven development refers to the historical process whereby the forms of intercourse become fetters on productive forces. The fettering of forces destroys the false consciousness of a seamless fit of forms and forces, which is replaced by the consciousness of that fit as illusory. The uneven development of forces and forms at the macro-level of historical stages is paralleled and constituted at the micro-level by the separation of social from personal identity. At this micro-level, false consciousness predisposes individuals to experience their existence and that of others as self-evident: as "organic" and "necessary," not "accidental" or "one-sided" in the sense of being conditioned by their material circumstances, not "determined" but ontologically given by nature, divinity, or some other source of the order of things. "But in the course of historical evolution, . . . there appears a division within the life of each individual insofar as it is personal and insofar as it is determined by some branch of labour and the conditions pertaining to it. . . . In the estate (and even more in the tribe) this is as yet concealed: for instance, a nobleman always remains a nobleman, a commoner always a commoner, apart from his other relationships, a quality inseparable from his individuality" (pt. 1, D). The increasing division between the personal and the sociomaterial that Marx describes is the precondition for the increasingly abstract ideas of universality needed to subtend division. We might identify as the micro-ideology of feudalism the illusion I've called aristocratic ideology and Marx and Engels argue was concealed in what they call the ideology of the estate. In the false consciousness of feudalism (to pursue the terms of my argument), it goes without saying that our consciousness of the socioeconomic reciprocity I've described is coextensive with and determinant of the way things are, just as we may take for granted that what seems our "external" condition is an expression of our "internal" being, and that both are inseparable parts of a greater whole. However, we've already encountered an important qualification of this model of false consciousness as far as the feudal regime is concerned.[39] Like all ideologies, feudal false consciousness conceived its universality as ontologically given, the way things are, rather than as a circumstance determined by the sociomaterial conditions of life. However, the sociomaterial conditions of life under feudalism reinforced this illusion because the actual interdependence of each hierarchical level determined that comparatively concrete social relations were also personal relations. Personal identity was palpably experienced as a saturated social being.

Part I of *The German Ideology* soon concludes with no more than a brief allusion to the ideology of the historical stage that succeeds it. So, the importance of this text for understanding the nature of capitalist universality lies not in concrete and detailed analysis but in its argument that universality is an illusion not only of capitalism but of all stages of historical development, mystifying conscious experience as ontologically autonomous and universal. However, a preview of the succeeding stage will appear in *Grundrisse*, where Marx argues that under social conditions in which labor becomes mobile and can itself be conceived as a "general abstraction," labor is separated from the individuals who customarily perform it and the two cease to be "organically linked" (104–105; I'll return to this argument below). These social conditions flourish during the Enlightenment, whose analytic impulse challenges this feudal false conviction that social being is organically—that is, tacitly—entailed in consciousness. At the same moment, the illusions of feudalism are challenged by those of capitalism. (How) are these two challenges related? To answer this question we must look to *Capital* for an extended account of its universalist ideology. We can then inquire into the relationship between capitalist and Enlightenment universality, and the relation of both to virtuality.

The Commodity Form

A brief review is in order before turning to *Capital*. Stuart absolutism deemed the domain of England the sovereign property of the crown. But the transition from a feudal system of politically constituted to one of economically constituted property replaced the traditional resources of estate revenue in taxes, rents, and office-holding by the requirement that landowners improve labor productivity in the face of a competitive market. Wealth, it was becoming clear, was produced not politically but economically and virtually, through the circulation and recirculation of commodities. Political absolutism devolved to the economic absolutism of private property. Locke theorized this devolution by arguing that property was an extension of the propriety of the body and became one's own by improving it through labor, and landowners capitalized on absolute ownership through long-term experiments in estate "improvement"—a double-edged term of art—and by increasing their competitiveness through investment.

With the invention of money, the actual marketplace had been supplemented by the virtual market, and barter in actual goods had been largely superseded by the abstract quantification of value and the exchange of virtual commodities. "Value" as a concept now applied not only to the qualitative nature of goods in use but also to the quantity of money for which goods circulated in market exchange. Over the course of the Enlightenment and aided by the Financial Revolution, the production of goods for the market in service to a more efficient and widespread circulation of commodities for consumption increasingly served as well the ambition to recirculate commodities and to accumulate value in exchange, or capital.

Commodity exchange made explicit the separability of the parts of the economic whole—production/consumption, use values/exchange values, value/price—and created conditions for greater access to goods and their wider distribution. On the one hand, by translating the qualitative differences between goods into a quantifying medium, both actual marketplaces and the virtual market made value universal, enabling consumers to exchange what they had, in greater quantity than they could use, for what they lacked and needed. On the other, in Marx's analysis the accumulation of capital expanded over time at a rate that outstripped the market's enablement of consumption, and its generation of universal value fostered a counterproductive "fetishism of commodities."

So, on the one hand, by systematically universalizing the production and circulation of goods and wealth, universal value created the conditions for universal access to goods and wealth. But on the other, the universalization of access was nugatory. In fact for Marx the emergent system both required that access be unequal and created the capitalist false consciousness of universality. This ideology went beyond the relatively concrete contexts and variants of doctrinal, professional, genealogical, environmental, and characterological consciousness to find its basis in the structurally abstract differential that was becoming truly universal to everyday experience, the default lowest common denominator of economic intercourse, the oppositional relation between value in use and value in exchange, the "twofold" structure of the commodity form. Common wisdom holds that the fetishism of commodities is a condition specific to the multitude of industrial laborers, who experience their subjective and social production of commodities as reified in the products of use value that are bought and sold as objects of exchange value. However, Marx's account of fetishism as a false consciousness generated through the entire system of capitalist production and through all who participate in it suggests that it's a global phenomenon.

The first volume of *Capital* is generously and copiously annotated with references to texts that have enabled Marx to conceive and formulate his thesis. Many of these are Enlightenment texts. Several paragraphs into *Capital*'s opening chapter, on the commodity, Marx, with a certain scholarly affection, cites a work by "old Barbon" in order to document his explication of the commodity as a whole that can be analyzed into two parts or kinds of value.[40] The use value of the commodity is the property of a single "useful thing." The commodity's exchange value is a property that's determined by its relation to other commodities. "As use-values, commodities differ above all in quality, while as exchange-values they can differ only in quantity, and therefore do not contain an atom of use-value. If then we disregard the use-value of commodities, only one property remains, that of being products of labour." Marx describes this as a process of abstraction: "If we make abstraction from [the product's] use-value, we abstract also from the material constituents and forms which make it a use-value. . . . This in turn entails the disappearance of the different concrete forms of labour," which are "reduced to the same kind of labour, human labour in the abstract." So, "when commodities are in the relation of exchange, their exchange-value manifests itself as something totally independent of their use-value." However, they contain a "residue of the products of labour. There is nothing left of them in each case but the same phantom-like objectivity; they are merely congealed quantities of homogeneous human labour" (128).

Several paragraphs later Marx writes, with a comparable scholarly self-awareness: "I was the first to point out and examine critically this twofold nature of the labour contained in commodities" (132). Marx displays here and throughout *Capital* a capacity for analytic abstraction, in part bequeathed by Enlightenment thought, and applies it to the understanding of capitalist abstraction. Capitalist universality secretes the concrete objectivity of the products of labor within the abstract, "phantom-like objectivity" of the commodity form. Enlightenment universality brings to light and makes legible the twofold nature of the commodity by disclosing the source of universal value in a multiplicity of concrete use values.

Capital is concerned not only to analyze but also to historicize the commodity form. A key to this process is the category of "appearance." The commodity "appears as the twofold thing it really is as soon as its value possesses its own particular form of manifestation, which is distinct from its natural form" and which it never has "when looked at in isolation, but only when it is in a value-relation or an exchange relation with a second commodity of a different kind" (152). This would seem to describe, in circular fashion, the condition of commodity circulation that defines the commodity form itself. Marx elaborates:

> It is only by being exchanged that the products of labour acquire a socially uniform objectivity as values, which is distinct from their sensuously varied objectivity as articles of utility. This division of the product of labour into a useful thing and a thing possessing value appears in practice only when exchange has already acquired a sufficient extension and importance to allow useful things to be produced for the purpose of being exchanged, so that their character as values has already to be taken into consideration during production. From this moment on, the labour of the individual producer acquires a twofold social character. (166)

Marx's specification of the moment when the exchange value of a product of labor "appears in practice" suggests that he's distinguishing between two kinds of "appearance." "As the commodity-form is the most general and the most undeveloped form of bourgeois production," he writes, "it makes its appearance at an early date, though not in the same predominant and therefore characteristic manner as nowadays. Hence its fetish character is still relatively easy to penetrate. But when we come to more concrete forms, even this appearance of simplicity vanishes" (176). Not that the twofold nature of the commodity form ceases at this point to appear. On the contrary, it no longer can be seen through because it has taken on the opacity of an illusion. This is the difference between the relatively manifest duality of its fetish character, which is legible and can be penetrated, and the fully developed socioeconomic system in which exchange value "transforms every product of labour into a social hieroglyphic" (167).[41]

The "phantom-like objectivity" of labor is its fetish character and underlies Marx's celebrated account of the fetishism of commodities:

> The mysterious character of the commodity-form consists therefore simply in the fact that the commodity reflects the social characteristics of men's own labour as objective characteristics of the products of labour themselves, as the socio-natural properties of these things. Hence it also reflects the social

> relation between objects, a relation which exists apart from and outside the producers. Through this substitution, the products of labour become commodities, sensuous things which are at the same time suprasensible or social.... It is nothing but the definite social relation between men themselves which assumes here, for them, the fantastic form of a relation between things. (164–165)

The commodity's "phantom-like" objectivity is its "fantastic" reflection of the social characteristics of men's own labor as objective characteristics of the products of labor themselves. Under feudalism, the system of commodity exchange is relatively undeveloped, and "because relations of personal dependence form the given social foundation, there is no need for labour and its products to assume a fantastic form different from their reality. They take the shape, in the transactions of society, of services in kind and payments in kind" (170). In the regime of capitalist universality, however, false consciousness has reached a point of abstraction that renders the commodity form illusory and illegible.

Marx's analysis of the commodity form is one of the great fruits of social scientific thinking. Its germination in the latter decades of the eighteenth century exemplifies the role of Enlightenment thought in separating out, sufficiently to raise the question of how they might be conflated, two fundamental categories: on the one hand, the material and social conditions of life; on the other, the conceptual structures of consciousness to which they correspond and with which they interact.[42] *Capital* pursues this question of conflation on two levels. First, on the level of content, it analyzes the apparently singular commodity form as having the twofold character of use value/exchange value, sensuous/suprasensible or social thing, social labor/universal value. Second, on the level of form or method, *Capital* undertakes a dialectical reflection on the capacity of conceptual forms of consciousness to reinforce or to countermand the productive forces of material life.

With the same intellectual energy he devotes to the insights of Enlightenment thinkers Marx pursues in *Capital* the "degree to which some economists are misled by the fetishism attached to the world of commodities" (176–177, also 171–175nn.).[43] What "appears valid" to these economists Marx accords the status both of illusion and of knowledge appropriate to or fitting its sociomaterial conditions. Exchange value and the measure of its magnitude "appear to the political economists' bourgeois consciousness to be as much a self-evident and nature-imposed necessity as productive labor itself" (174–175). "The categories of bourgeois economics ... are forms of thought which are socially valid, and therefore objective, for the relations of production belonging to this historically determined mode of social production" (169). "Later on, men try to decipher the hieroglyph, to get behind the secret of their own social product," and its "belated scientific discovery ... marks an epoch in the history of man's development, but by no means banishes the semblance of objectivity possessed by the social characteristics of labour. Something which is only valid for this particular form of production ... appears to those caught up in the relations of commodity production (and this is true both before and after the above-mentioned scientific discovery) to be just as ultimately valid as the fact that the scientific dissection of the air into its component parts left the atmosphere itself unaltered in its physical configuration" (167). That is, scientific analysis is right—even though it's finally of no material consequence for those caught up in illusion. To recall the terms of *The German Ideology*, bourgeois forms of thought are socially valid for this mode of production: they fit rather than fetter their productive forces.

But what of men like Marx himself? Isn't he, and others who "try to decipher the hieroglyphic," also "caught up in the relations of commodity production"? Or does Marx write at a historical moment of uneven development, when the commodity form is going out of sync with its forces of production (despite his apparent confidence that the opposite is the case) and becoming legible as an "accidental" and "one-sided" fetter? Indeed, is his ability to decipher it a sign of this development? Marx underscores the conditional nature of what is "socially valid, and therefore objective" by reminding us of how easily illusory forms can become fetters. "The whole mystery of commodities, all the magic and necromancy that surrounds the products of labour on the basis of commodity production, vanishes therefore as soon as we come to other forms of production" (167, 169). Marx then cites two other forms of production, one pertaining to feudalism, another imagined on Robinson Crusoe's island.

So, is this what it means to "come to" other forms: not a material transition but the conceptualization, the imagination, of an alternative? Marx's words require close attention. Now subtly heightened, his language distances us from the discursive nature of his topic and fabricates instead a scenario of forms and forces, a powerful but fleeting morality or mystery play. The "whole" mystery, "all" the magic: these words sum up and bring to a close the theatrical spectacle of the "fetishism" of commodities that has surrounded and captivated us but now will suddenly "vanish" before our eyes as though a wand has been waved or a curtain dropped. What's adumbrated is a sense that by imagining its alternative forms we may "come to" or be "caught up in" the forces of another mode of production—that what is may be accessible to what "appears" to be. Elsewhere, as we've seen, Marx suggests on the contrary that in his own time, the former relative ease of penetrating the fetishism of commodities—of separating their use from their exchange value—"vanishes" because it has attained the force of a fantastic illusion (176). Here it's the illusion that vanishes—or rather, what's illusory seems to have an aesthetic evanescence that allows for the suspension of disbelief. And we're reminded that Marx's famous turn of phrase for the commodity form characterizes a "consciousness" that is, from an analytic perspective, "false"—if not a dead metaphor, a self-conscious figure of speech, a trope.

The Trope of the Fetish

The term "fetishism" is an Enlightenment coinage, and by the end of the eighteenth century the discourse of fetishism was flourishing in a number of directions and applications.[44] Throughout their writings, Marx and Engels use the figure of the fetish to describe how capital, money, interest, and the commodity form abstract the social relations of laboring people into static things.[45] However, in *Capital* Marx acknowledges the figure's specific provenance: "In order, therefore, to find an analogy we must take flight into the misty realm of religion. There the products of the human brain appear as autonomous figures endowed with a life of their own. . . . So it is in the world of commodities with the products of men's hands. I call this the fetishism which attaches itself to the products of labour as soon as they are produced as commodities" (165). Marx's self-reference—"I call this"— (compare "I was the first to point out" [132]) draws attention to a stylistic feature of this passage that as in the one just discussed affords the fetish trope a self-conscious theatricality, but in a different register. Here the implication of the trope's extravagance concerns its religious content, although we soon learn that what makes the trope "misty" is as much its anachronism. That we must "take flight" to do justice to the commodity form may imply that to the degree that the fetish trope is apposite it's also far-fetched, its magical ambience of necromancy evocative not only of products endowed with a life of their own but also of the dead hand of the past brought back to life (165). The question that interests Marx concerns the relationship between the forms and the forces of production, and he continues to mull it over a few pages later. Does he ruminate on the fetish trope because it doesn't correspond historically to the modern forces of production he's describing, or because religion is so illusory as to beg the question of correspondence altogether? And yet religion won't go away; and so we must wait until the demise of capitalism before religion "vanishes" from the world with a nontheatrical finality: "The religious reflections of the real world can . . . vanish only when the practical relations of everyday life between man and man, and man and nature, generally present themselves to him in a transparent and rational form. The veil is not removed from the countenance of the social life-process, i.e. the process of material production, until it becomes production by freely associated men, and stands under their conscious and planned control" (173).

In the meantime, the notion that religious forms may correspond to productive forces, however compromised, bears further thought. Marx uses what might seem surprisingly similar terms to anticipate this postcapitalist possibility and to recall precapitalist actuality: the "ancient social organisms of production are much more simple and transparent than those of bourgeois society" and are based on "limited relations between man and nature." To be sure, these are likely to involve ancient forces of commodity production; but as we've seen, in its early stage "the commodity-form is . . . undeveloped" and "its fetish character is still relatively easy to penetrate" (173, 176). Here Marx uses the category of fetishism as he usually does, as a metaphor for the commodity form. But ancient society is also where fetishism has a literal existence. There the "limited relations between man and nature . . . are reflected in the ancient worship of nature, and in other elements of tribal religion" like the fetish form, which mediates the ancient worship of nature through the powers of contiguous magic. In other words, the fetish trope is appropriate for describing the early commodity form not only because it's metaphorically apposite but also because of its ancient metonymic conjunction with the literal practice of religious fetishism.

This may help explain why Marx applies the fetish trope to the advanced commodity form. What looks like extravagant anachronism is instead the basis for historical analogy.[46] Political economy's dogmatic faith, "misled by the fetishism attached to the world of commodities [and] by the objective appearance of the social characteristics of labour," treats "pre-bourgeois forms . . . in much the same way as the Fathers of the Church treated pre-Christian religions." That is, fetishism provides an ironic model not only for the doctrinal arrogance that replaced it, but also for the secular arrogance of the commodity form. To extrapolate: as monotheism abstracts from nature, exchange value abstracts from the social relations of material life, in favor of an illusion that appears to political economists a "self-evident and nature-imposed necessity" (175–176).[47] So, fetishism is a powerful figure for the putatively seamless fit between the forms and forces of commodity production central to capitalist universality. But it clearly isn't the religious form that actually provides that fit. However, Marx has already proposed the form that does fit those forces: "For a society of commodity producers, . . . Christianity with its religious cult of man in the abstract, more particularly in its bourgeois development, i.e. in Protestantism, Deism, etc., is the most fitting form of religion" (172).[48]

Parody

Marx gave a great deal of thought to the use of figures that possess a past resonance for conjuring up the present. Does the very promise of their former power warn that their reuse will seem far-fetched and backfire? Readers of *The Eighteenth Brumaire of Louis Bonaparte* (1852) may be excused for taking this to be Marx's single-minded lesson given his famous opening: "All great world-historical facts and personages appear, as it were, twice . . . the first time as tragedy, the second as farce." But Marx complicates this judgment in words that recall his ruminations on the "flight" enforced by the fetish trope. Recalling several such reuses, he writes: "The awakening of the dead in those revolutions therefore served the purpose of glorifying the new struggles, not of parodying the old; of magnifying the given tasks in imagination, not of taking flight from their solution in reality." The flight of the imagination from reality into the misty realm of pagan belief, if self-consciously undertaken, can serve reality. Precisely because of our historical detachment from it, the fetish trope makes us conscious of how false consciousness detaches us from our reality. However, the lesson is not that the fetish trope is simply false or wrong, but that it's historically serviceable. "Earlier revolutions required world-historical recollections in order to drug themselves concerning their own content. In order to arrive at its content," the present moment "must let the dead bury their dead," so as to discover for that content a form that fits not seamlessly but self-consciously, not like religion but as a trope of the imagination. This, at least, is what I suggest can be extrapolated from Marx's reflexive thoughts on his own thinking about the fetish form, which in the end sophisticates parody as having a twofold purpose: as not just a slavish imitation of the past—what's given—but as the key to how the past may be preserved, criticized, and superseded: "The parody of imperialism was necessary to free the mass of the French nation from the weight of tradition and to work out in pure form the opposition between the state power and society." In these terms, Marx deploys the dialectical, manifestly double movement of parody as the antidote to the mystifying twofold character of the commodity form.[49]

The Trope of the Invisible Hand

In *The Wealth of Nations* (1776) Adam Smith, in celebration of the commodity form, also has recourse to the analogy between the religious forms and the economic forces of production:

> Every individual necessarily labours to render the annual revenue of the society as great as he can. He generally, indeed, neither intends to promote the publick interest, nor knows how much he is promoting it. By preferring the support of domestick to that of foreign industry, [every individual] intends only his own security; and by directing that industry in such a manner as its produce may be of the greatest value, he intends only his own gain, and he is in this, as in many other cases, led by an invisible hand to promote an end which was no part of his intention. . . . By pursuing his own interest he frequently promotes that of the society more effectually than when he really intends to promote it. (456)

In contrast to the position Marx would take, Smith argued that commodity exchange created universal value that ensured the universal circulation and distribution of goods and wealth, redounding in general to all the particular parts of the economic whole. The success of capitalist universality was therefore evident. Particulars correlated with the general, individual interests and desires with the interest of society at large and with the objective means of their fulfillment.

I've argued elsewhere in this book that the Enlightenment impulse to render the tacit explicit contributed from many directions to the virtual coalescence and separation out of civil society from the state, and in turn to the separation from society of its actual individual components. In other words, what conceptually had been distinct but inseparable categories now gained autonomy and dynamic mobility, but by the same token lost a collectivity that could be taken for granted. The gap between individual and society, which was to become a defining feature of modern culture, was also evident to acute contemporaries like Smith, whose major works can fruitfully be seen as strategies aimed at achieving—because social collectivity could no longer be taken for granted—the explicit conflation of individuals with society, which is to say also with other individuals. In *The Theory of Moral Sentiments* (1759), Smith grounds the separation of individuals on the basic premise of empirical epistemology, which also grounds Enlightenment thought. That all knowledge is based in sense impressions precludes our knowledge of other people: "As we have no immediate experience of what other men feel," he writes, "we can form no idea of the manner in which they are affected, but by conceiving what we ourselves should feel in the like situation. Though our brother is upon the rack, as long as we ourselves are at our ease, our senses will never inform us of what he suffers. They never did, and never can, carry us beyond our own person, and it is by the imagination only that we can form any conception of what are his sensations."[50] The virtual reality of "society" itself is produced by imaginative acts of sympathy, which refine the actual particularity of others into the virtual particularity of others-as-ourselves, who thereby become susceptible to collective generalization. As when we are moved by seeing or reading a play, so when we sympathetically encounter other people, we experience a revival of the social coherence and solidarity of traditional cultures, but at the level of not physical presence but imaginative identification.

Like the social psychology of *The Theory of Moral Sentiments*, the political economy of *The Wealth of Nations* is concerned to conflate—in the language of capitalist universality, to find a fit between—individuals and society. Is a relevant connection to be found in the analogy between the capacity of sympathy to overcome emotional difference and the capacity of the market to overcome actual differences between objects of consumption? That is, can we say that the imagination bridges the gap between psychologies as it does the gap between actual use values and virtual exchange values? The question invites a deeper analysis, and here the analogy begins to lose its force. Sympathetic conflation requires individuals to imagine the minds of others, whereas market conflation may lead individuals to imagine that given objects have two different capacities—but nothing of relevance to the social relations of individuals. Still, it's on the higher level of market activity that Smith finds evidence of capitalist universality in the paradoxical conflation of individuals and society; yet here the analogy between sympathetic and market conflation falls apart. Sympathy brings individuals into sociable connection because they're motivated to imagine what others feel, whereas individuals are motivated to enter the market only because they intend to further their own self-interest. Even more, in order to refute mercantilist or protectionist doctrine Smith makes capitalist universality triumph despite paradox by expressly declaring it an unintended consequence. Individuals intend to fulfill only their own interests and have no wish or motive to further the interests of others.

If we set aside this triumph for a moment, other passages in *The Wealth of Nations* (let alone other of his writings) make clear that Smith had no illusions that the interest of the social whole was consistent with the self-interest of the majority of individuals. The impulse toward explicit analysis told him that some parts of the social whole, intent on serving the interests of their own lesser wholes, were able to prevent other parts from achieving a comparable self-service. And so Smith acknowledges that while English law prohibited workers from "combining" or unionizing, "masters are always and every where in a sort of tacit, but constant and uniform combination, not to raise the wages of labour above their actual rate," which was taken to be "the natural state of things which nobody ever hears of" (84).[51] This helps explain why Smith is content to treat the triumph of capitalist universality as something achieved by means beyond human will. Yet even his famous celebration of that triumph suggests that he was pulling his punches. Smith had a thorough knowledge of human theory and practice. Even if intent on paradox, why did he want it to stand alone, apart from political, social, or economic rationale, above the level of individual motive but below that of an invisible hand? Was he led to this uncharacteristic display by his antipathy toward mercantilist theory? Why does his advocacy of capitalist universality, diametrically opposed to Marx, dovetail with Marx's recourse to the misty realm of religion?

With reference to the world of Enlightenment Britain, the "invisible hand" connotes a monotheistic projection that might justify Marx's figure of flight better than Marx's pagan theology can do given the Christian association of the Deus absconditus with a supranatural heaven. More important, the invisible hand evokes a transcendence suggestive of the universality that both men associate with the promise of capitalism. However, Smith's earliest of three uses of the invisible hand trope complicates these associations. Speaking of the archaic world, he describes things as normally occurring "by the necessity of their own nature." "It is the irregular events of nature only that are ascribed to the agency and power of their gods," to "the invisible hand of Jupiter" and by implication the other gods, an ascription Smith calls "the lowest and most pusillanimous superstition." So, if the trope bears the same broad meaning in *Wealth*, it may suggest that capitalist universality is a superstition—a false consciousness—less credible even than the fetish trope.[52]

This view gains a degree of support from some of Smith's statements about his own religious beliefs. He wrote in *Theory* that having "created [man] after his own image" and recognizing the "obscurity and darkness" of his "faint and feeble" judgments, God "made man the immediate judge of mankind." But when men deem the judgment of "this inferiour tribunal" defective, they "feel that they may appeal" to "the tribunal in their own breasts," the "abstract man, . . . and substitute of the Deity," the "impartial spectator" and "supreme arbiter of his conduct" (128–130).[53] The false consciousness Smith's God exemplifies is doubly so. Implicitly the projection of human powers (an invisible *hand*), the illegibility of this absconded God requires his introjection as "their own consciences." The second falsehood cancels the first and makes true the consciousness of human powers as human. Smith's impartial spectator may be the limit case of Protestant internalization. And the devolutionary trajectory of his God in at least these selections of Smith's religious discourse divests capitalist universality of the invisible hand's preternatural authorization. So, from opposite directions, Marx and Smith self-consciously deploy the authority of religion—traditionally taken for granted, but not in an Enlightenment context where nothing can be granted without explicit inquiry—to represent capitalist universality as a knowing illusion, but no less effective for being that. Returning now to the terms of Marx's argument: on the one hand, the universal value of the commodity form is a creation of the market. On the other, the universal value of the commodity form, like the

Conceptual Abstraction

In *Grundrisse* Marx goes further than we've seen thus far in expanding the notion of universal value by isolating it not as a function of economic exchange but as an instrument of conceptual analysis; and he does this, strikingly, in his capacity as Smith's interpreter. I've suggested that the transit of accumulation and recirculation from the margins to the center of capitalist enterprise was facilitated by the realization of seventeenth-century English people, based on the evidence of commercial practices, that the amount and distribution of wealth and value were not fixed by political circumstance but generated economically by the indeterminate flow of goods as commodities. Smith's close analysis of the nature and causes of the wealth of nations in this period had given him an unrivaled knowledge of these developments. It may be for this reason that Marx attributed to Smith the conceptual abstraction, the method of mental discovery—what Marx in *Capital* will say Smith "deciphered," perhaps on analogy with his own decipherment of the commodity form—that enabled this practical discovery of how value is generated: "It was an immense step forward for Adam Smith to throw out every limiting specification of wealth-creating activity—not only manufacturing, or commercial or agricultural labour, but one as well as the others, labour in general. With the abstract universality of the object defined as wealth-creating activity we now have the universality of the object defined as wealth, the product as such or again labour as such, but labour as past, objectified labour" (104). Not (only) Smith's genius, but the historical moment in which he thought and wrote, facilitated this discovery:

> Indifference towards any specific kind of labour presupposes a very developed totality of real kinds of labour, of which no single one is any longer predominant. As a rule, the most general abstractions arise only in the midst of the richest possible concrete development, where one thing appears as common to many, to all. Then it ceases to be thinkable in a particular form alone. On the other side, this abstraction of labour as such is not merely the mental product of a concrete totality of labours. Indifference towards specific labours corresponds to a form of society in which individuals can with ease transfer from one labour to another, and where the specific kind is a matter of chance for them, hence of indifference. Not only the category, labour, but labour in reality has here become the means of creating wealth in general, and has ceased to be organically linked with particular individuals in any specific form. . . . The simplest abstraction, then, which modern economics places at the head of its discussions, and which expresses an immeasurably ancient relation valid in all forms of society, nevertheless achieves practical truth as an abstraction only as a category of the most modern society. (104–105)

What first must be said about this arresting passage is that it offers a close analogy to the simple circulation and exchange of commodities. As a conceptual process of virtualization, abstraction from concrete particulars to universal value is a self-consciously dialectical process that doesn't liquidate the particular or render it invisible but depends for its very coherence on the reciprocal relation of the abstract and the concrete. Consequently this conceptual conflation doesn't amount to a once-for-all positing of an abstract category that henceforth resides apart from the process of its ongoing production. The process is completed and resumed in the ongoing production and reproduction of the "mental product" "labor," as well as in that of other mental products. This is analogous to the abstraction of concrete use values to the universal medium of exchange, a process that's completed and resumed in the ongoing exchange of goods as commodities to be consumed. Just as use values are the "material bearers" of exchange value's abstract universality, so specific labors are the bearers of labor as such (*Capital*, 126, 295).

But second, the analogy of conceptual abstraction with commodity exchange fails in the case of advanced or capitalist exchange, where the reciprocity of the abstract and the concrete is lost because the abstract category of universal value conceals and absorbs the concrete particularity of both labor and consumption in service to the accumulation of capital. This difference is an index to the difference between capitalist and Enlightenment universality.

Capitalist and Enlightenment Universality

My ongoing contention is that the fundamental character of Enlightenment thought can be exemplified by a number of different but analogous intellectual pursuits. At one point in his account of simple commodity exchange in *Capital*, Marx's formulation calls to mind not only his account of Smith's insight into conceptual abstraction but also another innovation of Enlightenment thought, experimental method (to which I'll return later in this chapter). Marx writes: "Equality in the full sense between different kinds of labor can be arrived at only if we abstract from their real inequality, if we reduce them to the characteristics they have in common, that of being the expenditure of human labour-power, of human labour in the abstract" (166). "Indifference" toward any particular use value or kind of labor is paralleled by the experimental separation of "variables" from the coalescing category of the "constant," which also must presuppose a "very developed totality" of natural samples and their data before the discrimination and exclusion of variables becomes possible. The analogy with experimental method also brings into focus the temporal dimension of conceptual methodology. In the analogy of experimental and conceptual conflation, the point at which the abstract constancy of the entity under study is deemed probable corresponds, as a moment in the trial process, to the moment when the abstract universality of the concept coalesces. These examples testify to what's distinctive in the nature of Enlightenment thought: its commitment to the self-conscious separation out of categories that traditionally had been conceived as inseparable parts of greater wholes, and to the conflation of those parts as separate components in dialectical reciprocity with the new whole that they compose.

This pattern of separation and conflation is also a defining feature of Enlightenment universality, which returns us by a different route to the same question: What's the relationship between Enlightenment and capitalist universality? Marx appears to broach this very question in *Capital* when he recurs to his account, in *Grundrisse*, of Smith's "decipherment" of the concept of labor. But he answers it in terms not of their similarity and difference (as I've done in the preceding pages) but of the question of enabling priority: which precedes and lays the ground for the other? His point is that Smith's discovery wouldn't have been possible except under the following conditions: "The secret of the expression of value, namely the equality and equivalence of all kinds of labour because and in so far as they are human labour in general, could not be deciphered until the concept of human equality had already acquired the permanence of a fixed popular opinion. This however becomes possible only in a society where the commodity-form is the universal form of the product of labour, hence the dominant social relation is the relation between men as possessors of commodities" (152). This bold prioritization of capitalist universality belies some other evidence of Marx's thinking I've advanced, and is for this and other reasons subject to question. Still, as a temporal sequence it offers a clear hypothesis:

1. The standard of universality originated in the Enlightenment through the universalization of the commodity form and its dominance of social relations, and was therefore conceived first in the terms of capitalist universality.
2. This made possible the formation of the concept of human equality, which was the foundation of Enlightenment universality.
3. The concept of human equality enabled Smith to decipher the method of conceptual abstraction.
4. By implication, Smith's decipherment of conceptual abstraction facilitated Marx's decipherment of the commodity form, which is anticipated but not yet achieved in the first stage of this sequence.

Two parallel questions arise. First, how fundamentally, and with what implications, were concepts of Enlightenment universality shaped by the precedent capitalist concept of universality? Second (and by way of unfolding the first question), was capitalist universality susceptible to the penetration and influence of concepts of Enlightenment universality for which it had provided the initial impetus? In support of the latter notion, I've argued that in seeking to describe capitalist universality, Smith and Marx characterize the false consciousness of the commodity form as subtly defective in achieving a seamless fit with its material forces. On the basis of this argument I've suggested that our common assumptions about the nature of the relation between forms and forces may be defective, too reliant on the orthodoxy of capitalist universality and unmindful of the influence of Enlightenment universality. I'll now turn to a summary discrimination of the concepts of capitalist and Enlightenment universality, with, in deference to the temporal priority (for Marx) of capitalist universality, a specific focus on advanced commodity exchange. And because my discussion thus far has emphasized how Enlightenment universality has penetrated capitalist universality, I'll then conclude with a close exemplary reading of the reverse phenomenon. My ambition in this inquiry is not to show that one is prior to and determinant of the other. My aim is to disentangle the two: to separate Enlightenment from capitalist universality sufficiently to ensure that their conflation in modern thought is sustained with a consciousness of their difference. Marx's capitalism is a one-dimensional will to equalize and universalize by a standard of uniformity that conceals difference. Enlightenment universalism, conceiving the logic of equalization to derive from the premise of difference, is attuned to the dialectic between abstract and virtual generality and the concrete and actual particularity of its component parts. This contrast can be seen in the difference between the universality of the abstract concept, a secret whose decipherment Marx attributes to Smith, and the universality of the commodity form, the secret deciphered by Marx. As Marx tells it, what Smith discovered was a concept of the universality of labor that expresses the dialectical reciprocity of abstract generality and its concrete instantiations. This concept became explicit for Smith because it became evident over time as an abstract conflation of concrete instances that, being temporally disparate, bore no relation to each other apart from this conceptual conflation. In other words, the twofold nature of labor as having actual and virtual value was not mysterious to Smith but evident, not as a relation between concrete use values and abstract exchange value, but as empirically derived. The work of capitalist universality, by contrast, is to conceal the twofold character of labor by forgoing the evidence of temporal difference and exploiting the mysterious simultaneity of concrete and abstract value—that is, concealing the former within the latter—in the abstract commodity form.

Smith's abstract concept is a model of universality that entails a conflation that sustains and fulfills the value of concrete particularity, and it's the model that Enlightenment thought brings to bear on commodity exchange. By contrast, capitalist universality obscures this grounding of concrete particularity through the repeated and ongoing process of exchange, accumulation, and productivity. True, Enlightenment conflation is also one stage in a continuing process, founded on an awareness of the contingent and experimental nature of its results. To recall: traditional distinctions are analyzed explicitly and separated out from each other, which allows them to be either conceived as autonomous entities, subdivided into smaller categories, or conflated with other, newly separated categories to constitute new wholes. But the separate and integral categories that may be produced by conflation are at any point subject to a reconflation that amounts to the abstract representation of concrete behavior in the pursuit of any particular practical purpose. So, with respect to economy, Enlightenment thought conceives the purpose of the circulation and exchange of commodities to be the conflation of use values in the process of their exchange, but then their separation out in order to be distributed to and consumed by particular actual consumers and producers.

Yet we return to slavery: an institution that was grounded in the universality of the commodity form yet thrived in a setting attuned to Enlightenment universality. How can we understand this penetration of Enlightenment by capitalist universality? Locke's *Second Treatise of Government* allows us to pursue this question at the concrete level of close argument.

The *Second Treatise* is one of the great documents of Enlightenment thought. Its project is to refute the absolutist theory of the state as formulated by Sir Robert Filmer.[54] On the eve of civil war, Filmer had succumbed to the pressure of grave political crisis and made the tacit explicit by theorizing what traditionally was taken for granted and went without saying about how political power was exercised. Filmer's treatise was a triumph of traditional thought and also, because explicitly articulated, its death knell. And in this sense, the contractual or compact theory of the state, Locke's refutation of Filmer's absolutist theory of the state, was an affirmation and extension of Filmer's triumph in making the tacit explicit. Locke begins by distinguishing, then separating out, the several kinds of power, one of which is "Political Power." He hypothesizes a state of nature prior to polity and positive law that is composed of people all of whom are possessed of the natural *"Right of Self-preservation."* He describes how these fundamental parts of the whole of the state of nature establish a polity by entering into an explicit compact to cede their natural rights "to be Judges in their own Cases" to a common authority that will preserve their other rights, thereby establishing themselves as citizens equal under the law. With this compact, the natives of the state of nature formally authorize political power and enter into the first polity (paras. 2–3, p. 286; para. 11, p. 292; para. 13, p. 293).

We recall the notion that over the course of the seventeenth century, the "absoluteness" of Stuart monarchy devolved to the absolute private property rights of its landowning subjects. On this basis we might infer that the devolution of economic and the devolution of political power traditionally exercised by the state were coextensive, one through the transfer of public to private absolute ownership, and one through the formal provisions of the political compact. But then why does Locke stipulate that the right to private property be authorized apart from the political compact—that is, before it, according to the narrative framework of the transition from the state of nature to the political compact? And here another aspect of Locke's thinking should be recalled.[55] Because everyone has a property in their own person, whatever in nature they mix with their own labor they remove from the common state of nature, whereby it becomes their extended person or property. And because this is a right that prevails in the state of nature, the "self" whose preservation is fundamental to that state is that extended person or incorporated property.

Like the right to private property, the authorization of the marriage compact precedes the political compact. How is the marriage compact related to private property? Here Locke's (customary) designation of humanity by the male pronoun is given the lie by the need to make concrete reference to women. By the common law of coverture, a "woman's personal property, by marriage, becomes absolutely her husband's."[56] Within a decade of Locke's *Two Treatises* Mary Astell asked: "If Absolute Sovereignty be not necessary in a State, how comes it to be so in a Family?"[57] Locke may mean to defend this anomaly—absolutism within anti-absolutism—by designating *"Conjugal Society"* as the *"first Society,"* and therefore positing it as logically and chronologically prior to *"Political Society"* (paras. 77–78, p. 337). But his rudimentary defense of marriage itself avoids confronting its inequality by avoiding an account of coverture, and his claim that the *"Power of the Husband"* was "far from that of an absolute Monarch" (para. 82, p. 339) accords with his theoretical separation out of the several kinds of power but not with the actual law and practice of coverture. So, ensuring the prior authority of private property is a strong, if unstated, reason for also giving marriage priority over polity. (Marriage is also therefore deemed "natural," which of course serves male dominion.) The political compact subjects all legislation to its authority. But although property transactions in practice therefore will be subject to its oversight, the right of self-preservation that governs property transactions is a natural right that precedes political authority.

Still, Locke insists on stipulating the natural and moral law that also precedes political law and constrains the absoluteness of private property, as well as its limits. In accord with the principle of Enlightenment universality, God gave the land universally to all in common, and in England it continues to be used according to the common-law provision that land be parceled and shared subject to use rights that are limited by custom, and with the proviso that some waste lands be set aside for common use, like gathering wood for fuel.[58] But God also commanded us to labor, and man is *"Proprietor of his own Person,* and the actions or *Labour* of it" (para. 44, p. 316). The ductility of language registered the extension of personal propriety into private property. When we mix something in nature with our labor, Locke argued, we exclude the common right of others, and by appropriating and improving it we make it our own. Even so, universal access to land and its use isn't thereby endangered because the appropriation of property is limited by its being used before spoilage, and by enough being left for others to use (paras. 31, 33, pp. 308, 309).

However, the invention of money and the universal exchange value it enables removes these limits—not simply because exchange can obviate the problem of spoilage, but also because "the tacit Agreement of Men to put a value on [money] introduced (by Consent) larger Possessions, and a Right to them." Locke's point is by his own anti-absolutist standards "unenlightened": common practice can be construed as general tacit agreement—consent—to what may be its unintended consequences even if it's not explicitly given by all particular people. Although Locke isn't clear on this, it seems likely that what he's suggesting is, if not explicit consent to this agreement, a causal relation between it and what follows, "the desire of having more than Men needed [that] altered the intrinsick value of things, which depends only on their usefulness to the Life of Man" (paras. 37–38, pp. 311–312). What's clear is that Locke is describing the difference between use value and exchange value, or what Marx calls universal value. Moreover, his description rationalizes the function of universal value (exchange value) to satisfy desires that go beyond what's needed for use. To characterize circulation and exchange as having the function of universalizing access to the means for satisfying use needs would accord with Enlightenment universality. However, Locke's universal value satisfies desires for profit that are by definition extrinsic to use needs. In other words, rather than helping to universalize access to the means for satisfying use needs, his universal value satisfies desires for what can be gained through profitable exchange. Locke's story began as the repudiation of absolutism through the Enlightenment pursuit of universality as a matter of equality in difference. The story now shifts to the standard of capitalist universality as a matter of improved productivity.

Labor *"puts the difference of value* on every thing" (para. 40, p. 314). Henceforth the measure of value in exchange will make quantitative difference the universal standard of value by concealing qualitative difference and the standard of value in use. The value of land held in common will be defined negatively as the absence of productive improvement: "Land that is left wholly to Nature, that hath no improvement of Pasturage, Tillage, or Planting, is called, as indeed it is, *wast*" (para. 42, p. 315). The category "waste" is hereby transformed. A customary economy is superintended by a qualitative standard of value that limits individual use rights and reserves waste lands for common use. An economy in which the ownership of land is determined by improvement is superintended by the quantitative standard of absolute productivity, which redefines "waste" so as to equate the value of common use with the nonvalue of unimprovement. Both standards of value are based on a principle of universality: on the one hand, the qualitative equality of common use; on the other, the quantitative measure of overall productivity. Locke points out with respect to land that "the greatest part of all its useful Products" we owe to labor; by whom those products are used is another question (para. 43, p. 316).

By Locke's time England, widely improved and enclosed,[59] had been developed so far beyond where the story began that Locke must turn to an actually existing "state of nature": "In the beginning all the World was *America*" (para. 49, p. 319). The wit of Locke's allusion to Genesis distracts from its duplicity. "God gave the World to Men in Common" (para. 34, p. 309); but in Locke's America, productivity can be assessed by its proper standard of quantitative value without the complication, residual but still effective, of customary common rights and their standard of value: "An Acre of Land that bears here Twenty Bushels of Wheat, and another in *America*, . . . are, without doubt, of the same natural; intrinsick Value. But yet the Benefit Mankind receives from the one, in a Year, is worth 5 *l*. and from the other possibly not worth a Penny, if all the Profit an *Indian* received from it were to be valued, and sold here" (para. 43, p. 316). The intrinsic value of land, like the customary rights of English commoners and the natural rights of "Indians," is a matter of use, qualitative and manifold. Its profitability, a measure of its improvement, is determined by its market value, and the "Benefit Mankind" receives from it has the universality of maximum productivity but not the universality of equal access, least of all to its actual producers. Thus "Men have agreed to disproportionate and unequal possession of the Earth"; and "a man may fairly possess more land than he himself can use the product of, by receiving the overplus, Gold and Silver, which may be hoarded up without injury to any one, these metalls not spoileing" (para. 50, p. 320). But now Locke sets aside the other enlightened principle limiting the injury resulting from inequality, the requirement that enough be left for others. The new economy ensured that this requirement would not be met. The availability of money as capital and the potential for its "overplus" to be "hoarded," in concert with "the desire of having more than Men needed," would encourage what was already evident in England if not yet in America, the modulation of hoarding into accumulation and recirculation and the inevitable appropriation of what might have been left for others.[60] In Locke's narrative of property, Enlightenment universality has modulated at this point in the story to capitalist universality; put differently, Enlightenment universality has been penetrated by capitalist universality.

The universalizing assault on absolutism made explicit the separation out of all persons in the abstract equality of natural law. But it also entailed the devolution of absolute public sovereignty to the right of absolute private property. Locke's labor theory of property, transforming personal propriety into absolute property, was articulated at the same moment when the commodity form was transforming the propriety of use values through the universal medium of money. Slavery was coextensive with the Atlantic triangular trade. Does Locke's narrative suggest that the basis of the slave trade in the commodity form accommodated the notion that the propriety of a person can become the absolute property of another? Does it suggest that the equalizing exchange of unequal use values facilitated, within a deep commitment to equality, the concealment of its flagrant violation? What's written off as a failure of Enlightenment thought is often better seen as a failure of its posterity, or as an ideal demand for fully seasoned achievement that ignores the arguably greater achievement of innovation. However, slavery is rightly seen as a failure not only of the Enlightenment period but also of Enlightenment thought. I don't assume that its institution in the American colonies and republic was cynically condoned for the economic benefit of individual owners, or, by an invisible hand, of the nation; but it's hard to conceive by what other motives slavery might have seemed acceptable in an enlightened regime. Recourse to a broader perspective than personal choice may at least illuminate. At the Enlightenment moment, we might say, the American forces of production seized upon the fatal expedient of slavery, and their forms of intercourse, which might have fallen out of sync and become fetters upon those forces, instead fell into line.

However, slavery is a singular atrocity that can't be generalized. Locke's story begins in the Enlightenment assault on corporate political absolutism and crucially modulates into the single-minded pursuit of individual productivity through economic absolutism. This is also, in a longer chronology, the story of capitalism, whose later ramifications have been too easily laid at the door of the Enlightenment. The call for freedom from state monopolies in the seventeenth century is economically continuous but not intellectually consistent with the "neoliberal" advocacy three centuries later of an ongoing policy of free trade, one of whose milestones is monopoly capitalism. That these movements dovetail evinces another ground for the vindication of Enlightenment, the need to distinguish between the thought and the period—or better, between the thought and its unintended consequences.

Superstructure and Dialectics

I've argued that in his analysis of capitalist universality Marx builds on the footing of Enlightenment universality, which by this point I've associated with virtualization often enough to answer the question I posed at the beginning of this section: What's the relation between universality and virtuality in Enlightenment thought? "Virtualization" names a distinctive and innovative method of abstraction or generalization that's provisional because it entails a self-conscious awareness of its constitution by concrete, actual particulars, with which it sustains an ongoing dialectic. I've distinguished Enlightenment from capitalist universality, whose power lies in its occlusion of that dialectic. The importance of conceptualization to Marx's materialism is sometimes forgotten—acknowledged in the classic category "superstructure" but obscured by its reduction to a "vulgar" notion of ideology as illusory false consciousness (or, more lately and fully, by its transfiguration into the determinacy of the subject). Marx calls what he practices a materialist conception of history not because he denies the historical role of concepts but because he wrote for readers for whom the material basis of history most needed to be made explicit. The meaning of superstructure is defined by its relation to infrastructure, which is sometimes seen as, on the one hand, the illusion of a seamless fit between superstructural forms and infrastructural forces; and on the other, the illusion of superstructure exposed as a fetter on infrastructure. These dichotomous formulations belie the dialectical nature of Marx's thought. A more fruitful approach lies in recognizing that as an heir to Enlightenment thought, Marx was imbued with the conviction that the tacit must be made explicit. Forms and forces, former parts of the whole of economic production now separated out into self-conscious relationship, are susceptible to a conflation that bespeaks neither determinism nor idealism but the simultaneity of connection and disjunction. Superstructure is the conceptualization of infrastructural materiality; infrastructure is the materialization of superstructural conceptuality.

The comparative utility of these theoretical formulations is discovered in the analysis of any given historical practice. But often enough we also see Marx straightforwardly pursuing one dimension in provisional separation from the other. For example, he analyzes the circulation of commodities by separating its virtual from its actual capacity as "form" and "content": "If we disregard the material content of the circulation of commodities . . . and consider only the economic forms brought into being by this process, . . . money . . . is the first form of appearance of capital." "The direct form of the circulation of commodities is . . . selling in order to buy. But alongside this form we find another form, . . . the transformation of money into commodities, and the re-conversion of commodities into money: buying in order to sell." The payoff of this analysis is what Marx calls "The General Formula of Capital," its generality being the virtual summation of the particular forms of circulation (which in terms of their place in the structure of the analytic process I'm describing are "actual") (*Capital*, 247–248).

Marx's Enlightenment predecessors trace a similar analytic trajectory. A case in point is Smith's "decipherment" of the abstract concept, which requires him to separate out the multiple instances of actual labor in order to constitute the virtual category labor as such. Something similar occurs when Smith posits the virtuality of the invisible hand that coordinates the multiple self-interests of actual individuals to promote the general interest of society. True, sheer paradox would seem to obscure the self-conscious reciprocity of virtual and actual, general and particular. But if my reading is persuasive, Smith's conceptualization has the self-consciousness of a (religious) trope and draws attention to itself as notional, imagined, made. Or to put this differently, we become conscious of the form of Smith's discourse as though it were "literary" and a reflexive thematization of form on the level of content. Elsewhere Smith, confronting as given what I've suggested is the consequence of the Enlightenment "disembedding" of "individuals" from "society," supposes that the results of this separation can be conflated by the power of the sympathetic imagination, which generalizes the association of actual individuals by conflating them within the "society" of its own domain: "As we have no immediate experience of what other men feel, . . . it is by the imagination only that we can form any conception of what are [their] sensations" (*Theory*, 9). Again, only when categories are separated out can they be brought together—conflated— to achieve a kind of knowledge (sympathy is a good example) unavailable, because taken for granted, in a relation of tacit proximity.

The realm of the virtual makes explicit the gap between knowledge and what it knows. But in the comparative difference between specific instances of these gaps, Enlightenment thought also recognizes degrees of difference between modes of knowing: natural philosophy, moral philosophy, religious belief, and the imagination itself. Joseph Addison argues a profound analogy between the imagination and natural philosophy or the understanding, both empowered by their grounding in the actual materiality of the senses to achieve distinct kinds of epistemological "pleasure" through distinct degrees of virtualization.[61] Before the end of the century, the imagination will be accorded its own sphere of "aesthetic" cognition, one increasingly credited, as Smith's sympathy exemplifies, with a central role in knowledge through the reflexive conflation of the object and subject of knowledge.

I'll conclude the contrast between capitalist and Enlightenment universality with the idea of progress. The notion that the generation of wealth, and therefore material progress, is unlimited is built into the confidence of capitalist universality.

The Enlightenment idea of progress was more varied and circumspect. Progress as represented by "conjectural" history, for example, was real, but also inconsistent and ambivalent, especially as the stage of "civilization" was becoming complicated by the negative conditions that accompanied increasing urbanization and industrialization.

Conjectural History

Britons, grown accustomed to decades of commercial exchange and agrarian capitalist production and now in the early stages of industrialization, encountered lands and islands variously supported by hunting and gathering, herding, simple forms of agriculture, and the habits of commercial exchange they were pleased to identify with "civilization." They distinguished these forms of property holding and modes of material subsistence into separate categories that provided the basis for a "stadial" theory of cultural development.[62] They found in their own historical records evidence that they, too, had subsisted at comparable levels in the past, and on the basis of these current encounters they conjectured beyond historical documentation what the existence of their own island ancestors had been long before history had recorded it. This kind of speculation had been of interest much earlier than it became a discipline of study by Scottish scholars in the later Enlightenment. In 1590, for example, the illustrator of a travel narrative to Virginia interleaved with his engravings of New-World warriors an image from an *"oold English cronicle . . . for to showe how that the Inhabitants of the great Bretannie haue bin in times past as sauuage as those of Virginia."*[63] The most famous of the Enlightenment conjectures, also relatively early, is Locke's witty parody of the book of Genesis discussed in the previous section: "In the beginning all the World was *America*" (para. 34, p. 309). The line underscores the pastoralism of both the traditional and the Enlightenment versions of sovereignty, the delegation of Adam in the Garden of Eden and that of all people in the state of nature. Contemporaries also conjectured that the futurity of those cultures currently subsisting in simpler modes of production would one day resemble their own.

On the one hand, the accumulation of vast quantities of information about actual cultural practices; on the other, the analysis of correlations between material stages of economic production and virtual levels of what was only beginning to be called "culture": on this basis, a heuristic hypothesis took shape that over time all human cultures pass through the same three or four phases—the classic categories were "savage," "barbarian," and "civilized"—from the simplest to the most complex.

From a modern perspective it's hard not to read the first two terms pejoratively. This was also the perspective of some contemporaries; but as we've seen, the categories were also applied to European cultures, and their denotative use in service to this proto-ethnographic enterprise (wild, not civilized, outside civilization) took civility to be a temporal endpoint rather than a normative fulfillment. Adam Ferguson wrote that "property is a matter of progress." The savage was "not yet acquainted with property," whereas for the barbarian property was, "although not ascertained by laws, a principal object of care and desire." Progress is here a descriptive term that marks movement along a scale from "immediate use" or "the stores of the public" to private possession, which "requires such a habit of acting with a view to distant objects, as may overcome the present disposition either to sloth or to enjoyment." "Progress" in the sense of improved average standards of subsistence was generally affirmed, at least in the movement from savagery to barbarism; but positive and negative trade-offs were also observed. For Ferguson, the barbarian stage had already experienced the "infection" of "interest" introduced by the "commercial arts," the same "corruption" that is evident today in the civilized "poison which is administered by our traders of Europe."[64] Historians of the Enlightenment varied widely in the conclusions they drew from the innovative methods of conjectural history. Some commentators indulged the temptation to generalize and universalize "laws" of qualitative human progress. Others concurred with Ferguson that general material betterment was at odds with universal access.

Another Enlightenment idea of progress extrapolated in two respects from the Renaissance revival of classical learning. On the one hand, the late seventeenth-century Quarrel of the Ancients and Moderns (to which I'll return) laid the ground for the argument of *chronological* progress by asserting the superiority of modern over ancient learning. On the other, that argument was persuasive because of the discovery, in the method of modern science, of a model of *conceptual* progress that was unavailable not only to ancient science but also to the modern arts. The strength of this model of conceptual progress laid a more definitive ground for the separation of quantitative from qualitative, scientific from artistic, standards of value. Even so, for much of the British eighteenth century, theorists of the arts succeeded in creating a model of the arts that, because it was "aesthetic" and therefore grounded like science in empirical sense impressions, shared with science an experimental commitment to probable knowledge, and played a role in the conflation of the modes of knowledge that the Quarrel had separated out. By the turn of the nineteenth century, however, this conflation was already being forgotten.[65] Yet at the same time that the arts and the sciences were undergoing this more definitive separation, a more lasting extension of the scientific model was emerging in the form of the social sciences, first adumbrated by the stadial theory conjectured by Enlightenment historians.

Polity and Society

So far, I've been focusing attention on how economic ideas and practices were virtualized by the separation out of economy from polity and by the separations that transpired within economy itself. We can see a comparable process if we now turn our attention to polity and society. In the seventeenth century, the abstract category "society" (or "civil society") coalesced over against the polity or state to ground and situate all private English people apart from those associated with the public state and its apparatus. Civil society, unlike the tangible lands, villages, and cities that it abstracted from the royal estate, was a virtual entity that accounted for the new status of English people who were no longer subsumed within customary social relations or those of personal reciprocity that had been entailed in feudal hierarchy. But how were the public state and private civil society related to each other?

The Public Sphere

In the introduction to this volume I discussed Jürgen Habermas's celebrated account of the emergence of civil society and the public sphere in seventeenth-century England.[66] The public sphere, a virtual category composed of actual people, was a crucial mechanism in the development of democratic government in Britain because it facilitated the modern theory that it's the natural rights of the people that ground state sovereignty. Absolutism derived the legitimacy of the state from the top down. Its best-known scenario is Sir Robert Filmer's patriarchalist fiction of the Garden of Eden after the Fall, when God granted Adam, our first father, a sovereign authority that was identical with his paternal authority and characterized by a wholeness constituted from above. The paradigmatic alternative to the Garden of Eden is the fiction of the state of nature. Locke and Thomas Hobbes,[67] although at odds in other ways, concur that sovereignty is a bottom-up affair, the product not of divine creation but of the contractual consent of independent and autonomous parts—individuals—to a government that will represent them all. The multitude of private individuals does not only preexist the public state, as nature does culture. It also authorizes and constitutes the state from below as a virtual institution, an "imagined community" of its own making, providing the basis on which will rest the indefinite and ongoing inclusion of future citizens (the phrase is Benedict Anderson's).

The virtuality of the modern state recalls the sempiternity of the king's political body, but now perpetuated by a constantly changing multiplicity of human authorizations rather than by a singular and eternal divinity. Perhaps it's this act of self-authorization that we mean to acknowledge when we speak of the modern state as the "nation-state." I've just discussed the difference between Enlightenment and capitalist universality in these terms, among others. But it's important to see that the modern nation-state retains, as under absolute monarchy, the embodied identity of an actual public government administered by actual persons. What's referred to by the act of self-authorization expressed in the scenario of the state of nature is not this actual public nation-state but the virtual publicness of civil society, which has constituted, and can alter, the actual nation-state through the address of the people at large.

The emergent public sphere has been confused with, and criticized for, the failings entailed in its later deformation by the fully developed state-interventionist capitalism of the nineteenth and twentieth centuries. This confusion may be reflected in the translator's decision to render, "for better or worse," the *Burgerliche Offentlichkeit* of Habermas's title as "bourgeois" rather than "civil" public sphere (xv). For one thing, the constitution of the public sphere, although self-conscious, was not the function of class consciousness, which was only in the early process of coalescence at the turn of the eighteenth century. The reduction of the Enlightenment concept of the public sphere to illusory claims of its comprehensive practice is likely to stem from the analysis of the later devolution of the public sphere (which Habermas documents) owing to its infiltration by later capitalist ideologies and practices, which critics, flattening the process of historical change, have rendered coeval with Enlightenment thought.

Habermas's careful account of the public sphere as it emerged during the Enlightenment emphasizes its historically innovative significance as a concept that challenged the traditional public by opening up the theoretical inclusivity entailed in the idea of publicness, and it thereby had, as Habermas argues, a conceptual actuality. The concept had revolutionary implications for sociopolitical practice, which in this early development was primarily a future promise, although Habermas also describes its present instantiations in practice, paradigmatically the coming together of private citizens in public places, and in the virtual space of print, to discuss public matters. We gain perspective on the extent of this practice when we reflect on the three negative liberties from state interference for which the Enlightenment is celebrated: free trade, freedom of the press, and religious toleration or liberty of conscience. The reflex critique of such movements as subversion "always already" contained, which cynically assumes what needs to be shown, has some relevance to the ease with which Habermas is sometimes refuted.

The public sphere was first of all and crucially a matter of consciousness. The critical misconstruction of what Habermas means can be hard to fathom. He writes: "Not that this idea of the public was actually realized in earnest . . . but as an idea it had become institutionalized and thereby stated as an objective claim" (36). The public sphere "established the public as in principle inclusive. However exclusive the public might be in any given instance it could never close itself off entirely." "The public of the first generations, even when it constituted itself as a specific circle of persons, was conscious of being part of a larger public" (37). Yet one critic writes that "Habermas's account . . . stresses its claim to be open and accessible to all. . . . What are we to make of this historical fact of the nonrealization of the bourgeois sphere's ideal in practice?"[68]

According to Habermas, the public sphere engaged the public authorities of the state in debate, a "political confrontation" whose medium was "without historical precedent: people's public use of their reason" (27). Elaborating on this, he writes that the places where the public sphere came together "preserved a kind of social intercourse that, far from presupposing the equality of status, disregarded status altogether. The tendency replaced the celebration of rank with a tact befitting equals" (36). The critic I've just quoted takes this to mean that "merely private interests were to be inadmissible. . . . The result of such discussion would be public opinion in the strong sense of a consensus about the common good" (113). In other words, this critic believes that the rule of reason and the disregard for status militated against the discussion of private interests and the expression of private opinions (as though that's what "public opinion" has ever meant), achieving an agreement as if by the magical transcendence of difference. Again, this critic imagines that to Habermas, "exclusions and conflicts . . . appeared as accidental" (116). Another critic agrees: Habermas's account of the public sphere "misses the extent to which the public sphere was always constituted by conflict."[69] This is to assume that Habermas's idea of rational debate entails a temperate and disinterested arrival at agreement. Yet his evident meaning is not that participants either did not know or pretended not to know one another's status, or that interchange avoided conflict. On the contrary, the public sphere premise, that to engage in discourse whose publicness no longer took for granted the will of the traditional public elite, was by definition an exercise in conflict.

The resistance shown by these critics (and others) seems to derive from the notion that the Enlightenment public sphere is a creature of "bourgeois" ideology and the false consciousness that its own interests represent the universal standard of humanity. I've argued that even as an attribute of capitalist ideology in particular, the claim to inclusive universality needs to be considered more carefully. But in any case, this notion may underlie the supposition of the first critic that for the emergent public sphere to approach universal inclusion requires that it be understood as the "official" public sphere and to be supplemented by alternative publics, "counterpublics," or "subaltern counterpublics" (116, 123, 124, 127). However, this mistakes the innovative potentiality of the universal inclusion idea, which defines the nature of civil society, for the claim to having established its application in practice, which would tautologically be exclusive by virtue of its "official" sanction.

In short, the counterpublics argument misses the point. Using the terminology of my study, the public sphere reconceived the official whole of the traditional public that tacitly went without saying, seeking, with crucial intuition, to make explicit the part that until this moment had been not simply indistinguishable but invisible, the virtual modern public, a conflation of multiple interests that in their coherence were separate from that of the actual state institution. These are also Habermas's terms. The public sphere presupposed "the problematization of areas that until then had not been questioned," and undertook to "state explicitly what precisely in its implicitness for so long could assert its authority" (36–37). The public sphere idea of universal inclusion was first of all a radical idea whose very conception renders the idea of counterpublics gratuitous. The public sphere bespeaks not a (bad-faith) claim to equality of access and representation (which most contemporaries in any case would have dismissed frankly as neither possible nor desirable), but the hypothesis of a virtual collectivity of legitimate actual interests, beyond official tradition, and the capacity of civil society to account for them.

The Two Publics

Both the difference, and the relation, between the two kinds of public, the actual and the virtual, are clear in these reflections on the House of Commons as a representative government, made not long after Locke's version of the state of nature argument was published. In 1701, Sir Humphrey Mackworth affirmed that "an

Impeachment . . . is virtually the Voice of every particular Subject of this Kingdom." Addison wrote that the "House of Commons is the Representative of Men in my Condition. I consider my self as one who give [sic] my Consent to every Law which passes. . . . Such is the Nature of our happy Constitution, that the Bulk of the People virtually give their Approbation to every thing they are bound to obey, and prescribe to themselves those Rules by which they are to walk." And for Henry Care as well, political representation implicitly entailed a virtual obligation to, and authorization of, government that amounted to consent: "The Succession of the Crown hath been directed by Act of Parliament, in which, the Consent of the whole Nation is virtually included by their Representatives, so that it has been directed according to the presumed Will of the People, which is collected from what is most expedient."[70]

Care's specification of virtual consent to the royal succession was timely. In dynastic monarchies like England's, the legitimacy of royal sovereignty is grounded in the lineal actuality of genealogical inheritance. True, unavoidable gaps in the strict lineality of the royal succession had sometimes been officially papered over in the past in order to maintain the appearance of English sovereignty as an unbroken continuity, ordained by natural and divine law. However, the parliamentary deposal of James II in 1688, seen to be politically necessary, was justified by an argument from providence and the virtual consent of the people. In the words of Edward Stillingfleet, "A King de jure is one, who comes in by lineal Descent, as next Heir. . . . A King de facto is one, who comes in by Consent of the Nation." The rhetorical question was "whether Allegiance be not due where the Rights of Sovereignty are plac'd, by an extraordinary Act of Providence, and the concurrent Consent of the Nation."[71] From one perspective, this was pure cynicism. From another, it showed how traditional investment in supernatural virtuality could shore up modern investment in secular virtuality.

Decades later James Madison used a striking figure of speech to explain why the suffrage of private individuals, if virtualized through a representative system of government, is better than "pure democracy" at "controling the effects of faction." By delegating government "to a small number of citizens elected by the rest," republican representation is able "to refine and enlarge the public views, by passing them through the medium of a chosen body of citizens" who best generalize those views beyond "temporary or partial considerations." Care's figure of the "collected" will of the people is improved by Madison's image of the governmental public of representatives as passing the collected votes of individual citizens through a kind of sieve, which refines and enlarges them to the smooth consistency of a virtual public.[72] As a refinement of "pure" or direct democracy, representative democracy has the two-stage character of re-presentation. This same model of refining the actual into the virtual produced a number of other now-familiar notions of publicness. "Public opinion" cohered as a mass aggregation of actual opinions expressed in the public sphere, then concentrated and even quantified, as in today's opinion polls, so as to achieve a coherent and representative result. The innovative idea of the "reading public" referred both to the empirically existent totality of readers and to the distillation of that sum so as to quantify, as a virtual average, the qualitative particularity of individual reader responses. The idea of the "public domain" might seem to hark back to feudal reciprocity and the common-law provision of delimited rights to use common lands. But the idea was explicitly motivated by the aim to perfect the law of absolute individual ownership of literary property—itself a virtual entity—by a rational definition of its term limits.

Like the market, the emergent public sphere was a virtual realm that had no actual existence but promised actual consequences, and in theory both the market and the public sphere solicited belonging of all those who wished to belong. Both the market and the public sphere bracketed the qualitative differences between status groups with respectively one stipulation: the possession of property and the will to reproduce it in a virtual format. Anyone could play the market who had something to quantify and circulate through the medium of money, and anyone could enter the public sphere who had something to multiply and disseminate through the medium of publication. From a modern perspective these conditions rebut any claim to inclusivity. In the Enlightenment they were unprecedented inroads into the closed society of tradition.

The access to public policy that publication gave private citizens prompted self-conscious fantasies of a virtual alternative to the actual public or state authority, one that would caulk the cracks in the façade of social justice that state law neglected or ignored. Richard Steele, half in jest and half in earnest, undertook the role of modern public "Censor": "It is allowed, that I have no Authority for assuming this important Appellation. . . . But if in the Execution of this fantastical Dignity, I observe upon Things which do not fall within the Cognizance of real Authority, I hope it will be granted, that an idle Man could not be more usefully employed." Steele also presided, as Fielding did after him, over a virtual and highly elaborated "court of judicature" whose function was to consider cases of social impropriety whose "criminality" the actual state judicature was unable or unwilling to try.[73] The parodic judicial function of the public sphere as "court of public opinion" also was specified by contemporaries as the peculiar and public task of satire, which according to Swift was "first introduced into the World" "to supply such Defects as these."[74] In cases like these, the public sphere's parodic and fantastic virtuality, its ostentatious lack of actual authority, was the stealthy secret to its authority—that is, its publicity. This marks the beginning of journalism's most noble (and sometimes most ignominious) enterprise, the chastisement of those offenders against the public who have escaped official state punishment.

Locke gave this notion of the public sphere's virtual law a more philosophical formulation, making explicit what customarily "by a secret and tacit consent establishes it self in the several Societies" of the world. "The *Laws* that Men generally refer their Actions to, to judge of their Rectitude, or Obliquity, seem to me to be these three. 1. The *Divine* Law. 2. The *Civil* Law. 3. The Law of *Opinion* or *Reputation*, if I may so call it." Locke also calls this third kind of law, which judges whether actions are virtues or vices, "The Law of Fashion, or private Censure."

And he anticipates Steele in writing that this law "is nothing else, but the Consent of private Men, who have not Authority enough to make a Law: Especially wanting that, which is so necessary, and essential to a Law, a Power to inforce it." Nonetheless, "no Man scapes the Punishment of their Censure and Dislike, who offends against the Fashion and Opinion of the Company he keeps." For although as Locke himself was theorizing, the consent of citizens to establish "politick Societies" has required resigning "to the publick the disposing of all their Force, . . . yet they retain still the power of Thinking well or ill." This is the very essence of public sphere virtuality.[75]

The bookseller-translator Francis Kirkman imagined a different, more positive role for publication in the attribution of personal standing. When Kirkman first saw his name and "the honoured word Gent." on one of his title pages, he thought "that he was every Inch of him in his own imagination, and did believe that the so printing that word . . . did as much entitle him to Gentility, as if he had Letters Patents for it from the Heralds-Office: Nay, did suppose this to be more authentick because more publick." Kirkman's fantasy of the attributive powers of print (which the more modern development of social media has shown to be not so fantastic) reminds us that the replacement of the status system by a class system of social categorization at this time was itself a triumph of the virtual over the argument from physical actuality.[76]

By the end of the eighteenth century, stratification by qualitative status, which had been justified as incarnate in the noble blood of the body, had been disembodied and demystified by the abstract, quantitative criteria of income and class. Both status and class attitudes toward social relations were guided by the norm of personal virtue or merit. But the ideology of aristocratic honor claimed that honor-as-merit could be assumed to exist a priori in those through whose bodies flowed the physical fluid of noble blood, whereas its critics argued that honor-as-merit was demonstrated not by intrinsic bodily essence but by the empirical experience of meritorious achievements. Traditionally, honor was a tacit whole whose parts, rank and merit, were distinct but inseparable. Enlightenment analysis partialized honor, conceiving these parts as self-standing wholes and synonymizing honor with merit. Over the course of the Enlightenment, the predominant meaning of the word "honor" as a term of denotation shifted from "title of rank" to "goodness of character."[77] As long as the maxim "birth equals worth" commanded tacit consensus, no actual signifiers of honor were needed other than a general compliance with the notion that honor was an inherited trait in the biological as well as the genealogical sense of the term. It was only when skepticism about the physical basis of aristocratic honor began to grow that other, more ostensible signs of it were officially instituted. In 1665 Edward Waterhouse wrote that our ancestors distinguished between their social stations "not by sumptuary Laws, or Magistratique sanction, but by common agreement, and general understanding." In England, sumptuary legislation began only in 1337 and ended in several abortive attempts of the early seventeenth century. The Heralds' Visitations, aimed at testing existent and confirming new genealogical claims, began in 1529 and ended in 1686.[78] In other words, the very force with which the tacit "common agreement" that honor is heritable was reinforced by explicit laws and sanctions is a sign not of its strength but of its weakness. Some, like Delarivier Manley, betrayed the dependence of nobility on nurture or culture in the very process of seeking to affirm its naturalness: "It is easie to judge why Persons of Quality have generally more Penetration, Vivacity and Spirit, than those of a meaner Rank: For . . . good Nourishment, and the Juice of Nice Meats, which mixes with the Blood, and other Humours of the Body, subtilizes them, and renders them more proper for the Functions of Nature."[79] Defoe thought that gentlemen based their inordinate vanity "upon this imaginary honour," and he enjoyed making fun of the notion that nobility was heritable, "as if there were some differing Species in the very Fluids of Nature . . . or some Animalculæ of a differing and more vigorous kind."[80]

Print

Mechanical reproduction by movable type—not its invention, but its centrality to daily experience—offers an obvious parallel to the digital revolution we now experience. By the time of the Enlightenment, Britain was sufficiently saturated with the cultural implications and influence of typography to be characterized by modern historians as a "print culture." Only then was handwriting, and even speech, ceasing to count as the normative mode of communication through "publication"—that is, making public. In a play of 1662, one of Margaret Cavendish's characters knows that "those subjects that are only discourst off, in speach, flyes away in words; which vanisheth as smoak, or shadows, and the memory or remembrance of the Author, or Oratour, melts away as oyle, leaving no sign in present life, . . . when writeing, or printing, fixes it to everlasting time, to the publick view of the World." Echoing Cavendish at the turn of the eighteenth century, Defoe writes that "Preaching of Sermons is Speaking to a few of Mankind: Printing of Books is Talking to the whole World. . . . The Sermon extends no farther than the strength of Memory can convey it; a Book Printed is a Record, remaining in every Man's Possession, . . . and conveys its Contents for Ages to come, to the Eternity of mortal Time, when the Author is forgotten in his Grave."[81] Comparable to both wage payment and the detachment of property from propriety, mechanical reproduction by print separated the actions of the body both from their products and from actual contact with other bodies.

Print was also comparable to these phenomena in the ambivalence it generated. Protestantism put the Book into the hands of actual readers so as to prevent the perversion of its virtual teachings by the actual words of priestly mediators. Like many others, Andrew Marvell saw a fortuitous alliance in the fact that the printing press was "invented much about the same time with the Reformation." This alliance became especially evident with the full maturity of print culture after the Restoration of 1660, and in confrontation with the state prohibition of face-to-face dissenting conventicles, the virtuality of a nonconformist reading public was invaluable. As Marvell wrote in 1672, "There have been ways found out to banish Ministers, to fine not only the People, but even the Grounds and Fields where they assembled in Conventicles: but no Art yet could prevent these seditious meetings of Letters."[82] In another register, the Methodist Anne Dutton described print in 1743 as a short cut from the public sphere to the private faithful. Print, Dutton wrote, was "one Way of private Converse with the Saints: Only it is a more extensive one, of talking with Thousands, which otherwise could not have been spoke with, nor can ever be seen Face to Face in the Flesh."[83] But the virtual converse afforded by print, if a corrective to the absence of actual conversation, by the same token was a major force behind its disappearance. In John Aubrey's nostalgic words, "The fashion when I was a boy (before the Civill warres) [was] for the maydes to sitt-up late by the fire [and] tell old Romantique stories of the old time.... Before Printing, Old-wives Tales were ingeniose: ... now a-dayes Bookes are common, ... and the many good Bookes ... have put all the old Fables out of dores."[84]

The ambivalence of print has something to do with its doubleness. On the one hand, printed discourse is virtual in the sense that its form presupposes a dialogic, give-and-take exchange between actual speaker and auditors that has been disembedded from the occasional time and space of their exchange and depersonalized of their motives and agency. On the other, discursive exchange doesn't end with its virtualization; it shifts to a different level. Once published, discourse enters into a one-way exchange between author and the multiplicity of readers that constitute the reading public and generate the occasions of exchange in the public sphere, which are numerous but not dialogic. Typographical reproduction ensured that particular readers were precluded from responding to authorial discourse, and particular authors from responding to their construction by readers. (That printed debate developed as a response to this condition only underscores the basic difference between actual and virtual exchange.) Using the same metaphor as Cavendish, Marvell fears that fixing words in print so that they can't fly away may have a dampening effect on sociable conversation: "He that hath once Printed an ill Book, has thereby condenc'd his words on purpose lest they should be carried away by the wind; he has diffused his poison so publickly, in design that it might be beyond his own recollection [re-collection]; and put himself deliberately past the reach of any private admonition." Printed invective enjoyed impunity for violating the moral codes of sociability, to Marvell's mind like a ship sailing in international waters, where no single set of laws has force. Publication can become "a praedatory course of life, and indeed but a privateering upon reputation" and make one "an open Pirate of other mens Credit." For these reasons Marvell has decided "to go no more to Sea, having been sufficiently toss'd for one man upon the billows of applause and obloquy to put me in mind of a Shipwrack, which when the waves go high, may either way happen."[85]

The virtuality of print, at least in its public sphere capacity, has made it a frequent candidate for metaphorical actualization as sea travel; the application of "piracy" to the realm of publication that has survived to the present day was first made in the seventeenth century. An elaborate and brilliant application of this sort was achieved within two years of Marvell's by the nonconformist William

Okeley in the verses prefatory to a narrative of his travel to, captivity in, and deliverance from Algiers. Here are the first twenty-six lines of those verses:

> This Author never was in Print before,
> And (let this please or not) will never more.
> If all the Press-Oppressors of the Age
> Would so Resolve, 'twould Happiness presage:
> He should as soon another Voyage take,
> As be Oblig'd another Book to make.
> His Canvas Boat Escaped Seas and Wind,
> He fears this Paper-Vessel will not find
> Such gentle Gales, when every Reader hath
> Pow'r with a puff to sink the Writers Faith.
> For who so Prints a Book goes off from shore
> To hazard that which was his own before:
> As one poor Pinnace Over-match'd, that fights
> With an Armado, so doth he who Writes:
> If Books (like goodly Merchant-Ships) set forth,
> Laden with Riches of the greatest worth;
> With Councels, Fathers, Text-Men, School-Men Mann'd;
> With Sacred Cannon Mounted at each Hand;
> Are hard beset, and forc'd to make Defence
> Against Arm'd Atheism, Pride, and Impudence.
> How can this little Cock-Boat hope Escape,
> When Scripture Suffers Piracy and Rape?
> Noe's Ark (wherein the World Epitomiz'd,
> And Mankind in Octavo was Compriz'd.)
> Though in the Deluge 'twas preserved found,
> By Infidelity it self lyes drown'd.[86]

Marvell emphasizes the dangers of publication to participants in the public sphere in their capacities as readers; Okeley's concern is with them as authors. If venturing into print is like venturing out to sea, storms and hostile warships find their equivalent in a powerful and hostile reading public, which, signified by pirates, is doubly virtual. As setting to sea risks losing riches that were safe when under domestic protection, so publication, by making the private public, hazards that which was his own before. But midway through the lines I've quoted, Okeley also focuses on those peculiarly vulnerable publications that, like his own, defend religious faith against the warships of atheism and infidelity. In these troubled times even "Scripture Suffers Piracy and Rape." As I began by suggesting, the virtuality of the realm of God and the public sphere differ fundamentally in their ontological groundings, and the early modern proliferation of virtual entities authorized by humanity rather than divinity may have transformed the obvious dominance of the latter over the former into a more equal competition. Okeley's apprehension seems to be that entering the public sphere is injurious to the spiritualization of life here below. However much print may hold the promise of propagating the faith more efficiently than before, it propagates even more the enemies of faith, by transporting it from the realm of tacit belief to the arena of explicit debate. (Similarly, Filmer's theorization of patriarchalist principles, by making what goes without saying explicit, ironically jeopardized what publication was meant to empower.) Of course print is itself also a profane activity. And at a time when the weapons of empirical epistemology are gaining power, this change of venue is decisive. In fact maybe it's plausible to see Okeley's warning that to publish is to hazard what "was his own before" as presaging the long-term destiny of religious belief: its retreat beyond the range of public adjudication and into the province of the private.

Print depersonalized communication by virtualizing it. And yet as these passages suggest, the very distance authors felt from the multitude of strangers who might read their writing did not simply render vulnerable the privacy of those they wrote against. Publication played a powerful role in constituting privacy, that peculiarly modern and deeply personal sense of a virtual interior space properly set apart from, but profoundly susceptible to, public invasion.

Experimental Science

Defoe's empiricist refutation of aristocratic biologism reminds us that the most powerful force of all militating against habitual recourse to the actual in intellectual matters may have been the new philosophy, or science in the modern sense of the term. This may sound so counterintuitive as to be simply wrong. After all, empirical epistemology begins with the premise that all knowledge is gained through the bodily experience of sense impressions. However, from Francis Bacon onward, the second premise of the new philosophy was that the evidence of the senses alone can't provide a dependable guide to the knowledge of nature. If we would know "nature" well, we must separate it from the "art" or "culture" that inevitably clouds its individual perception and description—that is, from the punctual and local experience of its immediate knowing. "Art" and "culture" are in this sense umbrella terms for Bacon's four "Idols and false notions which are now in possession of the human understanding, and have taken deep root therein." To uproot these epistemological idols, the sensible data resulting from a multitude of individual experiences must be collected together and subjected to the methodical analysis of scientific experiment.[87]

Experimental method bears a close family resemblance to other modes of knowledge production that have come up in this account of seventeenth- and eighteenth-century virtual reality and that are discernible in the general model of empirical epistemology. In this model, knowledge is gained from the bottom up, by collecting data from a full range of actual, existent entities and abstracting from them a virtual representation (or re-presentation) of what they have in common. I want to emphasize the development of experimental method as a striking foray into virtual reality, but more broadly as an instance of Enlightenment innovation. As in other cases, the innovative nature of scientific experiment tends to be silently assumed or set aside in modern estimates of its significance in favor of a keen skepticism regarding its methodological rigor. Experiment was criticized from several perspectives in its own day; but as we might expect, for the most part they don't correspond to the doubts raised by historians of science. One problem with this skepticism is that it holds to account the earliest formulations of the new philosophy by standards established through three centuries of intellectual progress. In other words, it's not historical. I use the term "progress" advisedly. The idea of scientific progress has met much criticism, none of it more brilliant than the (genuinely historical) thesis that science proceeds not with the linear logic of successive discoveries but from one paradigm and its standard of "normal science" to another.[88] But that thesis is no more brilliant than the insight to which I've already alluded (and which I'll take up shortly in Bernard de Fontenelle's formulation) that scientific inquiry is progressive because it builds on itself as other kinds of inquiry do not.

A second case in point is the problem of induction. Some modern skeptics posit, in dichotomous opposition to deduction, a model of induction as a simple, unidirectional, and end-stopped generalization from particulars. This abstract model may then be complicated by acknowledging that early accounts of experiment also reverse the process by testing generalized hypotheses against the evidence of particulars and even by a species of "falsificationism."[89] The more trenchant critique is that seventeenth-century induction extended a method grounded in the material evidence of the senses to realms that exceed the limits of visual observation. This is evident in Bacon's theories of method, and Robert Boyle's recourse to corpuscularism is said both to acknowledge the problem and to compound it.[90] But as I've pointed out, Bacon's method is also grounded in the recognition that the sense perceptions of all individuals are demonstrably defective. Crucial to compensating for this apparent problem at the root of empiricism is the requirement that experimental results be based on a multiplicity of testimonies and procedural repetitions. Although this doesn't answer to the most subtle and acute objections to early experimental induction, the historian of science whose criticisms I've been adducing puts the problem in what seems to me a significant light: "Bacon is, in fact, at the origin of a confusion that has continued right down to the present."[91] In other words, for all their seasoned sophistication, modern theories of method reflect the failings of Bacon's. When the problems of modern science at its origins are silently intertwined with what's problematic in its most modern development, our sense of its achievement collapses along with the history of science. To this should be added that the extension of hypothesis beyond the direct evidence of the senses has long been a commonplace in modern scientific protocols, and was already gaining support in the Enlightenment practices of thought experiments, "virtual witnessing," and the ambition to extend "natural" to "moral philosophy" (on these see below in this chapter).

Other critics of seventeenth-century induction contend that apparently straightforward efforts to avoid bias in collecting observational data and in establishing experimental procedures were strategically skewed toward political partiality, even "masking," through a stealthy reliance on merchants in particular, the special interests of "the market system."[92] I think this hermeneutics of suspicion ignores what requires prior notice—the fundamentally innovative emergence of a fledgling impulse toward explicit empirical analysis in all spheres of Enlightenment inquiry. (To my knowledge it also skews the available evidence on whose testimony was actually relied on.) It's as though late modern skepticism, having learned to live with the hermeneutic circle, feels obliged to project back onto an earlier age an implausible degree of empirical positivism sufficient to require the bracing epistemological demystification that we ourselves have needed.

The problem of induction is related to a third complaint that tends to be implied rather than directly stated: that early experimentalism denied its status as a social process, in the sense both of its dependence on collective labors and of its procedure on the basis of shared "normal" conventions.[93] And this in turn is related to the reminder that because "experiment" and "experience" weren't pre-existing and self-evident categories before the seventeenth century but had to be formulated by contemporaries by means of "literary," "narrative," and "textual" "argument," they were not objective entities but expressive and rhetorical constructions.[94] This may be thought a salutary, even necessary, reminder in the late modern context of literary theory, but in the context of early modern understanding it's little more than a truism.

My aim to vindicate experimental method from misdirected criticisms like these is consistent with my aim to forestall judgments of its Enlightenment success or failure. The point here and elsewhere is to clear a space for recognizing the innovation of Enlightenment thought in its own right without the interference of perspectives derived from later developments.

The late seventeenth-century Quarrel between the Ancients and Moderns marks the final stage in a momentous diachronic separation out of two historical periods, a division whose origins lie in the earliest decades of the Renaissance. Why did the Quarrel also occasion the division between the arts and the sciences, the equally momentous first stage in a synchronic separation out of what were seen to be two fundamentally different modes of knowledge and practice? Ancients versus Moderns entailed arts versus sciences because the more closely moderns examined the grounds for claiming the superiority of either period over the other, the clearer it became that any claim to superiority turned on which kind of knowledge was under consideration. On the one hand, by the first years of the seventeenth century enough evidence had accumulated to show that in matters of what we call science and contemporaries called "natural" or "the new philosophy," Aristotle in particular had gotten much of it wrong. On the other, the excellence of Homer and Aeschylus, Virgil and Horace persisted over time in a way that seemed impervious to the sort of standard by which Aristotle confidently could be criticized. This was a standard of empirical demonstrability that dictated an inductive method of inquiry which, in the words of Bacon, "derives axioms from the senses and particulars, rising by a gradual and unbroken ascent, . . . opening and laying out . . . a road for the human understanding direct from the sense, by a course of experiment orderly conducted and well built up" (*NO*, I, aphs. 19, 82, pp. 261, 280).⁹⁵

The modern authority of experimental method should not lead us to suppose a more or less instantaneous success. Indeed, throughout the seventeenth century, "empirical" continued to possess largely pejorative connotations as an ungrounded practice (usually of a physician), based on observation and experience, whose efficacy could not be explained, in contrast to the dependably deductive knowledge obtained by "scientific" theory. This was John Dryden's usage in one of his dramatic prologues to Oxford University:

> Th' illiterate Writer, Emperique like, applies
> To minds diseas'd, unsafe, chance Remedies:
> The Learn'd in Schools, where Knowledge first began,
> Studies with Care th' Anatomy of Man;
> Sees Vertue, Vice, and Passions in their Cause,
> And Fame from Science, not from Fortune draws.⁹⁶

Nevertheless by the later decades of the seventeenth century, Baconian method was being adapted across a range of endeavors, and with it the premise that probable belief and knowledge are a function of sense experience.

Experience and Experiment

The late seventeenth-century Quarrel of the Ancients and Moderns played an important role in these developments. In Bernard de Fontenelle we read the earliest clear recognition that scientific knowledge is distinguished by the fact that it progresses:

> If the moderns are to be able to improve continually on the ancients, the fields in which they are working must be of a kind that allows progress [*encherir*]. Eloquence and poetry [*la poesie*] require only a certain number of rather narrow ideas as compared with other arts, and they depend for their effect primarily upon the liveliness of the imagination. Now mankind could easily amass in a few centuries a small number of ideas, and liveliness of imagination has no need of a long sequence of experiences nor of many rules before it reaches the furthest perfection of which it is capable. But science [*la physique*], medicine, mathematics, are composed of numberless ideas and depend upon precision of thought which improves with extreme slowness, and is always improving?⁹⁷

Fontenelle's notion of a kind of knowledge that "allows progress" because it slowly improves over time requires "a long sequence of experiences" the logic of whose ordering is determined by a "precision of thought" that successively derives "rules" from each experience to determine what the next one should be. This is the language of careful deliberation and temporal self-consciousness we associate with scientific experiment, which Fontenelle's contemporaries already were laboring to formulate. Indeed, his reference to "une longue suite d'experiences" might well be translated "experiments," since French has only the one term for both concepts.

For Bacon at the beginning of the century, the function of experiment was "exclusion":

> In the process of exclusion are laid the foundations of true Induction, which however is not completed until it arrives at an Affirmative.... The first work therefore of true induction (as far as regards the discovery of Forms) is the rejection or exclusion of the several natures which are not found in some instance where the given nature is present, or are found in some instance where the given nature is absent, or are found to increase in some instance when the given nature decreases, or to decrease when the given nature increases. Then indeed after the rejection and exclusion has been duly made, there will remain at the bottom, all light opinions vanishing into smoke, a Form affirmative, solid and true and well defined. (*NO* II, aph. 16, p. 320)[98]

The relation between exclusion and affirmation recalls the logic of quantification I described in the introduction to this volume. Quantification is not first of all a problem of partiality but a solution to it, because it vastly improves on the results of assessing the whole according to one or another standard that are qualitatively different and therefore inevitably partial. Bacon's expressive metaphors for the process and results of exclusion are worth noting. Observation confirms that the patterning in marble samples or in bouquets of pinks is invariable in all respects except for color, which varies widely, "from which we easily gather that colour has little to do with the intrinsic nature of a body, but simply depends on the coarser and as it were mechanical arrangement of the parts." Although each actual body we might examine evinces a complex and confusing mixture of natures and hence forms, there "are those which exhibit the nature in question naked and standing by itself, and also in its exaltation or highest degree of power; as being disenthralled and freed from all impediments" (*NO* II, aphs. 19, 16, 22, 24, pp. 322, 320, 328, 329).

Through observation, comparison, and repetition, the experimental process of controlling for variables is like alchemical transmutation (conceiving the natural as either purified vapor or material residuum); or like using a sieve to sift out coarser elements; or like the rare discovery of a singular instance in which a singular nature is already evident in itself, thrown into relief against its more usual and obscuring thralldom to other natures. Less susceptible to metaphor, finally, but crucial to these several evocations of experiment, is quantification. Rallying the faint of heart, Bacon denied that there is "any reason to be alarmed at the subtlety of the investigation, as if it could not be disentangled; on the contrary, the nearer it approaches to simple natures, the easier and plainer will everything become; the business being transferred from the complicated to the simple; from the incommensurable to the commensurable; from surds to rational quantities; from the infinite and vague to the finite and certain; as in the case of the letters of the alphabet and the notes of music. And inquiries into nature have the best result, when they begin with physics and end in mathematics" (*NO* II, aph. 8, p. 307). Quantification plays a role in experimentalism similar to that of commodification in the economy, making the incommensurable commensurable.

Bacon's metaphors are illuminating, but his literal terms overlap and need sorting out. What he calls a "simple nature" is a virtual conflation that emerges from the "given nature" that gradually coheres as the experimental process separates out and "excludes" from it those "several natures" that pertain to a multitude of concrete, actual bodies that have been collected, but not to the virtual conflation that's been abstracted by experiment, "the intrinsic nature of a body." The simple nature stands in relation to the complex process of its abstraction as a generality does to the multiplicity of particulars it generalizes.[99]

By the end of the century, experimental method was being described in familiar terms as a series of stages, and in sharp contrast to the way the arts undertake the knowledge of nature. In 1694 William Wotton wrote that the

> *Mathematical* and *Physical Sciences* . . . are Things which have no Dependence upon the Opinions of Men for their Truth; they will admit of fixed and undisputed *Mediums* of Comparison and Judgment: So that, though it may be always debated, who have been the best Orators, or who the best Poets; yet it cannot always be a Matter of Controversie, who have been the greatest *Geometers, Arithmeticians, Astronomers, Musicians, Anatomists, Chymists, Botanists*, or the like; because a fair Comparison between the Inventions, Observations, Experiments and collections of the contending Parties [namely, in our usage ancient and modern scientists] must certainly put an End to the Dispute, and give a more full Satisfaction to all Sides.
>
> The Thing contended for on both Sides is, the *Knowledge of Nature*. . . . In order to this, it will be necessary, (1.) To find out all the several Affections and Properties of Quantity, abstractedly considered; . . . (2.) To collect great Numbers of Observations, and to make a vast Variety of Experiments upon all sorts of Natural Bodies. . . . The most verbose Mathematicians rarely ever said any thing for saying Sake, theirs being Subjects in which Figures of Rhetorick could have no sort of Place, but they made every Conclusion depend upon such a Chain of Premises already proved, that if one link were broke, the whole Chain fell in Pieces.[100]

Wotton's account exemplifies how the comparison of the Ancients and Moderns seems to require a comparison between (in our terms) the arts and the sciences. If we would judge that, and how far, the Moderns excel the Ancients, we must isolate and describe a special mode of knowledge whose standards of comparison are "fixed" because its criteria of judgment are those of quantity, number, logical sequence, and abstraction. Experiment is the means by which these standards may be isolated and distinguished from those that pertain to other modes of knowledge, in which the qualitative judgment of "opinion" and "rhetoric" on the contrary plays an important role.

By the time Fontenelle and Wotton wrote, Thomas Sprat, first historian of the Royal Society, already had made his well-known effort to isolate the quantitative criteria of experimental method. The members of the Royal Society, Sprat wrote in 1667,

> have endeavour'd, to separate the Knowledge of *Nature*, from the Colours of *Rhetorick*, the Devices of *Fancy*, or the delightful Deceit of *Fables*. . . . They have tried to put it into a Condition of perpetual Increasing; by settling an inviolable Correspondence between the Hand and the Brain. They have studied, to make it not only an Enterprise of one Season, or of some lucky Opportunity; but a Business of Time; a steady, a lasting, a popular, an uninterrupted Work. . . . Those, to whom the Conduct of the *Experiment* is committed, . . . after they have perform'd the *Trial*, . . . bring all the *History* of its *Process* back again to the *Test*. Then comes in the second great Work of the *Assembly;* which is to *judge* and *resolve* upon the Matter of *Fact*. In this part of their Imployment, they us'd to take an exact View of the Repetition of the whole Course of the *Experiment;* here they observ'd all the *Chances*, and the *Regularities* of the Proceeding; what *Nature* does willingly, what constrain'd; what with its own Power, what by the succours of Art.[101]

And in the words of Robert Hooke, master experimentalist of the Royal Society,

> In the making of all kind of Observations or Experiments there ought to be a huge deal of Circumspection, to take notice of every the least perceivable Circumstance that seems to be significant either in the promoting or hindering, or any ways influencing the Effect. And to this end, . . . it were very desirable that both Observations and Experiments should be divers times repeated, and that at several Seasons and with several Circumstances, both of the Mind and of Persons, Time, Place, Instruments and Materials. . . . [These are the] ways by which Nature may be trac'd, by which we may be able to find out the material Efficient and Instrumental Causes of divers Effects, not too far removed beyond the reach of our Senses.[102]

Judging by the testimony of Sprat, Hooke, and Wotton, experiment is only a methodical exploitation of experience, which, gained through sense impressions, is in John Locke's vastly influential empirical epistemology the sole source of knowledge. But if we would know nature well we must separate it from the "art" that inevitably clouds its perception and description, which is to say from the punctual and local experience of its knowing. In this broad sense, art is not simply "rhetoric," "fancy," and "fables," but all those "artificial" factors that might complicate or confuse our engagement with "the matter of fact" in itself. Art is in this sense an umbrella term for Bacon's four "Idols and false notions which are now in possession of the human understanding, and have taken deep root therein," and "must be renounced and put away with a fixed and solid determination, and the understanding thoroughly freed and cleansed" (*NO* I, aphs. 38, 48, pp. 263, 274). Bacon's figures of "deep rooting" and "thorough cleansing," like those of purifying, sifting, and exalting, suggest that experience is to experiment as the sensible and social substratum of existence is to the process by which nature is extracted from that substratum. "Experience" is the product of the senses as they are deeply embedded in the temporal and spatial contingencies of social practice; "experiment" names the protracted and wide-ranging effort to disembed experience, to abstract what is generalizable—virtual nature as such— from the diversity of actual concrete practices. Our experiential knowledge of nature is, axiomatically, conditioned by our experience. Experiment seeks to "free" nature from those conditions by treating them (in modern terminology) as variables that can be controlled for by methods of quantification. Variable conditions can be recognized for what they are, and their effects can be neutralized, by multiplying the number of observations, observers, experiments, and experimenters so as to isolate that quantity "nature" that can be seen to persist, invariably, across a range of artificial variations. The persistence of nature is evident in its susceptibility to quantitative measures that show it to be the same under varying conditions; variations are qualitative in the sense that art adds to natural entities an element of difference that renders them unassimilable to, and incomparable by, a single standard of measurement.

Instruments: Experimental versus Artful

Bacon thought highly of the ambition to lay out "a road for the human understanding direct from the sense[s]"; but he also warned that "the greatest hindrance and aberration of the human understanding proceeds from the dulness, incompetency, and deceptions of the senses" (NO I, aphs. 82, 50, pp. 280, 267). The gap between these two sentiments was bridged by experiment, including the experimental use of what contemporaries most often called "instruments." In Wotton's words, the knowledge of nature requires that we "contrive such Instruments, by which the Constituent Parts of the Universe, and of all its Parts, even the most minute, or the most remote, may lie more open to view" (79). The microscope and the telescope were only the most celebrated instruments whose technological refinement during the seventeenth century had opened nature more clearly to view. And yet Bacon, writing when their invention was still very recent, approached the promise of these ocular aids with measured skepticism, distinguishing between experiment and instruments by the same logic that distinguished between experiment and the testimony of the senses: "For the subtlety of experiments is far greater than that of the sense itself, even when assisted by exquisite instrument" (PW, 250; see NO II, aph. 39, p. 351). Bacon's skepticism here is countered by his more general and spirited advocacy of instruments elsewhere, sometimes even in the same breath (see PW, 250; "Preface" to NO, p. 256, 257; NO I, aph. 2, p. 259), and it gives voice to a paradox central to the experimental method. The sieve through which method sifts out the refined uniformity of nature from the coarser elements of art—from socially skewed sense impressions—is itself an artfully constructed human technology. Remarking in 1666 that "Art . . . is apt to delude sense," Margaret Cavendish thought that "dioptrical instruments" like the microscope "can do no more than represent exterior figures in a bigger, and so in a more deformed shape and posture than they naturally are."[103]

Ten years later Samuel Butler satirically imagined a discovery made by the Royal Society through a telescope trained on the moon's nighttime surface. One of their number

> Apply'd one Eye, and half a Nose
> Unto the optick Engine close.
> For he had lately undertook
> To prove, and publish in a Book,
> That Men, whose nat'ral Eyes are out,
> May, by more pow'rful Art be brought
> To see with th' empty Holes as plain,
> As if their Eyes were in again:
> And, if they chanc'd to fail of those,
> To make an Optick of a Nose;
> As clearly it may, by those that wear
> But Spectacles, be made appear;
> By which both Senses being united
> Does render them much better sighted.

This ludicrous hypothesis prepares us for a scenario in which the "pow'rful Art" of the telescope, so far from sharpening the "nat'ral" senses, instead replaces their testimony by the artifice of illusion. The astonished virtuosi descry a pitched battle between two armies of lunar inhabitants and then an enormous lunar elephant, apparitions that are explained away when the telescope is opened to reveal, trapped in its tube, a swarm of flies and gnats and a solitary mouse.[104]

It would be easy to adduce many more instances of skeptical commentary on the way the artifice of experimental instruments distorts the senses, or, more often, colludes with the senses in distorting nature. What about the instrument of language? I've already suggested that for experimentalists like Sprat and Wotton, language—or its negative essence "rhetoric" or "eloquence"—encapsulates the artifice of the Baconian Idols, art in its capacity to obscure and obstruct nature. The best-known passage in Sprat's *History* is his self-consciously anti-rhetorical rhetoric (too often read as a naive affirmation of the prelapsarian origins of language) urging his readers "to return back to the primitive Purity and Shortness, when Men deliver'd so many Things, almost in an equal Number of Words . . . bringing all Things as near the mathematical Plainness as they can" (113). No doubt "the Ornaments of Speaking" were once "an admirable Instrument in the Hands of wise Men; when they were only employ'd to describe Goodness, Honesty; Obedience, in larger, fairer, and more moving Images; to represent Truth, clotah'd [*sic*] with Bodies; and to bring Knowledge back again to our very Senses, from whence it was at first deriv'd to our Understandings" (112). The implication is that in the beginning, figures of speech served an important function in materializing and objectifying oral discourse, which otherwise suffered the fate of oblivion. From this perspective, the arts of language might be seen as the original instrument by which experience is rendered experiment; but with writing and print, the disembedding and objectifying powers of language became so great as to be counterproductive, re-embedding "things" within the densely material superstructure of "words" themselves. Sprat does not put it this way, and his equivocal approach to the instrumentality of language is in any case mandated by its indispensability. Yet the systematic reformation of knowledge that's undertaken by experimentalism will render useless many technical terms of art that philosophy has relied on in the past. "But to supply their want, an infinite variety of *Inventions, Motions,* and *Operations,* will succeed in the place of words" (327).

Bacon seems to take a similar position. However difficult it may be to expunge the linguistic "Idols of the Market-place" (*NO* I, aph. 59, p. 269), language must be reformed, not replaced. We already know that memory alone will not do;

> yet hitherto more has been done in matter of invention by thinking than by writing; and experience has not yet learned her letters. Now no course of invention can be satisfactory unless it be carried on in writing. But when this is brought into use, and experience has been taught to read and write, better things may be hoped.... When all the experiments of all the arts shall have been collected and digested, and brought within one man's knowledge and judgment, the mere transferring of the experiments of one art to others may lead, by means of that experience which I term literate, to the discovery of many new things of service to the life and state of man. (*NO* I, aphs. 101, 103, p. 290)

The second generation of experimentalists elevated the indispensability of linguistic mediation to a role that might seem to challenge a principle basic to experimental epistemology, that data be derived from direct observation. This is the institution of what's been called "virtual witnessing," by which the number of witnesses who actually attended either an original laboratory experiment or one of its many replications might be multiplied by the assumption that those who read the textual account of the experiment also gave it their assent.[105]

However, the reform of language was also achieved by Locke's reconceptualization of its relation to the sensible world it represents. Because things are not immediately "present to the Understanding," ideas are needed as a mediation or "a Sign or Representation of the thing it considers," and words are needed as signs of our ideas so that we can mediate them to each other. "*Words* . . . excite in Men certain *Ideas,* so constantly and readily, that they are apt to suppose a natural connexion between them. But . . . they signify only Men's peculiar *Ideas,* and that *by a perfectly arbitrary Imposition.*" So, words are therefore both artful and "the great Instruments of Knowledge," but no more than our ideas are an artful extension of our bodies (4.21.4). Most notably, Locke models language formation on the experimental process by which a constant is abstracted from a multitude of variables:

> Since all things that exist are only particulars, how come we by general Terms, or where find those general Natures they are supposed to stand for? Words become general, by being made the signs of general *Ideas*: and *Ideas*

become general, by separating from them the circumstances of Time and Place, and any other *Ideas,* that may determine them to this or that particular Existence. By this way of abstraction they are made capable of representing more Individuals than one; each of which, having in it a conformity to that abstract *Idea,* is (as we call it) of that sort. (3.3.6)[106]

Locke's account of how words come to signify a "general nature" is a linguistic version of the Enlightenment schema whereby particulars are separated out from their traditional tacit distinction and conflated as a virtual whole, and it recalls not only Bacon's "simple nature" and Hooke's experimental abstraction from "persons, time, place," but also Smith's diachronic conceptualization of the "simple abstraction."[107]

Thomas Hobbes made no distinction between experiment and instruments, but only because he disputed the notion that experiment itself affords better access to nature than experience. For Hobbes, in fact, experience is nothing but "mean and common experiments," which thus understood are "a great deal better witnesses of nature, than those that are forced by fire."[108] In a tract that takes the form of a dialogue Hobbes's representative asks: "Are there not enough [experiments], do you not think, shown by the high heavens and the seas and the broad Earth?" His interlocutor protests: "There are some critical works of nature, not known to us without method and diligence; in which one part of nature, as I will say, by artifice, that is, produces its way of working more manifestly than in one hundred thousand of these everyday phenomena." But Hobbes's skepticism is unfazed, and elsewhere he describes the workings of Robert Boyle's air-pump, the experimental instrument he was most concerned to debunk, as no more than a "spectacle . . . of an amusing nature," an artful performance.[109]

For Hobbes, the artifice entailed in experimentalism was bound up with its commitment to an empirical method that begins at the level of sense perceptions and, by controlling for variables through instrumental improvements on the senses and the multiplication of experimental occasions, reasons upward toward general, virtual, and probable causes. Reasoning downward from causes to material effects, Hobbes's procedure eschewed the laborious experimental abstraction of experience through repetition, multiplication, and generalization because it was obviated by the generalizing authority entailed in the knowledge of causes itself. Experimentalists "fall back on this one thing," Hobbes writes, "that they procure new phenomena, when from the experience of one phenomenon alone the causes are known by reasoning about motion." For the experimentalists, a body of new phenomena is essential to the abstraction of nature from its concrete instances.[110] Not that "art" has no place for Hobbes in the pursuit of knowledge. Indeed, he believed that the most dependable sort of knowledge is of artifactual things like geometry and civic philosophy, because having made them we know the rules by which they were made and hence the causes by which they may be understood.[111] "The skill of making, and maintaining Commonwealths," Hobbes writes in *Leviathan*, "consisteth in certain Rules, as does Arithmetique and Geometry; not (as Tennis-play) on [sic] Practice onely."[112]

What seems anomalous to moderns as well as to some of his contemporaries is Hobbes's position that artificial objects are more susceptible to scientific understanding than are natural ones. Contemporaries more sympathetic than he was to experimental method are likely to have agreed with his critic John Bramhall that political philosophy is not easily compared to arithmetic or geometry: "State-policy, which is wholly involved in matter, and circumstances of time, and place, and persons, is not at all like Arithmetick and Geometry, which are altogether abstracted from matter, but much more like Tennis-play."[113] Bramhall's language is very close to that of the experimentalist Hooke, who thought the repetition of experiments was essential in order to control for the variables of "Persons, Time, [and] Place."[114] And as this might suggest, skepticism that the abstractive, quantifying powers of arithmetic give access to the concrete contingency of political philosophy doesn't persuade experimentalists to close the argument, but rather sets the stage for the attempt to know the state by experimental means. Is it possible to abstract time, place, and persons from politics without evaporating the object of knowledge? Nothing better expresses the ingenuity of Enlightenment thought than, having conceived experimentalism in natural philosophy, to experiment with extending it elsewhere.

Extending Experiment I: Political Philosophy

This can be seen in efforts to apply natural philosophy to political philosophy in the decades following the Restoration. Not long after Bramhall insisted that the involvement of politics in time, place, and persons made it resistant to arithmetic abstraction, William Petty formulated his method of "political arithmetic" (once again using tennis as the limit case of experimental application):

> Instead of using only comparative and superlative Words, and intellectual Arguments, I have taken the course (as a Specimen of the Political Arithmetick I have long aimed at) to express my self in Terms of *Number, Weight,* or *Measure;* to use only Arguments of Sense, and to consider only such Causes, as have visible Foundations in Nature; leaving those that depend upon the mutable Minds, Opinions, Appetites, and Passions of particular Men, to the Consideration of others: Really professing my self as unable to speak satisfactorily upon those Grounds (if they may be call'd Grounds), as to forecast the cast of a Dye; to play well at Tennis, Billiards, or Bowles, (without long practice,).... Now the Observations or Positions Expressed by *Number, Weight,* and *Measure,* upon which I bottom the ensuing Discourses, are either true, or not apparently false, and which if they are not already true, certain, and evident, yet may be made so by the Sovereign Power.[115]

Petty's discourse on method might appear to confound the experimental use of quantification—to generalize beyond the variables of "particular Men"—with the a priori and absolute privilege of one man in particular. If schematic, it may nonetheless be fruitful to consider this question in chronological terms.

1) Separating and Conflating Political Subjects

At the start of the seventeenth century, generalizations about the commonwealth of England and Scotland began and ended with the singular and mystical authority of its sovereign—which is to say, its royal—power; this is one of the implications of the doctrine of the king's two bodies. By the end of the century, an alternative model of assessing the commonwealth had gained widespread support, a quantifying model of generalization that required a "rational" accounting for and reconciling of the individual parts of the political whole. The watershed in this change was the experience of civil war; as George Monck put it on the eve of the Restoration: "Before these unhappy Wars the Government of these Nations was Monarchical in Church and State: these wars have given birth and growth to several Interests both in Church and State heretofore not known; though now upon many accounts very considerable. . . . I think upon rational grounds it may be taken for granted; *That no Government can be either good, peaceful or lasting to these Nations, that doth not rationally include and comprehend the security and preservrtion [sic] of all the foresaid Interests both Civil and Spiritual.*"[116] This alternative principle of political legitimacy also could be expressed without recourse to quantification through the potent figure, one indebted to the seventeenth-century revival of natural law theory, of the state of nature.

2) Imagining Separateness: The Political State and the State of Nature

The figure was susceptible to divergent interpretations. For Hobbes, the late Civil War had returned England and Scotland to the state of nature, "a time of Warre, where every man is Enemy to every man" because universal natural rights are unconstrained by the natural law that requires every man by contract *"to lay down this right to all things; and be contented with so much liberty against other men, as he would allow other men against himself"* (Leviathan, pt. 1, ch. 13, 14, pp. 62, 65). For Locke the state of nature is a more benign affair: *"Want of a common judge with Authority, puts all Men in a State of Nature: Force without Right, upon a Man's Person, makes a State of War,* both where there is, and is not, a common Judge" (Second Treatise, para. 19, p. 299). Hobbes notably suspends his commitment to reasoning downward from first principles, instead entering into the fiction that sovereignty derives from the agreement of "particular Men" to form a compact. But he thereby vindicates deduction from first principles by internalizing it within an inductive narrative whereby the compact of the many institutes absolute sovereignty and the rule of one. Locke's model government will conflate all separate persons but preclude absolutism by separating the powers by which they're governed. This separation was foreign to Hobbes's belief that only an absolute state could overcome the state of war that was coextensive with the state of nature and that prevailed in England after the defeat of monarchy.

But Hobbes and Locke agree on the basic proposition that political sovereignty flows not from on high but as it were "inductively," from the contractual willingness of all persons to cede their right of self-protection to a sovereign protector. The figure of the state of nature is a narrative experiment, a laboratory human polity so entirely stripped of variables that at the outset polity itself is absent, a condition that permits us to see the "arts" of government in their "natural" emergence and growth.[117] The heuristic hypothesis of the state of nature enables us to discover the nature of the state—not a priori, from the Garden of Eden down, but experimentally, generalizing upward from the sensible facticity of multiple persons to their agreement to enter into an *"original Compact"* (*Second Treatise*, para. 97, p. 350). Before it was experimentally put into practice, this narrative was rationalized in James Madison's advocacy of republican representation.[118] Like Bacon's experimental "exclusion," Madison's experimental representation works like a sieve to winnow out impurities so that the essence of not the natural but the public view stands revealed.[119] Madison's representative democracy aims to "include and comprehend" (in Monck's words) all the political interests whose diverse particularity is the inductive starting point for the methodical process of exclusion that produces legitimate government. By comprehending all interests such a government lays claim to being "disinterested," a normative term in modern scientific and artistic as well as political thought. Needless to say, the fulfillment of this claim through the universal extension of the franchise in formal terms waited until the early twentieth century and in factual terms continues to be violated.

Extending Experiment II: Beyond Observables

1) Religious Philosophy

The extension of natural philosophy's experimental method to what might be called "religious philosophy" would appear to be a contradiction in terms. One of the most rigorous exercises in experimental method outside the laboratory is David Hume's celebrated polemic against miracles. Experience is "our only guide in reasoning concerning matters of fact," Hume writes. A wise man "proportions his belief to the evidence," and in disputes about matters of fact such a man "considers which side is supported by the greater number of experiments." Judgments of probability suppose "an opposition of experiments and observations; where the one side is found to overbalance the other, and to produce a degree of evidence, proportioned to the superiority."

On this quantifying basis Hume lays out "a contest of two opposite experiences." The first is our experience of receiving witness testimony to the reality or truth of that to which it testifies. The second is our experience of miracles. Now, the first is a very common experience, and the reason "we place any credit in witnesses and historians is . . . because we are accustomed to find a conformity between" testimony and reality. The crucial words here are "we" and "accustomed," because they make clear that the standard of probability on which belief is based is temporally and "spatially" (i.e., inclusively) quantitative. Often enough we find ourselves skeptical about witness reports, but the testimony and the reality agree on average more often than they disagree, and therefore the balance falls on the side of crediting the testimony of witnesses with "a certain degree of assurance." But the second experience is so uncommon, whether it consists of our experience of the testimony of others or of our own sense perceptions, that on the average the credibility of miracles is nil. "Upon the whole, then, it appears, that no testimony for any kind of miracle has ever amounted to a probability, much less to a proof; and that, even supposing it amounted to a proof, it would be opposed by another proof, derived from the very nature of the fact, which it would endeavour to establish. It is experience only, which gives authority to human testimony; and it is the same experience, which assures us of the laws of nature." (Indeed, it is on the basis of this sort of inductive and arithmetically capacious survey of experience that we derive what then stand as seemingly deductive postulates, "the laws of nature.") "When, therefore, these two kinds of experience are contrary, we have nothing to do but subtract the one from the other, with that assurance which arises from the remainder."[120] Although he offers no comparably trenchant epistemological exercise in experiment, Hume's predecessor Locke uses criteria and terminology of empirical demonstration with which Hume's polemic is fully consonant (see *Essay*, 4.15.1–6, 4.16.1–11).

Of course, Hume's argument falls short of experimental method because he is content to assert his arithmetical data—whose force is to demonstrate an abstraction of what is constant in or "natural" to human belief from the variables that obscure it in individual cases of judgment—rather than actually to collect that data in the manner of a proto-sociological survey. Still, Hume's method here bears comparison to virtual witnessing, because his assertion of data is implicitly a rhetorical appeal to the experience of his readers, which he takes to confirm what he asserts.[121] In other words, Hume's assertion is the issue of a kind of "thought experiment," in which a hypothetical scenario substitutes—or prepares—for an actual experiment. Hume found the appeal to the experience of the reader so useful that elsewhere he makes it explicitly and often. In order to argue the correlation of simple ideas and simple impressions, for example, he first tells us that he has made "the most accurate examination, of which I am capable," then remarks that "the case is the same with all our simple impressions and ideas, 'tis impossible to prove by a particular enumeration of them. Every one may satisfy himself in this point by running over as many as he pleases."[122] With a similar blend of rhetorical suasion and empirical candor Locke, too, invites his readers to perform thought experiments: "Let any one examine his own Thoughts, and thoroughly search into his Understanding, and then let him tell me, Whether all of the original Ideas he has there, are any other then of the Objects of his *Senses;* or of the Operations of his Mind, considered as Objects of his *Reflection*" (2.1.5).

From Francis Bacon onward, empirical epistemology was overseen by two basic principles. First, empirical knowledge proceeds through the senses. The fallibility of the senses argued that individual sense impressions must be supplemented and reinforced by the protocols that define experimental method so that the evidence provided by the senses is an adequate basis for our knowledge of the world. Second, to attain probability, the tacit whole of knowledge must be explicitly analyzed and separated into its constituent parts: on the one hand, the external object of knowledge; on the other, the human subject or method by which the object is internally known.

In describing the major structural features of the mind, Locke accounts for how these two principles are ensured. He divides the whole of understanding into two operations, "sensation" and "reflection." First, sensation, or "the senses . . . from external Objects convey into the mind what produces there those *Perceptions*" that are the source of "most of the *Ideas* we have." Second, reflection sets the understanding "at a distance," self-consciously "turns inwards upon it self, *reflects* on its own *Operations*, and makes them the Object of its own Contemplation." That is, "External, Material things, [are] the Objects of *SENSATION*; and the Operations of our own Minds, within, [are] the Objects of *REFLECTION*." In its inward self-focus, reflection internalizes the external operation of sensation. "This Source of Ideas, every Man has wholly in himself: And though it be not Sense, as having nothing to do with external Objects; yet it is very like it, and might properly enough be call'd internal Sense" (2.1.3–4, 8). So, subject and object would appear to be separated through the separation of the two operations of reflection and sensation. Reflection concerns itself with the subject of understanding, while sensation is concerned with its object, and their separation from each other is made tangible in the difference between operations whose focus is, respectively, internal and partially external (the senses but also the perceptions) to the mind.

The problem with having insufficient distance from one's object of knowledge Locke illuminates in his critique of Protestant enthusiasm. If Hume's essay "Of Miracles" is the definitive experimental falsification of religious supernaturalism, Locke's critique of enthusiasm falsifies what might be called religious "subnaturalism," increasingly the normative marker of faith under the Protestant impulse to internalize and privatize religious experience. Even before it became firmly associated with modern science, the word "experiment" was already a religious term of art signifying the trials that were to be expected in the experience of a Christian, and especially a Protestant, professor of faith.[123]

The religious and the scientific usages have much in common. Jonathan Edwards is instructive on why Christianity is called the

> *experimental Religion*. For that Experience which is in these Exercises of Grace, that are found, and prove effectually at the very Point of Trial, wherein God proves which we will actually cleave to, whether Christ or our Lusts, are . . . the proper *Experiment* of the Truth and Power of our Godliness; wherein it's [sic] victorious Power and Efficacy, in producing it's proper Effect, and reaching it's End, is found *by Experience*. This is properly christian Experience, wherein the Saints have Opportunity to see, by actual *Experience and Trial*, whether they have a Heart to do the Will of God, and to forsake other Things for Christ, or not. As that is called experimental Philosophy, which brings Opinions

and Notions to the Test of Fact; so is that properly called experimental Religion, which brings religious Affections and Intentions, to the like Test.

On the face of it, Edwards's analogy between natural experiment and religious experiment—the divine trials that punctuate our daily experience—has some plausibility. Repetition and variation are important aspects of religious as of natural experiment: for "when there are many of these Acts and Exercises [of Grace], following one another in a Course, under various Trials, of every Kind, the Evidence is still heighten'd; as one Act confirms another." But even as Edwards describes this process as though it confirmed the spiritual condition of professors in the eyes of their peers, we realize that this is a very special kind of evidence. Professors are put to what is in effect an "Experiment of [their] Sincerity," and Edwards contrasts this kind of experiment with its negative counterpart, "a sort of external religious Practice, wherein is no inward Experience; which no account is made of in the Sight of God." But how is anyone besides God able to witness the evidence of an inward experience? Indeed, since God does not really need "Evidence himself of their Sincerity," religious experiment is "chiefly for their Conviction, and to exhibit Evidence to their Consciences."[124]

In other words, the witnesses who testify to the authenticity of these signs of grace are the professors themselves. Edwards brings us to the well-known nexus of antinomianism and predestination that led many Protestants to seek the signs of their election from the only available authority, their own convictions. The variable for which religious experiment cannot control is the intimate psychology of the individual professor.

This brings us very close to Locke's argument that "enthusiasm" or "internal Light" is by its very nature an unreliable ground of assent: "What I see I know to be so by the Evidence of the thing it self: what I believe I take to be so upon the Testimony of another: But this Testimony I must know to be given, or else what ground have I of believing?" (4.19.10) Enthusiasts

> see the Light infused into their Understandings, and cannot be mistaken. . . . They feel the Hand of GOD moving them within, and the impulses of the Spirit, and cannot be mistaken in what they feel. . . . What they have a sensible Experience of admits no doubt, needs no probation. . . . It is its own Proof, and can have no other. . . . This is the way of talking of these Men: they are sure, because they are sure: and their Perswasions are right, only because they are strong in them. [But] the strength of our Perswasions are no Evidence at all of their own rectitude. . . . If they say they know it to be true, because it is a *Revelation* from GOD, the reason is good: but then it will be demanded, how they know it to be a Revelation, from GOD. . . . Thus we see that the holy Men of old, who had *Revelations* from GOD, had something else besides that internal Light of assurance in their own Minds, to testify to them, that it was from GOD. . . . *Moses* saw the Bush burn without being consumed, and heard a Voice out of it . . . and yet he thought not this enough to authorise him to go with that Message, till GOD by another Miracle, of his Rod turned into a Ser-

pent, had assured him of a Power to testify his Mission by the same Miracle repeated before them, whom he was sent to.... Every Conceit that thoroughly warms our Fancies must pass for an Inspiration, if there be nothing but the Strength of our Perswasions, whereby to judge of our Perswasions: If *Reason* must not examine their Truth by something extrinsical to the Perswasions themselves; Inspirations and Delusions, Truth and Falshood will have the same Measure, and will not be possible to be distinguished. (4.19.10, 8 and 9)

2) Moral Philosophy

Locke's powerful critique of enthusiasm expresses the experimental principle that probability requires adducing evidence that is "extrinsic" to, detached or abstracted from, the knowledge it would confirm. The critique comes near the conclusion of Locke's *An Essay concerning Human Understanding* (1989), which begins with a candid acknowledgment that the question of the extrinsic is also central to his present undertaking: the "Understanding, like the Eye, whilst it makes us see, and perceive all other Things, takes no notice of it self: And it requires Art and Pains to set it at a distance, and make it its own Object" (1.1.1). Does Locke's experimental inquiry into the understanding, in which he criticizes enthusiasm for failing to separate the subject from the object of knowledge—does this *Essay* itself entail the same failure? As we've seen, Locke's account of the mind's structure is attentive to this question. As sensation makes external things its object, reflection, although a separate faculty, is an "internal sense" that on analogy with sensation behaves like an internal subject by taking its own operations as its object of knowledge. Hume takes up the question of moral philosophy where Locke leaves off. His *Treatise of Human Nature* (1739) is subtitled "Being an Attempt to Introduce the Experimental Method of Reasoning into Moral Subjects" (xi). In his "Introduction" Hume situates the origins of this philosophy within the larger context of the Quarrel of the Ancients and Moderns and the separation out of the "arts" from the "sciences," which here bears an unstated relation to the separation between the "moral" and the "experimental" (i.e., natural) philosophy, a separation that his and Locke's philosophical efforts aimed in part to overcome:

> 'Tis no astonishing reflection to consider, that the application of experimental philosophy to moral subjects should come after that to natural at the distance of above a whole century; since we find in fact, that there was about the same interval betwixt the origins of these sciences; and that reckoning from THALES to SOCRATES, the space of time is nearly equal to that betwixt my Lord BACON[125] and some late philosophers in England, who have begun to put the science of man on a new footing, and have engaged the attention, and excited the curiosity of the public.... For to me it seems evident, that the essence of the mind being equally unknown to us with that of external bodies, it must be equally impossible to form any notion of its powers and qualities otherwise than from careful and exact experiments.... Moral philosophy has, indeed,

this peculiar disadvantage, which is not found in natural, that in collecting its experiments, it cannot make them purposely, with premeditation.... But should I endeavour to clear up after the same manner any doubt in moral philosophy, . . .'tis evident this reflection and premeditation would so disturb the operation of my natural principles, as must render it impossible to form any just conclusion from the phaenomenon. (xvi–xvii, xviii–xix)

Hume uses the same terminology as Locke, but he takes a different approach to this problem. Regarding sensation, he writes "that nothing is ever really present with the mind but its perceptions . . . and that external objects become known to us only by those perceptions they occasion." Nonetheless we commonly "attribute a CONTINU'D existence to objects, even when they are not present to the senses; and . . . we suppose them to have an existence DISTINCT from the mind and perception." And so "I am naturally led to regard the world, as something real and durable, and as preserving its existence, even when it is no longer present to my perception." "Philosophers may distinguish betwixt the objects and perceptions of the senses," but "the generality of mankind" "never think of a double existence internal and external, representing and represented." This is because although our perceptions of objects are inevitably interrupted, we suppose "that these interrupted perceptions are connected by a real existence, of which we are insensible." The "smooth passage of the imagination along the ideas of the resembling perceptions makes us ascribe to them a perfect identity . . . by the fiction of a continu'd existence" (67, 188, 197, 202, 205).

Hume's principle of "double existence" may seem at first to take us, if by a different route, to Locke's separation of sensation from reflection, and thereby to the separation of the external object from the internal operations by which the subject comes to a knowledge of its objects. But for Hume, the problem concerns not the relation between sensation and reflection, but the relation between components of the operation of sensation in particular. And the meaning of Hume's principle is that the "real existence" of the external object that would be represented by sensation is unavailable to sensation's internal operations for representing it. This is in part because the interruption of our perceptions of the object interrupts our knowledge of it; but more fundamentally because it's in any case only our perceptions that are "ever really present with our minds." So we might say that for Hume, too, subject and object of knowledge are "separate"—but in the radical sense that not only in reflection but also in sensation we have access only to the inside. "Let us fix our attention out of ourselves as much as possible: Let us chace our imagination to the heavens, or to the utmost limits of the universe; we never really advance a step beyond ourselves, nor can we conceive any kind of existence, but those perceptions, which have appear'd in that narrow compass" (67–68).

Hume's words are deceptively but instructively similar to these words of Locke fifty years earlier: "All those sublime Thoughts, which towre above the Clouds, and reach as high as Heaven it self, take their rise and footing here: In all that great Extent wherein the mind wanders, in those remote Speculations, it may seem to be elevated with, it stirs not one jot beyond those *Ideas*, which *Sense* or *Reflection*, have offered for its Contemplation" (2.1.24). The comparison of these passages is instructive because it captures the coherence of Enlightenment empiricism in the very process of self-criticism. Lockean empiricism skeptically challenges the metaphysical view of mind, dividing and redividing it into its separate parts. Humean empiricism, inspired by Locke to a different thought experiment in moral philosophy, skeptically conflates these parts into a newly understood internal whole. The empirical analysis of material actuality bleeds into the empirical analysis of conceptual virtuality. Objectivity is the key to subjectivity; extrinsic evidence is always available, but according to a standard that's intrinsic to and determined by the given experimental framework.

In the introduction to this volume I pointed out that to limit empiricism to the realm of the material binds it too exclusively to a focus on its ostensible source and attends too little to the range opened up by focusing on it as method. This was perhaps a "naive empiricism" peculiar to early Enlightenment thinking (and one that valorized historicity as well as materiality as the privileged source of the empirical[126]). Extended beyond observables, the experimental method of natural philosophy opens up the invisible realm of mind to systematic analysis. Traditional faculty psychology had given names and functions to mental categories; however, these distinct categories were inseparable in the sense that they were conceived as parts of a hierarchically ordered micro-whole within a hierarchical system of corresponding and interdependent wholes, a macro-whole whose coherence consisted in its stasis and perpetuity. Like the parts of those other wholes—the body, the body politic, the sublunary sphere—Locke's partialization of mind conceives sensation and reflection as reciprocal but independent moving parts by virtue of functioning in different, external and internal, realms of being, a new conflation made possible by their explicit separation. Hume's analysis goes further, confirming the separation of sensation and reflection but as independent and nonreciprocal, hence unconflatable, realms of external objectivity and internal subjectivity. On the one hand, Hume's model fulfills the first principle of experimental method, the separation of subject and object, but with a finality that makes it not interactional but absolute and with the effect that mental experiment has no access to sensible experience. On the other, Hume's relocation of the two separate parts of mind within the same, internal realm of reflection reconceives their location but doesn't preclude their interaction and conflation.

Yet because Locke's model of analysis is structured as a movement from separation to conflation—a structure Hume adopted from Locke—he lays the ground for a conclusion similar to Hume's that differs from it only in conceiving that movement as functioning not only in the realm of reflection but also in that of sensation. Both are stages in the dialectical internalization of analysis whereby each new part, reconceived as a whole, becomes subject to further partialization. At each new stage of analysis, the structural separation between subject and object enables a conflation that provides a basis for further separations. In modern terminology, sensation breaks down into different sensory receptors—photo, haptic, taste, sound wave vibrations—and their electrical stimulation of the brain; reflection ramifies into the categories specific to different fields like Gestalt, cognitive psychology, neuropsychology, psychoanalysis, and quantum cognition, each of which conceives a separation of subject and object and the terms of their conflation. This psychological analysis, accomplished by means of language and conceptualization, might be compared to the division and redivision of images inaugurated in the seventeenth century by microscopy and extended by techniques like X-rays, CT scans, and microtomography.

Skeptics thought experimental instruments like the microscope produced artificial and illusory representations of nature, not nature as such. The modern extension of analysis deep into the unobservable and invisible dimensions of nature may invite a similar skepticism, but also the caveat that science has long since gone beyond the notion of a fundamental separation of the subject from the object of knowledge. This isn't to say that the classic model of experimentalism has become outmoded. On the contrary, the clinical trial, for example, is an indispensable practice in modern medicine. However, the contradiction disclosed by the idea of the hermeneutic circle, the inseparability of subject and object, is a modern problem because it follows from the modern separation out of categories that traditionally were distinct but inseparable. The circle doesn't return us to that traditional state of mind because as a product of the belief in their separability it prepares in turn for the modern, self-consciously conflationary way of knowing by moving back and forth between categories whose coherence is defined by their separation.

Yet the very term—the hermeneutic circle—reminds us that in the tradition of theology we may locate a state of mind closely analogous to our secular experimental epistemology. This is because in Christian thought, the opposition between matter and spirit, the profane and the sacred, is conceived as a relation in which the former category has the potential to accommodate the latter. The hermeneutic method of reading sacred texts would make immanent as though visible an invisible and transcendent truth. Similarly, the Protestant professor would confirm the inward experience of grace by outward trials. The outward trials of scientific experiment are artifactual structures that stand in relation to the truth of nature as do material signs, words, and artifacts to the truth of the spirit.

True, scientific experiment is distinctive in fashioning its material accommodation as a rigorous method of quantitative calibration and measurement: from data collection to the maintenance of standard uniformity, to the ongoing refinement of protocols of comparison and contrast, to the division of technical labor, to the multiplication and variation of conditions under which testing is accomplished. However, the quantitative standards of scientific experiment are on a continuum, in the most crucial respect, with the qualitative standards of theology. In the words of a commentator on metrology, the science of measurement: "Both metrology and theology are concerned with realizing, maintaining and disseminating the tangible representatives of something that is transcendent."[127]

Experimentalism and Christianity share the aim to purify experience of its temporal and spatial contingencies. Christian doctrine would accommodate the suprasensible realm of the Spirit to human understanding as experiment would understand nature according to the virtual category "natural law"; but both know the difference between methods of representation and the "presence" they would represent. And from this perspective, thought experiments and virtual witnessing are not only methods of virtualizing the conditions of the laboratory but also practical exercises in knowledge and self-knowledge that reflect the purposes of Enlightenment thought. In many passages Locke's *Essay* affirms that "every one may experiment in himself" (4.7.4); and another scholar observes that throughout this treatise Locke "appeals to the experimental method to extend our realm of experience by bringing customarily ignored mental phenomena into consciousness. His way of ideas becomes, in effect, an experimental technology for transforming implicit into explicit knowledge, for bringing ill-conceived or indistinct ideas into sharp focus. . . . An idea that has not been witnessed by our consciousnesses—that has not passed, however fleetingly, through our field of mental vision—is no idea at all."[128] With a simple candor Locke's observation that "I appeal to every one's own Experience" articulates the basic Enlightenment impulse toward universality (2.23.3).

The Imagination

Several times over the course of this chapter I've cited the misgivings of contemporaries at the notion that entities acknowledged to be imaginary are to be treated as substantial and real. Entry into the realm of the virtual is arguably made through the portal of the imagination; but prior to the period of our concern the imagination's powers of virtualization were feared as the means by which falsehood, madness, and the demonic gained traction in our minds. These fears didn't disappear;[129] but the imagination was transvalued in the seventeenth and eighteenth centuries, most famously on the coattails of artistic creativity and as a positive measure of human capacity. However, as this chapter has made clear, the reassessment of the imagination began long before the 1790s and the Romantic movement, and its implications extend well beyond the province of art and literature.[130] Moderns are accustomed to thinking of literature and science as antithetical modes of knowledge. But for some—notably John Dryden, Joseph Addison, and Samuel Johnson—the modern category of the aesthetic emerged as an active emulation of the scientific model. A category of empirical epistemology, the idea of the aesthetic applied the imagination to the project for which experimental method had been conceived, the creation of a virtual reality through the abstraction and refinement of the data of sensible experience. Addison's analysis in the *Spectator* papers (1712) provides an especially powerful illumination of the pleasures of the imagination by explicitly comparing and contrasting them with the pleasures of the understanding.

How is the culture of virtual reality a function of the Enlightenment project in making the tacit explicit—a question that returns to my earlier thoughts on the relation between virtualization and Enlightenment universality? Enlightenment techniques of self-conscious perception partialize the real, separating sensible actuality from the virtuality of the idols or variables that are produced by the imagination. These are experienced as illusions when contrasted to our perception of the actual, but at the same time as devoid of illusion by virtue of this reflexive awareness of their difference from actuality. The pleasure arising from this conflation comes from experiencing a reality distinct from empirical actuality but indebted to it for the effectual force that accrues to a mental investment that's individually willed and collectively performed. The paradigm case is those singularly modern entities: the public sphere, the nation-state, and market exchange. The force that enables them is not technology but techne, the technique of the imagination, whose extension of experimentalism into the domain of the aesthetic and realism was achieved with a degree of self-consciousness that dictates more detailed consideration in separate chapters.[131] Enlightenment virtual reality amounted to a discovery of the powers of mind, and its modern consequences are incalculable. But although the modern world has been shaped by this discovery, it has no awareness of its effect or significance. Evidence for this can be seen in our contemporary appetite for the technological construction of virtual reality, as though to achieve an end otherwise unavailable. If Enlightenment virtual reality entails the discovery of imaginative creativity, modern virtual reality, our discovery of technological aids to delude the senses, epitomizes the banality of modern culture.

4   Gender and Sex, Status and Class

The powerful appeal of the category "patriarchy" depends upon, but also is limited by, its implicit claim to a comprehensive application. In recent years it is the limitation of the term that has seemed most visible. In naming the persistent experience of male dominance—across cultures, across historical periods—"patriarchy" operates on a level of abstract reference that appears to posit an implausibly universal human nature and that, by seeming to explain everything, in the end explains very little. Some have argued that "patriarchy" more properly refers to the old regime of specifically patriarchal authoritarian rule within, and on the model of, the traditional family, and that it should be replaced by categories more concretely reflective of contextual variation. But any effort at historical or cultural specification requires a universalizing backdrop of the sort asserted by "patriarchy" to render its object intelligible as the singular instance of a general phenomenon.

In this chapter I aim to argue a broad thesis about how and why the modern systems of sex and class were established during the English Enlightenment. In making this argument I hope to exemplify how patriarchy may be historicized: how the history of male dominance may be understood to entail a general continuity complicated by specific and divergent discontinuities. Central to my thesis will be the view that to historicize patriarchy requires, among other things, an inquiry into the relationship between the modern systems of sex and class. Much of my argument will be based on evidence drawn from recent research into early modern political theory, marriage law, agrarian change, and the history of sexuality. It should go without saying that the entire argument is deeply indebted to the work undertaken by feminist studies and social history over the past several decades.

Some recent research substantiates and sophisticates received wisdom; some of it propounds new lines of thought. My procedure will be to use both kinds of research to formulate and develop a hypothesis that conceives the emergence of sex and class within the context of the early modern divisions of labor and knowledge.

From Patriarchalism to Modern Patriarchy

There is some value in employing the term "patriarchalism" to refer to the traditional regime that is replaced by the modern conception of gender difference. Although specifically associated with Sir Robert Filmer's theory of royal absolutism, "patriarchalism" also takes in, more inclusively, the set of ideas and social practices entailed in the analogy between the family and the state.[1] The patriarchal analogy works because it is based on a hierarchical notion of authority that is implicitly analogical: as in the microcosm, so in the macrocosm. In premodern England this analogy was "traditional" in the sense that it was entertained and acted upon as a tacit and unexamined article of belief—a way of giving to political arrangements the apparently integral and natural legitimacy of family arrangements. Puritan thought and the onset of political crisis in the seventeenth century forced this tacit knowledge to become explicit. Now the analogy between familial and political order had to be rationalized, and people were obliged to concretize both terms and acknowledge what was problematic in the comparison. The apparent integrity of patriarchal authority in the family was found in fact to consist of several distinct authorities—that of the father, the husband, and the master—whose compound complexity deviated from the simplicity of the model of absolute royal prerogative.[2] In this sense, Filmer marks not the triumphant ascendancy of patriarchal thought but its demise as tacit knowledge, the fact that it is in crisis. He wrote his *Patriarcha* on the eve of warfare between royalists and parliamentarians in 1642; it was published in 1680 and again in 1685, when the Exclusion Crisis renewed that conflict in similar terms.[3]

This is not to say, however, that Filmer's opponents were immediately prepared to reject the analogy. In 1644, the parliamentarian Henry Parker argued that because arbitrary power does not rule the family, therefore it is not to be endured in the state: "And who now hath any competent share of reason, can suppose, that if God and nature have been so careful to provide for liberty in Families, and in particulars; that Man would introduce, or ought to endure slavery, when it is introduced upon whole States and Generalities?"[4] In 1700, twelve years after the absolutist James II had been deposed, the proto-feminist Mary Astell reversed Parker's question: "If absolute Sovereignty be not necessary in a State, how comes it to be so in a Family? Or if in a Family why not in a State; since no reason can be alleged for the one that will not hold more strongly for the other?"[5] Although Filmer, Parker, and Astell disagree on the question of whether the family and the state are institutions grounded in absolute authority, they agree on the continued plausibility of the analogy between family and state. And yet the more the nature and terms of the analogy were subjected to self-conscious examination, the more inevitably its force was undermined. In his *Second Treatise of Government* (printed in 1690), John Locke took the next decisive step by arguing that "the Power of a *Magistrate* over a Subject, may be distinguished from that of a *Father* over his Children, a *Master* over his Servant, a *Husband* over his Wife, and a *Lord* over his Slave."[6] Locke divided the tacit whole of sociopolitical power into several separate parts. More specifically, he formalized, in terms of a liberal political theory, a two-part development whose cultural significance was far reaching. First, it articulated the growing conviction that the world of the family and that of the state were regulated by fundamentally different—respectively customary and contractual—principles. Second, by restricting female identity to that of wife and mother, roles whose customary authority in the broad domain of kinship was now gradually limited to the circumscribed domain of the household, it conceived the contractual affairs of the polity as an exclusively male preserve.[7]

The foundering of patriarchalist political theory at the end of the seventeenth century can be explained by reference to political developments, in particular to the succession crisis that dominated Restoration politics. Monarchal succession is based on a model of dynastic inheritance. Increasing suspicion of the heir to the House of Stuarts—James, Duke of York—culminated in the failed effort to exclude him from the royal succession, and in his successful deposal soon after he acceded to the throne in 1685. In the Hanoverian Settlement of 1689, England's rulers agreed that dynastic inheritance, and the patriarchalist principles on which it is based, may be diluted by pressing considerations. By implication, the interests of political subjects are not necessarily best served by the system of patrilineage.[8]

But the Hanoverian Settlement and the demise of patriarchalist political theory cannot be understood simply as a matter of constitutional politics. They also represent one outcome of a more general Enlightenment disenchantment with the status system of social relations, and in particular with aristocratic ideology. For present purposes, aristocratic ideology can be summarized as the set of related beliefs that birth makes worth, that the interests of the family are identified with those of its head, and that among the nobility and gentry, honor and property are to be transmitted patrimonially and primogeniturally, through the male line. The attack on these beliefs took many forms. It was even argued that honor of birth has nothing to do with internal virtue and competence—hence the depravity, corruption, and incompetence of male aristocrats. By this way of thinking, the aristocratic family subjugates its members to the unjust tyranny of patriarchal power and the rule of primogeniture.[9]

Enlightenment innovations in marriage law have an evident relevance to this widespread outcry against the monolithic injustice of the aristocratic family. The device of the "strict settlement" had the effect of emphasizing the partibility of the several family interests. It reinforced the patrimonial rights of the eldest son but strictly limited his powers of alienation; it attended to the bride's jointure should she be widowed; and it guaranteed provisions for daughters and younger sons. Thus the strict settlement separated out elements which, by the less scrupulous and self-conscious consensus of aristocratic ideology, were less problematically comprehended within the general category of "family." In a similar fashion, Enlightenment innovations in marriage settlements and separate maintenance contracts brought to fruition a long-term development of doctrines permitting married women to possess separate property. We have seen that the contractual assumptions of liberal political theory had no real application to the civil rights of eighteenth-century women.

As Susan Staves has showed, however, contemporary legal thinking went some distance toward applying contractual logic to the status of married women. After flourishing for the better part of a century, these legal devices were countered through an effort to reassert the common-law principle of coverture, the law that husbands and wives are legally one person and that husbands absorb most of their wives' property on marriage and logically cannot contract with them thereafter. But although this effort to restrict married women's separate property was in many ways successful, over the longer term the separability of married women's property interests from those of their husbands became an article of English marriage law.[10] However, even these failed campaigns to reform marriage law testify to a growing Enlightenment awarenesss that marriage was not only a customary tradition of family life that goes without saying but also a public institution subject to the influence of church, state, and commercial enterprise. This was most evident in the emergent genre of the novel.[11] The self-conscious critique of what formerly had been taken for granted can also be seen in the genre's decisive shift from a traditional and increasingly residual to an innovative and emergent ideology of marriage: from the dominance of parental authority through arranged marriages of "convenience" to the ascendancy of "marriage for love" based on the choice of the married couple. Ruth Perry has illuminated this shift as a movement from a "traditional" axis of kinship based on consanguineal ties or blood lineage to a "modern" axis based on the conjugal and affinal ties of the married couple.[12] Over the long term this is also a movement from a norm of the family unit as an extended, multigenerational household reflecting the value of diachronic extension over time to a norm of the "nuclear" household reflecting the value of synchronic depth fueled by powerful affective ties.

Thus far my argument concerning the death of patriarchalism has pursued what might be seen as a two-stage division. The family is increasingly separated from the state, while the component members of the family are increasingly separated from each other. If we pursue this phenomenon beyond the evidence of political, social, and legal ideology we arrive at the testimony of socioeconomic change. Although chapter 3 argues that we need a more informed understanding of the idea of the "public," what we have learned to call the separation of the public from the domestic sphere is materially grounded in the capitalist transformation of the English countryside. To put this another way, the emergence of modern patriarchy, and its system of gender difference, cannot be understood apart from the emergence of the modern division of labor and class formation. Although the complexity of the capitalist transformation of the countryside militates against precise chronology, it obviously both predates the Enlightenment and continues thereafter. Nevertheless, some crucial features of the change may be associated with the years from 1660 to 1760.

From Domestic Economy to Domestic Ideology

In the last few decades, the pioneering research of Alice Clark and Ivy Pinchbeck has been both corrected and confirmed by feminist historians interested in the nature of women's work in early modern England.[13] At the beginning of the sixteenth century, economic production was dominated by what historians have variously called the domestic system, the domestic economy, and the family economy—a system in which the household was the major unit of production. Attempts to generalize about how this domestic economy was undermined in early modern England are frustrated by crucial variations in households based on differences in region and social status. Still, it can be said that in 1500, all women were also housewives, involved in production both for the subsistence of the household and, often, for market.[14] The domestic economy operated according to a schematic sexual division of labor—between female "inside" work and male "outside" work—that was in practice rather flexible and scarcely operative on smaller holdings. In such an economy, husbands exercised the authority of the head of a household that was organized as an integrated working partnership.[15]

The breakdown of the domestic economy, and the concomitant withdrawal of women from work deemed economically productive, was most immediately the result of capitalist innovation. The flexibility of traditional work relations depended on customary arrangements that capitalist improvement rendered unprofitable. Enclosure and the consolidation of large estates increasingly denied to lesser farmers the subsistence conditions on which their households had depended. The loss of commons rights—not only grazing but gathering fuel and gleaning harvest leavings—deprived women in particular of customary labor. When farmers lost access to land, their wives lost the means to keep a cow and practice dairying, a common form of women's work. As a result, outside work traditionally available to women simply disappeared at the lower social strata. At the higher social strata, increased sensitivity to price levels and market demand marginalized dairying in favor of more profitable production, or transformed it into a commercial activity under the control of hired managers.[16]

What happened to that portion of the agrarian economy not organized through the household? Over the course of the eighteenth century, there was a general decrease in the agricultural employment of women, and work patterns for men and women outside the household diverged in a number of ways. Increasingly, female employment was concentrated in spring activities like dairying and calving, while male labor was specialized in the fall harvesting of cereal crops, which required heavier technology. Especially in the latter half of the century, moreover, male real wages rose as female real wages declined. By limiting quasi-independent domestic production, capitalist improvement exerted pressure on what was increasingly understood as "the labor market," so as to throw women into competition with men. This was especially true in the fall, when the vulnerability of laborers in cereal production to structural unemployment put a premium on the availability of nonharvesting jobs. That men tended to prevail in this competition was both a cause and a consequence of developing conceptions of familial income as primarily male income.[17]

At the higher social levels, the differential process of class formation led women (and men) who aspired to gentility to value idleness in women. In such households, women's work was increasingly oriented toward female accomplishments, while cheap wage labor did what was once the inside work of wives. In more modest households, husbands and wives turned increasingly to wage labor, seeking work outside the home. Both lost thereby the traditional liberty to define the tasks entailed in their work. But laboring women, as we have seen, were also losing the opportunity for this kind of employment as well. The decrease of female employment in the latter half of the eighteenth century is closely correlated with a rise in fertility, whose principal demographic causes are a fall in the age of women at first marriage and a rise in the number of women who married. It seems plausible to connect these two developments: "As female employment became more precarious and lowly paid, there were obvious motives to marry younger as defense against the unemployment which was increasingly the lot of women." Even as the incidence of marriage increased, however, wives were losing the flexibility once enjoyed in household labor, which was in the process of becoming "housework," the exclusive domain of women and increasingly denigrated as unproductive.[18] The process is reflected in contemporary religious teaching. Seventeenth-century Puritan divines relegated housework to the category of "private callings," and some went further to argue that what one did as a housewife had no bearing on salvation.[19] What might be seen as the secular equivalent of this demotion took longer to accomplish. What distinguished housework from other professions that political economy deemed unproductive was the fact that it was unwaged, and over time its unproductivity came to be understood as a function of its being nonmarket labor, a process reflected in the development of the British census. In 1851, nonmarket household work was listed among the female occupations. By 1881 it was relegated to the "Unoccupied Class," and in 1891 even this category had disappeared altogether from the occupational assessment, along with housework.[20]

Separate Spheres?

So, by the middle of the eighteenth century, the flexible distinction between female "inside" and male "outside" work had gone a long way—at least in the higher social orders—toward ossifying into the familiar, culturally ramified opposition between the domestic and the "public" realms.[21] For some time it's been received wisdom that in the latter years of the eighteenth century, the idea of "separate spheres" became institutionalized in thought and practice.[22] This is conceived as a division between the realms of male public and female private experience, based in a separation between outside and inside worlds, professional business and domesticity, breadwinner and homemaker, and broadly correlated with the formation and ideology of the middle class, the dominance of production for the market, and the takeoff of the industrial revolution, a separation that infiltrated most corners of British experience. We've seen the evidence for this understanding in the development of the agrarian economy. The evidence also argues that if the domestic labor of housewives was revalued as economically unproductive, the resettlement of wife and mother in the new and interiorized activity of housework was balanced by her new status as governor of the little commonwealth of the family. The new sexual modesty and purity of the modern married woman is justified and sustained by her new responsibility for inculcating techniques of internal self-regulation in her husband and children, who signify in their very embodiment her own regulated sexuality. She is not asexual or anti-sexual but the moral lodestar of sexuality.[23] However, in recent years the idea of a late eighteenth-century shift to an ideology of separate spheres has been questioned at the level of both myriad details and broad overviews, shedding doubt on the notion that it pervaded, especially this early, all social levels and geographical locales with the degree of uniformity implied by the blanket application of that phrase.[24] The modern ideology of separate spheres has a cultural authority whose force doesn't require demonstration. However, it systematizes and superintends a social practice whose complex variability belies the stark simplicity of the model.

The ramification of male and female labor in the early modern countryside would seem to bear a relation to the modern ideology and social practice of separate spheres. How can that relation be empirically concretized? My argument has been that the long-term and uneven shift from patriarchalism to modern patriarchy entailed a separation out of elements that formerly had been tacitly understood and experienced as parts of an integral whole—the cosmos, the social order, the family, economic production. Within each of these elements we see evidence of the same process of separation: what formerly were distinct parts of an integral whole were divided from each other to become separate wholes. This schematic distinction between "traditional" and "modern" ways of organizing experience may also be expressed as the difference between a "vertical" hierarchy of interlocking rungs and a "horizontal" differentiation of discrete interests. In the seventeenth century, the language of "interest" began to discriminate not only among private family members but also among private political, social, and economic agents over against the public interest of the sovereign power.[25] In the eighteenth century, the leveling of status hierarchy took shape in the emergence of the language and assumptions of "class," which is sanctioned not by vertical bonds of affiliation and interdependence but by shared interests and by horizontal solidarity over against other classes.[26] "Class" came into existence to demystify and replace a former rule of biological essence, the rule of inherited social status. "Class" named an increasingly conspicuous socioeconomic phenomenon and defined a way of thinking about human difference as not biologically given but socially variable: dynamic, conflictual, and alterable not only on the individual level of social mobility, but also on the macro-level of social change. Over time, "class" came to serve as the banner of a palpable revolution in social description, marking the long-term triumph of attitudes toward social relations based on principles of historical contingency over those, like status and caste, that are based on genealogical prescription. I want to suggest in what follows that the process of differentiation entailed in the rise of modern patriarchy can be illuminated by juxtaposing it with these contemporaneous developments—that the early modern emergence of class is one crucial element in the historicization of patriarchy. Before turning to sex and class, however, I'll pursue the model of change that organizes my argument about the emergence of Enlightenment thought in a direction whose focus is the category of sex as such.

Sex and Sex Consciousness

Although classes may have always existed, class consciousness emerged only in the Enlightenment. This may be a moderately surprising proposal; but it's not counterintuitive as the same proposal about sex is likely to be. Of course, human cultures have always been aware of sex. But the tacit category "sex" became explicit only during this period because it was then that sex, like class, was disembedded from the sociocultural, economic, and religious ground in which it traditionally had been a functional and purposive part.[27] The valorization of empirical knowledge, which gave nature a more sensible access and material foundation, encouraged the view that sex was natural and hence a thing in itself. The word "sex" was abstracted from its customary and particular reference to "the male sex" or "the female sex" and applied to the general category of "sex as such."[28] The relation between nature and nurture was traditionally a distinction for which the evidence of social determination coexisted with a belief in a species of natural social essence. For empirical epistemology nature and nurture became separate categories. The female capacity of childbirth was traditionally construed as the enabling condition for kinship and collectivity rather than as a marker of sexual difference and identity. "Identity" has only a notional application in traditional thought because the self was a fluid entity, variously constituted by kinship, age, social status, political clientage, legal standing, and religious affiliation. Until very recently (a stipulation I'll return to), modern selves have been accustomed to thinking of themselves as individuals defined first of all by the natural fact of sex. The physical capacity to bear children is the most important biological indicator of female identity, which is grounded in natural difference and, with male identity, provides the differential substratum for human personality. Traditional kinship ties, too, have a naturalizing force. But the authority of the natural in modern societies is of a different and far higher order, so much so that the natural and autonomous entity of "individual identity" renders the force of kinship ties between individuals relatively nugatory.

The Two-Sex Model?

In the seventeenth century, the traditional distinction between female and male work in the domestic economy was being hardened by capitalist production into a separation that fully justifies being called, in the modern locution, a "sexual division of labor." The foregoing evidence suggests that the form of modern patriarchy depends on the structural separation of the genders during the Enlightenment. Before "sex" was abstracted as a natural determinant, there was no general term for distinguishing between the sexes: the distinction between men and women was acknowledged without positing their separability, their difference. For this reason, Thomas Laqueur calls this traditional regime one of "gender" because "what we would take to be a cultural category, was primary or 'real.'"[29] The wit of this usage lies in the fact that it has both a familiar and an unlooked-for application. On the one hand, in modern thought "gender" names the social determination that subtly marks the dominance of apparently natural sexual identity. On the other, in traditional thought "gender" can name an all-inclusive and tacitly social realm that's unmarked by explicit sexual analysis and indicators. To hypothesize: the emergence of modern patriarchy is coextensive with the emergence of gender difference, whereby the genders took on the specific and dyadic character that's familiar to us in the modern world.

For the past three decades, the history of sexuality has been invigorated by the controversy engendered by Laqueur's brilliant and persuasively argued thesis that until the eighteenth century, the model of what he calls the "one-sex body" dominated thinking on gender relations. In the one-sex model, genital anatomy was differentiated, but not separated, along a hierarchical continuum that reflected the superiority of men and the inferiority of women. By this way of thinking, women have less bodily heat than men do, and women's sex organs are therefore morphologically underdeveloped, an inverted and internalized version of men's. Laqueur maintained that over the course of the seventeenth and eighteenth centuries, this traditional one-sex model of anatomy was incompletely challenged and replaced by the modern two-sex model, according to which the difference between men and women is not a matter of distinction along a common gradient but a radical separation based on fundamental physiological differences. Women are not an underdeveloped and inferior version of men; they are biologically and naturally different from them—not just the "other" but the "opposite" sex.

The thesis of an Enlightenment shift from a one-sex to a two-sex model of thought has an obvious resonance for the overarching model of historical change—from tacit distinction to explicit separation—that guides my argument in this study. From a whole differentiated by degrees there emerges, toward the end of the seventeenth century, the explicit imperative to partialize and separate differences of kind. It is a change from a system in which the tacitly acknowledged difference between men and women was experienced as inseparably interwoven with sociocultural factors to one in which the difference between men and women is understood as what renders the system systematic. I encountered this thesis years ago as my studies were leading me to find a similar pattern in other areas of Enlightenment thought, and it contributed to my growing sense that the analogy between these particular developments suggested a basis for generalizing about the significance of the Enlightenment in the transition from tradition to modernity. Later I was to see that it was over the course of the Enlightenment that this method of generalizing from particulars came into its own, along with the corollary that the legitimation of the general requires its regulation and adjustment based on the ongoing assessment of particulars. Laqueur's thesis was a case in point. A truly generative hypothesis, the one-sex/two-sex model, uncommonly compelling in its explanatory force for the overarching history of Western attitudes toward sex, was quickly taken up and submitted to empirical analysis by specialists in the particular periods and cultures it assembled.

As a result, the hypothesis has been modified in a number of respects. Most important, scholars have found that both models were articulated over the centuries that precede modernity, and this militates against the view that the eighteenth century was singular in propounding a two-sex model, and therefore in representing a definitive watershed from the one-sex to the two sex model.[30] What this suggests is that the evidence I'd taken to affirm the difference between the eighteenth-century experience and that of earlier periods is insufficient: that despite its correspondence to my model of an Enlightenment turn from the tacit to the explicit, the watershed thesis is, by the Enlightenment's own epistemological standards, too simple to be probable. However, it's worth considering the evidence that does exist. If the Enlightenment isn't the first period in which the two-sex model was entertained, is it the period that inaugurates the unprecedented dominance of a single model—the two-sex model—as witnessed by the nineteenth-century rise and longevity of separate spheres? By giving "nature" its modern meaning, the seventeenth-century revolution in empirical epistemology gave "sex" its modern meaning as a biological difference evinced by an empirically grounded morphological difference, one reflected in the two-sex but not in the one-sex model. Again, historical revision has shown that the concept of "natural" difference, and thereby the two-sex model, pre-existed this revolution, and so the two models variously coexisted in traditional cultures. Only now, however, did the idea of empirical difference gain the definitive force to ensure the uninterrupted persistence of the two-sex model that characterizes modern thinking.

But modern thinking is currently in flux. For the first time in the modern world, the biological determinacy of sex has for a great number of people become explicitly dubious rather than what goes without saying. The recent development of "sex reassignment" or "gender affirmation" surgery has challenged the notion that biological difference is natural and unalterable destiny. In fact, the contrasting use of these terms for the same operation succinctly reflects the significance of this transitional moment. I'll describe below how quickly the biologized notion of sex that emerged in the Enlightenment led some to question its absolute determinacy. Two centuries later and in the spirit of this same question, the term "gender" emerged (as I've said) to designate what seems biologically "sexual" but is contingent and socially determined. This is the connotation of "gender" in the current language of gender affirmation, a category that can be recognized and affirmed by de-emphasizing one's determined sexual nature. By contrast, the language of sex reassignment accepts that determination. Surgical intervention is then the most radical method, dictated by the prior recognition of either one's gender identity or one's sexual identity, of affecting the contingent or the determined nature of one's sexed body.

The Three-Gender System: Conflation I

The knowledge of where this skepticism about the force of the natural may take us lies in the future. To return to my present argument and to summarize thus far: the general hypothesis that the two-sex model emerged in the Enlightenment has been particularized, and thereby modified, by evidence of its pre-Enlightenment articulation. However, the significance of the Enlightenment version is that unlike earlier articulations it models gender difference in empirical terms as a function of sex difference, and therefore as grounded in nature with a fixity more secure and perdurable than before. Moreover an additional factor substantiates the status of this moment in the history of sexuality as a true watershed. Foucault located in the later nineteenth century the transition from "sodomy," defined as a category of behavior, to "homosexuality," defined as a category of persons.[31] However, Randolph Trumbach has shown that in England and much of Europe, "the change came around the turn of the eighteenth century" with the emergence of what he has called the third gender, the male effeminate sodomite, and with the origins of "a heterosexual majority and a homosexual minority." Although these terms are a later invention, "the behavioral patterns they described came into existence among men in the first generation of the eighteenth century" in the form of two genders: "the exclusive male heterosexual majority" and the male homosexual minority of the effeminate sodomite.[32] Trumbach's point is that the modern institution of gender opposition warrants the modern name "heterosexuality" as earlier versions of gender difference do not, and that what makes it different is the catalyst of "homosexuality"—that is, of effeminate sodomites, men who were like women.

In the old regime, sodomy was condemned as a detested activity even though temporarily indulged by a variety of men. In the new regime, the sodomite was condemned as a different sort of person and sodomy as coextensive with an evil mode of being and incompatible with masculine identity. By tradition, acceptably masculine behavior had entailed sexual relations with both women and adolescent males. The heterosexual role for men became solidified in the assumption that most men desired women, and that all masculine identity flowed from that desire. From the former whole of male sexuality were separated out two autonomous and dichotomous parts. Men no longer had sex with both boys and women; they had sex either with females or with males. To put this another way, an age-structured system of "sodomy" had moved in the direction of a gender-structured system of "homosexuality."[33]

Trumbach suggests that the exclusivity of the new heterosexuality created for most men a much greater intimacy with women, which in turn "could threaten the continuing male desire to establish domination." The third gender role "played its necessary part in the new relations between men and women . . . since it guaranteed that, however far equality between men and women might go, men would never become like women since they would never desire men."[34] In this view, the crucial part played by the third gender role follows from Trumbach's attribution to heterosexual men of a set of motives that, plausible in themselves, in my view need closer exposition and articulation to justify finding in them the explanation for so fundamental a phenomenon. However, what's crucial to Trumbach's suggestion is a broader structural framework whose explanatory force doesn't depend on the specific attribution of motive. To adopt the terms of the present study, we might say that it is only through the emergence of the new gender role that the two tacit genders became explicit as the normative choice of difference made intelligible by the alternative and negative choice of sameness. But "choice" may be the wrong word. The new exclusive heterosexuality owed its normativity to the fact that the three-gender system was established at the same moment that the two-gender model was gaining the unprecedented stability of being grounded in the naturalness of sexual difference. By this measure, effeminate sodomy was manifestly unnatural because it conflated the sexed male body with female behavior.[35]

Trumbach's research reinforces the standing of the Enlightenment as a watershed by virtue of the evidence he adduces that the modern system of three genders appeared at this moment. Moreover, it accords with my broad model of historical change in positing not only the separation of genders, or parts that had been distinguishable but not separable in the whole of tradition, but also their simultaneous conflation in the new category of the effeminate sodomite. This is the pattern that, I've argued, is characteristic of Enlightenment innovation. Only when the parts of a tacit whole are separated out sufficiently to be recognized as such can they be brought together with a self-consciousness that distinguishes the modern from the traditional conceptualization of categories. However, this conflation differs from others I've documented. In others, conflation is achieved on the very grounds of the separation that has constituted the two categories, and thereby through the dialectical discovery of a positive reciprocity between them. Here conflation is achieved through the creation of a negative category that stands apart from the two categories and represents their nonreciprocity. The difference is so striking as to suggest that the creation of the category of the effeminate sodomite is not a conflation but a failure to achieve conflation, and although the result of a very different development bears comparison to the anti-Enlightenment brutality of (Enlightenment) slavery. This lays the foundation for what comes to be called "homosexuality," and for the brutality of homophobia that stains much of modern culture.

The unnaturalness of effeminate sodomites marked them and made them conspicuous. In the early eighteenth century they acquired the nickname "mollies," and "molly-houses" became a topic of fascinated description as the most evident sign of an emergent London subculture. Alan Bray has remarked on its coalescence in public sphere consciousness as a visible social phenomenon distinguished paradoxically by its social separateness. "It was not mediated by existing social forms, of class or otherwise: it was set alongside them, a social institution in its own right [with] its own distinctive conventions: ways of dressing, of talking, distinctive gestures and distinctive acts with an understood meaning, its own jargon."[36] The palpability of the molly emergence, the coalescence of an alien culture both within and apart from the familiar London world, is suggested by a Restoration poem that traces the physical movements of the sexually ambiguous fop:

> Now wait on *Beau* to his *Alsatia*,
> A Place that loves no *Dei Gratia*;
> Where the Undoers live, and Undone,
> In *London*, separate from *London*;
> Where go but Three Yards from the street,
> And you with a new Language meet:
> *Prig, Prigster, Bubble, Caravan,*
> *Pure Tackle, Buttock, Purest Pure.*[37]

The molly subculture constituted itself as a singular social entity within a host culture whose intensified legal reprisals and public persecutions bespoke an increased recognizability that augured for traditional sodomy the far more explicit notoriety of homosexuality.

Gender as Culture: Conflation II

Like the two-sex model, the three-gender system conceives heterosexual gender as defined by the natural or biological sex of the male and female bodies. The third gender, although grounded in the male body, is unnatural by virtue of being a conflation of two different genders, yet also partakes, inevitably and ambiguously, of natural bodiliness. This understanding of "gender" as sexual nature is complicated by the fact that in modern usage, "gender" also has another meaning, which has undergone its own development. Well before the modern period, the word "gender" distinguished grammatically between "masculine" and "feminine" inflections without reference to male and female sexual difference, a usage that continues in modernity. In recent years, the grammatical meaning of gender was extended to include a sexual meaning—or more accurately, a gender meaning. That is, "masculine" and "feminine" are now commonly used to designate gendered or socialized difference as distinct from the sexual difference of male and female. This usage, and the insight it expresses, may also appear to be recent. But as might be expected given the historical logic I've been documenting, we first see it at the same time that gender as sexual nature emerges during the Enlightenment.

To recapitulate: earlier in this chapter I used "gender" to designate the traditional, pervasive, and unmarked condition of the whole. With the coming of sex and the modern system of sexuality—of sex and gender difference—"gender" is sometimes separated out from "sex" and made to stand for the countervailing force of sociocultural determination over against the biological naturalness of sex. In this usage it's as though gender, traditionally the suffusive, sociocultural medium of the distinction between men and women, now coheres and returns as "gender," defined over against nature as the substantial entity "society" and its punctual and concrete role in social determination.

The modern dominance of the natural both authorizes this exception to its sway and confoundingly militates against it. In the last several decades, the word "gender" has come to be used in contexts where the meaning is clearly sexual difference and not gender difference (in the sense of identity preference)—male versus female rather than masculine versus feminine—for example, in official forms that request basic personal information: name, date of birth, ethnicity, nationality, "gender." How can we account for this solecism? On the one hand, is "gender" being used as a polite euphemism for "sex"? Or on the other, is "gender" used strategically to subtly acknowledge the element of social determination in sexual categories? Both supposed reasons are implausibly naïve: the first in its basic disregard for what language means, the second in its presumption about how far language might be construed. However, what makes this late modern solecism interesting is its correspondence, although as its mirror image, to a phenomenon in the Enlightenment moment when the modern regime of the natural was only in formation. The late modern solecism issues from centuries of sophisticated experiment in conflating culture and nature. For those who first experienced the modern biologization of sex the challenge was how to discover a realm of freedom within the newly constraining bonds of the natural. The periodical papers of Richard Steele and Joseph Addison, indefatigably curious about everything including what we mean by male and female, are filled with manifold speculations on this topic. And on occasion we see them struggling to conceive what the limits of the incipient standard of the natural might be. What would it mean for women to be the "opposite" sex? How absolutely are our natures determined by the imperatives of nature?

In one of his papers Addison gamely affirms the naturalness of sexual difference, whether its cause is physiological or mental. But he also suggests that the power nature has over us may be mitigated by our consciousness of it:

> Women in their Nature are much more gay and joyous than Men; whether it be that their Blood is more refined, their Fibres more delicate, and their animal Spirits more light and volatile; or whether, as some have imagined, there may not be a kind of Sex in the very Soul I shall not pretend to determine. As Vivacity is the Gift of Women, Gravity is that of Men. They should each of them therefore keep a Watch over the particular Bias [sic] which Nature has fixed in their Minds, that it may not draw too much, and lead them out of the Paths of Reason.

Addison's figure gives sexual nature the power to skew the mind's direction out of what for lack of a better word he calls the straight path of reason. Being natural, this bias cannot be removed; but an awareness—"keeping a watch" on it—may keep it from too skewed a slant. The path we find ourselves following, he adds, "is not to be taken so strictly, . . . but only to set forth what seems to have been the general Intention of Nature."[38]

Steele, too, suggests that sexual identity is natural by writing that there is a sex in souls. But if there's a necessity in nature's dictates, we must be willing to excuse at least some of what can't be avoided. Affirming that "the Soul of a Man and that of a Woman are made very unlike, according to the Employments for which they are designed," he declares that "the Virtues have respectively a Masculine and a Feminine Cast." "But to make this State any Thing but a Burthen, and not hang a Weight upon our very Beings," men and women should realize that "there are many, many Things which grow out of their very Natures, that are pardonable."[39] What's striking in both men is that they see in natural dispensation not a positive and normative force but the danger of a determination so strong as to compel us to make the best of what we have not chosen. So, both seek ways to console their readers that nature is not all-powerful. It seems almost as though our sexual being, because it's rooted in nature, risks feeling unnatural, like an alien force that may take us away from ourselves and the self-evidence of what goes without saying.

This is the backward-looking response of commentators who are trying to make sense of what's new. But the emergent perspective, with which we are likely to be more familiar, was not slow in coming. What it demonstrates, as well as anything, is the Enlightenment capacity to recognize that the separation of categories traditionally no more than distinguishable (here, nature and culture, "sex" and gender) presents an opportunity to conflate them experimentally with a self-conscious intelligence unavailable to those predecessors for whom they were distinct parts of a greater whole. In 1723, Bernard Mandeville, a transplanted Dutchman whose genius suggests the indebtedness of the English to the Dutch Enlightenment, unmasks as an acculturation the apparent naturalness of female modesty (incidentally making explicit the connection between grammatical and sexual gender):

> The Lessons of [modesty], like those of *Grammar*, are taught us long before we have occasion for, or understand the Usefulness of them. . . . A Girl who is modestly educated, may, before she is two Years old, begin to observe how careful the Women, she converses with, are of covering themselves before Men; and the same caution being inculcated to her by Precept, as well as Example, it is very probable that at Six she'll be ashamed of shewing her Leg, without knowing any Reason why such an Act is blameable, or what the Tendency of it is.
>
> . . . .
>
> This strict Reservedness is to be comply'd with by all young Women, especially Virgins, if they value the Esteem of the polite and knowing World; Men may take greater Liberty, because in them the Appetite is more violent and ungovernable. Had equal Harshness of Discipline been imposed upon both, neither of them could have made the first Advances, and Propagation must have stood still among all the Fashionable People: which being far from the Politician's Aim, it was advisable to ease and indulge the Sex that suffer'd

> most by the Severity, and make the Rules abate of their Rigour, where the Passion was the strongest, and the Burthen of a strict Restraint would have been the most intolerable.
>
> . . . .
>
> The Multitude will hardly believe the excessive Force of Education, and in the difference of Modesty between Men and Women ascribe that to Nature, which is altogether owing to early Instruction. . . . It is Shame and Education that contains the Seeds of all Politeness.[40]

In Mandeville's argument, the developing notion of a naturally based difference between male and female sexual appetites provides the necessary foundation for the brilliant analysis of the gendered—that is, the acculturated—quality of behavior and of the virtues with which it's associated. The brilliance of the analysis is characteristic of an age that may justly be seen as witnessing, as a punctual corollary of the birth of "society," the birth of the sociological imagination, which demystifies what appears given by recognizing it as, not natural, but social or cultural. What must be recognized as well is the flip side of this insight: its dependence, as here, on a functional given, without which the demystification lacks coherence. At the most abstract level, the Enlightenment critique of the natural depends on the fundamental principle of empirical epistemology, the insistence that knowledge requires the self-conscious detachment of the subject from its object of knowledge. In this way, the empiricist hypothesis of a radical separation of subject from object enacts its wholesale repudiation of tacit knowledge. The separation isolates what is known from the familiar and customary matrix of its intelligibility. But in the same gesture, it also preserves, apart from this analysis, the framework in which the tacit is repudiated: the relation of subject to object. We might see this as a tacit embrace of that framework as what goes without saying. Better, we might see it as a self-conscious embrace of the oppositional framework needed for dialectical method to produce knowledge.

The Dialectic of Sexuality and Class

I've already alluded to a relationship between the anti-hierarchical, "horizontal" systems of sexuality and class difference as they emerge in early modern England. On the one hand, a suggestive analogy can be felt between these two systems, although it's loose and resistant to precise application. On the other, the two systems are involved in a differential interaction in which each appears to undertake the cultural labor formerly performed by the other. (This is a formal or structural and not a substantive undertaking: the thesis of an emergence precludes a continuity between "former" and "present" instantiations). I will suggest here some features both of the analogy and of the differential interaction.

In separating out what were formerly held together, the modern system of sexuality both criticized the traditional correlation of sex and gender as what goes without saying and self-consciously sophisticated it as a normative ground for modern personality. The modern system of class also emerged from a former unity that conjoined what we would separate as "status" or "rank" with "class" criteria—the genealogical prescriptions of blood on the one hand and financial/professional activity on the other.[41] To state this differently, the status assumption that birth automatically dictates worth was replaced by a class conviction that birth and worth are independent variables. The standard of class explicitly criticizes the tacit location of personal value in the bloodline, demystifying aristocratic honor as an arbitrary social construction. Defoe ridiculed the notion that honor is biologically inherited, "as if there were some differing Species in the very Fluids of Nature . . . or some *Animalculae* of a differing and more vigorous kind."[42] "Nor should I speak a syllable against Honours being Hereditary," said William Sprigg on the eve of the Restoration, "could the valour, Religion, and prudence of Ancestors be as easily intail'd on a line or family, as their Honours and Riches. . . . Could they transmit their vertues as well as names unto their posterity, I should willingly become the Advocate of such a Nobility."[43] Against the prescription of aristocratic honor, the standard of class propounds the empirical criterion of socioeconomic behavior and the fluidity of social mobility. Defoe's indignant lines of 1700 contributed to this emergent standard:

> What is't to us, what Ancestors we had?
> If Good, what better? or what worse, if Bad?
> . . . .
> For Fame of Families is all a Cheat,
> '*Tis Personal Virtue only makes us great.*[44]

The qualitative criteria of status were, strictly speaking, relevant only to nobility and gentility, who were colloquially referred to as "quality." By the end of the century their normative role in social description had been supplanted by the quantitative criteria of class—as in Thomas Malthus's reference to the "higher," "middle," and "lower" classes.[45]

Now, it would be naive to say that status prescriptions were simply and irresistibly replaced by the class conviction that personal achievement takes precedence over family and blood. Here as elsewhere, differences in social status ensured that change would be uneven. Just as the sexual division of labor (and hence the establishment of domestic ideology) proceeded more slowly at the lower social ranks, so common people clung, with increasing tenacity, to the traditional criterion of customary rights and privileges in the face of capitalist rationalization and "improvement." In apparent paradox, the persistence of the customary was instrumental in grounding the emergence of a radical working-class consciousness.[46] The paradigmatic class of the future was therefore resistant, at first, to the differential terms of class conflict in which it would learn in time to conceive its own identity. And in the fabrication of working-class solidarity, "class identity" was commonly felt as a distinctively physical condition—a matter of complexion, kinship, and modes of speech and self-articulation—and to be experienced as something whose loss could only be felt as a radical denaturing.[47]

But the undeniable overlap between "class identity" and "sexual identity" or difference should not obscure their fundamental differences. In fact, the relation between the modern systems of sexuality and class may plausibly be seen as one of inversion rather than analogy. Sexual difference was not invented in the early modern period; it ceased then to be embedded in the other registers of social situation and became relatively autonomized through association with biological condition. So in this respect, the modern coemergence of sexuality and class depended on a corollary *separation* of the sexual from the social. As a result of this separation, sexual "identity" became more rigidly defined, at the same time that socioeconomic "identity," freed of its traditional subservience to biological criteria of blood, became more variable. The emergent class system programmatically encourages mobility within its overarching structure of oppositional conflict, whereas the emergent system of sexuality exists to enforce an innovative standard of differential stasis.

These changes are reflected in the history of attitudes toward the use of clothing as a social or sexual discriminant. English sumptuary legislation, which flourished from the fourteenth to the seventeenth centuries, is a surprisingly late development. Like the brief heyday of patriarchalist theory, sumptuary legislation signaled not the strength but the instability of a once-tacit aristocratic ideology that now required explicit reinforcement. Edward Waterhouse knew this when, in 1665, he observed that our ancestors distinguished between their social stations by their "Garb, Equipage, Dyet, Housholdstuff, Clothes, [and] Education of Children not by sumptuary Laws, or Magistratique sanction, but by common agreement, and general understanding."[48] By the early eighteenth century, a double revolution was underway. The demise of status-based sumptuary laws signaled the challenge to status by class criteria, whose more fluid conception of social difference spurned the crudity of legally stipulated physical signs. However, the impulse to enforce difference by dress did not disappear in the modern world. Sumptuary laws were replaced by less formal means of social regulation, by private polemic rather than public legislation. When Richard Steele created the role of literary "censor" for the *Tatler* in 1710, he remarked that "among all the Irregularities of which I have taken Notice, I know none so proper to be presented to the World by a Censor, as that of the general Expence and Affectation in equipage. I have lately hinted, that this Extravagance must necessarily get Footing where we have no Sumptuary Laws."[49] But although Steele's immediate concern here is with codes of social status, polemic of the sort he is encouraging increasingly concentrated on the use of dress to regulate and discriminate genders far more than social orders.[50] In this way, the evident analogy between sexual and class criteria can be seen in their mutual challenge to more traditional status criteria even as the fundamental inverse reciprocity between the two systems is also evident.

The Common Labor of Sexuality and Class

It may be useful now to revise my earlier remark by suggesting that we see the difference between men and women, and the difference between one class and another, as overlapping regimes that jointly render the modern system systematic. The notion here of a common labor may seem at first unlikely. I've just made the case against conjoining the two systems according to any simple analogy. Moreover, the general modern tendency toward division has ensured in any case that sexuality and class customarily be taken to cover the territory of the modern according to a strict division of labor. In one familiar and reflexive conceptualization, the split is gendered as a division between internal affect and external enterprise, between the private and the public spheres. It may be more valuable, however, to see the two systems as fundamentally united in their attention to the realm that modernity deems its central field of work, the realm of the material, and divided only in the way each construes the nature of that work. For the primary focus of the sexual system is of course on the material as the biological, and the primary focus of the class system is on the material as the economic; whereas their effective overlap takes place on the ground of the social, where the unalterability of biological difference, mollified by the solvent of gender analysis, meets the alterability of socioeconomic situation. In other words, the social is the realm where the labor of sexuality and class find their conflation.

Sodomy and Aristocracy

Recent research into sodomy trials and the social composition of the molly clubs has corrected a long-standing misapprehension, based on the prevalence of pederasty in Tudor and Stuart court patronage, that early modern sodomy was largely an affair of the nobility and gentry. Historians may perhaps be excused for this error, since it is widely reflected in the views of contemporaries themselves. Why should this have been so? To answer this question I'll pursue what I've called the "common labor" of sexuality and class into the territory where modern gender roles first begin to cohere in complex association with modern class categorization.

Under aristocratic patriarchy, the criterion of difference had the crucial but limited responsibility of ensuring the transmission of the patrimony through the male line, a responsibility that was fully consistent with same-sex behavior. Under modern patriarchy, the criterion of difference superintends sexual identity as such, proscribing same-sex behavior for all who would be deemed masculine. The last generation to conceive masculinity as permitting a relatively inclusive sexual behavior was dominated by the paradigmatically masculine figure of the aristocratic rake of the Restoration, personified most notably by the celebrated libertine John Wilmot, Earl of Rochester.[51] In one of his songs, Rochester acknowledges this inclusiveness with an elegant brutality that affords sexuality a telling social dimension:

> Love a Woman! Th'rt an Ass!
>   Tis a most insipid passion
> To Chuse out for thy Happiness
>   The dullest part of Gods Creation.
>
> Let the Porter and the Groom,
>   Things design'd for dirty slaves,
> Drudg in fair *Aurelias* womb
>   To gett supplies for Age and Graves.
>
> Farewell *Woman*—I entend
>   Henceforth every Night to sitt
> With my lewd well natur'd Freind
>   Drinking to engender wit.
>
> Then give me health, wealth, Mirth, and wine,
>   And if buizy Love intrenches
> There's a sweet, soft Page of mine
>   Can doe the Trick worth Forty wenches.[52]

In Rochester's misogynist valediction, different-sex behavior is figured as the grim manual labor of menial servants who work their women to produce offspring. Sodomy is, by contrast, a supremely careless *otium*, suitably accessory to the gentlemanly Horatian retreat whose central pleasure is to "engender" not serviceable "supplies" but insubstantial "wit."

During the next few decades, Rochester's correlation of sodomy and aristocracy persists under the aegis of an increasingly definitive critique. This process may be figured as a dissection of the cadaver of male aristocracy, a division of parts that no longer were felt to cohere in a single normative social type. (Needless to say, the death of aristocracy as a cultural norm was consistent with its continued vitality as a social group.) Birth and worth were now surgically sundered. On the one hand, personal worth was relocated in the common woman, the repository of a normative honor that had been alienated from an undeserving male aristocracy and that would be apotheosized in the domestic virtues of the modern heterosexual family. This relocation was signaled by the way "honor" became, over the course of the seventeenth century, a common term for designating female chastity in its moralized enlargement.[53] On the other, the degeneration of aristocratic genealogy—not birth, but sterility and corruption—was reembodied in the effeminate "unreproductive" sodomite. From the interstices of these two gender types, the feminine and the effeminate, would emerge the modern category of the masculine. And for a while, at least, both femininity and effeminacy made positive contributions to the definition of modern masculinity.[54]

These complex developments can be documented in the literature of the period. Contemporaries record that in 1694, the younger son of an impoverished family, Beau Wilson, suddenly appeared on the London scene with an equipage whose splendor rivaled those of the greatest noblemen in the nation.[55] In the years that followed, the mystery of Wilson's extraordinary social elevation, which had preoccupied contemporaries, was solved by two narratives in two strikingly different ways.

In 1707 there appeared Delarivier Manley's highly circumstantial account of a story told by an elderly gentlewoman who had been unjustly cast aside by a well-situated "She-Favorite" at court. The story concerns that same female courtier and her comparable ingratitude toward Beau Wilson. In Manley's account, the unnamed courtier finds Wilson destitute; falls in love with him; and vows to raise his fortune to the level of his merit on the condition of utter secrecy. But when Wilson's devotion urges him to make their love public, his courtier patroness arranges to have him murdered. Already becoming famous for romans à clef of ingratitude in high places, Manley solves the mystery of Wilson's upward mobility through a characteristic plot of commoner virtue seduced and destroyed by noble perfidy. The not-unprecedented gender reversal—making the elevated and corrupt seducer not a man but a woman—gives to the male victim an aura of feminine passivity and innocence.[56]

Sixteen years later the mystery remains the same, but its solution has altered considerably. Wilson retains the "feminine" role, but now supposedly authentic letters between the principals reveal that his seducer is an unidentified nobleman, who has introduced the commoner simultaneously to astonishing luxury and to sodomy. A modulation of epistolary form into a third-person narration permits the anonymous author an explicit critique of the nobleman for unnatural love and misogyny, corruptions that here fill the role played in Manley's heterosexual plot by ingratitude and perfidy. So, by means of this structural proximity to culturally familiar stories of aristocratic degeneracy, sodomy becomes closely associated with the corruptions of aristocracy. And as though mindful of the heterosexual plot model that provides the basis for this association, the author ends his narrative with the interpolated story of Cloris, a young woman impregnated by the nobleman and destroyed by his careless vanity even as the affair with Wilson is still active. Thus the nobleman's bisexuality only justifies the plot device by which sodomitical and heterosexual corruption work to reinforce each other. Meanwhile, however, and despite his own misogyny, the effeminate commoner Wilson is tacitly ennobled by his foil relationship to the feminine commoner Cloris.[57]

Among the many sources that fed the early modern critique of aristocratic culture, there are some that must have played a special role in promoting the conjunction of aristocracy and sodomy. The general population decline of the later seventeenth century reduced the number of male births sufficiently to create a crisis in the highly visible inheritance patterns of the nobility, fueling widespread apprehension of aristocratic sterility and the failure of noble lineages.[58] These same consequences could also be attributed to the moral and physical corruption of modern gentility. According to one tract, the corruption of gentle lineages results from several causes. First, "the *French Pox*," and the heterosexual debauchery by which it is spread, leaves bodies that "are so much enervated, . . . that they beget a most wretched, feeble, and sickly Offspring: We can attribute it to nothing else but this, that so many of our antient Families of Nobles are of late extinct." Second, the traditional, spartan regimen for educating quality has been replaced of late by a method that treats boys as though they were girls:

> The Boy, thus spoil'd, becomes *Company* for none but Women, and . . . when our young Gentleman arrives to Marriage; . . . what can be expected from such an enervated effeminate Animal? . . . what can we hope from so crazy a *Constitution*? But a feeble, unhealthy Infant, scarce worth the rearing . . . Thus, unfit to serve his King, his Country, or his Family, this Man of *Clouts* dwindles into nothing, and leaves a Race as effeminate as himself; who, unable to please the Women, chuse rather to run into unnatural Vices one with another, than to attempt what they are but too sensible they cannot perform.[59]

By this account, the corruption of nobility is the generation of sodomy.[60] In the logical extension of the patrilineal contempt for women as the mere conduit of male value, women drop out of the circuit altogether. What remains is the ironic apotheosis of an aristocratic dynasticism that has lost the very capacity to reproduce itself. But the connection between sodomy and the aristocracy was not always expressed in explicitly causal terms. The normative model of male aristocracy traditionally shared some of the' standard markers of femininity—not only a fine luxuriance of dress, but also a softness and whiteness of complexion. By the mid-eighteenth century, however, these traits were being derided with reference both to the effete aristocrat and (in an almost insensible extension) to the depraved sodomite. One tract that connects the "Pretty Gentleman" to the molly subculture also associates him with the effeminacy of a refined gentility. In this economical formulation, the "Pretty Gentleman" is distinct from "common men" in the sense of both status and gender difference: "Observe that fine Complexion! Examine that smooth, that Velvety Skin! View that *Pallor* which spreads itself over his Countenance! Hark, with what a feminine Softness his Accents steal their Way through his half-opened Lips! Feel that soft Palm! . . . *The Pretty Gentleman* is certainly formed in a different Mould from that of Common Men, and tempered with a purer Flame. The whole System is of a finer Turn, and superior Accuracy of Fabric, insomuch that it looks as if Nature had been in doubt, to which Sex she should assign *Him*."[61] Here the ironic tone encourages us to see the molly as a parodic burlesque of the aristocrat. In another tract, the link between status and gender anomaly is so strongly felt that it entails an inversion whereby dressing like a woman runs the paradoxical risk of being mistaken for a commoner: "I am confident no Age can produce any Thing so preposterous as the present Dress of those Gentlemen who call themselves pretty Fellows: their Head-Dress especially, which wants nothing but a Suit of Pinners to make them down-right Women. . . . And yet with all this, the present Garb of our young Gentlemen is most mean and unbecoming. 'Tis a Difficulty to know a Gentleman from a Footman, by their present Habits."[62] We find ourselves here in the midst of the social transition of which I have already spoken, the transition from the polemical regulation of social orders to that of gender difference. It is in these years that flamboyant male dress is being proscribed in favor of less "effeminate" clothing.[63] In this particular passage, an increasingly antiquated status anxiety still has enough force to nourish a growing anxiety about gender, but the organizing dread of the upstart masquerading as quality has been overbalanced by dismay at the spectacle of quality caught in an involuntary devolution.

What is the social logic that informs the conjunction of sodomy and aristocracy during this period? Sodomy and aristocracy may be said to have analogous positions in the respective emergent systems of sexuality and class. On the one hand, a new standard of gender difference was achieved in part through the separation out of the limiting negative case for masculinity. On the other, the establishment of a new standard of social description was achieved in part through the critique of a corrupt and outmoded aristocracy. What aristocracy and sodomy shared was an increasingly anomalous status within their respective systems; or rather, what they shared was the function of establishing the regularity of those systems by the fact of their own anomaly.

Aristocracy was anomalous because it was a vestige of an increasingly obsolete status hierarchy—by definition not a class but an order—and it persisted into modernity like the relict of another world. Of course, these are not the formulations of contemporaries. But in their preoccupation with the enervation, the degeneracy, and the corruption of the nobility contemporaries addressed the crucially *historical* nature of the anomaly, which defined by its incipient anachronism the contrastive currency of class conflict. The proto-homosexuality of sodomy, on the other hand, functioned within the system of sexuality as a *structural* anomaly, bestowing on the difference between masculinity and femininity a normative coherence achieved through a mediating term that was at once both and neither.[64]

Types of Masculinity

During the first half of the Enlightenment, effeminacy was still sufficiently detachable from sodomy to play a positive role—in part, at least, as an allusive marker of cultural gentility—in the experimental construction of masculine norms. In several early papers of the *Tatler*, Steele and his correspondents provide a remarkable instance of this sort of experimental and characteristically Enlightenment undertaking, a minute and searching analysis of the "distinct Classes" of men encountered at the London coffee houses. One of the striking features of this proto-sociological survey is the degree to which its focus is concentrated strictly on gender characteristics—to the exclusion, for example, of professional and status discriminants. This is achieved by characterizing the several male types largely according to their disparate relations to women. In other words, it's as though the general rule of patriarchy, by which women are defined in terms of their relation to the father and the husband, at this particular moment takes on a certain gender reciprocity.

The survey begins in the impulse to distinguish the "Gentleman" from the "Pretty Fellow," and to subdivide the latter class into the "Coxcomb" and the "Fop." However, subsequent efforts to substantiate and articulate the general category "Pretty Fellow" only produce separate instances that require their own distinct categories: the "very Pretty Fellow" (also designated the "Woman's Man"); the "Smart Fellow" (whose sexual aggression and frequent recourse to the sword link him to the "Rake"); and "effeminate" "Persons of the Epicene Gender," who never receive a categorial label but seem clearly to be mollies. What the survey provides is therefore less an orderly taxonomy than a fluid continuum of male gender types principally distinguished—with a delicate self-irony but also with painstaking care—by details in the extravagance of their dress and in the extremity of their ingratiation with women. In one sense, of course, order has already been imposed: although sexual preference is by and large explicit, none of these types is evidently bisexual. Yet their subtle multiplicity, the plasticity of the range in which they are discriminated, most of all the way the male ingratiation with the female is used to distinguish a range of acceptable types of masculinity—all these bespeak a comparatively open-ended investigation of what soon will begin to close down. By the middle of the eighteenth century, the "Pretty Fellow," the "Pretty Gentleman," and the "Fop" are uncompromisingly denigrated in association with the sodomite.[65]

So, effeminacy made a surprisingly positive (if temporary) contribution to the early modern experimentation with masculinity. We are more familiar with the parallel role of femininity in this experiment—although recent work sometimes exaggerates the coherence and stability of early modern femininity itself.[66] Inner virtue, the great alternative both to corrupt aristocratic honor and to corrupt Roman Catholic hierarchy, was at first gender-neutral, and throughout the seventeenth century it was as likely to be associated with progressive male as with progressive female capacity.[67] Only by the middle of the eighteenth century was inner virtue becoming established as a peculiarly feminine trait, increasingly to be associated with the reformative powers of domesticity. But the coalescence of domestic ideology was greatly complicated by, among other things, the institutionalization of female authorship. If the message of much eighteenth-century women's writing was domesticating in its general import, the evident fact of women writing for publication and profit strikingly undercut that message. Still, the notion of female domestic virtue was sufficiently established by midcentury to provide, for the equally unstable category of masculinity, an ambivalently feminine ballast. The logic of this influence is clear enough. The idea of female virtue—the radical internalization of male honor—may be understood as one consequence of early modern cultural efforts to replace aristocratic notions of value. And it's not surprising that projects to establish normative masculine roles should have poached on feminine virtue even as they sought to establish a differential masculine standard of value. From this perspective, Richardson's impersonation of the virtuous Pamela Andrews and Fielding's characterization of the feminized Joseph Andrews are two sides of the same coin.

The type of the sentimental man in the early decades of the eighteenth century lent to the ungendered industrious virtue of Protestant descent a subtly feminine receptivity, and he pointed ahead to the cult of sensibility at midcentury. One facet of aristocratic ideology had been its claim that inner virtue was visibly manifested in the external phenomena of rank, regalia, personal display, even complexion. In its preoccupation with the blush, the tear, and the involuntary somatic signs of deep feeling, the cult of sensibility attempted to reinvent this notion of the body as a system of socioethical signification in terms of a biological materialism that would evade the ideology of aristocratic privilege. Crucial to this effort was the conception of feminine virtue as internalized honor. Yet the notion of the woman of feeling never attained any currency.[68] And the significance of the sensible Man of Feeling may be that, as a fully feminized hero, he strategically reclaimed a now recognizably *feminine* model of virtue as a distinctively *male* possession, reincorporating the newly normative *gender* traits within what a patriarchal culture persisted in seeing as the normative *sex*.

One reason the cult of sensibility was short-lived is because masculinity was elaborating successfully its own mode of "public virtue," alternative but complementary to the private domestic virtue of women. The solidification of this masculine ideal was inhibited by the influence of misogynist models of femininity. Modern male notions of value, for example, might seem on the face of it quite compatible with the anti-aristocratic heroism of the new economic man. But the extreme instance of economic value was exchange value, whose suspect insubstantiality could be associated with traits of imaginative fantasy, passion, and hysteria figured as female.[69] In his London journal of 1762–1763, the young James Boswell overcomes this problem with disturbing ingenuity. Boswell's journal enacts his coming of age as a vacillation between alternative career choices that are also masculine stereotypes—the dour Scots lawyer, the character of a gentleman, the character of a soldier, the "man of consequence," the "man of pleasure," the "man of economy." Boswell's tentative embrace of the latter role coincides with a crisis in his relationship with the actress Louisa, whom he has until now been pleased to consider a potential wife. The two plots are quite distinct; yet their momentary narrative entanglement suggests that Boswell exploits one to facilitate the other. A youth of uncommon spirit and fancy, Boswell is in the painful process of detaching from his severe aristocratic father's wish that he return to Scotland and extend the patriline. To stay in London and become a man of economy is an exhilarating alternative that he nonetheless frames in the symbolic terms of his dilemma. On the one hand it represents the sobriety and balance of careful "calculation," "management," and "prudent attention." On the other, the essence of this choice is the "sheer love of coin." He is "very fond of money": "making money is one of the greatest pleasures in life, as it is very lasting and is continually increasing." Yet "when we consider what one gains, it is merely imaginary." Earlier, when his relation with Louisa is consummated, Boswell's "lively imagination" recalls his other "conquests" and he styles himself a "Man of Pleasure." Yet he also imagines what seems a discordant pleasure: "I really conducted this affair with a manliness and prudence that pleased me very much. The whole expense was just eighteen shillings." When soon after Louisa modestly accepts his offer of a loan Boswell takes this as a sign that she's an avaricious whore. And the later passage on the man of economy coincides in the journal with Louisa's dignified return of the loan. Boswell feels at this "a strange kind of mixed confusion" that echoes the dilemma of his choice in life: the difficulty of reconciling prudence and pleasure, wife and whore, the purposive management of money and the imagination of money as an end in itself. Boswell displaces onto the woman all that's distressing about economy, securing for the man of economy a positive "manliness," at least to his temporary satisfaction, by detoxifying it of its feminine negativity.[70]

Boswell achieves through elaborate rationalization what his culture was to establish as a commonplace: the public virtue of economic man. There is no doubt a real danger in exaggerating the rigidity and circumscription of modern gender roles—and institutions. If the modern family came to be conceived as the living heart of private human feeling and the citadel of authenticity against worldly encroachment and corruption, it served thereby the needs of economic man quite as fully as it did those of domestic woman. But it may be fair to say that in the nineteenth century, the idea of the masculine would accommodate itself more successfully to the normative figure of the Public Man, defined by his economic activity, his occupational status, and his heterosexuality.

5 Biography, Fiction, Personal Identity

The title of this chapter consists of categories that might seem to be basic to human experience and therefore to have had a traditional existence. My aim will be to show their family resemblance to other branches of Enlightenment thought, and to document their emergence during the Enlightenment period.

Biography, Fiction, and the Common

Like their predecessors, early modern historians made ample use of concrete examples to teach abstract precept, a rhetoric of exemplarity that moves from the local instance to the general application. In traditional use, this rhetoric is persuasive because its examples are taken not from the realms of the local and the lowly but from the public precincts of greatness: only the lives of illustrious men and women can teach a pattern of virtue. By the same token, the distinction between historical and biographical writing, although traditionally understood as one between a regard for the public and for the private life, nonetheless took for granted that the exemplars even of private life would be great men, figures of public importance.

In the Enlightenment, however, biographical exemplarity underwent a revolution in which the illustrious was challenged by the private or common example. At midcentury Samuel Johnson wrote that "the business of the biographer is often to pass slightly over those performances and incidents, which produce vulgar greatness, to lead the thoughts into domestick privacies, and display the minute details of daily life, where exterior appendages are cast aside, and men excel each other only by prudence and virtue." The formulation recalls the experimental method of separating variables from the constants of nature. Johnson justifies this focus on the domestic because he believes that moral precepts are most reliably learned from the ethical examples of specifically private life: "The good or ill success of battles and embassies extends itself to a very small part of domestick life: we all have good and evil, which we feel more sensibly than our petty part of publick miscarriage or prosperity."[1] Contemporaries seconded Johnson's assessment of the business of the biographer. According to Oliver Goldsmith, "The relations of great events may surprise indeed; they may be calculated to instruct those very few, who govern the million beneath, but the generality of mankind find the most real improvement from relations which are leveled to the general surface of life; which tell, not how men learned to conquer, but how they endeavoured to live." And toward the end of the century John Bennett addressed "a young lady" on the topic of biography in similar terms: "Instead of wars, sieges, and victories or great atchievements, which are not so much within the province of a female, it presents those domestick anecdotes and events, which come more forcibly home to her bosom and curiosity." The language of interiority ("home to her bosom") strikingly discloses here the generality of human nature in the ultimate particularity of private sentiment. Another biographer writes that whatever people's outward differences, "yet follow them close, enter with them into their cabinets, or, which is still more, into their private thoughts, and the dark recesses of their minds, and they will be found pretty much on a level."[2]

What I have called a revolution in the rhetoric of exemplarity involves a revaluation of exemplary particularity from a means to the end of preceptual generality to an end in itself—that is, to an exemplification of the general in the sense not of qualitative greatness but of quantitative representativeness and inclusion. The most obvious cause of this revolution was the early modern decay of status hierarchy, a long-term process that challenged on several fronts the tacit coextension of lineage and virtue, birth and worth.[3] Personhood was disembedded from social practice, moral being became detachable from social rank, and the categories of birth and worth were explicitly reconceived as distinct, respectively "external" and "internal," manifestations of what traditionally had seemed a multiform but integral whole.[4] As Bennett's language reminds us, the consequent valorization of interiority had profound implications for ideas of gender difference; it also was deeply rooted in Protestant doctrine. Of course Christianity as such was founded on the paradox, exemplified by the life of Christ, that spiritual elevation was to be discovered among the lowly. Although this pattern was reflected often enough in Roman Catholic lives of the saints, in his *Book of Martyrs* (1563, 1570) John Foxe overlaid Roman Catholic absolutism with the state absolutism of the Marian persecutions so as to throw the spiritual authority of the English saint into the high relief of sociopolitical subjection, which Foxe reinforced with a plenitude of humble and homely details. Moreover, Protestant soteriology itself argued a degree of private responsibility that was emphasized by the triumphantly parodic figure of an aristocracy not of "honour" but of "grace." Thus Alice Driver is a common woman who "was an honest poor man's daughter, never brought up in the university but I have driven the plough before my father many a time." And after his conversion, Roger Holland, formerly an apprentice, tells his persecutors that he has replaced "that liberty under your auricular confession, that I made no conscience of sin, but trusted to the priest's absolution" by the strenuous conscientiousness of discipline in the calling.[5] In the seventeenth century Foxe's work was extended by practitioners of "spiritual biography" like Samuel Clarke, who collected and published scores of puritan lives between 1650 and 1683. Clarke also augmented the association, already apparent in Foxe, of the spiritually sanctified social humility of the saint with the historical authenticity of his or her life story. As Richard Baxter writes in the preface to Clarke's last collection, "He did not make the Histories, but take them made by faithful acquaintance of the dead. . . . To have made Stories himself had been unworthy a Historian."[6]

Energized by Protestant doctrine, by the middle of the eighteenth century common and domestic examples were thought able to do the sort of epistemological work that formerly had seemed to require a pedagogic fulfilment in the realm of the public. Or to put this differently, the aim to teach ethico-epistemological precepts of a general nature was no longer thought to depend on using examples of sociopolitical greatness. In one of the passages just quoted, Johnson commends biography for preferring "domestick privacies" to "vulgar greatness" because the differences that owe to "exterior appendages" are there "cast aside" and we confront more directly the realm of the ethical—of "prudence" and "virtue"—that we all inhabit in common. And a few lines earlier Johnson makes clear that the ultimate end of biographical particularization is generalization: "There is such an uniformity in the state of man, considered apart from adventitious and separable decorations and disguises, that there is scarce any possibility of good or ill, but is common to human kind." Johnson's remarks are relevant to the question of when and how the modern sense of identity—of the "self," the "person," the "subject," the "individual"—came into being.[7] Does the self-conscious experience of Renaissance "self-fashioning" express, as has been widely argued, the modern idea of coherent and integral identity—even more, a destabilizing skepticism about this already conventional idea? By Johnson's way of thinking, selfhood appears to be entailed not in the performance of particular social roles but in the constancy and uniformity revealed by stripping them away—or rather, in the dialectic between external particularity and internal generality that constitutes the self as a singular instance of a common kind. Indeed, "the common" is a fruitful term in this emergent sense of the self because its semantic richness mediates between these two realms. On the one hand, the common refers to what is "common to humankind," what is uniform in human nature and general to us all. On the other, the common inheres in "domestick privacies" and "the minute details of daily life," through whose legible familiarity we can learn more about a man "by a short conversation with one of his servants" "than might be collected from publick papers."[8]

We would be wrong to see Johnson as arguing either that the private lives of commoners or the testimony of common servants offers a privileged exemplary means for sifting the general from the particular. And yet both points seem implicit—even more so in Johnson's essay about the new species of fiction, written in the same year, 1750, as his commentary on "the business of the biographer." Here Johnson contrasts the "fiction" that is popular with "the present generation," which "exhibits life in its true state, diversified only by accidents that daily happen in the real world," with the fiction of the past, which had easy recourse to giants, knights, and "imaginary castles." "In the romances formerly written, every transaction and sentiment was so remote from all that passes among men that the reader was in very little danger of making any application to himself," since their protagonists "had neither faults nor excellencies in common with himself." "But when an adventurer is leveled with the rest of the world, [he] acts in such scenes of the universal drama, as may be the lot of any other man." "The task of our present writers ... requires ... that experience which must arise from general converse, and accurate observation of the living world Other writings are safe, except from the malice of learning, but these are in danger from every common reader; as the slipper ill executed was censured by a shoemaker who happened to stop in his way at the Venus of Apelles." Johnson's momentarily confusing analogy would stress not the special knowledge of the artisan but on the contrary the authority of the average man. Like the common shoemaker, that is, the "common reader" has an epistemological advantage that bears some relation to his sociopolitical status, which is that of the lowest common denominator, one to whose place the rest of the world has been leveled.[9] Like the idea of the common, the language of leveling Johnson shares with Goldsmith ("relations which are leveled to the general surface of life") and the anonymous biographer ("they will all be found pretty much on a level") points in two directions. On the one hand, the leveled is common in the sense of being general; on the other, the leveled has a sociopolitical commonness that gains access to the general by virtue of its being that "part of the universal drama" which, stripped of all status distinction, is truly universal.

Biography, Fiction, and the Actual

So for Samuel Johnson, both modern biography and modern fiction appeal to their readers by featuring protagonists who are common in both senses of the term. Yet, in the common appeal of fiction Johnson finds a danger that receives no such emphasis in his treatment of biography: "But if the power of example is so great ... care ought to be taken that ... the best examples only should be exhibited. ... It is therefore not a sufficient vindication of a character, that it is drawn as it appears, for many characters ought never to be drawn." From a modern standpoint Johnson's distinction is unimpeachable. A branch of history, biography draws life "as it appears" in actuality; whereas in Johnson's words, "historical veracity has no place" in fiction. In fact the orthodoxy of this distinction, although as old as Aristotle, is a recent development in European culture. Until the Renaissance, history and romance were, epistemologically speaking, only ill-distinguished from each other. Their modern divergence, and the emergence of "fiction" in the modern, explicit sense of the term, were determined by a range of factors, but the most evident cause was the scientific revolution and the rise of empirical epistemology—at least in the long run. In the short run and until the middle of the eighteenth century, the authority of a naive empiricism was so general that it had the opposite effect and carried all before it.[10] We can see this in the seemingly contradictory tendency to empiricize even religious narrative: for example, Baxter's insistence on the historicity of Clarke's puritan biographies, which implicitly functions as a material guarantor of their spiritual authenticity. We also can see this tendency in the way religious "apparition narratives" like Defoe's famous story about the ghost of Mrs. Veal stake their truth value on elaborately circumstantial claims to historicity.[11] This sort of appeal to the evidence of the senses also played a central role in what with hindsight we may recognize as the naive precursor of novelistic "realism." Defoe's *Robinson Crusoe* (1719) and *Moll Flanders* (1722), Swift's *Gulliver's Travels* (1726), Eliza Haywood's *The Fair Hebrew* (1729), and Samuel Richardson's *Pamela* (1740), to name only the best-known authors, self-consciously present themselves as "historical" in the sense of being about events that actually occurred, and they are narrated, either in the first or the third person, so as to appear either autobiographical or biographical. As their titles suggest, these narratives also are about the private lives of common people, and to different degrees they adduce the accessibility of their characters as testimony to their pedagogic exemplarity.

Biography, Fiction, and the Virtual

The claim to historicity amounted to a radical denial of conventionality. Did it also deny fictionality? This question is difficult to answer. "Fiction" had always possessed a broad and various range of reference, including reference to what is humanly made or made up as distinguished from what is actual or factual. But the most common use of the term was descriptive, not analytic, and plays and stories, except those about known figures of the past, were tacitly understood to be fictional. In the seventeenth century, the unprecedented force of empirical epistemology obliged all branches of knowledge to explicitly justify their truth value according to an epistemologically critical standard. However, the dominant pejorative for literature's falsehood was not "fiction" but "romance." The claim to historicity was a naively ontological defense against the critique of "romance" by means of an unmediated, literalistic notion of history. The claim had a popular but short-lived career before it was replaced by a more nuanced conception of historical truth, and by a more sophisticated view of literary fiction, which later came to be called "realism."[12]

Richardson's second novel—indeed, the second edition of *Pamela*, published three months after the first—already had compromised the claim to historicity, and authors like Swift indulged it only with a patently satiric motive. Such a motive is obvious in the very title of Henry Fielding's first narrative, *Shamela* (1741). So if the claim to historicity was the first attempt to practice the emergent genre of the novel according to empiricist protocols that crudely conflated the novel with biography, parodies like Swift's and Fielding's rejected that practice no less ostentatiously. And in the year after *Shamela* was published, Fielding's formal critique of the claim to historicity modulated into what is recognizably an early version of the modern doctrine of realism, a technique that accommodated the new genre to the standards of empiricism, but strictly in its own terms. In the middle of *Joseph Andrews* (1742), Fielding reflects on this practice, strikingly enough using the word "biography"—according to the *OED* a neologism then less than sixty years old—to name the form he is writing. "I describe not Men but Manners," Fielding declares; "not an Individual, but a Species." "Notwithstanding the Preference which may be vulgarly given to the Authority of those Romance-Writers, who intitle their Books, the History of England, the History of France, of Spain, &c. it is most certain, that Truth is only to be found in the Works of those who celebrate the Lives of Great Men, and are commonly called Biographers, as the others should indeed be termed Topographers or Chorographers." According to Fielding, the latter two justly describe the place and time in which the persons they treat have their existence. "But as to the Actions and Characters of Men, their Writings are not quite so authentic"—which for Fielding pointedly means they get their "facts" wrong. "Now with us Biographers the Case is different, the Facts we deliver may be relied on, tho' we often mistake the Age and Country wherein they happened." "Perhaps it will be answered, Are not the Characters then taken from Life? To which I answer in the Affirmative; nay, I believe I might aver, that I have writ little more than I have seen. The Lawyer [in *Joseph Andrews*] is not only alive, but hath been so these 4000 Years." Whereas what is commonly called history is "confined to a particular Period of Time, and to a particular Nation; [biography] is the History of the World in general." In this way Fielding's "general" factuality, not limited to the "particular" details of time and place, lays claim to a different kind of historicity and factuality, which become available only when the exemplary truth of action and characters is abstracted from the obfuscating details of a strictly empirical or actual particularity.[13] Clearly this is not the modern meaning of "biography." But it is interesting that Fielding should have chosen that term to name the sort of narrative that, while historical, nonetheless is not slavishly tied to the actualities of time and place. And it is no accident that this dyad recalls the debate over the pseudo-Aristotelian dramatic "unities," since Fielding's amusingly pedantic rejection of "chorography" and "topography" is consistent with the tendency, at least in England, to debunk the unities of time and place as a "rule" that misconceives the psychology of aesthetic response by confusing it with crudely empiricist standards of cognition.[14]

In this generalization of actual particularity Fielding's purpose is not only epistemological but also ethical and pedagogic. He aims "not to expose one pitiful Wretch, to the small and contemptible Circle of his Acquaintance; but to hold the Glass to thousands in their Closets, that they may contemplate their Deformity, and endeavour to reduce it, and thus by suffering private Mortification may avoid public Shame. This places the Boundary between, and distinguishes the Satirist from the Libeller; for the former privately corrects the Fault for the Benefit of the Person, like a Parent; the latter publickly exposes the Person himself, as an Example to others, like an Executioner."[15] Fielding's discrimination between libel and satire participated in a general debate that flourished for a half century or so and that drew comment also from Dryden, Shadwell, Congreve, Addison, Steele, Defoe, Swift, Pope, and Haywood, among others. And although the superiority of satire to libel frequently was rationalized on an ethical basis, the terms of the debate were generated by the state's legal efforts to subject the libel of public figures to prosecution. The direct effect of these efforts was limited, since attacks on well-known figures continued; but the danger of legal prosecution may have contributed to the ethical and epistemological arguments for detaching exemplary teaching from the realm of actuality.[16]

But if naive empiricism and the threat of libel prosecution might be overcome by reconceiving factuality as general not particular, virtual not actual, how could this be compatible with the emergent sense of biographical and fictional exemplarity as possessing the down-to-earth concreteness of private and common example? In the doubleness of the common, we recall, the concreteness of the local and familiar example is instrumental in ensuring its generalizability. Over the course of the seventeenth century, the unprecedentedly normative force of empirical actuality had both re-empowered exemplary concreteness and mandated the idea that concreteness depends on empirical—that is, actual—particularity. But Fielding's "biography" and nonlibelous satire are able to generalize about the individual life beyond the temporal and spatial registers of actual particularity only because they possess the concreteness of characterization needed to ensure that generalization. The demise of the naive claim to historicity marked the separation of fiction from biography, but it thereby encouraged a deeper recognition of their similarity. The concrete particularity of the narrative subject, under the aegis of naive empiricism assumed to inhere in and depend on his or her historico-personal actuality, became available as a species of virtuality, modeled on the particularity of the empirical subject but detached from the requirement of actual existence. To contemporaries this had important pedagogical implications. Only within the general realm of the virtual, it came to appear, could the private transaction of ethical improvement be achieved. To remain in the realm of actual particularity is, on the contrary, to resign oneself to libel, to the public exposure of the private, sacrificing the private to the public instead of bringing the private into public discourse. More broadly, the separation of virtual from actual particularity aided in the emergent division between the "literary" and the "biographical-historical" by substituting for the actual particularity of the novelistic claim to historicity the concrete particularity of probabilistic "realism," permitting literature to be "personal" in the sense of privacy and the familiarity of the common without also being "personal" in the sense of actual reference. In the modern world, "fiction" continues to have a broad and various reference. But in application to literature and especially to narrative, "fiction" has the refined meaning of realism: possessing the concrete particularity of biography and history but not their actual particularity.

The Self behind Self-Fashioning

As the interplay of epistemological, ethical, and legal motives makes clear, this division between the literary and the historical was broadly overdetermined. Nor was it forced only by modernizing developments like empiricism and the proliferation of print. In 1698, the Jacobite nonjuror Jeremy Collier ignited a major cultural controversy over what he called "the profaneness and immorality of the English stage." As Collier's assault makes clear, the public exposure of the personal met ethical opposition regarding not only print but also dramatic performance, and not only on the grounds that it injured exposed individuals but also because even if the exposure had no actual referent and made no pretense to personal representation, it nonetheless publicized and disseminated vicious example. For a poet "to descend to Particulars, and fall to Characterizing," Collier wrote, "is no better than Libel, and Personal Abuse"; hence "all Characters of Immodesty (if there must be any such) should only be hinted in remote Language, and thrown off in Generals." This stipulation anticipates Samuel Johnson. But Collier's position was more extreme than this. He flatly asserted that "'tis the Poet that speaks in the Persons of the Stage," and when those are vicious, the poet's "private Sentiments fall under Censure." Collier's insistence that the characterization of an evil person is necessarily an evil characterization forced his antagonists to make explicit the protocols of interpretation that tacitly obtained under customary conditions of theatrical performance and publication. According to William Congreve, nothing should be "imputed to the Persuasions or private Sentiments of the Author, if at any time one of these vicious Characters in any of his Plays shall behave himself foolishly, or immorally in Word or Deed." Similarly, James Drake warned against confusing the poets' "private or real sense" with the "Sentiments, which they are obliged sometimes to furnish Villains and Extravagants with in conformity to their Characters."[17] Again, what is new here is not the capacity to make a tacit distinction between fictional character and biographical author but the explicit separation out of character from author, of projected or performed self from self as such. Collier's antagonists hypostasize for literary characters a distinct realm of virtuality. For Collier, however, characters are simple empirical extensions of actual particularity, of actual authors, hence authors and characters constitute a continuous and homogeneous personality.

From Elizabethan through Enlightenment culture, the figure of the theater exercises a fascination for English people, expressing an extraordinary, perhaps also an increasing, power in the ontological intuition that to be in the world is to "act" on the "stage" of the world. By metaphorizing life as art, the figure of theatrical performance, like that of self-fashioning, gives voice to the understanding that actual persons are creatures, whether by the Creator or by the internalization of sociocultural "role" not naturally given but artfully made. Early on, the stress in the figure falls not on the nature and agency of the making but on the fact of madeness. But the increasingly explicit and general application of the figure of the theater also increased explicit inquiry into the empirical nature of the agency it implied. The gradual replacement of "soul"- by "self"-terms over the span of this period is one measure of that increase, as are the growth of both secularization and the sociological imagination. Of more immediate relevance here, however, is the way questions of agency increasingly broach questions of "identity" that posit a quasi-"natural" self-anterior to the artificial self that has been made.

In the earlier period, the experience of role-playing derives from the experience of having played other and different roles on other occasions. In the later period, the experience of role-playing derives from the sense of difference between any given role and the constant and continuous identity that it and all roles momentarily displace. The singularity of self-identity presupposes a "naturalness" of selfhood, conceived as a statistical generalization, of which it is a singular instance. The modern category of the self is constituted by this relationship between the singular and the general. "There is such an uniformity in the state of man," Johnson writes, "considered apart from adventitious and separable decorations and disguises, that there is scarce any possibility of good or ill, but is common to human kind." Collier's insistence that "the poet speaks in the persons of the stage" articulates, in the ethical and epistemological continuity between author and character, an assumption more local than, but analogous to, the assumption that the performance or fashioning of the self is coextensive with the self. The dramatists' rebuttal separates out the agency of author and character on analogy with the separation Johnson will argue between general selfhood and singular self-identity. But to formulate this analogy is also to recognize one dimension of disanalogy. There is a fundamental difference between the way authorial agency fashions virtual characters and the way actual, empirical persons exist apart from all such fashioning.

From Secret History to Novel

A summary overview of the changing relationship between biography and fiction during this period is provided by the fortunes of what contemporaries called the secret history.[18] The idea of a secret history presupposes the idea of a manifest and official but necessarily partial version of things. In the midst of civil war the Leveller Richard Overton posed the rhetorical question, "If the King conquer, the Parliament will be Traytours to posterity by Cronicle; for who writ the Histories of the Anabaptists but their Enemies?"[19] The secret history is both a logical entailment of and a solution to the problem of the fact that history gets written by winners.[20] The phrase "secret history" itself became familiar to Anglophone culture through the 1674 English translation of *The Anecdota* of Procopius (c. CE 550), whose title means "unpublished things."[21] The Procopian precedent quickly provided a popular model for the disclosure of state secrets. The material prefatory to a Restoration translation from the French praises the author for having written "a sort of Cabinet, Historical Inquisition" that "has refin'd upon Procopius his Pattern." But the "Author's Preface" to this translation also makes clear the broader relevance of the secret history to the eighteenth-century turn of biography toward the private and the common:

> The Historian considers almost ever Men in Publick, whereas the Anecdotographer only examines 'em in private. Th' one thinks he has perform'd his duty, when he draws them such as they were in the Army, or in the tumult of Cities, and th' other endeavours by all means to get open their Closet-door; th' one sees them in Ceremony, and th' other in conversation; th' one fixes principally upon their Actions, and th' other wou'd be a Witness of their inward Life, and assist at the most private hours of their leisure: In a word,

> the one has barely Command and Authority for Object, and the other makes his Main of what occurs in Secret and in Solitude . . .
>
> Not but that the Writer of *Anekdota* draws a Picture of Persons, as exact, and as faithful, at the least, as can be done by the Historian; but he does it after his own Mode: He represents only as much of the Man's Out-side, as is necessary to know his Inside; and as the good and bad dispositions of the Mind, are only to be disclos'd in the Manners, 'tis also for the Manners that he reserves his liveliest Colours, and finest Materials. . . . I pretend likewise to relate with a serious Air, the smallest trifles, when they have been th' Origine or occasion of the greatest Matters.

In the words of the translator, "Irresolution and Passion prevail equally in the Great, as in the Vulgar. And often a little Cabinet-pique, or Bed-Chamber Quarrel, occasions a rumbling World, and is the source of the greatest Transactions."[22]

As these words suggest, the significance of the private and the trivial in secret histories is that they bear an illuminating motivational relationship to great and public happenings. But the allure of the secret history was also that it might entail a stealthy political allegory: read aright, what appears to be an exotic tale or history turns out to have present and public application. Indeed, this may be the implication of the decision to reissue the 1674 translation of Procopius in 1682, although too late to fan the flames of the Exclusion Crisis, as *The Debauch'd Court. Or, the Lives of the Emperor Justinian, and His Empress Theodora the Comedian*. In other words, the mode of secret history that's inspired by the translation of Procopius draws strength from, and dovetails with, the mode of the roman à clef that had flourished at least since the beginning of the seventeenth century, which signals its secrecy through allegorical, amatory "romance" plots that sanction techniques of close reading to uncover their deepest public meaning. (Sometimes keys to the actual identities of the romance characters were published soon after the roman itself.) That is, the substantive, motivational relationship between the trivial-private and the great-public that organizes the Procopian secret history is expressed, in the roman à clef, as a formal relationship of signification between the trivial romance plot we read and the great historical plot we take it to mean. Once the historical meaning of the romance plot has been disclosed, however, the resulting public scandal may be either high or low, either political or sexual—or both by turns, as the roman à clef allegorizes state politics through the "sexual politics" of amatory intrigue and erotic romance. Indeed, in a nation-state like England, where royal sovereignty depends on familial-dynastic inheritance, the metonymic contiguity of the political and the sexual guarantees that political secrets will be understood in terms of sexual secrets. But as patriarchalism—the customary and tacit analogy between the family and the state—becomes increasingly explicit, hence strained, over the course of the seventeenth century, the separation out of the family from the state exerts pressure on their traditional, additionally metaphoric, relation as well. Under this pressure, the sexuality of political dynasty, the intimate privacy of the body natural that grounds the body politic, acquires the potential to undermine it, to desublimate the secret and scandalous truth of sovereignty so as to reveal that the "deepest meaning" of the story is in fact not public but disreputably private.

So the secret history operates along the differential axis of the public and the private, and in its gradual modulation toward the private realm it parallels the joint development of biography and fiction that I've already described. What bearing might this development have on the differential axis of actual and virtual particularity, in whose terms biography and fiction have, by the mid-eighteenth century, parted ways? The major romans à clef in the English tradition include Philip Sidney's *Old Arcadia* (1579–1581), John Barclay's *Argenis* (Latin 1621, trans. 1625, 1629), Mary Wroth's *The Countesse of Montgomeries Urania* (1621), the anonymous *Princess Cloria; or, the Royal Romance* (1661), Aphra Behn's *Love-Letters between a Nobleman and His Sister* (1684, 1685, 1687), and Delarivier Manley's *New Atalantis* (1709). By the time of Haywood's secret histories of the 1720s, a subtle, century-long transformation has been completed. This transformation has three interlocking features: the secrets concealed and revealed by the secret history have become primarily private and personal rather than public and political; the bi-leveled allegorical signification of public by private in the roman à clef has largely been displaced by a single literal narrative about private (i.e., domestic and sexual) affairs; and the resulting literal narrative retains the virtual particularity it possessed when it was no more than the signifier of actual particulars: history has become fiction. Although this is a work of time, Behn's *Love-Letters* is the single most consequential stage in this transformative process and may be summarized in its terms. Published in the aftermath of the Exclusion Crisis, Behn's roman à clef sets out to reveal and to vindicate the conditions of political subjection that should obtain under Restoration monarchy, using the disparate exemplary models available in her private, virtual plot as multiple and alternative foils for the normative subordination of actual subjects to actual king. But the circumstantial and affective detail with which Behn thickens her account of private, amatory affairs increasingly vies for attention with the political and military affairs it purports to signify. The result is less the direct "political" correlation of private character with public personage (e.g., Cesario with the Duke of Monmouth) than the construction of a broadly "ethical" grid of concrete examples that have both public and private relevance. Questions of state policy come to seem internalizable as questions of familial ethics. Over time, epistolary form gives way to third-person narration as the documentary and existential secrecy of letters is found to be less compelling than the subjective and psychological secrecy of the motives that lie behind and beneath them. In the end, the "key" that seems to open Behn's roman à clef is not the political identity of actual people but an ethical identification between readers and characters.

In modern practice, the difference between telling the stories of actual people and telling the stories of virtual people defines the boundary between biography and fiction. Indeed, it is our very confidence in this boundary that encourages us to experiment inventively at the borders of these two genres in a way that is not intelligible when the sense of borders is not explicit or coherent enough to make their crossing a fully stable concept. Yet there is a great difference between the tacit porousness of categories that is common in a culture that has not yet experienced a fundamental division of knowledge and the self-consciously reactive conflation of categories in a culture that has been marked by such division. But how do we bring this generalization into chronological specificity? We can draw a line at a specific point anywhere from 1600 to 1900; but by its very nature this falsifies the character of historical process, which at every moment consists in both continuity and discontinuity. Still, the implausibility of a parallel between early modern and postmodern culture may help where chronological precision does not. It seems implausible to me that contemporary readers of Foxe, Sidney, or Barclay experienced something akin to postmodern knowingness about the mixture of fact and fiction. Rather, they and those they read seem to move back and forth along the continuum of fact and fiction, life and art, nature and nurture, uncolored by the demystifying skepticism that fuels the very different sort of sophistication of postmodernity. But we do not need to wait until the twentieth century to see the latter mode in operation. I have already mentioned the fiction of Fielding and Sterne. As for biography, one of the ways in which the indefatigably opportunistic and intrusive James Boswell set the standard for the future in his *Life of Johnson* (1791) is expressed in the modern maxim that all biography is also autobiography. The maxim would have no point if we lacked an abiding conviction that the subject and the object of knowledge are separable from each other. This belief takes shape, over the course of the seventeenth century, in conjunction with the scientific revolution and the rise of empirical epistemology. The socio-ethical conviction that is analogous to and intertwined with this epistemological belief is the separability of individual or self from society, a belief that takes shape in conjunction with the seventeenth-century crises of status inconsistency and social mobility. It's also to these developments, I think, that we owe both the formation of, and the challenge to, the notion of personal identity or the self.

The Rise of Personal Identity

This dialectic of formation and challenge can be described in the terms that have become familiar over the course of this study, the movement from separation to conflation. I'll confine myself to philosophical discourse, the sort of evidence that lends itself most precisely to schematic abstraction, and suggest a correlation between John Locke and the argument of separation, and David Hume and the argument of conflation.

According to Locke in 1690, we call "our selves" "that thinking thing, that is in us" and that is "tied to a certain System of fleeting Animal Spirits." And "supposing a rational Spirit be the Idea of a Man, . . . whatever be the composition whereof the complex Idea is made, whenever Existence makes it one particular thing under any denomination, the same Existence continued, preserves it the same individual under the same denomination."[23] The marginal summary of the paragraph that contains the latter statement reads: "Continued Existence makes

Identity," and Locke maintains the continuity of personal identity as well. ("Person" he takes to be the same as "self.") (Locke, 346, 347, 348). Through a series of "thought experiments," Locke argues that thinking is coextensive with consciousness, from which it follows that consciousness is also necessary to personal identity (110). The continued existence of personal identity is a matter of its consciousness that it is identical with itself over time. "Personal Identity" is "the sameness of a rational Being: And as far as this consciousness can be extended backwards to any past Action or Thought, so far reaches the Identity of that Person; it is the same self now it was then; and 'tis by the same self with this present one that now reflects on it, that that Action was done." Locke recognizes that "our consciousness being interrupted, and we losing sight of our past selves, doubts are raised whether we are the same thinking thing; i.e., the same substance or no." But the question of personal identity is one not of substance but of consciousness. So that "as far as any intelligent Being can repeat the Idea of any past Action with the same consciousness it had of it at first, and with the same consciousness it has of any present Action; so far it is the same personal self" and "has existed in a continued Duration" (Locke, 335, 336, 345).

The grounds on which Hume criticizes Locke's account of personal identity are similar to those that underlie his broader criticism of Locke's epistemology (for an example, see chapter 1 in this volume), which the momentum of Enlightenment partialization leads him to deepen more than to refute. In his 1739 *Treatise* Hume writes: "There are some philosophers who imagine we are every moment intimately conscious of what we call our SELF; that we feel its existence and its continuance in existence; and are certain, beyond the evidence of a demonstration, both of its perfect identity and simplicity." "For my part," he continues, "when I enter most intimately into what I call myself, I always stumble on some particular perception or other. . . . I never catch myself at any time without a perception, and never can observe any thing but the perception." For Hume the two kinds of perception are impressions, which have greater "force and vivacity," and ideas. Given the supposed continuous existence of the self, "if any impression gives rise to the idea of self, that impression must continue invariably the same, thro' the whole course of our lives. . . . But there is no impression constant and invariable." This conclusion, which evokes the pristine standards of experimental method, is the product of the thought experiments that Hume must rely on in his effort "to introduce the experimental Method of Reasoning into Moral Subjects," and it diverges greatly from the conclusion produced by Locke's. In fact, Hume insists, our minds "are nothing but a bundle or collection of different perceptions, which succeed each other with an inconceivable rapidity, and are in a perpetual flux and movement." And the question becomes: "What then gives us so great a propension to ascribe an identity to these successive perceptions, and to suppose ourselves possest of an invariable and uninterrupted existence thro' the whole course of our lives?"[24]

To account for all the forces that persuade us of the existence of personal identity is beyond Hume's purpose. His concern is with the mental operations that promote our belief in it. Simply put, we attribute to the perceived object of knowledge a quality of the subjective mental operation by which we know it. We confound "the action of the imagination" "by which we reflect on the succession of related objects" with the action "by which we consider the uninterrupted and invariable object." Hume argues that "we often feign some new and unintelligible principle, that connects the objects together, and prevents their interruption or variation." And "where we do not give rise to such a fiction, our propension to confound identity with relation is so great, that we are apt to imagine something unknown and mysterious, connecting the parts, beside their relation." Hume's thought experiments ask us to focus on the ease with which our minds overcome the difference between "relation" and "identity." "The relation facilitates the transition of the mind from one object to another, and renders its passage as smooth as if it contemplated one continu'd object. This resemblance is the cause of the confusion and mistake, and makes us substitute the notion of identity, instead of that of related objects."

The question of identity can be asked of all objects of knowledge, and from this perspective personal identity need not be coextensive with one's own self: "In pronouncing concerning the identity of [another] person, [do] we observe some real bond among his perceptions, or only feel one among the ideas we form of them"? But it's with respect to our own identity that the role of temporal continuity is most crucially evident, and therefore also the role of memory. "As memory alone acquaints us with the continuance and extent of this succession of perceptions, 'tis to be consider'd, upon that account chiefly, as the source of personal identity." In fact, Hume goes so far as to write that "the memory not only discovers the identity, but also contributes to its production, by producing the relation of resemblance among the perceptions" (Hume, 254, 259, 261).

In these passages, Hume's language appears to describe two different states of mind that can encourage belief in one's personal identity. On the one hand, we might "feign" to ourselves the "fiction" of "some new and unintelligible principle" of connection. On the other, we might "imagine something unknown and mysterious, connecting the parts, beside their relation." Heuristically speaking, the first state of mind might be called a "motive" because it suggests a conscious act of will that purposefully fabricates the operation of something that goes against common sense. The second is more like a "cause" in that it's mysterious to us and therefore beyond our knowledge and powers, imagined but not therefore imaginary. On the evidence of other chapters in this study, Enlightenment thought was deeply preoccupied with the power of the imagination, the intimation of a realm of virtual existence not actual but real, and with what exerting pressure on the tacitness of traditional knowledge might disclose.

As we saw in chapter 4, the concept sex "as such" emerged during the Enlightenment in conjunction with a revolution in thinking about sex and gender that has led some historians of sexuality to predate by two centuries the broadly accepted view of the modern origins of the conception of male and female as "opposite" sexes; the discrimination between biological sex and socially constructed gender;

the reconception of sodomitical practice as definitive of an exclusive homosexual identity; and the complex entanglement of sex with a permanent realm of mentality unavailable to the conscious mind but accessible to the imagination. When Hume speculates on how some might come to the conviction that personal identity was, despite counterevidence, an uninterrupted and invariable mental capacity, his words adumbrate the words of contemporaries who are beginning to make explicit and to disembed sex as such from its traditional and definitive role in procreation. The historian Edmund Leites has connected the emergent understanding of sex to the influence of Protestant culture and the demand for constancy in the introspective scrutiny of conscience. His account of this connection brings us close to Hume's account of personal identity (Hume doesn't figure in his research), suggesting the proximity of conscience and personal identity as such, both being grounded in the permanence of sex as such.

In traditional thought, Leites maintains, the fluctuating and inconstant character of sexual interest and desire was consistent with the fluctuating nature of procreative activity, so that when we're not conscious of it sex is absent. But the Puritan sense of self is rooted in the constancy of conscience and its powers of self-regulation, which entails the constancy of what it regulates. So from the modern point of view, sexuality is constant, and when we're not conscious of it, it "can only appear to be absent, since it must always (really) be at work. Modern men and women thus suppose that sex is hidden (rather than absent) when it is not present. This makes sex fundamentally mysterious."[25]

Locke argued that the continued existence of personal identity is shown by the continuity of our consciousness of it. Hume threw this argument into doubt by showing that what we're continually conscious of is not an uninterrupted and invariable object—personal identity—but the succession of related objects that we imagine to be single and continuous. In the fifty years between Locke and Hume—in the Enlightenment—transpired the shift in English thinking about the self that we've become accustomed to postdating as a very recent transition from modernity to what we like to call "postmodernity." Needless to say, Hume didn't embrace this radical skepticism in pursuing his career as philosopher and historian, and the modern view of personal identity—less so sex—has for the most part lost its mysterious variability. Still, Hume's extreme analysis—external and separate relations absorbed as internal and continuous identity—brings to a fitting close this chapter's account of the disparate streams that fed the modern understanding of human existence. Unlike Hume's personal identity, these streams of thought did make a permanent contribution to our way of thinking, and they make tenable the view that in the Enlightenment was concentrated a remarkable network of innovations that was crucial to modern culture: the successive selves of role-playing grounded in an anterior and unchanging self; actual particularity re-presented by virtual particularity; the experience of commoners disclosed as the key to common humanity; the domestic signifier reconceived as signified; the abstract precept superseded by its example; the allegorical roman à clef leveled to the plain of the literal; history as biography; biography as autobiography; history as secret history.

6   *Historical Method*

Several years ago, the Mellon Foundation invited me to participate in a program aimed at developing seminars for graduate students who were writing their dissertations. The program had grown out of Mellon's aim to support and strengthen the structures of higher education in the humanities; the specific focus of the seminar was to be my decision. After some thought it occurred to me that the needs and concerns of students in the English graduate program at Rutgers University, where I then taught, might best be addressed by a workshop seminar in methods of historical interpretation for students of literature. The primary reading for this workshop would be chapters from the participants' dissertations supplemented by a selection of essays by a range of scholars on historical method. On the one hand, like most students in the field these days, ours were committed to the idea of historicizing literature. On the other, as students of literature rather than history, they had not received any training in historical method. What seemed to me significantly absent from their graduate education in this regard was not a knowledge of historiography, whether chronologically or thematically organized, but the ongoing practical expectation that their claims about the historical meaning of the texts they worked on had to be persuasive.

Through their training, I supposed, history students had internalized this requirement as a component of their habitual interpretive practice. Students of literature, however, were most likely to encounter the question of the criteria by which we assent to the claims of historical interpretation not at the level of practice but at the theoretical level of epistemology, where in recent decades the news has not been good.[1] To be sure, the critique of empirical epistemology in literary theory raises issues of central importance to historical practice. Yet its prominence in the milieu of literary studies over the last several decades has often seemed ungrounded in the sort of practical experience of interpretive historicization it aims to test. In the absence of that experience, it became too easy for literature students to embrace an abstract and absolute caveat against the legitimacy of historical interpretation as such, sidestepping a more searching effort to test against one another the relative adequacy of different modes of historicization. Moreover, the focus on historical epistemology in particular seemed blinkered. Profound theoretical skepticism about the grounds of objectivity, demonstration, and evidence in the representation of the past by the present coexisted with habits of close reading (the training literature students *do* receive and internalize) that seemed to me vulnerable—given that the present is to the past as the reader is to the text—but somehow immune to the same skepticism. True, the idea that history itself is a text promised illumination on both sides of the disciplinary divide. Yet in practice the analogy tended to work unevenly, reducing all history to naive history while ignoring, at least within the framework of disciplinary comparison, the implications of this sort of critique for literary criticism.

As I reflected on these issues, I formulated an idea of how the dissertation seminar might be motivated and organized. A skeptical approach to empiricism seemed to me not only compatible with, but essential to, historical method. But as this suggests, so is empiricism itself, because it is the basis on which any critique of historical method must be founded. Whatever misgivings we may have about the way empiricist standards of objectivity suffuse modern thinking, empiricism is, I believe, the only game in town. But the cultural credibility of empiricism is much younger than the ancient practice of history. When and why did they converge? Indeed, I wondered if this second-order kind of question, which in effect seeks to historicize historicism, might play a fruitful role in the study of historical method. How would this work? Not by research into intellectual history, certainly, but perhaps by generating a sustained awareness of the modern division of knowledge by which the disciplines of history and literature came to be separated out from each other, and both of them from the discipline of science. This became not the explicit plan by which the seminar proceeded but a periodic recourse that helped clarify what was at stake in our ambition to ask what makes historical readings of literature persuasive.

Lest my purpose be misunderstood, I should add that by "persuasive" I don't mean to suggest that this is an exercise in the "rhetoric" of history writing whose ultimate aim is to undercut it by showing that it is rhetorical and therefore, in the light of that demonstration, unpersuasive. Nor do I mean that by historicizing historical method I will practice a hermeneutics of suspicion, for which to historicize is to demystify by demonstrating that a category is not "natural" but "linguistic" or "constructed." To the modest extent that our seminar involved historical investigation rather than the study of historical method, we found ourselves interested in understanding how historical method, long before it became available for this modern sort of demystification, came into its own through an earlier stage of demystification that was fueled not by the critique of empiricism but by empiricism itself. In recalling some of the high points of the seminar, this chapter takes the following route. First, I describe how our seminar came to conceive that an effective historical method can be practiced through a method of inquiry that not only can begin the process of defining one's goals but also pursue and complicate those goals at every stage of study. Second, I use that method to open up, through a schematic series of operations, the territory of historical investigation.

Before turning to my argument, however, I'd like to reflect for a moment on the daunting question of the difference between literature and history in the Western tradition. The question has been asked from many directions. I'll address it from a historical perspective, and a particular one at that. From this perspective, the substantive difference between literature and history, although affirmed for centuries, resulted from an innovation in the means of cultural production that was at first devoid of conceptual implication but soon became grounded in and perpetuated by an oppositional way of thinking so stable as to condone, even invite, experimental challenge.[2] And the longer the difference between literature and history has endured as a modern norm, the more each has been conceived and written according to that norm.

In the beginning, all discourse was "poetic," marked by the insistence of a formal patterning whose purpose was to achieve the end of historical preservation by lodging discourse in consciousness and memory. As the mnemonic necessity of patterning was obviated by literate and typographical technologies of objectifying discourse, "literature" came to designate writing in which self-conscious patterning persisted as an end in itself, marking its objecthood as a special kind of writing that itself deserved the sort of attention and reference that writing as such bestowed on the world and its objects. Although they're not commonly rationalized by reference to a change in the means of cultural production, belief systems like structuralism and aestheticism appear to betray the mistaken assumption that if the marked quality of writing lacks a mnemonic end, writing itself has only the exclusive end of self-reference, rather than, as in oral culture, the end of double reference, to itself and to the world beyond itself. When we speak of literary "form" we mean the more or less ostensible patterning of its language, and in the process of learning to read literary texts we become increasingly conscious of the dense, virtual, and historically ramified network of formal signs—embedded in meter, syntax, diction, style, figuration, voice, allusion—that allows us to grasp and feel at a distance what others have written. Form is at the definitive heart of what we mean by literature, and its semantic force, both cognitive and affective, cannot be separated from the world to which those others referred.

Distance and Proximity

The most common experience in our workshop readings of dissertation chapters, familiar to anyone who has engaged in this sort of collective reading, was the encounter with perspectival difference. The question of perspective goes to the heart of the inescapable difference between being a reader of another's writing and being a reader of one's own—the difference between having the distance to see when and in what terms a claim requires support and being so close to a claim that it appears self-evident. In the great majority of our workshop cases, a consensus of disparate readers emerged to guide writers toward what we broadly agreed was the necessary sort of revision, which often enough took the form of providing better evidence. Along the way we tried to formulate some general principles of giving evidence that might cover the particular cases we had encountered. What are the standards of validity, probability, adequacy, and the like that we seek to satisfy when we give evidence? Do some kinds of evidence have greater intrinsic authority than others? What are the comparative claims of "quality" and "quantity"—of intentional statements, say, as opposed to the accumulation of data—in providing evidence for a historical interpretation? How much documentation is enough—or too much? Substantive answers to these questions are hard to come by, in large part because they must depend on and emerge from the nature of the project at hand. Later in the chapter I will return to the problem of evidence—and, more broadly, of perspective—in doing literary history. For the moment, however, the most useful principle may be no more than a rule of thumb based on the familiar workshop experience I have just mentioned: adducing satisfactory and plausible evidence requires the writer to be able to internalize self-consciously, within or alongside the relatively tacit standards of judgment one brings to one's own work, the standards of others. This is a principle of detachment or distance: for evidence to be credible it must be credible according to standards of judgment that go beyond those of the writer.

This rule of thumb is closely related to a central principle of empirical epistemology: to be credible, evidence must be separable from the phenomenon for which it provides evidence. John Locke, criticizing Puritan enthusiasts not on religious but on epistemological grounds, wrote that "if they say they know it to be true, because it is a *Revelation* from GOD, the reason is good: but then it will be demanded, how they know it to be a Revelation from GOD. . . . Every Conceit that thoroughly warms our Fancies must pass for an Inspiration, if there be nothing but the Strength of our Perswasions, whereby to judge of our Perswasions: . . . *Reason* must . . . examine their Truth by something extrinsical to the Perswasions themselves."[3] We readers are Locke's enthusiasts: to be persuasive we need to give evidence extrinsic to the self-evidence of our self-persuasion. But the principle has implications for us as readers not only of ourselves but also of seventeenth-century enthusiasts. What Locke requires as grounds for assent to propositions is the detachment or distance of the subjective process and norms of knowing from the object that's known. Whether we are historians who live in a later age, or, like Locke, contemporary with those enthusiasts, we cannot know them without having access to something beyond their own self-understanding. But what if our object of knowledge is not enthusiasts but poets like Milton and Dryden? Often enough the evidence on which we wish to base at least part of our interpretation of poetry is the judgment—the intentions and motives—of its authors. Indeed, this is also true of objects of knowledge like the enthusiasts themselves, because part of the knowledge we are after is knowledge of their subjective self-understanding. In such cases, it would seem, where the questions one asks about objects of historical knowledge call for answers that include the self-perceptions of those objects, subject and object must interpenetrate one another, and the principle of distance is joined by a principle of proximity. This means not that giving evidence in the pursuit of literary history—and any other historical inquiry that takes subjectivity as part of its object—therefore escapes the basic requirements of empirical method, but that we need a more nuanced understanding of empirical method.[4]

Historicizing Empiricism

For such an understanding we could do worse than return to Locke, because in the case of self-knowledge he recognized that the separation of object from subject is not available as a matter of course. "The activity of reflection," he wrote, is one in which "the Understanding turns inwards upon it self, *reflects* on its own *Operations*, and makes them the Object of its own Contemplation" (2.1.8) and he remarked that under normal circumstances, "the Understanding... takes no notice of it self: and it requires Art and Pains to set it at a distance, and make it its own Object" (1.1.1). If "sensation" is the means by which the subject gains knowledge of sensible objects that are external to it, "reflection" is a kind of "internal Sense" by which the subject gains self-knowledge (2.1.4). Fifty years after Locke's *Essay*, David Hume pursued this empiricist logic further than Locke had done. For Locke, the case of reflective self-knowledge was a skeptical complication, perhaps even an exception to the rule, of empirical epistemology.[5] Hume saw this exception to the rule as the rule itself, demonstrating that our sensible experience of the world cannot be separated from the experience of perceiving it.[6]

In the years following this brief but remarkable philosophical trajectory, Hume's argument commonly has been bracketed off from the mainstream practice of empiricism, following the example of Hume himself in his own philosophical career. This has left the Humean rapprochement of subject and object to be rediscovered most often as a critique of empiricism rather than as an extension of it, most famously, perhaps, in the thesis of the hermeneutic circle.[7] How is objective knowledge possible if its theoretically distinct categories can be felt, in interpretive practice, to interpenetrate or presuppose one another? Most often this thesis is formulated in terms other than those of subject-object relations. If the epistemological project begins inductively with particulars (or parts) in order to construct a knowledge of the general (or the whole) that is constituted by them, the nature of the whole is already predicated in, and determinant of, the conception of its parts as parts. A similar circularity obtains when we begin with a knowledge of the generality of the whole in order to construe the particular parts whose partial nature is already established by that condition of wholeness. Changing the terms from parts and whole to subject and object alters the argument to some degree but not in a way that challenges the basic circularity thesis: we can know an object only in the subjective terms available to us as subjects—or more simply, the unknown cannot be known except in terms of what we already know.

So, from one readily available perspective, the circularity of interpretation that's highlighted by the hermeneutic circle is by definition a logical contradiction that can't be reconciled with the idea of empirical knowledge. Broadly speaking, this is the perspective of the natural sciences, which emerged toward the end of the Renaissance as an offshoot of the Quarrel of the Ancients and Moderns. Elsewhere I've described how Enlightenment thinkers first divided the whole of knowledge or *scientia* into science on the one hand and the arts and humanities on the other.[8] Scientific method proceeds progressively by separating out hard knowledge of the object itself from the "subjective" variables of particular acts of knowing, whereas knowledge of the art object is suffused with the imaginative particularities of the singular knowing subject.

What about history and literature? Ever since its seventeenth-century formulation, scientific method has been the model by which all efforts to establish standards of credible and probable knowledge in both of these disciplines have proceeded. One might even say that the modern constitution of these disciplines has been a function of the way they have turned scientific empiricism to their own ends. The category "literature" cohered over the course of the eighteenth century in tandem with the explicit theorization of aesthetic judgment and response as an empirical mode whose relative detachment from the objective realm of the senses was achieved through the imagination, rather than through the understanding, of the knowing subject. The history of this theorization is a topic in itself to which I can only allude here,[9] and it separated literature not only from science but also from the discipline of history. However, literature was seen to be not only a special way of knowing the world, but also an object of knowledge that was itself susceptible to being known through the rapidly developing methods of literary criticism and literary history, which evidently shared the epistemological fortunes of historical method as such. Efforts at accommodating both history and literary history to the standards of science and its separation of subject from object have routinely punctuated the practice of historical method in the modern period.[10] But the most persuasive developments in historical method have been those that take the hermeneutic circle not as a logical contradiction that precludes real knowledge but as a historical contradiction that provides the key to its methodical acquisition. Is this an "empirical" procedure? If we take "empiricism" to apply only to the objectivity of knowledge from which subjectivity has been evacuated, the answer is no. But we arrive at a different answer if we see the separation of subject from object—a major premise of empirical epistemology—as the starting point of a method that in departing from the scientific does not depart from its empiricist grounding. As I turn now to describing, historical method involves a strategic and self-conscious oscillation between particularity and generality, parts and whole, a toggling back and forth between these poles in a process that successively adjusts the nature of each in turn by reference to the other, until a point is reached where knowledge of the object is felt to satisfy the standards of credibility, probability, sufficiency, or the like. One perspective on why this method of historical inquiry is an empirical epistemology is that the process I have just described—the dialectical movement between the division and the integration of categories—depends for its very intelligibility on the division of knowledge through which empiricism itself is constituted as a mode of knowledge.[11]

Historical Method: Matching Particulars and Generals

I've already alluded to the radical critique of historical method that dominated literary theory until rather recently. This critique may be known best for its blanket charge that the practice of history is committed to "binary" oppositions—for example, between the object and the subject. But this is to confuse opposition with dichotomy, provisional with absolute separation. It seems to me rather that the basic tool of historical method is the strategic dialectic between the division and the integration of categories. This tool becomes available as a practice by applying it as widely as possible to the broad range of experience we take to be historical. In other words, the dialectic of opposition is a tool of discovery, a way of opening up possibilities for the interpretation of any and all historical phenomena. This will become more concrete if we momentarily adopt from E. D. Hirsch a different set of terms for our basic polar opposition, one that grows out of the study of genre and thereby capitalizes on the notion that history is a text.[12] How do we recognize that a given text "belongs" to a certain genre? Whether we begin with the text or with its hypothesized genre, we gain confidence in assigning generic identity by successively "matching" the particular "traits" of the text to the general "type" of a given genre. The process begins on the basis of what may be a very loose expectation of how the match might be made, and as we continue the matching process we refine our understanding by reciprocal reconceptions of the nature of the generic type and re-examinations of the traits we take to characterize the text. The opposition between traits and type is methodologically useful because both categories are heuristic and therefore invite the revisionary process that in the end issues in a probable match. If such a match is not available, we may find ourselves speculating, as H. R. Jauss describes in his account of the aesthetics of reception, that the culturally given "horizon of expectations" that has guided our matching of traits to type has been exceeded and that the text at hand may contribute to the establishment of a new genre.[13]

The dialectical opposition between textual traits and generic type, although drawn from the precincts of genre theory, usefully illustrates the much broader province of hermeneutics. Traditionally a technique of reading a religious canon, hermeneutics construes the meaning of a "text"—commonly a word or a phrase—by methodically juxtaposing it with or within its enclosing linguistic context. This traditional, micro-level of matching text to context at the strictly linguistic level provides the model for the expanded, macro-level of hermeneutics, where the text is typically an entire book and its context is one particular part—political, social, intellectual—of the entire setting in which the book and its publication may be said to exist. There is an indefinite number of ways a context can be abstracted from its surrounds and conceived as the heuristic whole that best illuminates the text in question. No act of contextualization can be definitive; in fact, hermeneutic study commonly involves multiple re-entries into the text and reconceptions of context. These experimental substitutions of one interpretive context for another build on what has been learned, from each successive contextualization, about the likely construal of the text in question, moving toward an increasingly persuasive construal.[14] Historical interpretation has long found it fruitful to deploy a version of this process in which the text becomes not a word in a book or even a book but any other sort of historical entity—an event, institution, movement, culture—and the context becomes a yet more comprehensive historical entity. By successively matching and adjusting the lesser to the greater historical entity in the experimental process I have described, the historian arrives at a plausible understanding of what kind or "genre" of thing he or she is studying. As with the opposition of the particular and the general, the parts and the whole, and the traits and the type, historical text and context are heuristic categories that posit boundaries so as to fashion a two-part mechanism that construes meaning by crossing and recrossing those boundaries.

Many of the cases in which our seminar members were collectively successful in improving on one another's historical theses are well described as analyses of text and context. Is *Hamlet* a revenge tragedy? Is *Paradise Lost* a Renaissance poem? Is Milton a classical republican/civic humanist? Is Donne best seen as a Catholic or an Anglican poet? Is Swift's masterpiece a satire of the pride not only of Gulliver but also of the Houyhnhnms? Was seventeenth-century latitudinarianism a precursor of the eighteenth-century cult of sensibility? Should the rise of the public sphere in England be backdated to the middle of the seventeenth century (or even earlier)? Were the industrial revolution and the French Revolution revolutionary in comparable ways? As these examples make clear, to be hermeneutically useful, the relation of text to context need not conform to the single template of particular to general, of contained to container. In fact, the very diversity of these examples suggested to us that if we want the text-context opposition to provide practical guidance in discovering interpretive options, we need to think more analytically about how the relatively undifferentiated heterogeneity of these exemplary questions might be broken down into its component parts. Can we identify the several different kinds of oppositional sets that, taken together, schematically generate the range of possibilities for historical inquiry?

Dialectical Opposition I: History as Focalizations of Perspective

As I suggested earlier, the separation of scientific empiricism from historical empiricism grew out of the notion that science requires a separation of the knowing subject from the object of knowledge. At its most extreme, this separation is expressed in the antithesis between the qualitative terms of self-knowledge and the quantitative terms of enumeration and measurement. Perhaps the recognition that historical method cannot proceed on a strictly quantifying basis was the necessary precondition for recognizing that an analogous version of this opposition exists *within* the realm of historical method itself. If historical knowledge cannot claim the objectivity of scientific knowledge, it can profit from distinguishing what we might call more or less objective ways of doing history. The terminology most commonly used by historians for making this distinction opposes "explanation" on the one hand to "interpretation" on the other.[15]

There has been much interesting debate over the exact nature of this opposition, but for present purposes it may be enough to characterize it as the difference between distanced and proximate, "external" and "internal" approaches to a historical phenomenon, meaning by "external" either something like statistical quantification or the laws, whether physical or metaphysical, that account for history as it were from without, without reference to human will and motive. On the one hand, we can "explain" the past in causal terms that are not available to its own self-understanding. On the other, we can "interpret" the past in terms that are compatible with, even derived from, its own motives and conceptual-affective framework.

Both of these opposed methods have influentially been called "historicism." When Karl Popper argued "the poverty of historicism," he was criticizing the notion that doing history requires us to elaborate general laws—material and social but also psychological—as a foundation for explaining particular beliefs and behaviors "from the outside."[16] But "historicism" also, and more commonly, has been associated with the notion that doing history requires us to understand the meaning of the past within the context of, and in sympathy with, the intentional motives of its actors.[17] If we deploy the opposition between explanation and interpretation broadly enough, it becomes methodologically useful in the first instance because it organizes the bewildering heterogeneity of my list of exemplary questions in literary history that *have* been asked by sorting at least some of them into the sorts of questions that *might* be asked.

Now, there are obvious difficulties in the practical application of these categories. The coherence of the categories "external explanation" and "internal interpretation" is weakened as soon as we consider them in isolation rather than as antithetical and reciprocally constitutive parts of a greater methodological whole. Do we raise more questions than we answer when we lump together as "external" the kinds of determinacy advanced by economic materialism and psychoanalysis? The problem is even more evident in the case of "internal" interpretation. Even a small corner of the past—even a single consciousness—is populated by a multitude of motives, some of which even stand in relation to others as "external causes" to "internal motives."

Donne's motives, for example, become susceptible to the sort of complication entailed in juxtaposing the different implications of "faith," "belief," "affirmation," "profession," "practice," and "rule-bound behavior," not to mention the different sorts and degrees of intentional claim made by disparate kinds of text—poetry, sermons, letters, public documents—or the subtly distinctive intentional valences of oral, written, and printed (and for our era, digital) discourse. The question of Milton's sociopolitical convictions (was he a classical republican/civic humanist?), of a different order than that of Donne's religious beliefs, is perhaps more susceptible to being approached as an inquiry into the history of ideas. This sort of inquiry often identifies words, phrases, or other distinctive locutions that are at least partially representative or constitutive, especially in association with each other, of the idea under investigation. In the case of civic humanism, scholars have drawn our attention to the normative language of public virtue, landed property, and secularity, and to the negative status of fortune, luxury, corruption, and mercenary troops or standing armies. But these locutions and their norms play an active role as commonplaces in much of the discourse of Milton's period, and to assess his attitude toward classical republicanism, we need to interpret the kind and degree of intention that is implicit in each usage. Schematically speaking, that is, we need to construe each textual word or phrase in its immediate contextual passage in order to judge whether it is used there as a discursive "commonplace" that betrays a specifically classical-republican "ideology" or instead used with a discernible edge that turns it to ideological ends other than those of classical republicanism.[18]

Interpreting Swift's satiric norms (another classical republican/civic humanist possibility) in the fourth part of *Gulliver's Travels* invites attention to a full spectrum of evidence from the internal to the external because it addresses a textual crux that goes to the heart of Swift's personal, literary, ethical, sociopolitical, and existential identity. Why are the Houyhnhnms not, as their author is, Christian? How does their treatment compare with that of other figures in the first three parts of the book, who seem more clearly to be objects of either Swift's praise or blame? Are characteristic strategies to be found in Swift's satiric practice? Is *Gulliver's Travels* an "imaginary voyage"? How was Swift educated and what had he read? Who were his friends and what were his politics in 1726? What were his views on sex, race, and social status? How compatible are his own writings on sublimation with those of psychoanalytic theory (and does their compatibility matter as far as their interpretation is concerned)? The nature of our heuristic context, and of the scholarly search for evidence it dictates, will be defined in very different ways depending on which of these (or other) questions we undertake to answer. And in the pursuit of answers, new contexts and reading programs, new exercises in matching traits to type, and new judgments about the resulting matches and their plausibility necessarily will follow. (What does it mean to be Christian in 1726? Do the differences between the Houyhnhnms and the king of Brobdingnag outweigh their comparability? Does Swift's imaginary voyage better fit the model of More's *Utopia* or of Vairasse d'Allais's *History of the Sevarites*? Can we tell if Swift had actually read a book he possessed in his library? When was *Gulliver's Travels* [not printed but] composed? What were "sex" and "race" in Swift's age, and how can we reduce his ambivalence about aristocracy to a coherent "view"?)

What I want to emphasize is that these complications, although they appear to raise serious problems with the method of interpretation I propose, should be seen instead as stages in its practical unfolding and application. The defects of the way the explanation-interpretation, external-internal opposition is formulated do not compromise the utility of its explicitness, and its consequent availability as a tool that can be adjusted to different kinds and layers of discourse. Rather, the explanatory crudity of the opposition (e.g., its obliviousness of the fact that in Donne's England the sociopolitical and the religious were lived as thoroughly interpenetrating spheres of experience) is the precondition for its interpretive refinement. Deepening inquiry goes hand in hand with the recalibration of the methodological formulations themselves. For this reason, the most profitable opposition in heuristic terms may be the most general one—like the external versus the internal approach—and its invitation to enter more deeply into analysis in a methodical but open-ended fashion.

Dialectical Opposition II: History as Moments of Temporality

To some of my exemplary questions in literary history the dialectical opposition of external and internal would appear largely unhelpful—for example, whether the latitudinarianism of Restoration divines was a precursor of the sensibility movement a century later. Temporality is of course the existential medium most often associated with the domain of history: history, we like to think, happens in time. To understand the historical nature of sensibility, then, requires that we conceive the opposition "latitudinarianism-sensibility" along the temporal axis. Here contextualization is, broadly speaking, a matter not of mobility of viewpoint but of temporal potentiality. Temporal opposition does not in the first instance raise a question of determinacy on the schematic spectrum from cause to motive; it posits the field of temporality itself as flow or movement, a medium of becoming that schematically defines the difference between one precursory moment and the next. This understanding differs from that of the familiar theoretical charge against historical method that temporality—or its codified version, chronology—amounts to teleology. Behind this charge is the misconception that to posit a temporal relationship between a before and an after is to posit the latter as something like an evolutionary fulfillment of the former. This seems to me as mistaken as the belief that building a chimney establishes a normative hierarchy between its component bricks because some of them are higher than others. The policing of teleology as the quintessential tendency of temporal opposition also ignores the fact that for most of history it is not evolutionary but devolutionary thinking that has dominated the field.

How do temporal oppositions become methodologically dialectical? When a temporal question like that entailed in the latitudinarianism-sensibility opposition is answered in the affirmative, the implication is that the precursory status of the earlier formation is not only literally true but also expressive of a more particular kind of relationship to the later one, and earlier and later are experimentally reconceived as two moments in a single sequence of becoming. And if the evidence for a more particular relation between the two moments is compelling enough—that is, if it is a precursory relationship that goes well beyond the sheer necessity of the continuous temporal medium entailed in the very idea of becoming— we may wish to see the sequence more definitively as a "period." To posit a period no more entails perspectival determinacy than does positing a sequence. However, it invites us to ask further questions, about the nature of the moments that frame the period, which lead us into the dialectic of perspectives: questions about the motives that may be entailed in the textual usages by which we define those moments, as well as about the causes that may suggest a contextual but extraintentional relationship between those moments.

But the dialectic of temporality also has a distinct logic of its own. When we postulate periods, we generalize from evidence not just that the beginning and ending moments are connected to each other, but also that the moments between them are connected as well, and in ways that are related, whether more or less tangentially, to those that connect the two moments to each other. And as with the dialectical opposition between external and internal perspectives, although with different consequences, it is the revisionary movement back and forth between moments that thickens the texture of connection sufficiently to warrant identifying a sequence as a period. What's fundamental to this texture is neither the notion of a causal chain of moments nor the notion that each of them is intentionally motivated, but persuasive evidence of continuity. However, periodization is an extreme outcome of temporalization. More often the temptation to postulate a period is instead the prelude to the discovery of shorter sequences, within the potentiality of a period, that are more compellingly integral than is the period itself, no doubt in part because the territory they cover is less extensive and therefore more securely tied to the available evidence. I'll return to the topic of periods in a moment, but first I want to ask what other sorts of temporal discovery, falling short of periodization, may be thrown into relief by shuttling between discrete temporal moments.

Perhaps the most fruitful terminology for attaining this end by method is Raymond Williams's triad of the residual, the dominant, and the emergent, which transforms the paradoxically intransitive stages of historical temporality—past, present, and future—into a dynamic language of process. Here the isolation of the central term establishes, through its very dominance, the negative conditions under which pre- and postdominance coalesce into view. Needless to say, the transitive quality of Williams's categories militates against their stabilization—a point demonstrated by his effort to subtilize yet more the way dominance is infiltrated by emergence through the category of the "pre-emergent," and then more subtly yet by those "structures of feeling" famously put forth by Williams to identify meanings and values so deeply interwoven with lived social experience as not yet to have been "precipitated out" into semantic availability.[19] This is a good example of the way positing an opposition in one dimension (here, the temporal opposition of present and future) creates the opportunity for positing within one term of that opposition—in this case, the future—more precise versions of the opposition itself (dominant and emergent, emergent and pre-emergent, pre-emergent and structures of feeling) that recapitulate, and carry forward at a micro-level, the analytic work of the initial, macro opposition. Moreover, the category "structures of feeling" exemplifies how the methodological refinement of opposition within one dimension can create an opportunity for opening up opposition within another dimension—here, the perspectival dimension of external and internal. "Structures of feeling" not only (like "emergent" and "pre-emergent") recapitulates at the micro-level the initial terms of temporal opposition. It also does something similar within the perspectival dimension by conceiving an irreducibly singular moment of temporal futurity in perspectival terms, postulating a species of the internal ("feeling") so delicately delineated that it bleeds into its external, unmotivated causes (social "structure") without being reduced to or subsumed by them. So Williams's influential term raises questions of perspectival determinacy. As I will suggest in a moment, however, these questions may be more instructively seen as the issue of a third and final type of dialectical opposition.

Another temporal category that, like "emergence," has gained favor for its capacity to transform apparent dichotomy into dialectical opposition is "pre-history." When we speak of the pre-history of a phenomenon we attend to a temporal sequence as though through a magnifying glass, so that what had seemed to have no more than a sequential relationship to that phenomenon can be seen to be significantly related to it, although not in the fully constitutive way that would justify including it within the "history" of the phenomenon. The language of pre-history conveys a sense of permanent hypothesis, because the accumulation of evidence that confirms the probability of that term would likely result in the renaming of pre-history as history, turning the dialectic of separate parts into a whole made up of component parts. And in common with the other categories whose manipulation is central to this historical method, the transformation of pre-history into history is a heuristic enterprise that both establishes a new category of knowledge and solicits, on its own basis, the discovery of yet others, and perhaps even its own dissolution.

Using the category "labor" as his example, Marx offers the most nuanced and suggestive account I know of how a pre-history might be disclosed. "Labor seems a quite simple category," he writes. But in fact it is quite complicated, because "labor" is both immeasurably old and a product of the last century. According to Marx, Adam Smith's topic, "the wealth of nations," is a revolution in economic thought (although it has its own pre-history) because it is the result of generalizing, from the many kinds of labor he knew, to "the abstract universality of wealth-creating activity" or "labour as such." Smith was able to make this leap, Marx argues, because by the end of the eighteenth century, no single kind of labor was still predominant, and increased labor mobility—that is, both physical and social mobility—ensured that a given mode of labor no longer seemed "organically linked with particular individuals in any specific form." "The simplest abstraction, then, which modern economics places at the head of its discussions, and which expresses an immeasurably ancient relation valid to all forms of society, nevertheless achieves practical truth as an abstraction only as a category of the most modern society.... [Yet it] by no means begins only at the point where one can speak of it as such."[20]

What Marx calls the "simple abstraction" is a whole that encloses a dialectical opposition: on the one hand, a protracted temporal sequence of heterogeneous activity; on the other, the comparatively brief moment of its conceptual generalization. Only by toggling back and forth between both parts of this whole, he suggests, can we do justice to the nature of historical temporality. To a great extent, however, the force of Marx's argument comes from the nontemporal terms he uses here to describe the relationship between a historical phenomenon and its pre-history, namely the material and the conceptual. Now, the dialectical opposition between the material and the conceptual is recognizable as a version of the perspectival opposition between the external and the internal. The realm of material activity, by its nature objective, lies outside the realm of self-understanding and therefore is a source of historical explanation, whereas to conceptualize is a function of the subject and a precondition for, if not a guarantee of, interpretation. And although Marx finds material explanation essential to his work as a historian, he deploys it here not in a strictly oppositional mode, whereby conceptualization would be seen as the effect of a material cause, but as one part of a dialectical whole in which materiality and conceptualization have a fluid and reciprocal effect on one another. It's in this spirit that Williams formulated the category "structures of feeling."

Dialectical Opposition III: History as Levels of Structure

Although he didn't discover it and his historical materialism is not essential to it, the dimension of analysis represented by Marx's division and integration of the material and the mental is indispensable to historical understanding. Earlier I referred to the common notion that history can be equated with temporality. Marx repudiates this view by bringing into relation with the category of temporality the nontemporal category of structure. The result can be conceived as a grid composed of a "horizontal," temporal dimension and a "vertical" dimension that is atemporal in the sense that it amounts to something like a slice or cross-section of temporality by which is disclosed the structure of any given moment. The relationship between temporality and structure is fundamentally oppositional in the way that time and space are oppositional. But like time and space, the temporal and the structural axes are at every moment coextensive; to do history is to do justice to this coextension.[21] In Marx's analysis, structure, like temporality, can be divided and subdivided according to the local requirements of inquiry. The most general division is the opposition of material infrastructure to conceptual superstructure, in a familiar schematism "social being" to "consciousness." But in order to achieve greater specificity, Marx often enough opens up this opposition into the three-part relationship between material production, social relations, and consciousness, where the middle structure, by mediating between the other two, makes explicit their dialectical relationship by its appropriability to each of them. Once again, these structural divisions are heuristic: they posit opposed wholes that are susceptible both to dialectical relation as parts of greater wholes and to subdivision into their component parts.

In Marx's most general usage, there exists a causal—or better, a determinant—relationship between the "productive forces" and the "forms of intercourse," the material and the conceptual realms of historical structure. The determinacy of the material entails an ontological force that is effective in all structural and temporal spheres of life, and that ensures a correspondence between the material and the conceptual dimensions of existence that contemporaries feel to be natural, necessary, and organic. However, in the argument of Marx and Engels, "all collisions in history have their origin . . . in the contradiction between the productive forces and the form of intercourse." At such revolutionary moments, the external focus of analysis must shift from the general determinacy of productive forces to concentrate more internally on "various subsidiary forms" of intercourse—social, political, conceptual—that partake in the upheaval, and "from a narrow point of view one may isolate one of these subsidiary forms and consider it as the basis of these revolutions; and this is all the more easy as the individuals who started the revolutions had illusions about their own activity" and its determinacy. But if we must regard as a narrow perspective any internal focus that isolates forms of intercourse as being the basis of change that actually originates in the productive forces, it's only from a very general and external perspective that the internal focus on revolutionary actors can be fully divided from the external. In fact, from a yet more general point of view, the illusions of individuals play an indispensable role in historical change: "The conditions under which individuals have intercourse with each other, . . . which appear first as conditions of self-activity, later as fetters upon it, form in the whole evolution of history a coherent series of forms of intercourse, the coherence of which consists in this: in the place of an earlier form of intercourse, which has become a fetter, a new one is put, corresponding to the more developed productive forces and, hence, to the advanced mode of the self-activity of individuals—a form which in its turn becomes a fetter and in then replaced by another." "The conditions under which individuals have intercourse with each other" sum up the multiple structures—say, the social, political, institutional, familial, personal, intimate—that compose the dimension of the superstructural. From being forms that correspond to the developed productive forces to being contradictory fetters upon them, these superstructural conditions fail to develop evenly with those forces, and it is this "uneven development" that is the primary motor of historical change. The contradiction in which this uneven development culminates can be hypothesized in somewhat different terms. Although superseded, "the various stages and interests" of these conditions of intercourse "are never completely overcome, but only subordinated to the prevailing interest and trail along beside the latter for centuries to come." And so "an earlier interest" of this sort, "the peculiar form of intercourse of which has already been ousted by that belonging to a later interest, remains for a long time afterwards in possession of a traditional power in the illusory community . . . , which has won an existence independent of the individuals; a power which in the last resort can only be broken by a revolution."[22] Both scenarios call to mind how temporal process may be analyzed as the overlay of residual and emergent moments within the dominant. Here the close analysis of the relation between atemporal structures discloses a temporal relation between "earlier" and "later" interests that influence the "prevailing" one.

Marx famously uses the language of uneven development to describe the radical but nonrevolutionary contradiction between forces of artistic production and artistic forms of intercourse—"the uneven development of material production relative to e.g. artistic development"—when he raises the discrepancy between ancient Greek art and the rudimentary technology that produced it.[23] Is there perhaps a negative correlation between the quality of cultural products and the quantifying sophistication of their production? Perhaps Marx here falls under the spell of the romantic construal of the division of knowledge whose seeds were planted by the Enlightenment.[24] In any case, he elsewhere articulates and to some degree rationalizes the discrepancy by principle: "Consciousness can sometimes appear further advanced than the contemporary empirical relationships, so that in the struggles of a later epoch one can refer to earlier theoreticians as authorities."[25] Marx is thinking of prolepsis in discursive and explanatory contexts; but the concept of uneven development may be more interesting—and less able to be explained away—in the case of art. The temporal and structural, the formal and substantive complexity of a work like *Paradise Lost*—at the least its enactment of a Hegelian *aufhebung*, whereby the past is preserved and superseded in the present—might be repaid by reading it in terms of uneven development.[26]

The philosophers and historians of the Scottish Enlightenment may be the first to have put into concerted practice the model of historical interpretation that coordinates temporal sequence with inquiry into the structure of historical phenomena at any given stage in that sequence. Adam Ferguson wrote that if we would know the character of our distant past, of which little or no material evidence remains, we might conjecture it by observing similarities between cultures at comparable stages of development. One celebrated outcome of this sort of "conjectural" history, as it came to be called, was the stadial theory of human civilization, whose conceptual and empirical appeal was tempered by its susceptibility to teleological uses.[27]

Although the temporal and the structural axes of historical method are interdependent, their utility goes far beyond the dubious possibility of constructing a model that can predict the future development of a given culture. A familiar terminology for the temporal and the structural axes of history is the opposition of "diachrony" to "synchrony." Ferdinand de Saussure formulated this opposition to designate "the axis of successions" and "the axis of simultaneities" in linguistic study, an "opposition" that "is absolute and allows no compromise" because "the diachronic perspective deals with phenomena that are unrelated to [structural] systems although they do condition them."[28] The temptation to extrapolate Saussure's innovative opposition from the study of language to the formulation of analogous axes in the study of literature (syntagm and paradigm, metonymy and metaphor), and thence to the study of history, has been both productive and problematic. Saussure's structuralist followers have tended to correlate the "diachrony-synchrony" opposition within language with a "history-structure" extrapolation, thereby contributing to the reduction of history to temporality—a theoretical confusion that can devolve into the reduction of temporality to teleology.[29] In historical practice, diachronic and synchronic analyses are not "absolute" but dialectically intertwined. This can be seen in the way historical periods coalesce as probable categories of study when we oscillate back and forth between discrete moments in a temporal sequence until this multiplicity of traits is seen to possess the family resemblance of a general type. At this point, the diachronic study of history is operationally coextensive with its synchronic study because a period is nothing but a synchronic unit defined in its wholeness by its separation out from the temporal sequence of which it is also a part.

Of course a period, however much its identification as a synchronic structure depends on its abstraction from diachrony, also possesses in itself a diachronic dimension, and it therefore cannot be said to be an "atemporal" structure. Nor can the length of a posited period be radically reduced so as to make it devoid of temporality. On the one hand, the very definition of a period entails temporality;

on the other, it is in the nature of time to be indefinitely divisible without sacrificing its temporal status. And just as diachrony is composed of moments each of which has a synchronic dimension, so synchronic structures, which are parts of a diachronic whole, are composed of parts whose coherence at a single moment is determined by a distinct temporal development: thus crisis is manifested by the uneven development of infrastructure and superstructure. The temporality of structures may also be seen in the analysis of a cultural product like a literary work into its dominant, residual, and emergent elements.[30] In short, the reciprocity of diachrony and synchrony ensures the concrete historicity of the phenomena to whose analysis they are methodologically applied, which is the same as saying that their reciprocity tests the historicity of those phenomena. Even period categories that attain the structural stability of habitual usage, like "the Renaissance," are heuristic in the sense that their quasi-institutional claim to plausibility is an open invitation to experiments in reformulation, as the recent advocacy of the category "early modern" exemplifies. The protest against the reifying tendencies of periodization, like that against "binaries," misconceives categorization to be a dogmatic strategy for closing down understanding rather than the first step in opening it up to questions that otherwise would never be asked. The synchronic challenge posed by the utter singularity of *Paradise Lost* may be less significant than the diachronic challenge posed by its belatedness as a Renaissance artifact. But of this we might ask: What is thereby challenged: the status of *Paradise Lost* as a Renaissance poem or the status of the Renaissance as a period category capable of coordinating its temporality structurally, that is, across national lines? The answer to this question, which generates new ones in turn, depends on whether the literary historian is most interested in bringing the instrument of dialectical opposition to bear on issues of generic or of period inclusiveness.

In the preceding pages I've tried to describe a historical method that has a theoretical grounding but whose major value lies in its practical applicability to concrete problems in doing literary history. And history as such: for in the end, the opposition between "literary history" and "other sorts of history," while useful in emphasizing the special incentives of the former (e.g., a sensitivity to the implications of formal usage, from voice and meter to genre and medium), is perhaps even more useful in obliging us to see analogous demands that are inherent in doing history as such. The method I've outlined is practical because it involves practices that are intelligible and determinate as concrete operations. The central practice is the deployment of oppositions between the whole and its parts in a dialectical fashion, discovering the coherence of former parts as integral wholes and the status of former wholes as parts of new wholes. At the primary stage of analysis, I've outlined three broad dimensions in which this method can be pursued: those of perspectival focus, temporal moments, and structural levels. Succeeding stages of analysis are dictated by choices made at the primary stage and are likely to involve the following two methodological shifts. First, within any one of these three dimensions, the relationship between oppositional terms at the primary level of analysis can be adapted to a more closely concentrated analysis of, and within, a single one of those terms. Second, all three of the dimensions can lead analysis into and out of any other dimension.

By what evaluative criteria are methodological choices made? Near the beginning of this chapter I reduced the thesis of the hermeneutic circle to its bare bones: the unknown cannot be known except in terms of what we already know. And yet in practice, gaining new knowledge is a rather common experience. The categorical aura of the hermeneutic circle is a function of the conciseness with which it's formulated. The more fully its circularity is opened up, the more it becomes recognizable as, not the dead end of repetition, but a methodological process of understanding whereby what we know is incrementally and differentially matched and rematched—increasingly with by-products that have been thrown up by the process itself—through a series of operations that leaves us in the end where we have not been before. How do we know when we have finished? Given that there is no end to the process of gaining historical knowledge that exists outside the process itself, we decide we have completed our task when (however forced this may be by the practical limits of time, opportunity, access to sources, and the like) we are satisfied with the results.

Throughout this chapter I have used words like "satisfactory," "adequate," "sufficient," "persuasive," "plausible," "probable," even "valid," to signify, with respect to standards of epistemology and method, the positive evaluations both historians and their readers make of their work. These evaluations judge the degree to which there is a match, across the entire spectrum of the most particular to the most general levels of discourse, between explanatory and interpretive claims on the one hand and the evidence adduced to support them on the other. Entered into through the dialectic of oppositions, the three dimensions of perspective, temporality, and structure offer a method of discovery that is both economical in its operation and open-ended in its reach. The criteria by which we judge the match between claims and evidence are empirical in the same way that the hermeneutic matching of text to context is empirical. In the early modern period it became common to compare the reading of scripture with the reading of God's other book, nature, and at least for a while both science and history took seriously the techniques of biblical exegesis as a model for their own enterprises. The discipline of history came into its own when it embraced the methodological requirement that knowledge of the past be grounded in "texts" whose objectivity, even in the most inclusive sense of that term, is also a function of subjective interpretation—that is, interpretation by a subject. This is the objectivity not of deconstructive "textuality" but of empirical hermeneutics. To recall the purpose with which I began this chapter, students of literary history may gain their best access to historical method less through exposure to the training historians may customarily receive than by reflecting self-consciously on their own training in the close reading of written texts as the basis for extrapolating outward and upward to the realm of history as such.

Acknowledgments

I'm deeply grateful to the many critics, scholars, colleagues, friends, and family who over the years have aided my thought and writing with unflagging intelligence and generosity. Rather than acknowledge everyone who has helped me by naming them individually, I'll confine myself to highlighting those whose work has energized mine early on, in recent years, or at each stage of my intellectual development: György Lukács, Jean-Paul Sartre, Claude Lévi-Strauss, R. H. Tawney, Christopher Hill, E. P. Thompson, Ellen Meiksins Wood, Raymond Williams, Jürgen Habermas, Randy Trumbach, Ruth Perry, and Douglas Lane Patey.

Notes

INTRODUCTION

1. The Enlightenment period was a broadly European phenomenon that varied according to differences in chronology, national character, and contextual circumstance. For example: the Enlightenment is associated with the eighteenth century, but the Dutch and English Enlightenments are thought to have begun earlier, in the mid-seventeenth century, than the French and German. To generalize about the nature of Enlightenment thought even within a single national culture is a notional enterprise. If we ask nonetheless what's central to the Enlightenment, the most common answer to this question, then and now, is the rational and empirical critique of religion. But rationalism is often aligned with French and Cartesian Enlightenment, whereas empiricism is often associated with British and Lockean Enlightenment. Is the broadly European coherence of "the Enlightenment" challenged by this philosophical difference? I don't think so. But the difference between a philosophical foundation in reason, and in the empirical evidence of the senses, has major consequences for the nature and direction of the French and British Enlightenments. This study concentrates on the British first of all because it's the field I know; but then because empiricism offers a more dependable method of approaching the singular understanding that Enlightenment thought brought to the transition from tradition to modernity. This was most evident to me early on in the specialist field of literature and aesthetic cognition, where the differences between French and Anglo-Scottish-American innovation in the field are crucial. But what I learned there I found borne out in other fields, as well as in the comparative emphases of these two cultures in pursuit of enlightenment. It seems to me that they define alternative but complementary approaches to understanding without presuppositions, augmenting the capacity of each to this common end. But the great liability of the category reason is its tendency to be hypostatized or substantialized as Reason, not only the means to that end but also the end itself. (The emphasis on reason rather than empiricism in the French Enlightenment is related to the persistence of absolutist political institutions until the end of the eighteenth century. That Foucault gives his "Classical Age" the same chronology has a great deal to do with the fact that his historical focus is France.) The empirical pursuit of sense perceptions isn't lacking in liabilities. But an attention to evidence and its implications, modeled on the analysis of sense perceptions but susceptible to extrapolation as a self-conscious method of inquiry, has a capacity for ongoing self-correction that might be said to enact the methodical component of methodology. This introduction will describe the enlightenment scrutiny of tradition in terms that express this empirical method of analysis.

2. Robert Wokler, "Introduction," in *The Enlightenment and Modernity*, ed. Norman Geras and Robert Wokler (New York: St. Martin's, 2000), x.

3. This may sound surprising to historians of the Enlightenment, who recently have seen an extensive, and to some degree revisionary, debate on the common view that the Enlightenment was critical of religious belief. I think this is a reaction to the critique of the Enlightenment I've described, but one that both accepts and interprets it in terms that the Enlightenment has made available; see ch. 2 in the present volume.

4. See, e.g., Max Horkheimer and Theodor W. Adorno, *Dialectic of Enlightenment* (1944), trans. John Cumming (New York: Herder and Herder, 1972); Peter Gay, *The Enlightenment: An Interpretation*, 2 vols. (New York: Knopf, 1966–1969); Margaret Jacob, *The Radical Enlightenment: Pantheists, Freemasons and Republicans* (London: George Allen and Unwin, 1981); Roy Porter and Mikuláš Teich, eds., *The Enlightenment in National Context* (Cambridge: Cambridge University Press, 1981); James Schmidt, ed., *What Is Enlightenment? Eighteenth-Century Answers and Twentieth-Century Questions* (Berkeley: University of California Press, 1996); William Clark, Jan Golinski, and Simon Schaffer, eds., *The Sciences in Enlightened Europe* (Chicago: University of Chicago Press, 1999); Jonathan Israel, *Radical Enlightenment: Philosophy and the Making of Modernity 1650–1750* (Oxford: Oxford University Press, 2001); Stephen Eric Bronner, *Reclaiming the Enlightenment: Toward a Politics of Radical Engagement* (New York: Columbia University Press, 2004); Jonathan Sheehan, *The Enlightenment Bible: Translation, Scholarship, Culture* (Princeton, NJ: Princeton University Press, 2005); Sarah Knott and Barbara Taylor, eds., *Women, Gender, and the Enlightenment* (Houndmills, England: Palgrave Macmillan, 2005); Clifford Siskin and William Warner, eds., *This Is Enlightenment* (Chicago: University of Chicago Press, 2010); Daniel Carey and Lynn Festa, eds., *The Postcolonial Enlightenment: Eighteenth-Century Colonialism and Postcolonial Theory* (Oxford: Oxford University Press, 2013); Ulrich Lehner, *The Catholic Enlightenment: The Forgotten History of a Global Movement* (Oxford: Oxford University Press, 2016); Ritchie Robertson, *The Enlightenment: The Pursuit of Happiness 1680–1790* (London: Allen Lane, 2020).

5. The following list might be expanded at will: Matthew C. Augustine, John Bender, Terry Castle, Lisa Forman Cody, Elizabeth L. Eisenstein, Kevis Goodman, J. Paul Hunter, Paula McDowell, Douglas Lane Patey, Ruth Perry, Joanna Picciotto, John Richetti, Pat Rogers, Wolfram Schmidgen.

6. See chs. 3 and 5 in the present volume.

7. Of course, the Enlightenment was the period when in England, at least, the category of the "modern" took on enormous ideological and cultural meaning, stimulated by the Quarrel of the Ancients and Moderns but soon acquiring its own complex and distinctive character. Although it's obviously relevant, this is not the meaning of the modern that I aim to designate in my use of the period term.

8. For a discussion of periodization as method, see ch. 6 in the present volume.

9. The language of wholes and parts introduced in this section should not be taken to attribute an evaluative standard of wholeness to the discourses under discussion either as their own representational goal or as a formal criterion by which they are critically evaluated. Rather, it is a method of describing the variable structural importance of discourses relative to one another.

10. Although the distinction between tacitly and explicitly held principles is not commonly conceived as chronological, I apply it schematically to the difference between traditional and modern mentalities. I think the rationale for so broad an application will become clear to the reader.

11. These fields include tradition and ideology, religion and secularization, positive and negative liberty, actual and virtual reality, Enlightenment and capitalist universality, state and civil society, the public sphere, imperialism and slavery, experience and experiment, the imagination, gender and sex, social status and class, individuality and personal identity, the arts and the sciences, mimesis and realism, the historicity of conventions, the historicity of genres, the historicity of political poetry, parody as a model of historical change.

12. Subhabrata Bobby Banerjee and Diane-Laure Arjaliès, "Celebrating the End of Enlightenment: Organization Theory in the Age of the Anthropocene and Gaia (and Why Neither Is the Solution to Our Ecological Crisis)," *Organization Theory* 2, no. 4 (2021): 2, 6.

13. Nancy Hartsock, "Foucault on Power: A Theory for Women?," in *Social Theory: The Multicultural and Classical Readings*, ed. Charles Lamert (Boulder, CO: Westview, 1993), 545, 548.

14. Mark Poster, *Foucault, Marxism and History: Mode of Production versus Mode of Information* (Cambridge: Polity Press, 1987), 11, 66.

15. Mary Poovey, "Financing Enlightenment, Part One. Money Matters," in Siskin and Warner, *This Is Enlightenment*, 328.

16. Robert Langbaum, *The Poetry of Experience: The Dramatic Monologue in Modern Literary Tradition* (New York: Norton, 1957), 11, 14.

17. Rajani Sudan, *Fair Exotics: Xenophobic Subjects in English Literature, 1720–1850* (Philadelphia: University of Pennsylvania Press, 2002), 9, 12.

18. Richard Rorty, *Consequences of Pragmatism (Essays 1972–1980)* (Minneapolis: University of Minnesota Press, 1982), 193.

19. Alasdair MacIntyre, *After Virtue: A Study in Moral Theory* (Notre Dame, IN: Notre Dame University Press, 1981), 78.

20. Horkheimer and Adorno, *Dialectic of Enlightenment*, 14 (further citations appear parenthetically in the text).

21. Michel Foucault, *The Order of Things: An Archaeology of the Human Sciences*, trans. Alan Sheridan (New York: Vintage, 1970), 125–128 (further citations appear parenthetically in the text).

22. For an intelligent discussion that engages several of these issues, see Alan Mikhail, "Enlightenment Anthropocene," *Eighteenth-Century Studies* 49, no. 2 (Winter 2016): 211–231. Mikhail's modus operandi is to sustain a comparison of the two that's thoughtful enough to belie its ongoing reduction of the Enlightenment to the Anthropocene. (He treats the former as dating from 1800.) For a discussion of these issues that's a good deal less thoughtful, see Banerjee and Arjaliès, "Celebrating the End of Enlightenment." Much of the discussion of the Anthropocene turns on its view of the relation between

nature and culture compared to that of tradition. For a consideration of this relationship as reflected in the development of pastoral poetry in the British Enlightenment, see *Historicizing the Enlightenment*, vol. 2, ch. 4.

23. For the moment I pass over legitimate questions that have been raised about the theorization and practice of this method because they would distract from my present and central point, the significance of experimentalism in the historical context of what it sought to supersede. These questions concern the problem of induction, the criterion of falsifiability, the sometimes virtual status of empirical testimony, and the concepts of the paradigm and "normal science." I take them up in ch. 3 in the present volume, nn.87–93.

24. For a recent overstatement of the virtues of quantification, see Steven Pinker, *Enlightenment Now: The Case for Reason, Science, Humanism, and Progress* (New York: Penguin, 2018). Pinker claims a direct continuity between the Enlightenment and Now, which he discovers by ignoring all qualitative evidence. This claim rests on Pinker's conviction that quantity has a positive supremacy over quality, a conviction that is the mirror image of its negative "domination" for Horkheimer and Adorno. Although Pinker takes himself to be a champion of the Enlightenment, this conviction exemplifies the modern, anti-Enlightenment failure to sustain Enlightenment principles, partializing them as the unqualified and absolute will to quantify, which the authors of *Dialectic of Enlightenment* attribute to the Enlightenment itself.

25. Jürgen Habermas, *The Structural Transformation of the Public Sphere* (1962), trans. Thomas Burger and Frederick Lawrence (Cambridge, MA: MIT Press, 1989), 89. For Habermas's evaluation of *Dialectic of Enlightenment*, see *The Philosophical Discourse of Modernity: Twelve Lectures*, trans. Frederick G. Lawrence (Cambridge, MA: MIT Press, 1987), ch. 5.

26. Ch. 3 of the present volume is devoted to a discussion of this Enlightenment realm of virtual reality.

27. For example, see Nancy Fraser, "Rethinking the Public Sphere: A Contribution to the Critique of Actually Existing Democracy," in *Habermas and the Public Sphere*, ed. Craig Calhoun (Cambridge, MA: MIT Press, 1994), 109–142; Geoff Eley, "Nations, Publics, and Political Cultures: Placing Habermas in the Nineteenth Century," in Calhoun, *Habermas and the Public Sphere*, 289–339.

28. Partha Chatterjee, *Nationalist Thought and the Colonial World: A Derivative Discourse* (Minneapolis: University of Minnesota Press, 1986), 168.

29. Michel Foucault, *Discipline and Punish: The Birth of the Prison*, trans. Alan Sheridan (New York: Vintage, 1979), 222.

30. John Roberts, *The Reasoning of Unreason: Universalism, Capitalism, and Disenlightenment* (London: Bloomsbury, 2018), 101, 104.

31. *The Economist*, 338, no. 7957 (March 16, 1996): 97.

32. See ch. 3 in the present volume.

33. Sankar Muthu, *Enlightenment against Empire* (Princeton, NJ: Princeton University Press, 2003), 345.

34. In *The German Ideology*, Marx and Engels use the figure of forms becoming fetters to describe a number of the above historical developments. Friedrich Engels and Karl Marx, *The German Ideology* (writ. 1845–1846, pub. 1932), pt. 1, D, https://www.marxists.org/archive/marx/works/download/Marx_The_German_Ideology.pdf.

35. Pheng Cheah, *Spectral Nationality: Passages of Freedom from Kant to Postcolonial Literatures of Liberation* (New York: Columbia University Press, 2003), 3, 6.

36. Patrick Williams and Laura Chrisman (eds.), *Colonial Discourse and Postcolonial Theory: A Reader* (New York: Columbia University Press, 1994), 8.

37. Lisa Lowe, "Decolonization, Displacement, Disidentification: Asian American 'Novels' and the Question of History," in *Cultural Institutions of the Novel*, ed. Deirdre Lynch and William Warner (Durham, NC: Duke University Press, 1996), 106.

38. Henry Louis Gates Jr., *The Signifying Monkey: A Theory of African-American Literary Criticism* (New York: Oxford University Press, 1988), 130.

39. Daniel Carey and Lynn Festa, "Introduction," in Carey and Festa, *Postcolonial Enlightenment*, 1–34.

40. See, e.g., Alasdair MacIntyre, *After Virtue: A Study in Moral Theory* (Notre Dame, IN: Notre Dame University Press, 1981), chs. 5 and 6. John Gray borrows this phrase from MacIntyre, uses it throughout, and in his title turns its anticipation into retrospection: *Enlightenment's Wake: Politics and Culture at the Close of the Modern Age* (London: Routledge, 1995).

41. See James Delbourgo and Nicholas Dew, "Introduction," in *Science and Empire in the Atlantic World*, ed. James Delbourgo and Nicholas Dew (New York: Routledge, 2008), 1–28. See also Jonathan Lamb, Vanessa Smith, and Nicholas Thomas, "Introduction," in *Exploration and Exchange: A South Seas Anthology 1680–1900*, ed. Jonathan Lamb, Vanessa Smith, and Nicholas Thomas (Chicago: University of Chicago Press, 2000), xiii–xxv; Dorinda Outram, *The Enlightenment* (Cambridge: Cambridge University Press, 1995), 63–65.

42. Michael Hechter, *Internal Colonialism: The Celtic Fringe in British National Development*, 2nd ed. (London: Routledge, 1999); Katie Trumpener, "The Abbotsford Guide to India: Romantic Fictions of Empire and the Narratives of Canadian Literature," in *Cultural Institutions of the Novel*, ed. Deidre Lynch and William B. Warner (Durham, NC: Duke University Press, 1996), 193–221.

43. For an amplification of this argument, see *Historicizing the Enlightenment*, vol. 2, ch. 4.

44. Vico (1725), Montesquieu (1748), and the later eighteenth-century writers of the Scottish Enlightenment.

45. For two judicious studies, see Mark Salber Phillips, *Society and Sentiment: Genres of Historical Writing in Britain, 1740–1820* (Princeton, NJ: Princeton University Press, 2000), ch. 7; and Frank Palmeri, *State of Nature, Stages of Society: Enlightenment Conjectural History and Modern Social Discourse* (New York: Columbia University Press, 2016).

46. Although the term itself doesn't arise in the following excerpts, it seems just to read them as an indictment of the knowledge conjectural history produces: "The

Enlightenment invention of the primitive" is an instance of "chrono-politics," "a *civilizational* principle that serves to ostracize all who do not conform to the modern conventions of time, that devalues 'subalterns' for being slow and not racing toward death, which in the rhetoric of modernity is translated as 'progress and development'. Chrono-politics . . . served . . . during the Enlightenment, to detach European modernity from the 'primitives.'" Walter D. Mignolo, *The Darker Side of Western Modernity: Global Futures, Decolonial Options* (Durham, NC: Duke University Press, 2011), 177, 178. If "the invention of the primitive" has reference to the word itself, its Enlightenment meaning was "simple," "a predecessor," "a foundation," "a root" (as opposed to a derivative), an early Christian (*OED* online: "primitive": A. I. 1. b., 2 a., 4, B. I. 1, 2, 3). In an age on the cusp of one of the greatest revaluations in Western history, from the normative status of what's traditional and old to that of what's innovative and new, the term "primitive" resists easy appraisal. If "the invention of the primitive" refers to the theory of conjectural history, it's hard to reconcile the author's assumption of division and exclusion with the inclusive mixture and expansion the theory actually opened up.

47. See, e.g., Pinker, *Enlightenment Now*, 11.

48. For a range of sources on these several facets of the topic, see Roxann Wheeler, *The Complexion of Race: Categories of Difference in Eighteenth-Century British Culture* (Philadelphia: University of Pennsylvania Press, 2000); Gretchen Holbrook Gerzina, *Black London: Life before Emancipation* (New Brunswick, NJ: Rutgers University Press, 1995); Andrew S. Curran, *The Anatomy of Blackness: Science and Slavery in an Age of Enlightenment* (Baltimore: John Hopkins University Press, 2011); Nicholas Hudson, "From 'Nation' to 'Race': The Origin of Racial Classification in Eighteenth-Century Thought," *Eighteenth-Century Studies* 29, no. 3 (Spring 1996): 247–264, and "'Hottentots' and the Evolution of European Racism," *Journal of European Studies* 34, no. 4 (December 2004): 308–332; Mary Nyquist, *Arbitrary Rule: Slavery, Tyranny, and the Power of Life and Death* (Chicago: University of Chicago Press, 2013).

49. See Jill Lepore, *These Truths: A History of the United States* (New York: Norton, 2018), 115–116, 130–131, 175, 701; *The 1619 Project: A New Origin Story*, ed. Nikole Hannah-Jones, Caitlin Roper, Ilena Silverman, and Jake Silverstein (New York: One World Books, 2021).

50. Related testimony can be seen in the sudden brutalization—and modernization—of attitudes toward sodomy at the turn of the eighteenth century; see ch. 4 in the present volume. In Anglo-American experience, there's a profound analogy between the exploitation of wage laborers and the forced labor of enslaved people. The analogy may be illuminated by the parallel between pastoral—country and city—and "macro-pastoral"—colony and metropolitan—relations; see *Historicizing the Enlightenment*, vol. 2, ch. 4.

CHAPTER 1 — TRADITION AS TACIT KNOWLEDGE

1. I use the term throughout not in the literal and restricted sense of "silent" but in the more general sense of "implicit" or "inferred."

2. *Commons Debates 1628, 21 April–27 May 1628*, ed. Robert C. Johnson et al. (New Haven, CT: Yale University Press, 1977), 3:578–579.

3. "The King's Answer to the Nineteen Propositions," June 18, 1642, in *The Stuart Constitution 1603–1688: Documents and Commentary*, ed. J. P. Kenyon (Cambridge: Cambridge University Press, 1966), 22–23. Charles here invokes his father's precepts, whose very explicitness, belying the tacitness they demand, itself conveys a crisis in tacit knowledge: "That which concerns the mystery of the King's power is not lawful to be disputed; for that is to wade into the weakness of Princes, and to take away the mystical reverence that belongs unto them that sit in the throne of God.... It is presumption and high contempt in a subject to dispute what a King can do, or say that a King cannot do this or that." James I, *Political Works of James I*, ed. C. H. McIlwain (London, 1918), 333, as quoted in J. R. Tanner, *English Constitutional Conflicts of the Seventeenth Century 1603–1689* (Cambridge: Cambridge University Press, 1928; rpt., 1961), 20.

4. George Monck, "A Letter of General George Moncks Dated at Leicester 23 January, and Directed unto Mr. Rolle to Be Communicated unto the Rest of the Gentry of Devon...," in *A Collection of Several Letters and Declarations Sent by General Monck* ... (London, 1660), 19. The related observation of George Savile, Marquess of Halifax, emphasizes the epistemological more than the political effects of the civil war: "The liberty of the late times gave men so much light, and diffused it so universally amongst the people, that they are not now to be dealt with, as they might have been in an age of less inquiry." Quoted in Derek Hirst, *England in Conflict 1603–1660: Kingdom, Community, Commonwealth* (New York: Oxford University Press, 1999), 328.

5. Edward Waterhouse, *The Gentleman's Monitor: or, A Sober Inspection into the Vertues, Vices, and Ordinary Means, of the Rise and Decay of Men and Families* (London: Printed by T. R. for R. Royston, 1665), 261–262. Cf. Sir William Davenant in 1654: "And subjects should receive good education from the State, as from vertuous Philosophers, who did anciently with excellent success correct the peoples manners, not by penall Statutes and Prisons, but by Moral Schooles and Heroick Representations at the publick charge.... Armies ... are improper to command belief and conformity, because they do it by compulsion; for the minde ... should be govern'd by the insinuations of perswasion" (Sir William Davenant, *A Proposition for Advancement of Moralitie, by a New Way of Entertainment of the People* [1654], 2, 5; reprinted in James R. Jacob and Timothy Raylor, "Opera and Obedience: Thomas Hobbes and *A Proposition for Advancement of Moralitie* by Sir William Davenant," *The Seventeenth Century* 6, no. 2 [1991]: 243). Davenant's proposal is to revive ancient methods of obtaining "a quick and implicit obedience" to state authority by "civiliz[ing] the people" through theatrical and operatic productions. But he is also mindful that now "Perswasion must be joyn'd to Force" (5, 11; 242–243, 244). Foucault's followers sometimes take him to be arguing that Enlightenment discipline "dissociates power from the body" in the sense of elaborating methods of "discursive" persuasion to achieve the ends of social control that traditionally had been undertaken by physical force alone (Michel Foucault, *Discipline and Punish: The Birth of the Prison*, trans. Alan Sheridan [New York: Vintage, 1979], 138). The testimony of Waterhouse and Davenant suggests that what is new is not "disciplinary" persuasion but the separation out of persuasion and force as parts of the former whole "domination" (or, of discourse

and bodily power as parts of the former whole "discipline") as different methods that can be exploited in different ways.

6. The "traditional" idea of the public interest presumed its coextension with the royal interest. "Significant discussion about the public interest begins with the Civil War": J.A.W. Gunn, *Politics and the Public Interest in the Seventeenth Century* (London: Routledge, 1969), 1.

7. See Eric Hobsbawm, "Introduction: Inventing Traditions," in *The Invention of Tradition*, ed. Eric Hobsbawm and Terence Ranger (Cambridge: Cambridge University Press, 1984), 1–14.

8. For a recent and deeply informed engagement with these issues, see Paula McDowell, *The Invention of the Oral: Print Commerce and Fugitive Voices in Eighteenth-Century Britain* (Chicago: University of Chicago Press, 2017).

9. See in general Jack Goody and Ian Watt, "The Consequences of Literacy," in *Literacy in Traditional Societies*, ed. Jack Goody (Cambridge: Cambridge University Press, 1968), 27–68.

10. *Religio Laici or A Laymans Faith. A Poem* (1682), in *The Works of John Dryden*, vol. 2, *Poems 1681–1684*, ed. H. T. Swedenberg Jr. and Vinton A. Dearing (Berkeley: University of California Press, 1972), ll. 270–275, 305–306, 350–353, 386–389, 400–403. That Dryden misrepresents Roman Catholic "tradition" as exclusively oral does not compromise the force of his argument for present purposes.

11. Davies, *Irish Reports* (1612), quoted in J.G.A. Pocock, *The Ancient Constitution and the Feudal Law: A Study of English Historical Thought in the Seventeenth Century* (New York: W. W. Norton, 1967), 32–33.

12. William Blackstone, *Commentaries on the Laws of England: In Four Books*, ed. Thomas M. Cooley (Chicago: Callaghan and Cockcroft, 1871), 1:63.

13. The first phrase is Pocock's, *Ancient Constitution*, 46; the second is Christopher Hill's: see *The Century of Revolution, 1603–1714*, 2nd ed. (New York: W. W. Norton, 1980), 54; John Warr, *The Corruption and Deficiency of the Laws of England* (1649), in *Harleian Miscellany* (1744–1746), 3:240, quoted in Christopher Hill, *The World Turned Upside Down: Radical Ideas during the English Revolution* (New York: Viking Press, 1973), 219. It is in this sense that Ellen Meiksins Wood can speak of "the British ideology of tradition": *The Pristine Culture of Capitalism: A Historical Essay on Old Regimes and Modern States* (London: Verso, 1991), 76. As I argue below, however, "tradition" and "ideology" may usefully be seen to have a special relationship that complicates this sort of usage.

14. Francis Bacon, *Of the Proficience and Advancement of Learning, Divine and Human* (1605); "Author's Preface," *Of the Wisdom of the Ancients* (Latin 1609), in *The Philosophical Works of Francis Bacon*, ed. Robert L. Ellis and James Spedding, rev. John M. Robertson (London: Routledge, 1905), 121, 124, 822. Bacon's skepticism in the latter work justifies the cheerful negligence of his own rereadings of the ancient fables: "The wisdom of the primitive ages was either great or lucky. . . . My own pains, if there be any help in them, I shall think well bestowed either way: I shall be throwing light either upon antiquity or upon nature itself" (824).

15. Thomas Hobbes, "Preface to the Readers" (1649), *De Cive* (1642), trans. and ed. Richard Tuck and Michael Silverthorne as *On the Citizen* (Cambridge: Cambridge University Press, 1998), 9.

16. *The Works of the Honourable Robert Boyle*, 3rd ed., ed. Thomas Birch (London: J. and F. Rivington, 1772), 1:304.

17. John Locke, *An Essay concerning Human Understanding* (1689), ed. Peter H. Nidditch (Oxford: Clarendon Press, 1975), bk. 4, ch. 19, sec. 14; bk. 4, ch. 16, sec. 10 (pp. 664, 704). Although the "discovery" of tradition, especially through technological innovation, is most powerfully conceived as a once-and-for-all revolution in consciousness, its multiple and overlapping nature can be seen in the plausible argument that the epistemological separation of the subject and object of knowledge was achieved first of all by Plato, under the more or less direct influence of the literacy revolution; see Eric A. Havelock, *Preface to Plato* (Cambridge, MA: Harvard University Press, 1963), chs. 11–12.

18. *Christianity Not Mysterious*, 2nd ed. (London, 1696), 58; Bernard Mandeville, *Origin of Honour* (London, 1732), 40–41; both quoted by the editor in Mandeville, *The Fable of the Bees* (1705, 1714), ed. F. B. Kaye (Oxford: Clarendon Press, 1924), 1:46–47n.1. For Mandeville's earlier usage, see "An Enquiry into the Origin of Moral Virtue," in *Fable of the Bees*, 1:41–57.

19. Francis Bacon, *Novum Organum* (1620), in *Philosophical Works*, 265, in specific reference to the Idols of the Theater.

20. *Essay concerning Human Understanding*, IV, xix (697–706); Locke to Damaris Cudworth, later Lady Masham, April 6, 1682?, in *The Correspondence of John Locke*, ed. E. S. de Beer (Oxford: Oxford University Press; Clarendon Edition of the Works of John Locke, 1976), 2:500.

21. Swift's other two realms are variously "empire" and "knowledge," "empire" and "philosophy," and "faction" and what we might call "popular culture"; see Swift, "A Discourse concerning the Mechanical Operation of the Spirit" (1704) and "A Tale of a Tub" (1704, 1710) in *A Tale of a Tub to Which Is Added The Battle of the Books and The Mechanical Operation of the Spirit*, 2nd ed., ed A. C. Guthkelch and D. Nichol Smith (Oxford: Oxford University Press, 1958), 266–267, 162, 62–63.

22. Robert Filmer, *Patriarcha* (writ. c. 1640, pub. 1680), in *Patriarcha and Other Political Works*, ed. Peter Laslett (Oxford: Blackwell, 1949), 54; Algernon Sidney, *Discourses concerning Government* (writ. 1680–1683, pub. 1696), ed. Thomas G. West (Indianapolis: Liberty Fund, 1996), I, iii (pp. 12–13).

23. John Locke, *An Essay concerning the True Original, Extent, and End of Civil Government (The Second Treatise of Government)* (1690), in *Two Treatises of Government*, ed. Peter Laslett, 2nd ed. (London: Cambridge University Press, 1967), bk. 2, ch. 8, sec. 119 (pp. 365–366). The problem of tacit consent provided Dryden the opportunity for a reductio ad absurdum that implied an anti-Christian tendency in contractarian thinking: "If those who gave the Scepter, could not tye/By their own deed their own Posterity,/How then coud Adam bind his future Race?/How coud his forfeit on mankind take place?/Or how coud heavenly Justice damn us all,/Who nere consented to our Fathers

fall?": *Absalom and Achitophel* (1681), ll. 769–774, in *Works of John Dryden*, 2:28. Cf. Sir John Vanbrugh's Lady Brute, whom the playwright economically employs to satirize in the same breath contractarianism, tacit consent, and patriarchalism: "Why, what did I vow? I think I promised to be true to my husband. Well; and he promised to be kind to me. But he hasn't kept his word. Why then I'm absolved from mine. Aye, that seems clear to me. The argument's good between the King and the people, why not between the husband and the wife? Oh, but that condition was not expressed. No matter, 'twas understood": Sir John Vanbrugh, *The Provok'd Wife* (1697), ed. Anthony Coleman (Manchester: Manchester University Press, 1982), I.i:69–76 (pp. 59–60).

24. See Claude Lévi-Strauss, *The Savage Mind* (Chicago: University of Chicago Press, 1966), ch. 1.

25. *The Doctrine & Discipline of Divorce Restor'd to the Good of Both Sexes . . .* (1644), in *Complete Prose Works of John Milton, 1643–48*, ed. Don M. Wolfe et al. (New Haven, CT: Yale University Press, 1959), 2:222–223.

26. Bernard Mandeville, "Remark (C.)," *Fable of the Bees*, 1:69.

27. Mary Astell, *A Serious Proposal to the Ladies for the Advancement of Their True and Greatest Interest*, pt. 1, 3rd ed. (1696), in *The First English Feminist: Reflections upon Marriage and Other Writings by Mary Astell*, ed. Bridget Hill (Aldershot, England: Gower/Maurice Temple Smith 1986), 147–148.

28. Enlightenment educational theory sought to acknowledge the role of implication in the pedagogic process. Cf. Fenelon's "indirect instructions" and Locke's idea of inculcation by "insensible degrees," and see generally Richard A. Barney, *Plots of Enlightenment: Education and the Novel in Eighteenth-Century England* (Stanford, CA: Stanford University Press, 1999), ch. 1.

29. David Hume, *A Treatise of Human Nature* (1739–1740), ed. L. A. Selby-Bigge and P. H. Nidditch, 2nd ed. (Oxford: Oxford University Press, 1978), I, iii, sec. 8 (pp. 102–103). For relevant reflections on the paradigm figure, see Thomas S. Kuhn, *The Structure of Scientific Revolutions*, 2nd ed. (Chicago: University of Chicago Press, 1970), 23–25, 176–179.

30. Michael Polanyi, *The Tacit Dimension* (Gloucester, MA: Peter Smith, 1983), 20, 87, 61–62. For his acknowledgment of earlier work by Polanyi, see Kuhn, *Structure*, 44, 191.

31. The recognition has been had in other areas as well; cf. the notion of "implication" in hermeneutics, "latent content" and "the unconscious" in psychoanalysis, etc. Issues of tacit knowledge also may (although they need not) be pertinent to contemporary second-order, methodological debates about whether the social sciences should "interpret" or "explain" their objects of study: whether they should understand their objects from the "inside" or from the "outside," according to concepts "internal" or "external" to them, by reference to "motives" or by reference to "causes." For an illuminating discussion, see Alasdair MacIntyre, "The Idea of a Social Science," in *Against the Self-Images of the Age: Essays on Ideology and Philosophy* (Notre Dame, IN: University of Notre Dame Press, 1978), 211–229.

32. This concept of ideology has been elaborated most influentially by Antonio Gramsci as that "level" in "the complex of superstructures" that has the "function of 'hegemony' which the dominant group exercises throughout society": *Selections from the Prison Notebooks of Antonio Gramsci*, ed. and trans. Quintin Hoare and Geoffrey Nowell Smith (London: Lawrence and Wishart, 1971), 12.

33. Jürgen Habermas, *Toward a Rational Society: Student Protest, Science, and Politics*, trans. Jeremy I. Shapiro (Boston: Beacon Press, 1970), 99.

34. Alvin W. Gouldner, *The Dialectic of Ideology and Technology: The Origins, Grammar, and Future of Ideology* (New York: Seabury Press, 1976), 30, 36.

35. Michael Oakeshott, *Rationalism in Politics and Other Essays* (London: Methuen, 1974), 122–123.

36. Clifford Geertz, "Ideology as a Cultural System," in *The Interpretation of Cultures: Selected Essays* (New York: Basic, 1973), 219 and n.42.

37. Raymond Williams, *Marxism and Literature* (New York: Oxford University Press, 1977), 115–116.

38. The uncertain relationship of tradition and ideology as modes of tacit knowledge is expressed by John Plamenatz in *Ideology* (London: Praeger, 1970), 21: "Though the term ideology is by no means confined to explicit beliefs it is in practice seldom used to refer to the beliefs of primitive peoples. I do not know why this should be so."

39. Daniel Defoe, *The Compleat English Gentleman* (writ. 1728–1729), ed. Karl D. Bülbring (London: D. Nutt, 1890), 13.

40. Thomas Paine, *Rights of Man*, pt. 1 (1791), in *Common Sense and Other Political Writings*, ed. Nelson F. Adkins (Indianapolis: Bobbs-Merrill, 1953), 89, 108, 111.

41. Karl Marx, *Grundrisse: Foundations of the Critique of Political Economy*, trans. and ed. Martin Nicolaus (Harmondsworth, England: Penguin, 1973), 110.

42. Gouldner, *Dialectic*, 211, 214, 222.

43. See Louis Althusser's pursuit of the analogy through the idea of "interpellation": "Ideology and Ideological State Apparatuses," in *Lenin and Philosophy and Other Essays*, trans. Ben Brewster (London: New Left Books, 1971), 162–170. The relationship between ideology and tradition can also be felt in Althusser's emphasis on "education" at the root of "ideological state apparatuses"; see 144–145.

44. Friedrich Engels and Karl Marx, *The German Ideology* (written 1845–1846, pub. 1932), pt. 1, D, https://www.marxists.org/archive/marx/works/download/Marx_The_German_Ideology.pdf. They go on to formulate the corollary principle of "unequal development": "The various stages and interests are never completely overcome, but only subordinated to the prevailing interest and trail along beside the latter for centuries afterwards."

45. Hans-Georg Gadamer, *Truth and Method*, trans. William Glen-Doepel (London: Sheed and Ward, 1979), 244.

46. Edmund Burke, *Reflections on the Revolution in France* (1790), ed. Thomas H. D. Mahoney (Indianapolis: Bobbs-Merrill, 1955), 69; cf. 70–71 (further citations appear parenthetically in the text).

47. See n.17.

48. For Marten, see n.2.

49. James Boswell, *Life of Johnson* (1791), ed. R. W. Chapman (Oxford: Oxford University Press, 1980), 316, 317. To perceive the "accidental" nature of social forms is therefore not necessarily (as in Marx's ideology theory) to experience them as "fetters." Rather, it confirms the impersonal and rule-bound nature of "the great system of society"—that is, its systematicity.

50. The following three paragraphs draw on my essay "The Origins of Interdisciplinary Studies," *Eighteenth-Century Studies* 28, no. 1 (Fall 1994): 22–23.

51. Addison, *Spectator*, nos. 411, 418 (June 21 and 30, 1712), in *The Spectator*, ed. Donald F. Bond. (Oxford: Clarendon Press, 1965), 3:537–539, 568–569.

52. See Aristotle, *Poetics*, in *Introduction to Aristotle*, trans. Ingram Bywater, ed. Richard McKeon (New York: Modern Library, 1947), 1448b; Samuel Taylor Coleridge, *Biographia Literaria* (1817), ed. George Watson (London: J. M. Dent, 1965), II, xiv (p. 169). Cf. John Dryden, *Of Dramatic Poesy: An Essay* (1668), in *Of Dramatic Poesy and Other Critical Essays*, ed. George Watson (London: Dent, 1964), 50–52, 62; Edmund Burke, *A Philosophical Inquiry into the Origin of Our Ideas of the Sublime and the Beautiful* (1757), ed. J. T. Boulton (London: Routledge, 1958), 44–51, 91; Samuel Johnson, "Preface" to *The Works of William Shakespeare* (1765), in *The Yale Edition of the Works of Samuel Johnson*, ed. Arthur Sherbo (New Haven, CT: Yale University Press, 1968), 7: 76, 78. Coleridge had earlier described this effect with regard to the reading not of poetry but of the novel; see *Critical Review*, 2nd ser., 19 (February 1797): 195, quoted in Joseph F. Bartolomeo, *A New Species of Criticism: Eighteenth-Century Discourse on the Novel* (Newark: University of Delaware Press, 1994), 140.

53. Anon., *The Gentleman's Magazine* 40 (October 1770), in *Novel and Romance 1700–1800: A Documentary Record*, ed. Ioan Williams (New York: Barnes and Noble, 1970), 274–275.

54. Clara Reeve, *The Progress of Romance through Times, Countries, and Manners* (Colchester, 1785), 1:111.

55. Henry Mackenzie, *The Lounger*, 20 (Saturday, June 18, 1785); Thomas Monroe, *Olla Podrida*, 15 (June 23, 1787); both in Williams, *Novel and Romance*, 330, 350. Cf. Davenant's proposal to revive "heroick representations," in this chapter, n.5.

56. William Enfield, *The Monthly Review*, ser. 2, 15 (November 1794), in Williams, *Novel and Romance*, 393.

57. Collins, "An Ode on the Popular Superstitions of the Highlands of Scotland, Considered as the Subject of Poetry," ll. 18–21, 32–35, 172–173, 185–191, in *The Poems of Thomas Gray, William Collins, and Oliver Goldsmith*, ed. Roger Lonsdale (London: Longman, 1976), 503–516.

58. Schiller's distinction between the "childish" and the "childlike" elements of the naive parallels my argument concerning the ambivalence with which Enlightenment thought "discovered" tradition; see Friedrich Schiller, "Naive and Sentimental Poetry" (1801), in *Naive and Sentimental Poetry and On the Sublime*, trans. and ed. Julius A. Elias (New York: Ungar, 1966), 87–90.

CHAPTER 2 — CIVIL AND RELIGIOUS LIBERTY

1. The first version of this chapter was written for a conference entitled "Civil and Religious Liberty: Ideas of Rights and Tolerance in England 1640–1800," held at Yale University, July 23–26, 2008. My thanks to Blair Worden, a co-organizer of the conference, for bringing this passage to my and others' attention. John Milton, *Considerations Touching the Likeliest Means to Remove Hirelings Out of the Church* . . . (London, 1659), sig. a5r.

2. John Milton, *Of Education. To Master Samuel Hartlib* (London, 1644), 2.

3. George Herbert, "Redemption" (1633), in *George Herbert: The Complete English Poems*, ed. John Tobin (London: Penguin, 1991), 35–36.

4. This paragraph is taken in part from Michael McKeon, *The Origins of the English Novel, 1600–1740* (Baltimore: Johns Hopkins University Press, 1987), 178.

5. Although the focus of this chapter is on conceptual change, the material history in which this intellectual history was situated was of course crucial to the debate.

6. Roger Manwaring, *Religion and Allegiance: In Two Sermons Preached before the Kings Maiestie* . . . (London, 1627), 5, 13–14, 20, 23–24, 24–25, 26–27.

7. The literature on the opposition between positive and negative liberty is extensive, as is disagreement on the meaning of the two terms. (My interpretation of it corresponds to and illuminates the change in thinking from the early seventeenth to the early eighteenth century. For a more skeptical response to the petition see Chap. 1 in this volume." This chronology correlates positive liberty with cultures that put a premium on a collective principle of social, political, and economic well-being and entail a sanction against the autonomy of the individual. But positive liberty is also the guiding principle of modern socialist and communist movements, which would build upon the economic productivity of capitalism to establish societies based on sociopolitical values of the collective that are consistent with the development of individual potential.) For a range of interpretations, see G.W.F. Hegel, *Reason in History: A General Introduction to the Philosophy of History* (1837), trans. Robert S. Hartman (New York: Liberal Arts, 1953), ch. 3; Isaiah Berlin, "Two Concepts of Liberty," in Isaiah Berlin, *Four Essays on Liberty* (Oxford: Oxford University Press, 1969), 118–172; Charles Taylor, "What's Wrong with Negative Liberty," in *The Idea of Freedom: Essays in Honour of Isaiah Berlin*, ed. Alan Ryan (Oxford: Oxford University Press, 1979), 175–193; Lawrence Crocker, *Positive Liberty: An Essay in Normative Political Philosophy* (The Hague: Martinus Nijhoff, 1980); and Quentin Skinner, "The Idea of Negative Liberty: Philosophical and Historical Perspectives," in *Philosophy in History: Essays on the Historiography of Philosophy*, ed. Richard Rorty, J. B. Schneewind, and Quentin Skinner (Cambridge: Cambridge University Press, 1984), 193–219.

8. Robert Filmer, *Patriarcha* (1680), in *Patriarcha and Other Political Works*, ed. Peter Laslett (Oxford: Blackwell, 1949), 55.

9. Thomas Hobbes, *Leviathan* (London, 1651), ch. 21:107, ch. 29:169.

10. For example, see John Ley, *Light for Smoke* (London, 1646), 6–7, who distinguishes between a "State or publique conscience" and "a personal/ and particular conscience."

Controversialists even used the phrase "publike liberty of conscience" (to refer to a policy of religious toleration): see [Dudley Fenner], *An Antiquodlibet, or An Aduertisement to Beware of Secular Priests* (Middelburgh: by R. Schilders, printer to the states of Zealand [Denmark]: 1602), 103.

11. John Locke, *Two Treatises of Government* (1690), ed. Peter Laslett, 2nd ed. (Cambridge: Cambridge University Press, 1967), bk. 2, ch. 1, sec. 2 (p. 268).

12. See *OED* online: "civil": A.I. 1–3, II.12; B.1.a. "civil society": 1.

13. See Jürgen Habermas, *The Structural Transformation of the Public Sphere: An Inquiry into a Category of Bourgeois Society*, trans. Thomas Burger and Frederick Lawrence (Cambridge, MA: MIT Press, 1989), 30.

14. See the discussion in Christopher Hill, *The Century of Revolution, 1603–1714* (1961; 2nd ed. rpt., New York: W. W. Norton, 1980), 126–127.

15. See Locke, *Two Treatises*, bk. 2, ch. 5 (pp. 303–320).

16. Robert Brenner has argued that the separation of the economy from the polity was central to England's early development from a feudal system of "politically constituted property" to a capitalist system of "economically constituted property"; see his "The Agrarian Roots of European Capitalism," in *The Brenner Debate: Agrarian Class Structure and Economic Development in Pre-Industrial Europe*, ed. T. H. Ashton and C.H.E. Philpin (Cambridge: Cambridge University Press, 1985), 291–299; and his *Merchants and Revolution: Commercial Change, Political Conflict, and London's Overseas Traders, 1550–1653* (1993; rpt. London: Verso, 2003), 647–553. See also Ellen Meiksins Wood, *The Origins of Capitalism: A Longer View* (London: Verso, 2002), esp. 55–56, 171–174.

17. John Lilly, *The Practical Register* (1719), quoted in G. E. Aylmer, "The Meaning and Definition of 'Property' in Seventeenth-Century England," *Past and Present* 86 (1980): 95.

18. Joseph Addison, *Spectator*, no. 69 (May 19, 1711), in *The Spectator*, ed. Donald F. Bond (Oxford: Clarendon Press, 1965).

19. Daniel Defoe, *The Compleat English Gentleman* (writ. 1728–1729), ed. Karl D. Bülbring (London: Nutt, 1890), 62–63.

20. George Monck, "A Letter of General George Moncks...directed unto Mr. Rolle...[and] the rest of the Gentry of Devon," January 23, 1660, in *A Collection of Several Letters and Declarations Sent by George Monck*... (London, 1660), 19.

21. Richard Cumberland, *A Philosophical Enquiry into the Laws of Nature* (Latin 1672; trans. J. Towers 1750), 307, quoted in J.A.W. Gunn, *Politics and the Public Interest in the Seventeenth Century* (London: Routledge and Kegan Paul, 1969), 285.

22. [Edward Hyde, Earl of Clarendon], *Second Thoughts, or, the Case of a Limited Toleration, Stated according to the Present Exigence of Affairs in Church and State* (1663), 4; 3; 4–5 (further citations appear parenthetically in the text).

23. John Locke, *An Essay concerning Toleration* (writ. 1667), in *A Letter concerning Toleration and Other Writings*, ed. Mark Goldie (Indianapolis: Liberty Fund, 2010), 125, 129 (further citations appear parenthetically in the text).

24. John Foxe, *The Acts and Monuments of John Foxe* (1563; enlarged ed., 1570), ed. Stephen R. Cattley (London: Seeley and Burnside, 1839), 8:475.

25. OED online: "Conscience" I.

26. See Christopher Hill, "Covenant Theology and the Concept of 'A Public Person,'" in *The Collected Essays of Christopher Hill* (Amherst: University of Massachusetts Press, 1986), 3:300–324.

27. See Conal Condren, *The Language of Politics in Seventeenth-Century England* (New York: St. Martin's, 1994), 46, 47.

28. Andrew Marvell, *The Rehearsal Transpros'd*, pt. 1 (1672), ed. Martin Dzelzainis, in *The Prose Works of Andrew Marvell: 1672–1673*, ed. Annabel Patterson, Martin Dzelzainis, N. H. Keeble, and Nicholas von Maltzahn (New Haven, CT: Yale University Press, 2003), 1:192 (further citations appear parenthetically in the text).

29. [Samuel Parker], *A Discourse of Ecclesiastical Politie Wherein the Authority of the Civil Magistrate over the Consciences of Subjects in Matters of Religion Is Asserted, the Mischiefs and Inconveniences of Toleration Are Represented, and All Pretenses Pleaded in Behalf of Liberty of Conscience Are Fully Answered* (London, 1669), 89, 91, 308.

30. William Penn, *The Great Case of Liberty of Conscience . . .* (London, 1670), 26.

31. [William Lloyd], *The Late Apology in behalf of the Papists Re-Printed and Answered, in behalf of the Royallists* (London, 1667), 40.

32. R. T. [Peter Pett], *A Discourse concerning Liberty of Conscience, in Which Are Contain'd Proposalls, about What Liberty in This Kind Is Now Politically Expedient to Be Given, and Severall Reasons to Shew How Much the Peace and Welfare of the Nation Is Concern'd Therein* (London, 1661), 15–16, 19–20 (further citations appear parenthetically in the text).

33. Thomas Sprat, *The History of the Royal Society of London, for the Improving of Natural Knowledge* (London, [1667], 3rd ed., 1722), 63.

34. This usage was more common before the Civil Wars: see [William Perkins], *A Discovrse of Conscience . . .* (Cambridge: Universitie of Cambridge, 1596), 96–97; John Robinson, *Ivstification of Separation from the Church of England* (Amsterdam, 1610), 30.

35. Roger L'Estrange, *Interest Mistaken, or the Holy Cheat . . .* (London, 1661), 6–7.

36. John Corbet, *Discourse of the Religion of England . . .* (London, 1667), 23, 26.

37. Charles Wolseley, *Liberty of Conscience, upon Its True and Proper Grounds, Asserted & Vindicated* (London, 1668), 59.

38. Herbert Thorndike, *A Discourse of the Forbearance or the Penalties Which a Due Reformation Requires* (London: J. M., 1670), 165–166.

39. Samuel Parker, "Preface" to *Bishop Bramhall's Vindication of Himself . . . Together with a Preface Shewing What Grounds There Are of Fears and Jealousies of Popery* (1672), sig. a2; on dissent and trade see, e.g., Marvell, *Rehearsal*, 1:47, 56–57.

40. John Dryden, *Religio Laici or a Laymans Faith. A Poem* (1682), in *The Works of John Dryden*, vol. 2, *Poems 1681–1684*, ed. H. T. Swedenberg Jr. and Vinton A. Dearing (Berkeley: University of California Press, 1972), ll. 376–385, 388–397.

41. See this chapter, nn.32-33.

42. In his most famous poem, published a year before *Religio Laici*, Dryden reflects the skeptical historicism of his period by fashioning a synthesis of typological and allegorical signification that self-consciously displays a rhetorical brilliance serviceable to epistemological analysis rather than to metaphysical affirmation. See Michael McKeon, "Historicizing *Absalom and Achitophel*," in *The New Eighteenth Century*, ed. Laura Brown and Felicity Nussbaum (New York: Methuen, 1987), 23-40.

43. [John Dryden], "To the Reader," prefixed to *The Hind and the Panther* (1687), in *The Works of John Dryden*, vol. 3, *Poems, 1685-1692*, ed. Earl Miner and Vinton A. Dearing (Berkeley: University of California Press, 1969), 120.

44. [William Lawrence], *Marriage by the Morall Law of God Vindicated against all Ceremonial Laws* (n.p., 1680), 101-102.

45. Thomas Shadwell, *The Lancashire Witches* (1682), in *The Complete Works of Thomas Shadwell*, ed. Montague Summers (1927; rpt. New York: Blom, 1968), 4:111.

46. Richard Steele, *Spectator*, no. 298 (February 11, 1712), in Bond, *The Spectator*.

47. See n.26 in this chapter.

48. For an excellent account of this movement as of 2003, see Jonathan Sheehan, "Enlightenment, Religion, and the Enigma of Secularization: A Review Essay," *American Historical Review* 108, no. 4 (October 2003): 1061-1080.

49. Sheehan, "Enlightenment," 1079.

50. Sheehan, "Enlightenment," 1074.

51. The normative value of "privacy" is unknown in premodern culture, for which to be "private" connotes privation, to be deprived of connection to what is most central and important. The modern value of privacy is related to the modern value of negative liberty. See Michael McKeon, *The Secret History of Domesticity: Public, Private, and the Division of Knowledge* (Baltimore: Johns Hopkins University Press, 2005), esp. xix, 228, 469.

52. *OED* online: "religion": "Etymology."

CHAPTER 3 — VIRTUAL REALITY

1. For a historically informed and authoritative discussion of virtual reality, see Martin Lister, Jon Dovey, Seth Giddings, Iain Grant, and Kieran Kelly, *New Media: A Critical Introduction*, 2nd ed. (London: Routledge, 2013), ch. 2. See also *Wikipedia*, s.v. "Virtual Reality," last modified November 14, 2022, https://en.wikipedia.org/wiki/Virtual_reality; "Virtual Reality Apps," VRS, accessed November 24, 2022, https://www.vrs.org.uk/virtual-reality/apps.html; *Investopedia*, s.v. "Virtual Reality"; "The Science of Virtual Reality," Franklin Institute, accessed November 24, 2022, https://www.fi.edu/virtual-reality/the-science-of-virtual-reality; and Rae Earnshaw, Michael Gigante, and H.U.W. Jones, "Introduction," in *Virtual Reality Systems*, edited by Rae Earnshaw, Michael Gigante, and H.U.W. Jones (Amsterdam: Elsevier, 1993), xix-xxii.

2. Tom Boellstorff, *Coming of Age in Second Life: An Anthropologist Explores the Virtually Human* (Princeton, NJ: Princeton University Press, 2008), 6.

3. See *Wikipedia*, s.v. "Metaverse," last modified November 21, 2022, https://en.wikipedia.org/wiki/Metaverse; *New York Times*, October 30, 2021, A1. *Meta Incognita*, "beyond the unknown" or "the unknown beyond," is the name Elizabeth I gave in 1577 to the land Admiral Martin Frobisher hoped to use as a base for his expedition in search of the Northwest Passage to China.

4. This chapter will discuss three areas in which the virtual extension of the body was undertaken: 1) the extension of experimentalism from the analysis of the objective world to the analysis of the virtual realm and productions of the subject; 2) the disembodiment and extension of the propriety of the self to the virtual ownership of objective property; 3) the extension of the actual private self to the virtual realm and publicness of print.

5. See *Historicizing the Enlightenment*, vol. 2, ch. 2.

6. See Jürgen Habermas, *The Structural Transformation of the Public Sphere: An Inquiry into a Category of Bourgeois Society* (1962), trans. Thomas Burger and Frederick Lawrence (Cambridge, MA: MIT Press, 1989); Benedict Anderson, *Imagined Communities: Reflections on the Origin and Spread of Nationalism* (London: Verso, 1983); and Charles Taylor, *Modern Social Imaginaries* (Durham, NC: Duke University Press, 2004).

7. This brief discussion continues the reflections on secularization that conclude ch. 2 in this volume.

8. Defoe's *Robinson Crusoe* (1719) is an acute narration of this dialectic of human motive and divine purpose: see Michael McKeon, *The Origins of the English Novel, 1600–1740* (Baltimore: Johns Hopkins University Press, 1987, 2002), ch. 9.

9. See Conal Condren, *The Language of Politics in Seventeenth-Century England* (New York: St. Martin's Press, 1994), 46, 47; and Max Weber's classic thesis in *The Protestant Ethic and the Spirit of Capitalism* (1904–1905), trans. Talcott Parsons (New York: Charles Scribner's Sons, 1958), more fully grounded in the European historical context by R. H. Tawney, *Religion and the Rise of Capitalism: A Historical Study* (London: John Murray, 1926).

10. For examples of these inroads, see McKeon, *Origins*, 65–89, 91–96, 189–200.

11. On these matters, see Ernst H. Kantorowicz, *The King's Two Bodies: A Study in Medieval Political Theology* (Princeton, NJ: Princeton University Press, 1957), esp. ch. 4, sec. 3; ch. 5, secs. 1 and 2.

12. In order to sustain the continuity of my presentation at this point I'm obliged to repeat the argument of several pages in *Historicizing the Enlightenment*, vol. 2, ch. 4.

13. Karl Marx, *Capital: A Critique of Political Economy* (1867), trans. Ben Fowkes (London: Penguin Books, 1976), 1:170 (further citations appear parenthetically in the text).

14. Raymond Williams, *The Country and the City* (New York: Oxford University Press, 1973), ch. 2.

15. Jonathan Parry and Maurice Bloch, eds., *Money and the Morality of Exchange* (Cambridge: Cambridge University Press, 1989), intro., 29.

16. Cf. Francis Bacon's usage in "Of the True Greatness of Kingdoms and Estates," no. 29 in *Essays or Counsels Civil and Moral* (1612), in *The Philosophical Works of Francis Bacon*, ed. Robert L. Ellis and James Spedding, rev. ed. John M. Robertson (London: Routledge, 1905), 770–774 (further citations appear parenthetically in the text).

17. Daniel Defoe, *The Compleat English Gentleman* (writ. 1728–1729), ed. Karl D. Bülbring (London: Nutt, 1890), 62–63.

18. See Robert Brenner, "The Agrarian Roots of European Capitalism," in *The Brenner Debate: Agrarian Class Structure and Economic Development in Pre-Industrial Europe*, ed. T. H. Ashton and C.H.E. Philpin (Cambridge: Cambridge University Press, 1985), 291–299; and Robert Brenner, *Merchants and Revolution: Commercial Change, Political Conflict, and London's Overseas Traders, 1550–1653* (1993; rpt. London: Verso, 2003), 647–653. My summary of Brenner's hypothesis is indebted to Ellen Meiksins Wood, *The Origin of Capitalism: A Longer View* (London: Verso, 2002).

19. Henry Robinson, *The Office of Addresses and Encounters* (1650), 2, 4; Henry Fielding, *A Plan of the Universal Register Office*, 2nd ed. (1752), 5, 7–8, 9, 17–18.

20. For a concise and lucid account of the relation between William III's need to finance wars against Louis XIV and the establishment of these financial institutions, see John Richetti, *The Life of Daniel Defoe* (Oxford: Blackwell, 2005), 149–150.

21. Joseph Addison, *Spectator*, no. 69 (May 19, 1711), in *The Spectator*, ed. Donald F. Bond (Oxford: Clarendon, 1965).

22. Jean-Christophe Agnew, *Worlds Apart: The Market and the Theater in Anglo-American Thought, 1550–1750* (Cambridge: Cambridge University Press, 1986), 41–42, and ch. 1. throughout.

23. On the imaginative virtuality of the emergent market, see also the frontispiece to *Historicizing the Enlightenment*, vol. 2, which depicts these several "walks" within the Royal Exchange. As we've seen, the actual/virtual difference can also be expressed in terms of an overt/covert (Agnew) and a direct/indirect (Brenner) difference.

24. Thomas Scott, *The Belgick Pismire* (1622), 32, 34.

25. See Margot C. Finn, *The Character of Credit: Personal Debt in English Culture, 1740–1914* (Cambridge: Cambridge University Press, 2003).

26. Jonathan Swift, *The Examiner*, no. 13 (November 2, 1710), and no. 34 (March 29, 1711), in *The Prose Works of Jonathan Swift*, ed. Herbert Davis (Oxford: Blackwell, 1940), 3:6–7, 119.

27. Daniel Defoe, *A Review of the State of the English Nation* 3, no. 126 (October 22, 1706); 5, no. 107 (December 2, 1708); 6, nos. 31, 32 (June 14 and 16, 1709); Addison, *Spectator*, no. 3 (March 3, 1711).

28. John Graunt and William Petty, *Natural and Political Observations Mentioned in a Following Index, and Made upon the Bills of Mortality* (1662), 21; Samuel Pepys, *The Diary of*

Samuel Pepys, ed. Robert Latham and William Matthews (Berkeley: University of California Press, 1995), 5 (February 2, 1664).

29. Nicholas Barbon, *A Discourse concerning Coining the New Money Lighter* (1696), 43; *A Discourse of Trade* (1690), 15; both quoted in Joyce Oldham Appleby, *Economic Thought and Ideology in Seventeenth-Century England* (Princeton, NJ: Princeton University Press, 1978), 229, 169.

30. Natalie Roxburgh has used this financial term of art to coordinate a number of topics under the aegis of public credit; see *Representing Public Credit: Credible Commitment, Fiction, and the Rise of the Financial Subject* (London: Routledge, 2016).

31. Andrew Brown, *A Second Essay concerning the Land Mint* (Edinburgh, 1705), 13–14.

32. Adam Smith, *An Inquiry into the Nature and Causes of the Wealth of Nations* (1776), ed. R. H. Campbell, A. S. Skinner, and W. B. Todd (Indianapolis: Liberty Classics, 1981), vol. 2 of *The Glasgow Edition of the Works and Correspondence of Adam Smith*, 321 (further citations appear parenthetically in the text).

33. See John Locke, *Second Treatise of Government*, in *Two Treatises of Government* (1690), ed. Peter Laslett, 2nd ed. (Cambridge: Cambridge University Press, 1967), "Of Property," paras. 25–51, pp. 303–320 ("propriety," paras. 36, 37, pp. 311, 313) (further citations appear parenthetically in the text).

34. In part because they go in directions different from my own, I've been stimulated by the arguments about capitalist universality of three writers in particular: Immanuel Wallerstein, "The Ideological Tensions of Capitalism: Universalism versus Racism and Sexism," in Etienne Balibar and Emmanuel Wallerstein, eds., *Race, Nation, Class: Ambiguous Identities* (London: Verso, 1991), 29–36; Todd McGowan, "The Particularity of the Capitalist Universal," *Continental Thought and Theory* 1, no. 4 (October 2017), 473–494; and Moishe Postone, *Time, Labor, and Social Domination: A Reinterpretation of Marx's Critical Theory* (Cambridge: Cambridge University Press, 1993).

35. Friedrich Engels, letter to Franz Mehring, in *Karl Marx and Friedrich Engels: Selected Works in Two Volumes* (Moscow: Foreign Languages Publishing House, 1950), 2:451. The critique of ideology extends the critique of tradition by making explicit not only the epistemological but also the material bases of tacit knowledge; see ch. 1 in the present volume.

36. Karl Marx, "Preface," *A Contribution to the Critique of Political Economy* (1859), https://www.marxists.org/archive/marx/works/1859/critique-pol-economy/preface.htm.

37. Friedrich Engels and Karl Marx, *The German Ideology* (written 1845–1846, pub. 1932), pt. 1, D, https://www.marxists.org/archive/marx/works/download/Marx_The_German_Ideology.pdf (further citations appear parenthetically in the text).

38. See Karl Marx, *Grundrisse: Foundations of the Critique of Political Economy* (written 1857–1858, pub. 1953), trans. Martin Nicolaus (Harmondsworth, England: Penguin, 1973), 109–111 (further citations appear parenthetically in the text). This isn't a case of false consciousness because what the forms exhibit is autonomy, not determinacy, of the forces of

production. *Grundrisse* is a rough draft in seven notebooks written in the period between *The German Ideology* and *Capital*.

39. See this chapter, nn.12–15.

40. For Nicholas Barbon see n.28.

41. Another well-known example of two "appearances" or stages in the development of the commodity form is the schematic distinction between the early or simple and the later or advanced stage of commodity production in terms of the difference between the predominant motives that lead people to enter the market (of course both motives are present in both stages). The early stage is primarily motivated by "selling in order to buy": "Consumption, the satisfaction of needs, in short use-value, is therefore its final goal." The later, capitalist stage is motivated by "buying in order to sell": "Its driving and motivating force, its determining purpose, is therefore exchange-value" and the accumulation and recirculation of money or capital. Marx represents these two stages by the formulae C-M-C and M-C-M', in which the prime symbol signifies an indeterminate ambition to accumulate and recirculate (*Capital*, 176, 247–257, 953).

42. In the later history of Marxist thought, one of the most powerful theories of this relationship is that of the "hegemonic" determinacy of capitalist domination, which, along with modern theories of acculturation, socialization, incorporation, introjection, advertising, and the like account for what rose from the ashes of tacit knowledge once the effects of the Enlightenment revolution in explicit knowledge had subsided. Antonio Gramsci's category "hegemony" has been taken up and elaborated by no one more resourcefully and brilliantly than Raymond Williams; see his "Base and Superstructure in Marxist Cultural Theory," in *Problems in Materialism and Culture: Selected Essays* (London: Verso, 1980), 31–49. See also Antonio Gramsci, *Selections from the Prison Notebooks of Antonio Gramsci*, ed. and trans. Quintin Hoare and Geoffrey Nowell Smith (London: Lawrence and Wishart, 1971), e.g., 12–13. One great task of (modern) hegemony was to recognize how thoroughly the process of separation and conflation inaugurated during the Enlightenment undermined and dissolved the body of tacit knowledge it inherited. Only on this basis was it able to apply and augment Enlightenment principles to the traditional knowledge that persisted or was transformed under the pressure of Enlightenment critique, and to engage the massive conceptual structures of modern thought that had been sophisticated by that critique. I think Williams is drawn to "hegemony" because it takes "practical consciousness [to be] inseparable from all social material activity," and seems thereby to improve on "ideology" by accounting for the whole or "totality" of life without dividing it into parts. Raymond Williams, *Marxism and Literature* (New York: Oxford University Press, 1977), 38. By contrast, classical Marxism conceived consciousness as a species of ideology and as a separable category of "superstructure" over against "infrastructural" social material activity. However, Gramsci, by no means a classical Marxist, is content to describe hegemony as the function of one of two "superstructural 'levels'" (*Prison Notebooks*, 12). And it seems to me that by insisting on a category whose working parts are distinct but not separate, Williams evokes the ideal of a whole that goes without saying under modern conditions of knowing by means of parts that actually work, by virtue of their explicit division. (It might be argued that the

traditional principle of distinction without separation has an equivalent in what Marxism criticizes as "false consciousness"; see above, nn.35–38.) Only when parts are detached and separated from each other sufficiently to be conceived as such can they be entered into active relation. The Enlightenment division of totality into its parts, here consciousness and materiality, created the conditions for their conflation, for the empirical and rational analysis of their relation. The experimental separation of infrastructure from superstructure is the first stage in the ongoing dialectical refinement of analysis. Williams's supreme sensitivity to the liabilities of division encourages him, I believe, to throw out the totality of the baby with the solvent of the bath water. For further thoughts on Williams's approach to this problem, see ch. 6 in the present volume.

43. On "the fetishism of the political economists," see also the originally planned part seven of *Capital*, published in vol. 1, 983.

44. See William Pietz, "Fetishism and Materialism: The Limits of Theory in Marx," in *Fetishism as Cultural Discourse*, ed. Emily Apter and William Pietz (Ithaca, NY: Cornell University Press, 1993), 130–131.

45. For an especially concentrated discussion, see *Capital*, vol. 3 (1894), ed. Friedrich Engels, ch. 24, which begins: "The relations of capital assume their most externalized and most fetish-like form in interest-bearing capital. We have here M-M', money creating more money, self-expanding value, without the process that effectuates these two extremes. . . . The social relation is consummated in the relation of a thing, of money, to itself. Instead of the actual transformation of money into capital, we see here only form without content. . . . In M-M' we have the meaningless form of capital, the perversion and objectification of production relations in their highest degree. . . . As interest-bearing capital, . . . capital assumes its pure fetish form" (266, 267), http://www.marxists.org/archive/marx/works/download/pdf/Capital-Volume-III.pdf.

46. In another context Marx explicitly if indirectly refutes a thesis that might be taken to justify this anachronism, the thesis of a "direct transition" to modernity from either religious or economic fetishism in antiquity. Scorning what he takes to be Frédérique Bastiat's proposal that wages have been the fixed form of remunerating labor "from the semi-savage state into the modern," Marx argues that wage labor has undergone a long and complicated historical development. "The direct transition from the African's fetish to Voltaire's supreme being, or from the hunting gear of a North American savage to the capital of the Bank of England, is not so absurdly contrary to history as is the transition from Bastiat's fisherman to the wage labourer" (*Grundrisse*, 890, 891).

47. However, the value of the fetish concept as a tool of analysis shouldn't be confused with its having a substantive value. To treat religious fetishism as superior to the *deus absconditus* of Christian belief because its alienation of human powers is comparatively proximate would run counter to Marx's judgment that fetishism is an illusion.

48. Marx here conflates, without explicit analysis, the Catholic and the reformed churches as two parts of the Christian whole. For a different view see his trenchantly

dialectical analysis in Introduction to *A Contribution to the Critique of Hegel's Philosophy of Right* (1844), https://www.marxists.org/archive/marx/works/1843/critique-hpr/intro.htm.

49. Karl Marx, *The Eighteenth Brumaire of Louis Bonaparte* (1852), excerpted in Robert C. Tucker, *The Marx-Engels Reader* (New York: Norton, 1978), 594, 596, 597, 614.

50. Adam Smith, *The Theory of Moral Sentiments* (1759), ed. D. D. Raphael and A. L. Macfie, (1976; Indianapolis: Liberty Classics, 1982), vol. 1 of *The Glasgow Edition of the Works and Correspondence of Adam Smith*, 9 (further citations appear parenthetically in the text).

51. As Smith's language in the latter passage suggests, the modern concept of ideology sublates—preserves and supersedes—the tacit knowledge of tradition. For fuller discussion, see ch. 1 in the present volume.

52. Adam Smith, *The History of Astronomy*, in *Essays on Philosophical Subjects* (1795), ed. W.P.D. Wightman and J. C. Bryce, vol. 3 of *The Glasgow Edition of the Works and Correspondence of Adam Smith* (1980; Indianapolis: Liberty Classics, 1982), 3, 49–50.

53. I quote principally from a passage in the text of the 1759 ed. that was revised in the ed. of 1790.

54. Sir Robert Filmer, *Patriarcha* (writ. c. 1640, pub. 1680), in *Patriarcha and Other Political Works*, ed. Peter Laslett (Oxford: Blackwell, 1949).

55. See note 33 in this chapter.

56. William Blackstone, *Commentaries on the Laws of England*, 12th ed. (London: A. Strahan and W. Woodfall, 1793), 1:445. On patriarchy in Enlightenment thought, see ch. 4 in the present volume.

57. Mary Astell, *Reflections Upon Marriage* (London, 1700), 3rd ed. (1706), in *The First English Feminist: Reflections upon Marriage and Other Writings by Mary Astell*, ed. Bridget Hill (Aldershot, England: Gower, 1986), 102.

58. Locke acknowledges this custom but signals his skepticism, perhaps in anticipation of his later introduction of exchange value, although here with no reference to the productivity of property: removing something from the state of nature *"begins the Property; without which the Common is of no use"* (para. 28, p. 307).

59. By 1699, 71 percent of England was already under enclosure; see J. R. Wordie, "The Chronology of English Enclosure, 1500–1914," *Economic History Review*, 2nd ser., 36, no. 4 (November 1983), esp. 502.

60. My thoughts on this question have been informed by Ellen Meiksins Wood, "Capitalism or Enlightenment?," *History of Political Thought* 21, no. 3 (Autumn 2000): 405–426.

61. On Addison, see *Historicizing the Enlightenment*, vol. 2, ch. 1.

62. See Introduction to this volume, nn. 44–46.

63. Thomas Hariot, *A Briefe and True Report of the New Found Land of Virginia*, with engravings by Theodore de Bry (London, 1590).

64. Adam Ferguson, *An Essay on the History of Civil Society* (1764) (New Brunswick, NJ: Transaction, 1980), 80, 102–103.

65. For a fuller argument, see *Historicizing the Enlightenment*, vol. 2, ch. 1.

66. Jürgen Habermas, *The Structural Transformation of the Public Sphere* (1962), trans. Thomas Burger and Frederick Lawrence (Cambridge, MA: MIT Press, 1989) (further citations appear parenthetically in the text).

67. Thomas Hobbes, *Leviathan, or The Matter, Forme, & Power of a Common-Wealth Ecclesiasticall and Civill* (1651).

68. Nancy Fraser, "Rethinking the Public Sphere: A Contribution to the Critique of Actually Existing Democracy," in *Habermas and the Public Sphere*, ed. Craig Calhoun (Cambridge, MA: MIT Press, 1994), 118 (further citations appear parenthetically in the text).

69. Geoff Eley, "Nations, Publics, and Political Cultures: Placing Habermas in the Nineteenth Century," in Calhoun, *Habermas and the Public Sphere*, 306.

70. Sir Humphrey Mackworth, *A Vindication of the Rights of the Commons of England* (London, 1701), 32; Joseph Addison, *The Free-Holder, or Political Essays* (London, 1716), 2; Henry Care, *English Liberties, or the Free-Born Subject's Inheritance*, 4th ed. (1719), 125.

71. Edward Stillingfleet, discourse of 1689 and c. 1705, quoted in Gerald M. Straka, *Anglican Reaction to the Revolution of 1688*, State Historical Society of Wisconsin (Madison: University of Wisconsin Press, 1962), 55, 33.

72. James Madison, *Federalist*, no. 10, in Alexander Hamilton, John Jay, and James Madison, *The Federalist* (1787–1788), ed. George W. Carey and James McClellan (Indianapolis: Liberty Fund, 2001), 42–49.

73. Richard Steele, *Tatler*, no. 144 (March 11, 1710); nos. 110, 116 (December 22, 1709, January 5, 1710), in *The Tatler*, ed. Donald F. Bond (Oxford: Clarendon, 1987); Henry Fielding, *Champion* 1, December 22, 1739, in *The Champion*, 2 vols. (1739–1740).

74. Jonathan Swift, *The Examiner*, no. 38 (April 26, 1711), in Davis, *Prose Works of Jonathan Swift*, vol. 3.

75. John Locke, *An Essay concerning Human Understanding* (1689), ed. Peter H. Nidditch (Oxford: Clarendon Press, 1975), bk. 2, ch. 28, paras. 7–13 (pp. 352–357) (further citations appear parenthetically in the text in this form: 2.28.7–13).

76. Francis Kirkman, *The Unlucky Citizen Experimentally Described in the Various Misfortunes of an Unlucky Londoner* (1673), 181–182.

77. C. L. Barber makes this generalization on the basis of usage in seventeenth-century drama in *The Idea of Honour in the English Drama, 1591–1700* (Gothenburg: Elanders, 1957), 330–331. I think it can be extended to other kinds of discourse as well.

78. Edward Waterhouse, *The Gentleman's Monitor: or, A Sober Inspection into the Vertues, Vices, and Ordinary Means, of the Rise and Decay of Men and Families* (1665), 261–262. On the Heralds' Visitations and sumptuary legislation, see Christopher Hill, *Pelican Economic History of Britain*, vol. 2, *Reformation to Industrial Revolution 1530–1780* (Harmondsworth:

Penguin, 1971), 49, 51; N. B. Harte, "State Control of Dress and Social Change in Pre-Industrial England," in *Trade, Government, and Economy in Pre-Industrial England*, ed. D. C. Coleman and A. H. John (London: Weidenfeld and Nicolson, 1976), 132–165.

79. Delarivier Manley, *The Secret History of Queen Zarah, and the Zarazians* (1711), 2, 126.

80. Defoe, *Compleat English Gentleman*, 171, 16.

81. Lady Sanspareille in Margaret Cavendish, Duchess of Newcastle, *Youths Glory, and Deaths Banquet*, in *Playes* (1662), II.v.131–132; Daniel Defoe, preface to *The Storm: Or, a Collection of the Most Remarkable Casualties and Disasters Which Happen'd in the Late Dreadful Tempest, Both by Sea and Land* (1704), A2r–v (font reversed).

82. Andrew Marvell, *The Rehearsal Transpros'd*, pt. 1 (1672), in *The Prose Works of Andrew Marvell*, vol. 1, *1672–1673*, ed. Martin Dzelzainis and Annabel Patterson (New Haven, CT: Yale University Press, 2003), 45.

83. Anne Dutton, *A Letter to Such of the Servants of Christ, Who May Have Any Scruple about the Lawfulness of Printing Any Thing Written by a Woman* (1743), in *Women in the Eighteenth Century: Constructions of Femininity*, ed. Vivien Jones (London: Routledge, 1990), 158, 159.

84. John Aubrey, *Remaines of Gentilisme and Judaisme*, in *Three Prose Works*, ed. John Buchanan-Brown (Fontwell, England: Centaur, 1972), 445, 289–290. For some suggestive reflections on Aubrey's perspective with regard to the idea of tradition, see Paula McDowell, *The Invention of the Oral: Print Commerce and Fugitive Voices in Eighteenth-Century Britain* (Chicago: University of Chicago Press, 2017), 47–48.

85. Marvell, *Rehearsal Transpros'd*, pt. 2 (1673), in Dzelzainis and Patterson, *Prose Works of Andrew Marvell*, 1:238, 240, 247.

86. William Okeley, *Eben-Ezer: or, A Small Monument of Great Mercy, Appearing in the Miraculous Deliverance of . . . from the Miserable Slavery of Algiers* (London: Nat. Ponder, 1675), "Upon This Book and Its Author."

87. Francis Bacon, *The New Organon* (1620), pt. 1, aph. 38, p. 263, in *The Philosophical Works of Francis Bacon*, ed. Robert L. Ellis and James Spedding, rev. ed. John M. Robertson (London: Routledge, 1905). Further citations appear parenthetically in the text keyed to the following abbreviations: "NO I" for *The New Organon* (1620), pt 1; "NO II" for *The New Organon* (1620), pt. 2; "PW" for "The Plan of the Work" prefixed to *The Great Instauration* (1620).

88. Thomas S. Kuhn, *The Structure of Scientific Revolutions* (Chicago: University of Chicago Press, 1962).

89. See Ernan McMullin, "Conceptions of Science in the Scientific Revolution," in David C. Lindberg and Robert S. Westman, eds., *Reappraisals of the Scientific Revolution* (Cambridge: Cambridge University Press, 1990), 27–92. On falsification, see Karl Popper, *The Logic of Scientific Discovery* (London: Routledge, 1959). The reversal of direction from the general category to the evidentiary testing of its particular parts can also be recognized in temporal terms in the repetition of trials that, as we'll see, the early accounts of experiment advocate.

90. See McMullin, "Conceptions," 30, 51–54. On Boyle's corpuscularism, see also Helen Thompson, *Fictional Matter: Empiricism, Corpuscles, and the Novel* (University of Pennsylvania Press, 2017).

91. McMullin, "Conceptions," 51.

92. Mary Poovey, *A History of the Modern Fact: Problems of Knowledge in the Sciences of Wealth and Society* (Chicago: University of Chicago Press, 1998), ch. 3. In passing, I think this argument skews the evidence of experimental standards by giving undue weight to the testimony of merchants and disregarding that of other sources.

93. See Richard Rorty, *Consequences of Pragmatism (Essays: 1972–1980)* (Minneapolis: University of Minnesota Press, 1982), 194–195.

94. See Peter Dear, "Narratives, Anecdotes, and Experiments: Turning Experience into Science in the Seventeenth Century," in Peter Dear, ed., *The Literary Structure of Scientific Argument: Historical Studies* (Philadelphia: University of Pennsylvania Press, 1991), 135–163.

95. Like all "revolutions," the "Scientific Revolution" of the early seventeenth century has a prehistory that is crucial to its existence and that belies the punctual implications of the term. On the "practical knowledge" that was rooted in the humanist arts of discourse and in the application of geometry to the technology of spatial diagram and design, and that precipitated the emergence of both the "arts" and the "sciences," see Henry S. Turner, *The English Renaissance Stage: Geometry, Poetics, and the Practical Spatial Arts 1580–1630* (Oxford: Oxford University Press, 2006).

96. John Dryden, "Prologue, To the University of *Oxon., Spoken by Mr. Hart, at the Acting of the* Silent Woman," ll. 22–27, in *The Poems and Fables of John Dryden*, ed. James Kinsley (London: Oxford University Press, 1962), 305.

97. Bernard Le Bovier Fontenelle, "A Digression on the Ancients and Moderns," trans. John Hughes (with revisions) (1719), in *The Continental Model*, ed. Scott Elledge and Donald Schier, rev. ed. (Ithaca, NY: Cornell University Press, 1970), 362. See Fontenelle, "Digression sur les anciens et les modernes" (1688), in *Entretiens sur la pluralité des mondes. Digression sur les anciens et les modernes*, ed. Robert Shackleton (Oxford: Clarendon, 1955), 166: "Cependant afin que les modernes puissent toujours enchérir sur les anciens, il faut que les choses soient d'une espéce a le permettre. L'éloquence et la poésie ne demandent qu'un certain nombre de vues assez borné, et elles dépendent principalement de la vivacité de l'imagination; or les hommes peuvent avoir amassé en peu de siécles un petit nombres de vues, et la vivacité de l'imagination n'a pas besoin d'une longue suite d'expériences, ni d'une grande quantité de régles pour avoir toute la perfection dont elle est capable. Mais la physique, la médecine, les mathématiques, sont composées d'un nombre infini de vues, et dépendent de la justesse du raisonnement, qui se perfectionne avec une extréme lenteur, et se perfectionne toujours." The "Digression" first appeared in Fontenelle's *Poesies pastorales* (1688). The significance of the Quarrel for the modern division between the arts and the sciences receives excellent treatment by Douglas Lane Patey in "Ancients and Moderns," in *The Cambridge History of Literary Criticism*, vol. 4, *The Eighteenth Century*, ed. H. B. Nisbet and Claude Rawson (Cambridge: Cambridge University Press, 1997), 32–71.

As in the case of the "Scientific Revolution," the oppositional categorization of the "arts" and the "sciences" was far less definitive, even by the end of the eighteenth century, than historical hindsight might presume. For a more detailed and less tidy account of this development, see David Spadafora, *The Idea of Progress in Eighteenth-Century Britain* (New Haven, CT: Yale University Press, 1990), ch. 2.

98. "When I speak of Forms, I mean nothing more than those laws and determinations of absolute actuality, which govern and constitute any simple nature, as heat, light, weight in every kind of matter and subject that is susceptible of them" (*NO* II, aph. 17, p. 321).

99. As an example of Enlightenment thinking, Bacon's "simple nature" might be compared to the "simple abstraction" of labor Marx attributes to Smith, which required an "indifference towards any specific kind of labour [that] presupposes a very developed totality of real kinds of labour, of which no single one is any longer predominant" (see above, "Conceptual Abstraction").

100. William Wotton, *Reflections upon Ancient and Modern Learning* (1694), 78–79, 340 (further citations appear parenthetically in the text).

101. Thomas Sprat, *The History of the Royal Society* (1667; 3rd ed., 1722), 62, 99 (further citations appear parenthetically in the text).

102. Robert Hooke, "A General Scheme, or Idea of the Present State of Natural Philosophy . . ." (c. 1668), in *The Posthumous Works of Robert Hooke*, ed. Richard Waller (1705), 61–62, ed. Theodore M. Brown (facs. rpt. London: Cass, 1971).

103. Margaret Cavendish, Duchess of Newcastle, *Observations upon Experimental Philosophy . . .* (1666; 2nd ed., 1668), 3, 7, 12.

104. Samuel Butler, "The Elephant in the Moon," ll. 65–78, in *The Genuine Remains in Verse and Prose of Mr. Samuel Butler*, ed. R. Thyer (London, 1759), 1:6.

105. See Steven Shapin and Simon Schaffer, *Leviathan and the Air-Pump: Hobbes, Boyle, and the Experimental Life* (Princeton, NJ: Princeton University Press, 1985), 60–65.

106. My discussion has benefited from Richard Bauman and Charles L. Briggs, "Language Philosophy as Language Ideology: John Locke and Johann Gottfried Herder," in *Regimes of Language: Ideologies, Polities, Identities*, ed. Paul V. Kroskrity (Santa Fe, NM: School of American Research Press, 1999), 139–204.

107. This is also the pattern English theorists conceive in their formulation of aesthetic epistemology; see *Historicizing the Enlightenment*, vol. 2, ch. 1.

108. "Decameron Physiologicum" (1678), in *The English Works of Thomas Hobbes of Malmesbury*, ed. Sir William Molesworth (London: John Bohn, 1839–1845), 7:117, quoted in Shapin and Schaffer, *Leviathan and the Air-Pump*, 128. Cf. Sprat's implication (n.102 in this chapter) that the "forcing" of nature—so that we can observe "what Nature does willingly, what constrain'd; what with its own Power, what by the succours of Art"—is one fruitful potential of experimental method rather than its general and suspect tendency.

109. Thomas Hobbes, *A Physical Dialogue, or a Conjecture about the Nature of the Air Taken Up from Experiments Recently Made in London at Gresham College* (1661), trans. from the Latin, in Shapin and Schaffer, *Leviathan and the Air-Pump*, 351, 346.

110. Thomas Hobbes, *Examinatio et Emendatio Mathematicae Hodiemae* (1660), in *Thomas Hobbes Malmesburiensis Opera Philosophica quae Latine Scripsit Omnia*, ed. Sir William Molesworth (London: John Bohn, 1839–1845), 1:228, quoted in Shapin and Schaffer, *Leviathan and the Air-Pump*, 115.

111. See Shapin and Schaffer, *Leviathan and the Air-Pump*, 146–154.

112. Thomas Hobbes, *Leviathan, or The Matter, Forme, and Power of a Common-Wealth Ecclesiasticall and Civill* (London, 1651), pt. 2, ch. 20, p. 107 (further citations appear parenthetically in the text).

113. John Bramhall, *Castigations of Mr. Hobbes . . .* (1657), 507.

114. See n.103 in this chapter.

115. William Petty, *Political Arithmetick* (writ. 1670s, pub. 1690), "Preface," sig. a3v–a4r, a4v.

116. George Monck, "A Letter of General George Moncks . . . directed unto Mr. Rolle . . . [and] the rest of the Gentry of Devon," January 23, 1660, in *A Collection of Several Letters and Declarations, Sent by General Monck . . .* (London, 1660), 19.

117. The early novel undertakes this narrative experiment in order to trace the emergence and growth of this and other human institutions; see *Historicizing the Enlightenment*, vol. 2, ch. 1.

118. See note 74 in this chapter.

119. Madison, *Federalist*, no. 10.

120. David Hume, *Enquiry concerning Human Understanding* (1748; 1777), sec. 10, ed. L. A. Selby-Bigge and P. H. Nidditch, 3rd ed. (Oxford: Clarendon, 1975), 110, 111, 113, 127.

121. See Shapin and Schaffer, *Leviathan and the Air-Pump*, 60–65; in the present case Hume uses something like virtual witnessing to assess the testimony of actual witnessing.

122. David Hume, *A Treatise of Human Nature* (1739), ed. L. A. Selby-Bigge and P. H. Nidditch, 2nd ed. (Oxford: Clarendon, 1978), bk. 1, pt. 1, sec. 1 (pp. 3–4) (further citations appear parenthetically in the text).

123. See William Haller, *The Rise of Puritanism* (New York: Harper, 1957), 299.

124. Jonathan Edwards, *A Treatise concerning Religious Affections* (Boston, 1746), 314, 334–335.

125. "Mr. *Locke*, my Lord *Shaftsbury* [sic], Dr. *Mandeville*, Mr. *Hutchinson* [sic], Dr. *Butler*, &c." (Hume's note).

126. See *Historicizing the Enlightenment*, vol. 2, ch. 1.

127. Joseph O'Connell, "Metrology: The Creation of Universality by the Circulation of Particulars," in *Social Studies of Science*, 23 (1993): 171n.56.

128. Peter Walmsley, *Locke's Essay and the Rhetoric of Science* (Lewisburg, PA: Bucknell University Press, 2003), 80, 81.

129. Sometimes they were colored by an emergent impulse to psychologize the imagination. Warning against masturbation, an anonymous moralist was careful that he not

"betray my Readers into the Remembrance of what it is much better that they should for ever forget, as they would not then be able to set a watchful Guard upon their Thoughts and Fancies, but that some foul or filthy Desires would in Spight creep in; the least imagination only of which, would render them Odious in God's sight, who seeth the Heart." *Onania; or, the Heinous Sin of Self-Pollution*, 8th ed. (London, 1723), 115.

130. On these matters, see *Historicizing the Enlightenment*, vol. 2, intro.

131. See *Historicizing the Enlightenment*, vol. 2, chs. 1 and 2.

CHAPTER 4 — GENDER AND SEX, STATUS AND CLASS

1. On the currency of the analogy in early modern English thought, see Gordon J. Schochet, *Patriarchalism in Political Thought: The Authoritarian Family and Political Speculation and Attitudes Especially in Seventeenth-Century England* (New York: Basic Books, 1975); Susan D. Amussen, *An Ordered Society: Gender and Class in Early Modern England* (Oxford: Blackwell, 1988), ch. 2.

2. Amussen, *Ordered Society*, 38–39, 57.

3. Schochet, *Patriarchalism*, 116.

4. Henry Parker, *Jus Populi, or, A Discourse* (London, 1644), 42, quoted in Amussen, *An Ordered Society*, 58.

5. Mary Astell, *Some Reflections upon Marriage* (London, 1700), 28–29.

6. John Locke, *Two Treatises of Government*, ed. Peter Laslett, 2nd ed. (Cambridge: Cambridge University Press, 1967), 286.

7. For a lucid discussion of these matters, see Ruth Perry, "Mary Astell and the Feminist Critique of Possessive Individualism," *Eighteenth-Century Studies*, 23 (1990): 444–457.

8. See Michael McKeon, *The Origins of the English Novel, 1600–1740* (Baltimore: Johns Hopkins University Press, 1987), 181–182.

9. See generally McKeon, *Origins*, chap. 4.

10. See Susan Staves, *Married Women's Separate Property in England, 1660–1833* (Cambridge, MA: Harvard University Press, 1990), 1–5, 178–195. On coverture, see William Blackstone, *Commentaries on the Laws of England*, 12th ed. (London: A. Strahan and W. Woodfall, 1793), vol. 1, ch. 15, 441–445.

11. In more recent criticism, see Lisa O'Connell, *The Origins of the English Marriage Plot: Literature, Politics, and Religion in the Eighteenth Century* (Cambridge: Cambridge University Press, 2019); Melissa J. Ganz, *Public Vows: Fictions of Marriage in the English Enlightenment* (Charlottesville: University of Virginia Press, 2019).

12. See Ruth Perry, *Novel Relations: The Transformation of Kinship in English Literature and Culture, 1748–1818* (Cambridge: Cambridge University Press, 2004).

13. Alice Clark, *Working Life of Women in the Seventeenth Century* (London: Routledge, 1919); Ivy Pinchbeck, *Women Workers and the Industrial Revolution, 1750–1850* (1930; London: Virago, 1981).

14. See Susan Cahn, *Industry of Devotion: The Transformation of Women's Work in England, 1500–1660* (New York: Columbia University Press, 1987), 33.

15. See Cahn, *Industry*, 46, 80–81, 89–90; Amussen, *An Ordered Society*, 43, 68–69; Bridget Hill, *Women, Work, and Sexual Politics in Eighteenth-Century England* (Oxford: Blackwell, 1989), 35.

16. Hill, *Women*, 36–37, 50–51; Cahn, *Industry*, 38–39; K.D.M. Snell, *Annals of the Laboring Poor: Social Change and Agrarian England, 1660–1900* (Cambridge: Cambridge University Press, 1985), 22, 62. See Deborah Valenze, "The Art of Women and the Business of Men: Women's Work and the Dairy Industry c. 1740–1840," *Past & Present*, 130, no. 1 (1991): 142–169.

17. See Snell, *Annals*, 21–22, 37, 45, 51, 58–62, 157–158. Snell's data come entirely from the south of England.

18. See Hill, *Women*, 47–48, 49–50; Cahn, *Industry*, 43–44, 47, 99, 120, 158; Snell, *Annals*, 53, n.36, 215–218, 311–312, 348–349 (quotation, 348). On the rise in fertility, see generally E. A. Wrigley, "The Growth of Population in Eighteenth-Century England: A Conundrum Resolved," in *People, Cities, and Wealth: The Transformation of Traditional Society* (Oxford: Blackwell, 1987), 215–241.

19. Cahn, *Industry*, 71.

20. See Nancy Folbre, "The Unproductive Housewife: Her Evolution in Nineteenth-Century Thought," *Signs* 16 (1991): 470–473.

21. Cahn, *Industry*, 22, 157–158.

22. See, e.g., Leonore Davidoff and Catherine Hall, *Family Fortunes: Men and Women of the English Middle Class, 1780–1850* (Chicago: University of Chicago Press, 1987); Anna Clark, *Women's Silence, Men's Violence: Sexual Assault in England, 1770–1845* (New York: Pandora, 1987).

23. For further discussion see Michael McKeon, *The Secret History of Domesticity: Public, Private, and the Division of Knowledge* (Baltimore: Johns Hopkins University Press, 2005), 149–152, 297–298.

24. See, e.g., Amanda Vickery, *The Gentleman's Daughter: Women's Lives in Georgian England* (New Haven, CT: Yale University Press, 1998); Robert B. Shoemaker, *Gender in English Society 1650–1850: The Emergence of Separate Spheres?* (London: Longman, 1998).

25. See J.A.W. Gunn, *Politics and the Public Interest in the Seventeenth Century* (London: Routledge, 1969).

26. See Harold Perkin, *Origins of Modern English Society* (London: Routledge, 1969), 176–177.

27. Michel Foucault affirms that sex became an explicit discourse at this time; see *The History of Sexuality*, trans. Robert Hurley (New York: Vintage, 1990), 1:33, 37–39. However, Foucault's account of its emergence is marred by his thesis of an epistemic break at the end of the eighteenth century, which leads him to ignore most of the Enlightenment discourse that for the first time made sex explicit.

28. See *OED*, s.v. "sex," 1.a (1382 first-use citation) and 3 (1631 first-use citation).

29. See Thomas Laqueur, *Making Sex: Body and Gender from the Greeks to Freud* (Cambridge, MA: Harvard University Press, 1990), 8.

30. Many scholars have contributed to what now might tentatively be called a consensus. Most of the findings have been published in article form; the most careful and comprehensive guide to the scholarship I know of is Helen King, *The One-Sex Body on Trial: The Classical and Early Modern Evidence* (Farnham, England: Ashgate, 2013).

31. Foucault, *History of Sexuality*, 1:43.

32. Randolph Trumbach, *Sex and the Gender Revolution*, vol. 1, *Heterosexuality and the Third Gender in Enlightenment London* (Chicago: University of Chicago Press, 1998), 4 (further citations appear parenthetically in the text). The considerable part of Trumbach's book that documents the role of the third gender organizes and refines his many earlier articles on this subject, which will be extended and amplified in the forthcoming *Sex and the Gender Revolution*, vol. 2, *The Origins of Modern Homosexuality*.

33. Trumbach, *Sex and the Gender Revolution*, 3–22.

34. Trumbach, *Sex and the Gender Revolution*, 9.

35. The gender total was still limited to three at this time, Trumbach suggests, because for most of the eighteenth century it was still understood that women who had sexual relations with other women also desired men. This would begin to change toward the end of the century with the emergence of the social type of the sapphist; see Randolph Trumbach, "London's Sapphists: From Three Sexes to Four Genders in the Making of Modern Culture," in *Third Sex, Third Gender: Beyond Sexual Dimorphism in Culture and History*, ed. Gilbert Herdt (New York: Zone Books, 1994), 111–136; "Review Essay: The Origin and Development of the Modern Lesbian Role in the Western Gender System: Northwestern Europe and the United States, 1750–1990," in *Historical Reflections/Réflexions Historiques* 20, no. 2 (Summer 1994): 288–320.

36. Alan Bray, *Homosexuality in Renaissance England*, 2nd ed. (London: Gay Men's Press, 1988), 86.

37. *Mundus Foppensis: Or, the Fop Display'd* (1691), 13, in *Mundus Foppensis (1691) and The Levellers (1703, 1745)*, ed. Michael S. Kimmel, *Augustan Reprint Society*, no. 245 (1988). The author of *Mundus Foppensis* appends a "Short Supplement" that translates cant terms and expressions (25–26) and, like John Gay's "Alphabetical Catalogue" appended to *The Shepherd's Week* (1714), suggests a quasi-anthropological interest similar to Gay's in another subculture, common rural life (on Gay, see *Historicizing the Enlightenment*, vol. 2, ch. 4). Alsatia was a criminal sanctuary in Whitefriars.

38. Joseph Addison, *Spectator*, no. 128 (July 27, 1711), in *The Spectator*, ed. Donald F. Bond (Oxford: Clarendon Press, 1965).

39. Richard Steele, *Tatler*, no. 172 (May 16, 1710), in *The Tatler*, ed. Donald F. Bond (Oxford: Clarendon Press, 1987).

40. Bernard Mandeville, "Remark (C.)," *The Fable of the Bees* (1705, 1714), ed. F. B. Kaye (Oxford: Clarendon Press, 1924), 1:69–72.

41. On the transition from status to class in early modern England, see McKeon, *Origins*, 159–171.

42. Daniel Defoe, *The Compleat English Gentleman* (writ. 1728–1729), ed. Karl D: Bülbring (London: D. Nutt, 1890), 16.

43. William Sprigg, *A Modest Plea for an Equal Common-Wealth against Monarchy* (London, 1659), 77–78.

44. Daniel Defoe, *The True-Born Englishman. A Satyr* (London, 1700), 70–71.

45. T. R. Malthus, *An Essay on the Principle of Population* (1798), ed. Donald Winch (Cambridge: Cambridge University Press, 1992), 7, 25, 26, 274, 277, 278.

46. On the erosion of customary relations and its effect on social conflict in the eighteenth century, see E. P. Thompson, *Customs in Common: Studies in Traditional Popular Culture* (New York: New Press, 1991).

47. More generally, "class distinctions are linked in the most varied ways with status distinctions": Max Weber, "Class, Status, Party," in *From Max Weber: Essays in Sociology*, ed. H. H. Gerth and C. Wright Mills (New York: Oxford University Press, 1958), 187.

48. Edward Waterhouse, *The Gentleman's Monitor: or, A Sober Inspection into the Vertues, Vices, and Ordinary Means, of the Rise and Decay of Men and Families* (London, 1665), 261–262.

49. *Tatler*, no. 144 (March 11, 1710), in Bond, *The Tatler*.

50. For a complex and striking example of such discourse, see *Tatler*, nos. 48, 96, 116, 151, 243, in Bond, *The Tatler*; *Spectator*, nos. 15, 41, 57, 66, 73, 81, 104, 127, 129, 435, in Bond, *The Spectator*. In many of these papers, the law of the land has been replaced by the far more volatile and intractable "law" of gender fashion.

51. See Trumbach, *Sex and the Gender Revolution*, 1:73–75; Randolph Trumbach, "The Birth of the Queen: Sodomy and the Emergence of Gender Equality in Modern Culture, 1660–1750," in *Hidden from History: Reclaiming the Gay and Lesbian Past*, ed. Martin B. Duberman, Martha Vicinus, and George Chauncey Jr. (New York: New American Library, 1989), 130–131; Randolph Trumbach, "Sex, Gender, and Sexual Identity in Modern Culture: Male Sodomy and Female Prostitution in Enlightenment London," in *Journal of the History of Sexuality* 2, no. 2 (1991): 189.

52. *The Works of John Wilmot Earl of Rochester*, ed. Harold Love (Oxford: Oxford University Press, 1999), 38.

53. See McKeon, *Origins*, 157–158. Among the gentry, this enlargement entailed an "inheritance" of the duties of charity and care for the poor formerly proper to the aristocratic paterfamilias.

54. As Kristina Straub has shown, the figure of the dramatic player is an acute index to the instability of gender categories in the eighteenth century; see *Sexual Suspects: Eighteenth-Century Players and Sexual Ideology* (Princeton, NJ: Princeton University Press, 1992). For a different, but comparably suggestive, approach to the same subject, see Lynne Friedli, "Passing Women—A Study of Gender Boundaries in the Eighteenth Century," in *Sexual Underworlds of the Enlightenment*, ed. G. S. Rousseau and Roy Porter (Manchester: Manchester University Press, 1987), 234–260.

55. For contemporary accounts, see G. S. Rousseau, "An Introduction," in Rousseau and Porter, *Sexual Underworlds*, 48–53.

56. See [Delarivier Manley,] *The Lady's Packet of Letters*, appended to Marie Catherine D'Aulnoy, *Memoirs of the Court of England: In the Reign of King Charles II*, 2nd ed. (1708), 3–24. Cf. Manley's *Secret History of Queen Zarah and the Zarazians* (1705) and *Secret Memoirs . . . from the New Atalantis* (1709). For the gender reversal, cf. Aphra Behn, *The Fair Jilt* (1696). For attempts to illuminate the ideology of these plots in Manley and Behn, see McKeon, *Origins*, 232–233, 258–260, 263.

57. *Love-Letters between a Certain Late Nobleman and the Famous Mr. Wilson* (1723, 1745), reprinted in *Journal of Homosexuality* 19 (1990): 11–44. Like Rochester in his "Song," the correspondents link the heterosexual love of women with "base, low, dull" vulgarity; see *Love-Letters*, 11, 12, 25–26. For an extended discussion of the two Beau Wilson narratives, see McKeon, *Secret History of Domesticity*, 569–587. On the familiarity of stories of aristocratic degeneracy, see McKeon, *Origins*, ch. 6.

58. See McKeon, *Origins*, 153.

59. Anon., *Satan's Harvest Home* (London, 1749), 33, 49–50. In its account of a "race" of men acculturated into sodomy, this story exhibits the contradictory doubleness of the modern system of sexuality. The emphasis on the central role of education in the constitution of the sodomite both abets the emergent notion of sodomy as a matter of persons rather than actions, and augments the emergent sociological insight (cf. Mandeville in this chapter, n.33) that persons are socially constructed. For an analysis related to that of this tract, see [Lancaster,] *Pretty Gentleman*, 14, 31. For ideologically diverse accounts of the degeneration of the English gentry and nobility into a soft "effeminacy," see Daniel Defoe, *Review*, 3, no. 10 (January 22, 1706); "Mrs. Crackenthorpe," *The Female Tatler*, no. 5 (July 15–18, 1709); Jonathan Swift, *Intelligencer*, no. 9 (1728), in *The Prose Works of Jonathan Swift*, ed. Herbert Davis, vol. 12, *Irish Tracts: 1728–1733* (Oxford: Blackwell, 1955), 46–53; [John Brown,] *An Estimate of the Manners and Principles of the Times*, 2nd ed. (1757), esp. 30.

60. The causes of this corruption are for the most part English; but it is notable that the author adds to the French pox the metaphorically contiguous "Contagion" of men kissing each other and the opera's "Corruption of the English Stage," both of which are of Italian extraction (*Satan's Harvest Home*, 51, 55).

61. [Lancaster,] *Pretty Gentleman*, 25–26. Lancaster is at pains to explicitly associate with sodomy the foppish Fribble in Garrick's recently produced *Miss in Her Teens* (1747).

62. *Satan's Harvest Home*, 50. The passage is unusual in maintaining a balance between status- and gender-related sumptuary concerns; see this chapter, n.37.

63. In the formulation of J. C. Flügel, this is "the great masculine renunciation"; see John Carl Flügel, *The Psychology of Clothes* (London: Hogarth Press, 1930).

64. However, the aristocracy may also be said to have functioned as a structural anomaly—as a term mediating between an emergent middle class and an emergent working class—in the sense that it not only was neither of these but also partook of both

of them. On the one hand, an influential strain of aristocratic conservatism anticipated and articulated an anti-capitalist ideology that it self-consciously linked to the proto-proletarian interests of the laboring poor. On the other, from the beginning the ideology of the middle class has been defined in part by the self-canceling impulse to assimilate upward. Indeed, in its oscillation between the will to assimilate into and the will to supersede the aristocracy, the middle class has displayed the ambivalence—the intertwined attraction and repulsion—that we have come to associate with the modern critique of homosexuality. In the terms of this argument, the conservative exposure of anti-aristocratic progressive ideology as stealthily celebrating the rise of a "new aristocracy" is analogous to the outing of the homophobe. On anticapitalism, assimilationism, supersessionism, and the "new aristocracy," see McKeon, *Origins*, 162, 171, 174.

65. *Tatler*, nos. 14, 21, 24, 26, 27, 28 (May 12–June 14, 1709), in Bond, *The Tatler*. For an acute discussion of these and related papers, see Erin Mackie, *Market à la Mode: Fashion, Commodity, and Gender in the* Tatler *and the* Spectator (Baltimore: Johns Hopkins University Press, 1997). For the "Pretty Fellow," the "Pretty Gentleman," and the "Fop" at mid-century, see *Satan's Harvest Home*, 50; [Lancaster,] *Pretty Gentleman*, 6, 12; Trumbach, "Birth," 130–135.

66. Nancy Armstrong's claim that the modern category of subjectivity is gendered feminine at the outset is not borne out by the evidence—either that of the early novel or that of other discourses; see Nancy Armstrong, *Desire and Domestic Fiction: A Political History of the Novel* (New York: Oxford University Press, 1987), esp. 4, 14–15.

67. See McKeon, *Origins*, 148–159, 218–226, 255–265.

68. But see the interesting discussion in Janet Todd, *Sensibility: An Introduction* (New York: Methuen, 1986), ch. 7.

69. However, J.G.A. Pocock makes an unwarranted inference (and generalization) from this association in claiming that in the eighteenth century, economic man "was seen as on the whole a feminized, even an effeminate, being." *Virtue, Commerce, and History* (Cambridge: Cambridge University Press, 1985), 114.

70. See *Boswell's London Journal, 1762–63*, ed. Frederick A. Pottle (New York: McGraw-Hill, 1950), 139–140, 185–187.

CHAPTER 5 — BIOGRAPHY, FICTION, PERSONAL IDENTITY

1. Samuel Johnson, *Rambler* no. 60 (October 13, 1750), in *The Rambler*, ed. W. J. Bate and Albrecht B. Strauss, vol. 3 of *The Yale Edition of the Works of Samuel Johnson* (New Haven, CT: Yale University Press, 1969), 321; Johnson to Joseph Baretti, December 21, 1762, in James Boswell, *Life of Johnson* (1791), ed. R. W. Chapman (Oxford: Oxford University Press, 1980), 269.

2. Oliver Goldsmith, *The Life of Richard Nash, Esq.; Late Master of the Ceremonies at Bath*, 2nd ed. (1762), 2–3; Rev. John Bennett, Letter 51 in *Letters to a Young Lady on a Variety of Useful and Interesting Subjects* (1789), 184; and *Memoirs of the Life and Times of Sir Thomas Deveil* (1748), 1, quoted in Mark Salber Phillips, *Society and Sentiment: Genres of*

Historical Writing in Britain, 1740–1820 (Princeton, NJ: Princeton University Press, 2000), 135, 133, and 136, respectively; on these matters, see generally his ch. 5.

3. The following paragraph is elaborated on in Michael McKeon, *The Origins of the English Novel 1600–1740*, 2nd ed. (Baltimore: Johns Hopkins University Press, 2002), ch. 4.

4. For a penetrating account of these developments in association with the eighteenth century see Karl Marx and Friedrich Engels, *The German Ideology* (written 1845–1846, pub. 1932), pt. 1, D, https://www.marxists.org/archive/marx/works/download/Marx_The_German_Ideology.pdf.

5. *The Acts and Monuments of John Foxe* (1563, enlarged 1570), ed. Stephen R. Cattley (London: Seeley and Burnside, 1839), 8:493–495, 473–476.

6. Samuel Clarke, *The Lives of Sundry Eminent Persons in This Later Age. In Two Parts, I. Of Divines. II. Of Nobility and Gentry of Both Sexes* (London: 1683), preface by Richard Baxter, "To the Reader," a4r.

7. The terms are obviously distinct but to different degrees overlapping. For an illuminating historical semantics of these and related categories, see Amelie Oksenberg Rorty, "Characters, Persons, Selves, Individuals," in *Mind in Action: Essays in the Philosophy of Mind* (Boston: Beacon Press, 1988), 78–98.

8. Johnson, *Rambler*, no. 60.

9. Samuel Johnson, *Rambler*, no. 4 (March 31, 1750), in Bate and Strauss, *The Rambler*, 3:19–21. Johnson alludes here to Pliny's *Natural History*, bk. 35, ch. 36, sec. 85.

10. Fictionality, traditionally tacit, became explicit with the emergence of the category "fiction" under the pressure of empirical epistemology. For a fuller argument, see *Historicizing the Enlightenment*, vol. 2, ch. 2.

11. Daniel Defoe, *A True Relation of the Apparition of One Mrs. Veal the Next Day after Her Death to One Mrs. Bargrave at Canterbury the 8th of September, 1705* (1706).

12. On realism as the narrative version of the aesthetic, see *Historicizing the Enlightenment*, vol. 2, chs. 1 and 2.

13. Henry Fielding, *The History of the Adventures of Joseph Andrews, and of His Friend Mr. Abraham Adams. Written in Imitation of the Manner of Cervantes, Author of Don Quixote*, vol. 1 (London: 1742), in *Joseph Andrews and Shamela*, ed. Douglas Brooks-Davies and Thomas Keymer (Oxford: Oxford University Press, 1999), bk. 3, ch. 1, 164, 162.

14. On that debate see *Historicizing the Enlightenment*, vol. 2, ch. 2.

15. Fielding, *Joseph Andrews*, bk. 3, ch. 1, 164–165.

16. On the contrast between libel and satire, see Michael McKeon, *The Secret History of Domesticity: Public, Private, and the Division of Knowledge* (Baltimore: Johns Hopkins University Press, 2005), 368–372 and 95–99, respectively.

17. Jeremy Collier, *A Second Defence of the Short View of the Prophaneness and Immorality of the English Stage* (1700), 104; Jeremy Collier, *A Defence of the Short View of the Prophaneness and Immorality of the English Stage* (1699), 10–11; see also William Congreve, *Amendments of Mr Collier's False and Imperfect Citations, &c.* (1698), 9; and James Drake, *The*

Antient and Modern Stages Survey'd (1700), 222. All quoted in Aubrey Williams, *An Approach to Congreve* (New Haven, CT: Yale University Press, 1979), 61, 78.

18. For a fuller discussion, see McKeon, *Secret History*, pt. 3.

19. Richard Overton, *The Arraignement of Mr Persecution* (1645), in *Tracts on Liberty in the Puritan Revolution, 1638–1647*, ed. William Haller (New York: Columbia University Press, 1933), 3:230.

20. For a reading of Milton's *Paradise Lost* (1667, 1674) as a secret history, see *Historicizing the Enlightenment*, vol. 2, ch. 6.

21. Procopius, *The Secret History of the Court of the Emperor Justinian* (1674). On Procopius and the seventeenth-century English secret history, see McKeon, *Secret History*, ch. 10.

22. [Antoine Varillas,] *Medicis. Written Originally by That Fam'd Historian, the Sieur de Varilles. Made English by Ferrand Spence* (1686; French 1685), "Epistle Dedicatory," a4v–5r, a6r, and "Author's Preface," a4v–a5r, a8r.

23. John Locke, *An Essay concerning Human Understanding* (1689), ed. Peter H. Nidditch (Oxford: Clarendon Press, 1975), bk. 1, ch. 1, para. 1 (p. 43) (further citations appear parenthetically in the text in the form: 1.1.1).

24. David Hume, *A Treatise of Human Nature* (1739), ed. L.A. Selby-Bigge, 2nd ed., rev. Peter H. Nidditch (Oxford: Clarendon Press, 1978), bk. 1, pt. 4, sec. 6 (pp. 253, 254) (further citations appear parenthetically in the text in the form 1.4.6).

25. Edmund Leites, *The Puritan Conscience and Modern Sexuality* (New Haven, CT: Yale University Press, 1986), 143–144.

CHAPTER 6 — HISTORICAL METHOD

1. The skeptical critique of empirical epistemology was central to those movements, poststructuralism and deconstruction, that dominated the heyday of "theory" in the latter decades of the last century, and it persists in less programmatic form today in much criticism that has been influenced by those movements. A case in point is the assemblage of practices that in the 1980s came loosely to be called "the new historicism." It seems to me that the thread that connected these practices was the unfulfillable aim to return literary criticism to historical study, which seemed to have been abandoned when the theory movements were ascendant, without sacrificing the radical skepticism that was theory's hallmark.

2. See Eric A. Havelock, *Preface to Plato* (Cambridge, MA: Harvard University Press, 1963).

3. John Locke, *An Essay concerning Human Understanding* (1689), ed. Peter H. Nidditch (Oxford: Clarendon Press, 1975), bk. 4, ch. 19, secs. 2, 14 (pp. 702, 704) (further citations appear parenthetically in the text in the form: 4.19.2).

4. For a thoughtful discussion of distance and proximity in eighteenth-century histories and historiography, see Mark Salber Phillips, *Society and Sentiment: Genres of Historical Writing in Britain, 1740–1820* (Princeton, NJ: Princeton University Press, 2000), esp. "Conclusion."

5. But see ch. 3 in the present volume on Locke's flexibility in this regard.

6. David Hume, *A Treatise of Human Nature* (1739), ed. L. A. Selby-Bigge and P. H. Nidditch, 2nd rev. ed. (Oxford: Clarendon Press, 1978), bk. 1, pt. 4, secs. 2, 6, 7 (pp. 187–218, 251–274).

7. The most fundamental and influential commentators on this concept are the nineteenth-century German philosophers Friedrich D. E. Schleiermacher and Wilhelm Dilthey.

8. See ch. 3 nn.96 and 98 in this volume. See also *Historicizing the Enlightenment*, vol. 2, ch. 1 nn.1–6.

9. For a fuller account, see *Historicizing the Enlightenment*, vol. 2, ch. 1.

10. For a powerful and notorious example, see Carl G. Hempel, "The Function of General Laws in History," in *Theories of History*, ed. Patrick Gardiner (New York: Free Press, 1959), 344–356.

11. For a related approach to empiricism as an epistemological method that might be extended beyond the material and historical, see the intro. to the present volume.

12. E. D. Hirsch Jr., *Validity in Interpretation* (New Haven, CT: Yale University Press, 1967), ch. 3.

13. Hans Robert Jauss, "Literary History as a Challenge to Literary Theory," in *Toward an Aesthetic of Reception*, trans. Timothy Bahti (Minneapolis: University of Minnesota Press, 1982), 3–45.

14. The hermeneutics of sacred texts bears comparison with scientific experiment: see ch. 3 in the present volume.

15. Even on the level of terminology (which in this field tends to derive from German usage) this oversimplifies things, because "understanding" is a fairly common alternative to (but not a synonym for) "explanation," and to a lesser degree even to "interpretation." For a sense of the range of discussion during a particularly fruitful period of exchange, see Alasdair MacIntyre "Symposium: The Idea of a Social Science," *Proceedings of the Aristotelian Society, Supplementary Volumes* 41 (1967): 95–114, reprinted in MacIntyre's *Against the Self-Images of the Age: Essays on Ideology and Philosophy* (Notre Dame, IN: University of Notre Dame Press, 1978), 211–229; Paul Ricoeur, "The Model of the Text: Meaningful Action Considered as a Text," *Social Research* 38, no. 3 (Autumn 1971): 529–562, reprinted in *Interpretive Social Science: A Reader*, ed. Paul Rabinow and William M. Sullivan (Berkeley: University of California Press, 1979), ch. 2, 73–101; and Charles Taylor, "Interpretation and the Sciences of Man," *Review of Metaphysics* 25, no. 1 (1971): 3–51, reprinted in Rabinow and Sullivan, *Interpretive Social Science*, ch. 1, 25–71.

16. K. R. Popper, *The Poverty of Historicism* (London: Routledge and Kegan Paul, 1957).

17. See, e.g., Erich Auerbach, "Vico and Aesthetic Historism," in *Scenes from the Drama of European Literature: Six Essays* (New York: Meridian, 1959), 183–198. For a discussion that aims to integrate into a single method these two senses of "historicism," see Karl Mannheim, "Historicism," in *Essays on the Sociology of Knowledge*, ed. Paul Kecskemeti (London: Routledge and Kegan Paul, 1952), 84–133.

18. For a fuller argument, see Michael McKeon, "Civic Humanism and the Logic of Historical Interpretation," in *The Political Imagination in History: Essays concerning J. G. A. Pocock*, ed. D. N. Deluna, assisted by Perry Anderson and Glenn Burgess (Baltimore: Archangul Foundation, 2006), 59–99. The opposition between "commonplace" and "ideology" is a version of the "external"-"internal" dialectic internalized, as it were, within the realm of the internal.

19. See Raymond Williams, *Marxism and Literature* (Oxford: Oxford University Press, 1977), 133–134.

20. Karl Marx, *Grundrisse* (writ. c. 1857–1861), trans. Martin Nicolaus (Harmondsworth, England: Penguin, 1973), "Introduction," 103–106.

21. A classic example of this truth, alluded to above, is the way the temporal distinction between the Ancients and the Moderns disclosed the structural distinction between the arts and the sciences.

22. Karl Marx and Friedrich Engels, *The German Ideology* (written 1845–1846, pub. 1932), pt. 1, D, https://www.marxists.org/archive/marx/works/download/Marx_The_German_Ideology.pdf.

23. Marx, *Grundrisse*, 244–246.

24. See *Historicizing the Enlightenment*, vol. 2, ch. 1.

25. Marx and Engels, *German Ideology*, pt. 1, D, 53.

26. For an attempt to do something like this, see *Historicizing the Enlightenment*, vol. 2, ch. 6.

27. Adam Ferguson, *An Essay on the History of Civil Society* (Dublin, 1767), pt. 2, sec. 1.

28. Ferdinand de Saussure, *Course in General Linguistics*, ed. Charles Bally, Albert Sechehaye, and Albert Reidlinger; trans. Wade Baskin (New York: Philosophical Library, 1959), 80, 83, 85.

29. Saussure himself disputed the correlation of "diachrony-synchrony" at the linguistic micro-level with "history-structure" at the macro-level; see *Course in General Linguistics*, 79–81.

30. Marx provides a parallel account of the production of use values by analyzing in minute and fascinating detail how the labor process uses use values that are the products of previous labor to produce use values that will in turn be a means of production in a later process; see *Capital* (1867), Volume 1, trans. Ben Fowkes (London: Penguin, 1990), pt. 3, ch. 7, sec. 1, 283–292.

Source Notes

CHAPTER 1 — TRADITION AS TACIT KNOWLEDGE

This chapter is based on an essay that first appeared as "Tacit Knowledge: Tradition and Its Aftermath" in *Questions of Tradition*, ed. Mark Salber Phillips and Gordon Schochet (Toronto: University of Toronto Press, 2004), 171–202. Copyright © University of Toronto Press Incorporated. Reprinted with permission of the publisher.

CHAPTER 2 — CIVIL AND RELIGIOUS LIBERTY: A CASE STUDY IN SECULARIZATION

This chapter is based on an essay that first appeared as "Civil and Religious Liberty in Seventeenth-Century England: A Case Study in Secularization," in *Representation, Heterodoxy, and Aesthetics: Essays in Honor of Ronald Paulson*, ed. Ashley Marshall (Newark: University of Delaware Press, 2014), 157–187. Copyright © Rowman and Littlefield Publishing Group, Inc. All rights reserved. Reprinted with permission.

CHAPTER 4 — GENDER AND SEX, STATUS AND CLASS

This chapter is based on an article that first appeared as "Historicizing Patriarchy: The Emergence of Gender Difference in England, 1660–1760," *Eighteenth-Century Studies* 28, no. 3 (Spring 1995): 295–322. Copyright © 1995 Johns Hopkins University Press. Reprinted with permission of the publisher.

CHAPTER 5 — BIOGRAPHY, FICTION, PERSONAL IDENTITY

This chapter is based on an essay that first appeared as "Biography, Fiction, and the Emergence of 'Identity' in Eighteenth-Century Britain," in *Writing Lives: Biography and Textuality, Identity and Representation in Early Modern England*, ed. Kevin Sharpe and Steven N. Zwicker (New York: Oxford University Press, 2012), 339–356. Reprinted with permission of the publisher.

CHAPTER 6 — HISTORICAL METHOD

This chapter is based on an essay that first appeared as "Theory and Practice in Historical Method," in *Rethinking Historicism from Shakespeare to Milton*, ed. Ann Baynes Coiro and Thomas Fulton (Cambridge: Cambridge University Press, 2012), 40–64. Copyright © 2012 Cambridge University Press. Reprinted with permission of the publisher.

Index

abolition movement, 25–26
absolutism, 20, 51, 53, 56, 57, 58, 59, 141, 168; devolution of, from public sovereignty to private property, 21, 79–80, 87, 101–105
accommodation, doctrine of, 49–54, 63, 68, 73
Addison, Joseph, 44–45, 55, 81, 106, 139, 154
Adorno, Theodore W., 11, 12, 20
aesthetic, the, as modern replacement of tradition, 42–48
allegory, 23, 82, 176, 177, 181
Anecdota, The (Procopius), 175
Anglican Church. *See* Church of England
Anthropocene period, 13
arcana imperii, 29, 34, 35
Argenis (Barclay), 177
aristocratic ideology, 18, 39, 143, 159–163, 234n64; as ideology of feudalism, 86
Aristotle, 11, 120, 170
Artaud, Antonin, 75
Astell, Mary, 36, 142

Bacon, Francis, 12, 13–14, 32, 33, 118, 122–123, 125, 128
Barbon, Nicholas, 83
Barclay, John, 177
Baxter, Richard, 168
Behn, Aphra, 177
Bennett, John, 167–168
biography: actual and, 170–171; common and, 167–170; virtual and, 171–173. *See also* fictionality
Blackstone, William, 31
Book of Martyrs (Foxe), 59–60, 168
Boswell, James, 43, 165–166, 178
Boyle, Robert, 32–33, 35, 119, 128
Bramhall, John, 129
Bray, Alan, 152
Brenner, Robert, 80, 216n16
Burke, Edmund, 42–43
Butler, Samuel, 126

Capital (Marx), 87–90, 97, 98, 99, 223n45
Care, Henry, 112
Catholic Church. *See* Roman Catholicism
Cavendish, Margaret, 115, 125
Charles I (king), 28–29, 31, 49, 51, 57

Charles II (king), 49, 56, 58
Church of England, 50–51, 60, 62–64, 67
Cicero, 73
civil society, 17, 54–56
Clarendon, Edward Hyde, Earl of, 57–58, 59, 67
Clark, Alice, 144
Clarke, Samuel, 168
class, 157–159, 233n47; as emergent category, 18–19, 147–148, 157
Classical Age, 12–13, 203n1
Coleridge, Samuel, 45, 73
Collier, Jeremy, 173–175
Collins, William, 46–48
commodity fetishism, 88, 89–93. *See also* fetishism; exchange value
commodity form, 87–91, 222n41. *See also* form; exchange value
common, commoners, the common, 18, 21, 31, 80, 81, 101, 102–103, 145, 162–163, 167–170, 173
common law, 31, 143–144
conjectural history, 24–25, 107–108, 207n46
conscience, liberty of, 53, 57–67, 70–72, 181, 215n10; as liberty of consciousness, 60
conscience, public, 57, 61
consciousness; class, 148, 157; false, 74, 84–87, 221n38; gender, 148, 152, 154; the public sphere and, 110; sex, 148, 158
Conventicle Act (1664), 56, 69
Corbet, John, 67
corporation, idea of, 77–78
Corporation Act (1661), 56
corpuscularism, 119
Countesse of Montgomeries Urania, The (Wroth), 177
coverture, common law principle of, 102, 143–144
Cromwell, Oliver, 49
Cumberland, Richard, 57

Davenant, William, 209n5
Davies, John, 31
Debaucht Court Or, the Lives of the Emperor Justinian, and His Empress Theodora the Comedian, The (Procopius), 176
Declaration of Breda (1660), 56

Declarations of Indulgence, 56, 57
Defoe, Daniel, 39, 55–56, 81, 82, 115, 118, 157, 170–171
Descartes, René, 12, 65
diachrony and synchrony, temporality and structure, 24–25, 107–108, 195, 197–198
Dialectic of Enlightenment (Horkheimer and Adorno), 11, 12
Dilthey, Wilhelm, 238n7
Discourse of Ecclesiastical Politie (Parker), 61, 68
dissent and dissenters, 56, 58–61, 67–68, 70, 115
distinction-separation-conflation, historical schema, 8, 9–10, 22, 26–27, 54, 81, 130–131, 152, 178
domestic economy, 144–146
domestic ideology, 144, 146–147, 164–166. *See also* domestic economy
Donne, John, 189, 190, 191
Don Quixote (Cervantes), 46
double consciousness of aesthetic attitude, 45, 47
"double existence" of objects and perceptions (Hume), 136
double movement of parody, 93–94
double ("two-fold") structure of commodity form (Marx), 88
Drake, James, 174
Dryden, John, 30–31, 37–38, 69–70, 121, 218n42
Dutton, Anne, 116

education, 36, 155–156
Edward, Thomas, 59
Edwards, Jonathan, 133–134
effeminacy, 151–152, 160, 162–164, 235n69
Eighteenth Brumaire of Louis Bonaparte, The (Marx), 93
empiricism, 6–8, 136–139, 182–183, 185–187
Engels, Friedrich, 24–25, 40, 74, 84–87
English Civil Wars (1642–1660), 28, 49, 51, 54, 56, 59–60, 62, 209n4
Enlightenment period, overview, 2–6
Enlightenment project, as phrase, 23, 207n40
Enlightenment thought, overview, 1–10, 19–22; English vs. French, 75, 203n1
Essay concerning Human Understanding, An (Locke), 127–128, 139
exchange value: abstracted from use value (Marx), 88, 98; historical emergence of, 82–83, 87–91; how discovered: Locke, 102–103; Marx, 91, 93; Smith, 100
Exclusion Crisis, 53, 59, 70, 142, 176, 177
experiment, experimental method: 13–15, 118–121; beyond the observable, 131–139; compared to conceptual abstraction, 98;

experience and, 8, 121–125; experimental vs. artful, 125–129

family romance, 176
femininity, 153, 160, 235n66. *See also* gender
Ferguson, Adam, 107–108, 197
fetishism: change in legibility of, in commodity, 89, 90, 91; of the commodity, 88; religious source of, acknowledged, 92–93, 223n47
feudalism, 21, 22, 51, 55, 78–80, 86–87, 90, 113
fictionality, 167, 175, 178, 236n10. *See also* biography
Fielding, Henry, 80–81, 165, 171–173
Fielding, John, 80–81
Filmer, Robert, 34, 52, 53, 101, 109, 141–142
Five Mile Act (1665), 56
Fontenelle, Bernard de, 121–122, 123
form: Bacon on, 122, 228n98; circulation of commodities, form of, 105–106; commodity, 87–91, 94, 222n41; literary, 183–184. *See also* forms and/as fetters; forms of intercourse and forces of production; superstructure and infrastructure
forms and/as fetters, 22, 41, 85–86, 91, 104, 105, 196, 207n34, 214n49. *See also* superstructure and infrastructure; uneven development
forms of intercourse and forces of production, 40–41, 85–86, 91, 94, 195–196. *See also* superstructure and infrastructure; uneven development
Foucault, Michel, 12–13, 203n1, 231n27
Foxe, John, 59–60, 168

Gangroena (Edward), 59
gender: as acculturation, 153–156, 234n59; as difference, 149–150, 151–153, 232n35; as euphemism for sex, 154; as traditional regime, 148–149, 153. *See also* patriarchalism; sex, as emergent category; women
German Ideology, The (Marx and Engels), 84–87
Goldsmith, Oliver, 167
Gramsci, Antonio, 222n42
Graunt, John, 82
group formation, sociology of, 57–59
Grundrisse (Marx), 87, 97, 99, 221n38
Gulliver's Travels (Swift), 171, 191

Habermas, Jürgen, *The Structural Transformation of the Public Sphere*, 17–18, 54, 109–111
Hanoverian Settlement (1689), 143
Haywood, Eliza, 171
Hegel, G. W. F., 22, 197

hegemony, 39, 213n32, 222n42
Henry VIII (king), 77
Herbert, George, 50
Hirsch, E. D., 188
historical materialism, 21, 105
History of the Rebellion and Civil Wars in England (Clarendon), 58
History of the Royal Society, The (Sprat), 65, 123–124, 126–127
Hobbes, Thomas, 32, 52–53, 57, 109, 128, 130
Holland, Roger, 168
Home, John, 47
homophobia, 152
homosexuality, 151–153, 163, 181, 235n64. *See also* sodomy
honor, 18, 48, 114–115, 143, 157, 160
Hooke, Robert, 124, 128, 129
Horkheimer, Max, 11, 20
House of Stuarts, 51, 53–54, 59, 64, 72, 84, 87, 101, 143, 159
Hume, David, 3, 36–37, 131–137, 179–181, 186

identity, 148, 158; personal identity, 178–181
ideology, as false consciousness, 84–87; as modern articulation and replacement of tradition, 37–41
imagination, 37, 39–40, 43–45, 82, 93, 95, 106, 139–140
impartial spectator, the (Smith), 96
imperialism, 22–23, 24–27
interest, 10, 16, 37–40, 56–59, 67, 85, 94–95, 110–111, 147, 196, 210n6
invisible hand, the (Smith), 94–97, 104, 106

James, Duke of York, later James II, 56, 142, 143
Jauss, H. R., 188
Johnson, Samuel, 43–44, 139, 167, 169–170, 174–175
Joseph Andrews and Shamela (Fielding), 171

King's two bodies, doctrine of, 51, 77–78, 130
Kirkman, Francis, 114
Kuhn, Thomas, 36–37

Lacquer, Thomas, 149–150
Leviathan (Hobbes), 129, 130
Lévi-Strauss, Claude, 35
liberty, positive vs. negative, 16–17, 49, 51–53, 55, 56–57, 58, 65–71
liberty of conscience, 62–63, 65–66, 71
Life of Johnson (Boswell), 178
Lilly, John, 55
literature, 183–184
Lloyd, William, Bishop of Worcester, 62

Locke, John: on empiricism, 3, 42, 124, 133; on epistemology, 33, 34, 132–139, 185; *An Essay concerning Human Understanding*, 139; on group formation, 59; on language formation, 127–128; on the law of opinion, 113–114; on the marriage compact, 101–102; on personal identity, 178–179; on the political compact, 34–35, 101–105, 107, 142; on propriety and property, 55, 83–84, 87; *The Second Treatise of Government*, 101–102
Love-Letters between a Nobleman and His Sister (Behn), 177

Mackworth, Humphrey, 111–112
macro-pastoralism, 23–24. *See also* pastoral, pastoralism
Madison, James, 112
Malthus, Thomas, 157
Mandeville, Bernard, 33, 36, 37–38, 155–156
Manley, Delarivier, 161, 177
Manwaring, Roger, 51–53, 63–64
market, the: actual vs. virtual, 22, 81, 87–88, 113; compared to sympathy, 95; Financial Revolution and, 81–83
marriage, 101–102, 143–144, 146–147. *See also* coverture, common law principle of
Marten, Henry, 28, 29, 43
Marvell, Andrew, 60–61, 68–69, 115–117
Marx, Karl: *Capital*, 87–90, 97, 98, 99, 223n45; on commodity form, 87–91, 222n41; on economy, 79, 84, 105–106; *The Eighteenth Brumaire of Louis Bonaparte*, 93; on exchange value and commodity exchange, 88, 91, 93, 98; on fetishism of the commodity, 88–93, 223n47; on forms and/as fetters, 41, 85–86; *The German Ideology*, 84–87; *Grundrisse*, 87, 97, 99, 221n38; on history, 24–25, 40, 105, 194–196, 223n46; on ideology, 74, 84–85; on uneven development, 86, 196
Marxism, 18–19, 213n44, 222n42
masculinity, 153, 160, 163–166. *See also* gender
materialism, 10, 21, 52, 105, 158, 159, 165, 190, 195
mercantilism, 82, 96, 105
Metaverse, as term, 75
Milton, John, 35–36, 49–50, 197, 198
Moll Flanders (Defoe), 171
mollies, molly-houses, 152–153
Monck, George, 29, 56, 57, 64–65, 130
monotheism, 73, 93, 96. *See also* religion
"Mr. Spectator" (speaker in *The Spectator*), 55, 71, 81. *See also Spectator, The* (publication)
Mysteries of Udolpho, The (Radcliffe), 46

nature, state of, 53, 62, 83, 101, 103, 109, 130–131, 224n58
New Atalantis (Manley), 177
nonconformists and nonconformity, 56, 57–58, 61–62, 66–67, 115, 116–117

"An Ode on the Popular Superstitions of the Highlands of Scotland" (Collins), 46–47
"Of Miracles" (Hume), 133
Okeley, William, 116–118
Old Arcadia (Sidney), 177
Order of Things, The (Foucault), 12
Overton, Richard, 175

Paine, Thomas, 39–40, 42
Palmer, Roger, Earl of Castlemaine, 62
Pamela (Richardson), 171
Paradise Lost (Milton), 197, 198
Parker, Henry, 142
Parker, Samuel, 61, 68
parody, 93–94, 107
pastoral, pastoralism, 16, 23, 24
Patriarcha (Filmer), 53, 142
patriarchalism, 16, 141–144
Pepys, Samuel, 82–83
periodization, 2–6, 192–194
Perry, Ruth, 144
Petition of Right (1628), 28
Pett, Peter, 62–65
Petty, William, 82, 129–130
Pinchbeck, Ivy, 144
Pinker, Steven, 206n24
Polanyi, Michael, 37
political arithmetic, 129
Popper, Karl, 190
Princess Cloria; or, the Royal Romance, 177
print, print culture: 30–31, 40, 75–76, 115–118
privacy, 18, 67, 118, 176–177, 218n51
Procopius, 175–176
progress, 106–108, 119
property: conditional use-rights to *vs.* absolute ownership of, 21, 102, 103; devolution of private from public domain, 21, 79–80, 87, 101–105; from "direct" to "indirect" mode of relations of, 80, 87; institution of, as index of cultural stage, 107–108; labor theory of (Locke), 83, 87, 102, 104; propriety, and, 55, 83–84, 87, 115; rights of married women, 102, 143–144; right of private precedes political compact, 101–102
Property Qualifications Act (1711), 82
Protestantism, 50–51, 64–65, 69, 115
public, actual *vs.* virtual, 16–17, 111–115
public opinion, 17, 32–33, 112–113

public sphere, 17–19, 54, 76, 109–111, 112–114, 116–118, 140, 152
Puritans, Puritanism, 57–58, 60, 77, 142, 146, 185

quantification, 6, 7, 15–16, 122–123
Quarrel of the Ancients and Moderns, 108, 120, 121, 135, 186, 204n7

racism, 26. *See also* slavery
réalité virtuelle, as term, 75
"Redemption" (Herbert), 50, 69
Reeve, Clara, 45
reflexivity, 54, 56, 62, 93, 106, 110, 140, 159
Reformation, Protestant, 50, 51, 77, 115
Religio Laici (Dryden), 37, 69–70, 218n42
religion: the aesthetic a secularization of, 45–46; economic theory informed by, 91–97; etymology of, 73; as experiment, 133–139; as false consciousness, 74, 84–85; modernity of, 72–73, 76–77; religious subsumed under civil liberty, 49–74; as tacit knowledge, 34
representative democracy, 16, 112, 131
residual-dominant-emergent, temporal stages (Williams), 193, 196
Restoration period, 29, 53, 56–57, 115, 177
Richardson, Samuel, 45, 165, 171
Robinson, Henry, 80
Robinson Crusoe (Defoe), 171
Rochester, John Wilmot, Earl of, 159–160
Roman Catholicism, 30, 37, 50–51, 57, 59, 70–71, 76, 168
romance, 46, 47, 169–171, 176
romans à clef, 161, 176–177, 181
Royal Exchange, 55, 81
Royal Society, 13–14, 62, 65, 123–124, 126

Saussure, Ferdinand de, 197, 239n29
Savile, George, Marquess of Halifax, 209n4
Schiller, Friedrich, 47, 214n58
Schleiermacher, Friedrich D. E., 238n7
scientific revolution, 170, 178, 227n95, 227n97
Scottish Highlands, 46–48
Second Anglo-Dutch War (1667), 58
Second Thoughts (Clarendon), 67
Second Treatise of Government, The (Locke), 53, 101
secret history, 175–178
secularization, 49, 71–74. *See also* religion
self-fashioning, 173–175
sensibility, 46, 165, 189, 191–192
separate spheres, 146–148
sex: as emergent category, 148, 150, 181; female modesty and, 146–147, 155–156; sex

consciousness, 148, 158; sexuality and, 148–153, 156–163, 234n59. *See also* gender
Shadwell, Thomas, 71
Sidney, Algernon, 34
Sidney, Philip, 177
Simon, Richard, 30
slavery, 25–27, 101, 142
Smith, Adam, 81, 83, 106, 128, 194; *The Theory of Moral Sentiments*, 94–95; *The Wealth of Nations*, 94, 95
society, 17–19
sociology of group formation, 57–59
sodomy, 151–152, 159–163, 208n50, 234n59
Spectator, The (publication), 139. *See also* "Mr. Spectator" (speaker in *The Spectator*)
spheres of discourse, 62–65
Sprat, Thomas, 123–124, 228n108
Sprigg, William, 157
stadial theory, 25, 107, 108, 197
state of nature, 16, 53, 62, 83, 101, 103, 109, 130–131, 224n58
statistical analysis, 6, 15, 175, 189
Staves, Susan, 143
Steele, Richard, 113, 154, 155, 158
Stillingfleet, Edward, 112
structuralism, 12, 195–199
Structural Transformation of the Public Sphere, The (Habermas), 18
structures of feeling (Williams), 194–195
sumptuary legislation, 29, 158
superstructure and infrastructure, 21–22, 24, 40–41, 91, 105–107, 195–198. *See also* forms and/as fetters; forms of intercourse and forces of production
Swift, Jonathan, 34, 82, 171, 191, 211n21

tacit vs. explicit knowledge, 7–9, 28–30, 34–35, 40
Tatler, The (publication), 158, 163

Test Act (1673), 56
Theory of Moral Sentiments, The (Smith), 94–95
Thorndike, Herbert, 67–68
thought experiment, 132, 137, 139, 179
Toland, John, 33
Toleration Act (1689), 56
Trumbach, Randolph, 151–152

uneven development, 22, 40, 84–87, 91, 196–198
Uniformity Act (1662), 56, 57
Universality, universalism, 19–22, 84, 95–96, 98–105

virtuality, virtualization: analogy of, with experimental method, commodity exchange, conceptual abstraction, 98, 118–119; as Enlightenment discovery, 75–76; Enlightenment universality and, 105; virtual witnessing and, 119, 127, 139, 229n121

Warr, John, 31
Waterhouse, Edward, 29, 114, 158, 209n5
Wealth of Nations, The (Smith), 94, 95
"What Is Critique?" (Foucault), 12
"What Is Enlightenment?" (Foucault), 12
Williams, Raymond, 79, 193, 222n42
Wolseley, Charles, 67
women: agricultural work of, 144–146; marriage and, 146; property rights of married, 143–144; separate spheres and, 146–148; socialization of, 36. *See also* gender
Wotton, William, 123
Wroth, Mary, 177

Zuckerberg, Mark, 75

About the Author

MICHAEL MCKEON is Board of Governors Distinguished Professor Emeritus at Rutgers University–New Brunswick in New Jersey. He is the author of *Politics and Poetry in Restoration England: The Case of Dryden's "Annus Mirabilis," The Origins of the English Novel, 1600–1740, The Secret History of Domesticity: Public, Private, and the Division of Knowledge*, and scores of articles, as well as the editor of *Theory of the Novel: A Historical Approach*.

Printed in the United States
by Baker & Taylor Publisher Services